Perspectives in Law, Business and Innovation

Over the last three decades, interconnected processes of globalization and rapid technological change—particularly, the emergence of networked technologies—have profoundly disrupted traditional models of business organization. This economic transformation has created multiple new opportunities for the emergence of alternate business forms, and disruptive innovation has become one of the major driving forces in the contemporary economy. Moreover, in the context of globalization, the innovation space increasingly takes on a global character. The main stakeholders—innovators, entrepreneurs and investors—now have an unprecedented degree of mobility in pursuing economic opportunities wherever they arise. As such, frictionless movement of goods, workers, services, and capital is becoming the "new normal".

This new economic and social reality has created multiple regulatory challenges for policymakers as they struggle to come to terms with the rapid pace of these social and economic changes. Moreover, these challenges impact across multiple fields of both public and private law. Nevertheless, existing approaches within legal science often struggle to deal with innovation and its effects.

Paralleling this shift in the economy, we can, therefore, see a similar process of disruption occurring within contemporary academia, as traditional approaches and disciplinary boundaries—both within and between disciplines—are being re-configured. Conventional notions of legal science are becoming increasingly obsolete or, at least, there is a need to develop alternative perspectives on the various regulatory challenges that are currently being created by the new innovation-driven global economy.

The aim of this series is to provide a forum for the publication of cutting-edge research in the fields of innovation and the law from a Japanese and Asian perspective. The series will cut across the traditional sub-disciplines of legal studies but will be tied together by a focus on contemporary developments in an innovation-driven economy and will deepen our understanding of the various regulatory responses to these economic and social changes.

The series editor and editorial board carefully assess each book proposal and sample chapters in terms of their relevance to law, business, and innovative technological change. Each proposal is evaluated on the basis of its academic value and distinctive contribution to the fast-moving debate in these fields.

More information about this series at http://www.springer.com/series/15440

Marcelo Corrales · Mark Fenwick ·
Helena Haapio
Editors

Legal Tech, Smart Contracts and Blockchain

 Springer

Editors
Marcelo Corrales
Institute of European and American Studies
Academia Sinica
Taipei, Taiwan

Mark Fenwick
Faculty of Law
Kyushu University
Fukuoka, Japan

Helena Haapio
School of Accounting and Finance
University of Vaasa
Vaasa, Finland

ISSN 2520-1875   ISSN 2520-1883 (electronic)
Perspectives in Law, Business and Innovation
ISBN 978-981-13-6085-5   ISBN 978-981-13-6086-2   (eBook)
https://doi.org/10.1007/978-981-13-6086-2

Library of Congress Control Number: 2018967430

This Springer imprint is published by the registered company Springer Nature Singapore Pte Ltd.
The registered company address is: 152 Beach Road, #21-01/04 Gateway East, Singapore 189721, Singapore

Preface

This volume is part of the book series: *Perspectives in Law, Business and Innovation*. The aim of this series is to provide a forum for the publication of cutting-edge research in the fields of innovation and the law from a global perspective. The series aims to cut across the traditional sub-disciplines of legal studies, but is tied together by a focus on deepening our understanding of the various responses to technological, economic and social change.

This volume constitutes the result of a joint cooperative effort drawing on the extensive global network of three academic institutions: The Institute of European and American Studies, part of the Academia Sinica (Taipei, Taiwan), the Graduate School of Law, part of Kyushu University (Fukuoka, Japan) and the School of Accounting and Finance, Business Law, part of the University of Vaasa (Vaasa, Finland). Contributors to this book—including business, management, software engineering, design and legal scholars and practitioners from Europe, East Asia and the Americas—attempt to provide some of the latest thinking and assessment of current challenges and opportunities with regard to Smart Contracts, Blockchain and Legal Tech and Design.

The main target audience of the book comprises two different groups. The first group belongs to the legal community—particularly, legal scholars, law students and practitioners—in the field of technology or contract law who are interested in an up-to-date legal analysis of current trends. The second group are experts in the fields of Cloud Computing, Smart Contracts and Blockchain—including, service and infrastructure providers, IT managers, chief executive officers (CEOs), chief information officers (CIOs), designers and software developers—who are interested in, and influenced by, some of the shortcomings and benefits of the current legal issues under scrutiny in this work.

The editors would like to thank the Editor-in-Chief of this book series, Prof. Toshiyuki Kono, for opening the doors to this project and for his support. The editors are also indebted to the authors and co-authors of each chapter for their hard work, patience and cooperation throughout the whole process from initial concept to the final manuscript. Finally, the editors are grateful to the Springer staff for their support and efforts in ensuring final publication.

Taipei, Taiwan   Marcelo Corrales
Fukuoka, Japan   Mark Fenwick
Helsinki, Finland   Helena Haapio

Contents

Editors and Contributors

About the Editors

Marcelo Corrales is Attorney-at-Law specializing in intellectual property, information technology and corporate law. He is currently a Visiting Scholar at the Institute of European and American Studies, Academia Sinica in Taiwan. He has a Doctor of Laws (LL.D.) degree from Kyushu University in Japan. He also holds a Master of Laws (LL.M.) in international economics and business law from Kyushu University, and an LL.M. in law and information technology and an LL.M. in European intellectual property law, both from the University of Stockholm in Sweden. His most recent publications include *New Technology, Big Data and the Law* (Springer, 2017). His past activities have included being a research associate with the Institute for Legal Informatics and IT Law at Leibniz Universität Hannover (Germany) from 2007 to 2018.

Mark Fenwick is Professor of International Business Law at the Faculty of Law, Kyushu University, Fukuoka, Japan. His primary research interests are in the fields of white-collar and corporate crime, and business regulation in a networked age. Recent publications include *New Technology, Big Data and the Law* (Springer, 2017) and *The Shifting Meaning of Legal Certainty in Comparative and Transnational Law* (Hart, 2017). He has a Master's and a Ph.D. degree from the Faculty of Law, University of Cambridge, and has been a visiting professor at Chulalongkorn University, Duke University, the University of Hong Kong, Shanghai University of Finance and Economics, the National University of Singapore, Tilburg University and Vietnam National University.

Helena Haapio is Associate Professor of Business Law at the University of Vaasa, Finland, and a Contract Innovator at Lexpert Ltd., Helsinki. After completing legal studies at the University of Turku, Finland, and Cambridge University, England, she served for several years as in-house Legal Counsel in Europe and the USA. A pioneer of the Proactive Law approach, she has for many years promoted the use of simplification and visualization in commercial contracting. Her multidisciplinary research focuses on ways to enhance the functionality and usability of contracts through design. Her books include *Next Generation Contracts: A Paradigm Shift* (Lexpert, 2013) and two titles co-authored with Prof. George Siedel, *A Short Guide to Contract Risk* (Gower, 2013) and *Proactive Law for Managers: A Hidden Source of Competitive Advantage* (Gower, 2011). She also acts as arbitrator in contract disputes.

Contributors

Thomas D. Barton California Western School of Law, San Diego, CA, USA

Marcelo Corrales Institute of European and American Studies, Academia Sinica, Taipei, Taiwan

Mark Fenwick Faculty of Law, Graduate School of Law, Kyushu University, Fukuoka, Japan

Helena Haapio Business Law, School of Accounting and Finance, University of Vaasa, Vaasa, Finland

Margaret Hagan Legal Design Lab, Stanford University, Stanford, CA, USA

James G. Hazard CommonAccord.org, Sacramento, CA, USA

Paulius Jurčys Nanomolar, Inc., California, CA, USA

George Kousiouris Department of Informatics and Telematics, Harokopio University of Athens, Athens, Greece

Charlotta Kronblad Department of Technology Management and Economics, Chalmers University of Technology, Gothenburg, Sweden

Cecilia Magnusson Sjöberg Faculty of Law, Stockholm University, Stockholm, Sweden

Stefania Passera Legal Tech Lab, Helsinki University, Helsinki, Finland

Johanna E. Pregmark Department of Technology Management and Economics, Chalmers University of Technology, Gothenburg, Sweden

Ivar Timmer Research Program Legal Management, Amsterdam University of Applied Sciences, Amsterdam, The Netherlands

Rory Unsworth Swiss Re, Head Contracts Centre and Smart Contracts Counsel, Zurich, Switzerland

Erik P. M. Vermeulen Department of Business Law, Tilburg University, Tilburg, The Netherlands;
Legal Department, Philips Lighting, Amsterdam, The Netherlands

Sam Wrigley Faculty of Law, University of Helsinki, Helsinki, Finland

Acronyms

AEPD	Agencia Española de Protección de Datos (Spanish Data Protection Agency)
AGI	Artificial General Intelligence
AI	Artificial Intelligence
APIs	Application Programming Interfaces
ARTIST	Advanced Software-based Service Provisioning and Migration of Legacy Software
AUAS	Amsterdam University of Applied Sciences
B2B	Business-to-Business
B2C	Business-to-Consumer
BCRs	Binding Corporate Rules
CAS	Contract Automation Software
CEOs	Chief Executive Officers
CFOs	Chief Financial Officers
CIOs	Chief Information Officers
CJEU	Court of Justice of the European Union
CM	Contract Management
CRM	Customer Relationship Management
DAO	Decentralized Autonomous Organization
DLT	Distributed Ledger Technology
DM	Data Management
DNA	Deoxyribonucleic Acid
DPD	Data Protection Directive
EEA	European Economic Area
EU	European Union
EU DPA	European Union Data Protection Authority
EULA	End-User License Agreement
FCPA	Foreign Corrupt Practices Act
FINRA	Financial Industry Regulatory Authority
FTP	File Transfer Protocol

GDPR	European General Data Protection Regulation
GUI	Graphical User Interface
HTML	Hypertext Markup Language
IaaS	Infrastructure as a Service
IACCM	International Association for Contract and Commercial Management
ICO	UK Information Commissioner's Office
ICT	Information and Communication Technology
IoT	Internet of Things
IP	Internet Protocol
IRS	Internal Revenue Service
ISO	International Standardization Organization
ISP	Internet Service Provider
IT Law	Information Technology Law
JSON	JavaScript Object Notation
LeDA	Legal Design Alliance
Legal Tech	Legal Technology
NDA	Non-disclosure Agreement
NLP	Natural Language Processing
OECD	Organization for Economic Cooperation and Development
OPTIMIS	Optimized Infrastructure Services
PaaS	Platform as a Service
PbD	Privacy by Design
PCs	Personal Computers
PPL	Proactive/Preventive Law
PSI	Public Sector Information
QoS	Quality of Service
SaaS	Software as a Service
SCCs	Standard Contractual Clauses
SL	Source Language
SLAs	Service-Level Agreements
SMEs	Small- and Medium-Sized Enterprises
TCP	Transmission Control Protocol
TL	Target Language
UK	United Kingdom
UML	Unified Model Language
UN	United Nations
US	United States
USD	United States Dollars
VMs	Virtual Machines
XML	eXtensible Markup Language

Digital Technologies, Legal Design and the Future of the Legal Profession

Marcelo Corrales, Mark Fenwick and Helena Haapio

Abstract Legal Technology—or "Legal Tech"—is disrupting the traditional operations and self-understanding of the legal profession. This chapter introduces the central claim of this book, namely that these developments are having and will continue to have a disruptive effect on the work of lawyers and that adapting to this new operating environment is crucial for legal professionals remaining relevant in an increasingly technology-driven world. The chapter outlines some of the main features of this on-going transformation process, describes some of the pressures it is creating for lawyers, and provides short summaries of the chapters that comprise this collection.

Keywords Legal Tech · Blockchain · Smart contracts · Cryptocurrency · Legal design · Legal profession

1 Introduction

Legal Technology, or "Legal Tech,"[1] is a term that broadly refers to the adoption of innovative technology and software to streamline and enhance legal services. Legal Tech companies are generally startups founded with the specific purpose of disrupting the operation of the (traditionally conservative) legal profession.[2]

---

[1] Other synonyms which are used interchangeably are "law tech," "LegalIT," "legal informatics."
[2] Bues and Matthaei (2017), p. 90.

M. Corrales (✉)
Institute of European and American Studies, Academia Sinica, Taipei, Taiwan
e-mail: marcelo.corrales13@gmail.com

M. Fenwick
Faculty of Law, Graduate School of Law, Kyushu University, Fukuoka, Japan

H. Haapio
School of Accounting and Finance, University of Vaasa, Business Law, Vaasa, Finland

© Springer Nature Singapore Pte Ltd. 2019
M. Corrales et al. (eds.), *Legal Tech, Smart Contracts and Blockchain*,
Perspectives in Law, Business and Innovation,
https://doi.org/10.1007/978-981-13-6086-2_1

Three stream categories can be distinguished within Legal Tech: (i) technologies facilitating the access to and processing of data; (ii) support solutions; and, (iii) substantive law solutions.[3]

The first stream is the most general and consists of "enabler technologies"—such as Cloud storage tools and cybersecurity solutions—that would facilitate access to lawyers and legal data (i.e., information retrieval). This category attempts to support the competitiveness of the legal market and legal research.[4]

The second stream comprises "support-process" tools to adopt more effective case management and "back-office" systems in order to maximize the potential of the law firm's administration. These processes vary from the management of human resources and customer relationships to other functions largely related to the performance of accounting, billing, payrolls and other administrative tasks.[5]

The third stream adopts solutions which assist or even replace legal advice from lawyers in the execution of specific legal tasks. This category takes a broader view and includes various subfields such as automated contracts, e-discovery, online dispute resolution, legal analytics, Blockchain-based technologies and, in particular, Smart Contracts.[6]

The content of this book focuses primarily on the third category and how lawyers could tap into the potential power of these developments. This chapter introduces the main aspects of Blockchain technology, Smart Contracts, and what we call the Legal Design of Smart Contracts. Section 2 outlines in simple terms how Blockchain and Smart Contracts work and suggests that they have the potential to revolutionize multiple aspects of social and economic life. Section 3 introduces how and why developments in the context of Legal Tech place a new emphasis on Legal Design. Section 4 suggests that these developments will continue to have a disruptive effect on the legal profession and that adapting to this new operating environment is crucial in order for lawyers to remain relevant in a technology-driven world. Finally, Sect. 5 briefly summarizes each of the chapters and identifies key themes.

2 Blockchain and Smart Contracts

The Blockchain is a decentralized and distributed cryptographic digital "ledger" that is used to record transactions. The principles underlying this technology allows people who do not know or trust each other to build a large digital record of "who owns what" that will enforce the consent of everyone concerned.[7]

---

[3]Bues and Matthaei (2017), p. 90.
[4]Bues and Matthaei (2017), p. 90.
[5]Bues and Matthaei (2017), p. 90.
[6]Bues and Matthaei (2017), p. 90.
[7]The Economist (2015a).

The Blockchain "acts as a consistent transaction history on which all 'nodes' eventually agree."[8] It is essentially a public database with the potential to store and transfer tangible assets (physical properties such as cars, real estate property, etc.) and intangible assets (such as votes, genomic data, reputation, intention, information, software and even ideas).[9]

The Blockchain is also a verification system that enables—*among other things*—crypto-currencies such as Bitcoin, Ethereum, Ripple, etc. For this reason, distributed ledgers in the form of Blockchain promise to be a technology that will revolutionize the business world and virtually every aspect of record-keeping or exchange that we currently have.[10] This technology enables not only crypto-currencies but also different kinds of applications, platforms, information storage and distribution systems.[11] At a governmental level, the Blockchain could be used to leverage the monitoring and controlling of certain tasks such as voting systems, tax collection, issuing passports, record land registries, delivering grants and other benefits.[12]

In other words, the Blockchain allows parties to send, receive and store value or information through a distributed peer-to-peer network of several computers. Each transaction is distributed across the entire network and is recorded on a "block" only when the rest of the network ratifies the validity of the transaction based on past transactions considering the previous blocks.[13] Each block follows the other one successively and this is what creates the Blockchain.[14]

To put it in simple terms, the technology behind the Blockchain could be compared to that of a database, although the way of interaction is different in a sense that it is maintained and updated by a network of participating computers rather than a single computer of a company or organization.[15] For this very reason, the Blockchain can be regarded as an authoritative public database with a very high level of trust.[16]

Using a clear analogy from everyday life, it would be like when you try to erase an old message in a group conversation on WhatsApp in order to hide certain information. This could not be done in the Blockchain, since it contains the complete history of all transactions that have been made in the network.

---

[8]Wattenhofer (2016), p. 85.

[9]Swan (2015), p. 16.

[10]Walch (2018), p. 245.

[11]Tomas (2017), Introduction.

[12]Asharaf and Adarsh (2017), p. 33.

[13]Kost de Sevres (2016).

[14]Mougayar (2015).

[15]Mougayar (2015).

[16]Stark (2016).

As such, the Blockchain creates more transparency and allows otherwise mutually distrustful parties to contract safely without intermediaries.[17] This is because the pervasive nature of the Internet allows that the node of a Blockchain can be supported outside of the organization by a neutral third party.[18] Therefore, it is fair to say that the Blockchain itself becomes the trusted (distributed) third party. This also enables the Blockchain to act as mediator in conflict situations.[19]

In the same way that the Internet decentralized the information, what the Blockchain is essentially trying to achieve is to decentralize the certification processes by acting as a database that holds records of every transaction executed in the network.[20] That is, decentralizing the "trust" that is usually deposited in intermediary institutions (banks, credit card companies, governments, etc.) and transferring it directly to the network of individuals that are part of the Blockchain.[21]

If we take Bitcoin as an example, the "coins" themselves are not physical assets, not even digital files, but entries in a public ledger using its own unit of account. Therefore, owning a Bitcoin is more like a declaration of owning something, which is recorded on the Blockchain.[22] Satoshi Nakamoto (a pseudonym that refers to a person or a group of people) is credited for mining the first block of the Bitcoin back in 2008.[23] Bitcoin was created as a cryptocurrency to prevent "double spending," acting as a decentralized public ledger for all transactions made on the Bitcoin network. The first Blockchain was therefore an essential feature of Bitcoin and this is the reason why the Blockchain is widely associated with Bitcoin.[24]

Take for instance a bank transaction. Imagine that a person called Anna would like to send money to another person called Bob. The normal procedure is to wire the money through a bank which is acting as an intermediary. In this case, Anna would ask her bank to transfer the money to Bob. The transaction may take a few minutes or several days, depending on the amount, the bank and the country in which the transfer is made. The transaction does not really need a transfer of bank notes, but the intermediary banks would rather make a simple change in the balance of their accounts with the use of a computer software. The problem here is that neither Anna nor Bob have any control over the process, since only the banks have all the information. Both depend entirely on those banks (and their commissions) to carry out the transaction.

---

[17]Kosba et al. (2015), p. 1.

[18]Linthicum (2016).

[19]Wattenhofer (2016), p. 88.

[20]Morabito (2017), p. 167; Drescher (2017), p. 5.

[21]Huang (2015), p. 3.

[22]The Economist (2015b).

[23]Bues and Matthaei (2017), p. 90.

[24]Prusty (2017), p. 14; Williams (2017), p. 44.

What the Blockchain basically proposes is to eliminate intermediaries and decentralize the entire management system, providing a high level of security and integrity by acting as a database that contains records of each transaction executed on the network. The control of the process would rely directly on the users, not on the banks anymore as in the previous example. In this case, both Anna and Bob would become participants and managers of the bank account books. This example can be extrapolated to other types of transactions and not only to money transfers. This is why the Blockchain represents a profound paradigm shift in the entire financial structure that we currently use.

Cryptocurrencies based on decentralized Blockchains, such as the abovementioned examples, have allowed the emergence of the so-called: "Smart Contracts."[25] According to Kost De Sevres, Smart Contracts are "self-executing, autonomous computer protocols that facilitate, execute and enforce commercial agreements between two or more parties."[26] Another definition of Smart Contracts that focuses on Blockchain technologies is given by Wattenhofer as "an agreement between two or more parties, encoded in such a way that the correct execution is guaranteed by the Blockchain."[27]

The idea of Smart Contracts was popularized by computer scientist Nick Szabo. He suggested that many kinds of contracts can be embedded in computer software and hardware architecture. A typical example of a Smart Contract in its earliest and most simple form is the vending machine, which is designed to transfer the ownership of a good (e.g., a can of soda) for the exchange of money. The vending machine is in control of the property—by being physically sealed—thus can enforce the "contract" that is called a "contract with bearer,"[28] since anyone with money can engage in a transaction with the vendor.[29]

By extending the logic underlying mechanical devices such as the vending machine, Szabo suggested that the computer code could be used in place of vending machines. This idea could be implemented to negotiate more complex transactions, forging strategic relationships, and coordinating transactions arising under diverse jurisdictions. Instead of transferring the ownership of a can of soda, a Smart Contract could transfer ownership of shares, real estate, intellectual property rights, etc.[30]

Among the most important advantages of the Blockchain and Smart Contracts are the reduced transaction costs originating from intermediary third parties. In the same way, the Blockchain accelerates the transactions because it works 24 hours a day, 7 days a week. Imagine how long it takes to transfer money to another country using a bank as an intermediary. In short, with Blockchain, time and transaction costs could be reduced to a minimum, which would, in turn, translate into greater efficiency when doing business in the long term.

---

[25]Weber et al. (2016), p. 330.

[26]Kost de Sevres (2016).

[27]Wattenhofer (2016), p. 88.

[28]Szabo (1997a).

[29]Szabo (1997b).

[30]Stark (2016).

However, since the Blockchain is a relatively new and disruptive technology, its current implementation remains difficult. It takes time to get the specialized personnel to implement it within the structure of the systems of governments and companies. This process of adaptation can take several years and is one of the main objectives of this book. To reduce the information gap and spark new research on Blockchain-based technologies.

Another fundamental problem is that of anonymity, especially with regard to the use of cryptocurrencies. As some of the cryptocurrencies offer special characteristics of anonymity, they could facilitate certain criminal activities such as: money laundering, sale of drugs online, etc. This leads to the raising of some legal issues not yet contemplated in our legal system. It could be said that, there is a kind of "status quo" in this respect; and the lack of regulation generates at the same time a stagnation in the development and evolution of this technology.

Understanding and navigating the new environment created by the above technologies clearly requires a high degree of technical competency, as multiple technologies need to be gathered together and integrated into products and services relevant in a legal context. But, there is also a design challenge created by these disruptive innovations. In this context "design" focuses on understanding an area of human experience and then developing a product service or interface to improve that experience and empower people in new and previously unimagined ways. The next section considers the application of human-centered design to prevent or solve legal problems that new technologies are creating, focusing on the key issue of Legal Design.

3 The Legal Design of (Smart) Contracts

Legal Design is an umbrella term for merging forward-looking legal thinking with design thinking. It takes an interdisciplinary and proactive approach to contracts and law, covering not only legal information and documents, but also legal services, processes, and systems.[31]

In the context of contracts, the focus is on supporting collaboration, driving desirable outcomes, creating opportunities, and preventing problems before they arise. This requires contracts and processes that make sense for business and the people who work with those contracts. Their needs are not being served well by contracts' current design (or lack of design), whether those contracts are smart or "dumb."[32]

As Tim Cummins, the then CEO of the International Association for Contract and Commercial Management (IACCM) put it: "Impenetrable, incomprehensible, confusing and downright boring. These are a few of the words commonly associated with contracts. Whether it is the way they are designed, or the way they are worded,

---

[31]For Proactive Law and Proactive Contracting, see Siedel and Haapio (2011) and Haapio (2006). For Legal Design, see Hagan (n.d.) and "What is Legal Design?" at LeDA/Legal Design Alliance (n.d.).

[32]For "dumb" contracts, see Lipshaw (2018).

the overwhelming majority of contracts merit those descriptions."[33] The look and feel of Smart Contracts is not likely to improve the situation for human readers. Even if Smart Contracts offer perfect performance, humans will remain in the picture for the foreseeable future.

Legal Design is about applying human-centered design to prevent or solve legal problems. It prioritizes the point of view of the "users" of the law—not only lawyers and judges, but also citizens, consumers, and businesses.[34] The approach is particularly important in the context of Legal Tech and Smart Contracts, where the choices the builders and users make can have a huge impact on both the processes and systems as well as their outputs. Legal designers can bring a new perspective to Smart Contract planning and making by asking questions such as:

i.   How can we make "good" Smart Contracts?
ii. How can we build user-friendly systems, interfaces, and editors that facilitate the making of "good" Smart Contracts—and what does "good" mean here?
iii. How can we make sure Smart Contracts capture the intent of their parties?
iv. How can we secure successful implementation of Legal Tech and transformation from "dumb" to Smart Contracts?
v.   How can we build powerful interface tools that empower individuals to make the best choice for them at the Smart Contract planning and making stage?

Where people are needed to initiate a contract or to translate some obligations of the contract into action, they need to be aware of their roles and responsibilities, and what they need to do when. This requires interfaces that are easy to use and information that it is easy to understand. How best to do all of these things, is a question deeply rooted in the discipline of information design.[35] Legal information design is about organizing and displaying information in a way that maximizes its clarity and understandability. It focuses on the needs of the users who may need to grasp both the big picture and the details and switch between these two views. Even in the era of Smart Contracts, the need remains to create contracts and guidance that users can understand and put into practice.

Legal Design stresses the importance of visual communication. Visualizing helps humans to think, communicate, make assumptions visible, and secure understanding across disciplines. The goal is not to create images—the goal is to create understanding. In the context of Smart Contracts, visualization can help create functional, useful, and usable processes, systems, and outcomes. It can help lawyers, technologists, and business people see the big picture and communicate and share solutions.

No law requires contracts to look and feel like legal documents, and they do not have to be text-only. Visualization—here understood as adding graphs, icons, tables, charts and images to supplement text—can help human readers in navigating contract text, opening up its meaning, and reinforcing its message. At the contract planning

---

[33]Cummins (2016).

[34]LeDA/Legal Design Alliance (n.d.).

[35]Haapio and Passera (in press).

stage visualization can help identify the parties' goals and expectations, align these, and capture them in a record.

Different jurisdictions have different requirements for valid contracts, but by and large, the freedom of contract allows the parties to choose whether, when and to whom they want to commit themselves through a contract. The parties are not only free to choose and agree upon the contents of their contract, they are also free to choose its form (except when the law requires a special form, such as in the case of sale of real property). As long as the arrangement and the parties' intent to commit (or not to commit, as the case may be at the preliminary stages) are clear, the parties have a freedom to tailor their affairs and to design their contracts the way they want, according to their own needs and interests. If they want to, they can choose to deviate from the traditional paradigm in which the contents of contracts are expressed as text only.[36] They can choose to use code, a visual user-friendly interface, or both for their contracts—something that is already happening with the Creative Commons licenses, for example.[37]

What, then, is the true purpose of contracts? We are likely to obtain different answers from different people. Even lawyers may not agree among themselves. For some, winning possible future disputes and litigation is key, for others preventing these is what matters. If we take the view that contracts exist because of business deals and relationships, contracts become business tools rather than merely legal tools, and the role of contract lawyers changes: "like engineers, [they] want to make something useful that works for their clients."[38] Contracts themselves can be viewed as interfaces,[39] and information design methods and strategies can be used to simplify them.[40] Legal Design can help change mindsets, too, so the move toward a new paradigm—we call it Next Generation Contracts—can begin.

With the help of Legal Design, we can supplement text or code with layers of explanatory diagrams, examples, plain language translations, audio, or video. Merging Legal Tech with Legal Design helps switch between the different versions of the same content and facilitates the making of "good" contracts, whether smart or otherwise. With the help of code, we can also build better human-contract interfaces and arrive at "wise contracts"[41]—Smart Contracts that work for people and machines: contracts that are simple at the front, but smart—from a legal and technological perspective—at the back (Table 1).

---

[36]Haapio (2013), p. 79.

[37]See "Three "Layers" of Licenses" at Creative Commons (n.d.).

[38]Howarth (2013), p. 67.

[39]Haapio and Passera (in press).

[40]Waller et al. (2017).

[41]Hazard and Haapio (2017).

Table 1 Moving to next generation contracts

From This …	… To This
Legally perfect contracts that prepare for failure and seek to allocate all risk to the other party	**Usable** contracts that facilitate and guide desired action and help implement what is agreed
Contracts are **legal** tools, made to win in court: legally binding, enforceable, must cover all conceivable contingencies	Contracts are **business** tools: must be clear and easy-to-use to achieve business goals for a win-win deal
Contracts allocate **risk**. They are needed only when things go wrong	Contracts add **value**. They enable business success and prevent problems and disputes
Contracts are **text-only**	Contracts can be **presented as text, code, visuals, audio, video, or hybrids**, depending on the needs of the audience

Adapted from Haapio (2013), pp. 41–42 and Waller et al. (2017)

4 The Future of the Legal Profession?

In general, the image of lawyers as innovators or constructive partners in innovation is not positive. Entrepreneur and venture capitalist, Steve Blank, leaves little room for doubt when he claims that lawyers have always been poor at running innovative companies and that they often hold back such companies.[42] The traditional issues with lawyers are well-known: they are constantly "over-lawyering" and killing innovation; they are notorious for failing to prioritize issues, instead focusing on what are—from a business point of view—trivialities or irrelevancies; they have poor listening skills; they are inflexible and unresponsive.

These problems become even worse in the context of digital technologies. For a start, lawyers tend to zoom in on the "privacy" and "data protection" issues raised by new technologies, such as artificial intelligence or Blockchain. Or, they will explain how current rules don't allow for the use of "Big Data." They even argue that we need stricter rules and regulations to deal with IP infringements, for instance. In short, lawyers are constantly holding back innovation, rather than facilitating it. Lawyers are creating problems, rather than working to find solutions.

The traditional approach of lawyers is clearly wrong and short-sighted. Lawyers need to be much smarter about new technologies and their role in building a better future. This is not only necessary to remain relevant in a fast-changing digital world, but also to contribute to a better society for all.

So, what should lawyers be doing? In short, adapting and taking advantage of new opportunities. Here are three things that lawyers could be doing in order to add value. First, lawyers need to work with new technologies. Existing and new clients have to prepare for a new digital and innovation-driven economy. They want to get a better idea of how their businesses can benefit from Blockchain, Smart Contracts and algorithms. Such clients will expect their lawyers to understand these technologies

---

[42]https://thinkgrowth.org/why-lawyers-dont-run-startups-25c5e0c877ed.

in order to provide strategic business and legal advice. If lawyers are not able to give a satisfying answer to their clients, they run the risk that their clients will switch to another law firm or consultant. Being tech-savvy will be essential in building and maintaining "brand" loyalty.

Second, lawyers need to come up with "smart" solutions. We believe that digital technology has the potential to contribute to a better, healthier and safer world. Yet, there are challenges that we shouldn't ignore. We need to be smart about digital technologies. In order to come up with the best possible solutions, lawyers (and other consultants) need to have a detailed and accurate understanding of the new technologies in order to play a role in identifying such solutions.

Third, lawyers must learn to work together with designers and "technologists." We strongly believe that pro-active and tech-savvy lawyers can play a crucial role in the further development of the digital economy. This doesn't mean passively "applying" current rules and regulations to a new technology in order to constrain innovation. This is the type of lawyer that Steve Blank objects to. Rather, it requires new and different skills. The "best" lawyers of the future will be those that understand the need to work together with designers and technologists in order to find user-friendly technological solutions that can help generate confidence in the technology, *as well as* meeting the regulatory requirements.

This means going beyond a pure compliance role and instead focusing on adding genuine value by utilizing the current technological developments and Legal Design methodologies. For instance, how can we create an easy-to-use system in which autonomous and connected devices can build reputation and trust, and ensure that the collected data will only be shared with other trusted devices. Such an approach addresses privacy and data protection concerns, but also makes a product more attractive in today's marketplace.

5 Chapters

Each of the chapters collected here addresses different aspects of the above themes and issues.

The first chapter, by Rory Unsworth, focuses in more detail on what the widespread use of "self-executing" contracts means for the future of contracting. For certain standard contract types with simple and well understood provisions, little geographical variation, no intermediation and short execution periods, change is already occurring without great difficulties. However, in the case of more complex, more entrenched, and less agile sectors of the global economy, there are multiple hurdles to overcome and more time will be needed for implementation. The arrival of this new technology presents important questions about the future of contracting, as well as about traditional legal practice within both legal departments and law firms, calling for new forms of cooperation between business and their lawyers. Given that the natural reaction to change is resistance, that companies are having ever-greater challenges navigating international regulation and that as a result legal departments within companies tend to exert a strong influence out of line with the number of employees they include, the power of institutional resistance to delay adoption of the change will be considerable. To achieve these objectives, the chapter stresses the importance of a well thought through Digital Contract Optimization plan, supported by new technologies, as a means to mitigate the various risks associated with Smart Contracting.

Thomas D. Barton, Helena Haapio, Stefania Passera, and James G. Hazard also focus on contracting in commercial settings. They introduce one of the central problems with traditional contracts, namely that they are "documents written by lawyers, for lawyers," artifacts of a negotiated exchange wrapped tightly in pages of clauses intended to insulate the agreement against litigation attacks. Such verbose language and structure come at high costs, namely such contracts decrease accessibility, functionality, and efficiency. Reforms to the classic forms and mentality surrounding contracting have recently been proposed, several of which look to insights and methods outside the legal system. This chapter outlines two such recent efforts: information design and computer codification. Such methods can enhance communication, participation, and usefulness across the entire life-cycle of contracting: assessment of needs, gathering background resources, negotiation, commitment, implementation/monitoring, adjustment, and sometimes dispute resolution. Although challenging to integrate, better design and codification can re-conceptualize contracting in order to generate value and better manage business enterprises.

Margaret Hagan presents new models for the presentation of contracting terms and interactions, based on user research and design work in the context of consumer contracts. As more contracts become machine-readable, questions emerge over how people will interact with such contracts. Drawing on work at the Stanford Legal Design Lab, several new contract designs have been developed, tested and improved. This initial study led to the identification of key principles and best practices that demonstrate how consumer contracts can be more comprehensible, engaging, and effective. Such research can serve all of the stakeholders by improving disclosures, terms of service, privacy policies, and various other aspects of business-to-consumer contracts. Moreover, it links the literature of contract design for improved usability and outcomes with behavioral economist concerns over choice engines and decision making, legal scholarship on the effectiveness of disclosure as a regulatory mechanism, and HCI research on how best to engage users and help them navigate complex systems.

Charlotta Kronblad and Johanna E. Pregmark focus on the legal industry and highlight how the vast majority of law firms have remained the same without responding to the rising opportunities created by Legal Tech. This reluctance on the part of the mainstream legal industry to adopt new digital technologies has created a bifurcation with a minority of technology enthusiasts, on one side, and traditional sceptics on the other. This chapter examines the reasons for this situation and discusses the connection between industrial diffusion and the capacity for change of individual firms. The chapter argues that, for the moment, most law firms have neither the technological capabilities nor the economical motivation to change, and why digitalization has, instead, become a source of fear. However, in order to seize digital opportunities and adapt to the constantly, and rapidly, changing environment, law firms need to overcome this fear and develop the organizational capacity to change.

Ivar Timmer provides a case study of the Dutch experience with Legal Tech, focusing on the issue of contract automation. It is suggested that the number of organizations that are actively deploying contract automation is still relatively small, but growing. Contract automation can improve legal service delivery to consumers and SMEs, as well as contracting processes within organizations, and several organizations studies as part of this research report positive results. However, successfully implementing contract automation, especially for internal use within organizations, is not simple. Tight budgets, resistance to change and poor integration with other software are some of the problems that organizations encounter. Generally, human and organizational factors are often at least as important as the technological aspects. Nevertheless, in spite of these difficulties, the use of contract automation software in Dutch legal practice can be expected to increase in the near future as more law firms and companies expand their activities. The chapter concludes by exploring the thought that the increased use of contract automation will drive a further harmonization of contracts within various sectors and facilitate other technological applications, such as the automated analysis of contracts. In this way, automation brings multiple potential efficiency gains.

Cecilia Magnusson Sjöberg identifies a range of issues that are raised by "legal automation," which—as elsewhere in this book—is understood broadly as the use of modern information and communication technologies in a legal context. In particular, the chapter discusses the role of education as the need arises both for IT-professionals to be somewhat in command of IT Law as well as for lawyers to grasp Legal Tech. Another key issue is digital resources management, both within and outside the legal domain. The analysis concerns rights of access, on the one hand, and corresponding restrictions, on the other. For instance, freedom of expression and information are limited by personal data protection, transparency by secrecy, open data by information security and re-use of public sector information (PSI) by intellectual property, etc. Such a "legal landscape of contradictions" is generally speaking why artificial intelligence (AI) comes into the picture as lever of legal system management. At the same time, it is important to remember that there have been attempts to automate law in a broad sense for decades, and that quite a few of the main challenges concerning decision making systems are still valid. In response to the legal implications of today's AI developments and implemented applications a new legal entity—digital person—is introduced. The overall purpose is to acknowledge the need for a conceptual model for legal reasoning supplementing the well-established notions of "natural person" and "legal person."

Marcelo Corrales, Paulius Jurčys and George Kousiouris analyze some of the main legal requirements laid down in the new European General Data Protection Regulation (GDPR) with regard to hybrid Cloud Computing transformations. Significantly, the GDPR imposes several restrictions on the storing, accessing, processing and transferring of personal data. This has generated concerns with regard to its practicability and flexibility given the dynamic nature of the Internet. The current architecture and technical features of the Cloud do not allow adequate control for end-users. Therefore, in order for the Cloud adopters to be legally compliant, the design of Cloud Computing architectures should include additional automated capabilities and certain "nudging" techniques to promote better choices. The chapter explains how to fine tune and effectively embed these legal requirements at the earlier stages of the architectural design of the computer code. The discussion focuses on Smart Contracts and Service Level Agreements (SLAs) frameworks, which include selection tools that take an information schema and a pseudo-code that follows a programming logic to process information based on that schema. The pseudo-code is essentially the easiest way to write and design computer code, which can check automatically the legal compliance of the contractual framework. This raises a set of legal questions that have been specifically designed to urge Cloud providers to disclose relevant information and comply with the legal requirements established by the GDPR.

Sam Wrigley also examines how automation of contracting will create new legal risks. His chapter focuses on the GDPR, specifically the issue of how data controllers are only allowed to recruit data processors who provide "sufficient guarantees" that they will comply with data protection law. Given the wide definitions of the key terms "processing," "controller" and "processor," it seems likely that we will see many situations where at least one of those parties is not acting in a professional capacity, but still comes under the remit of the GDPR (e.g., if the personal data is being processing in a Blockchain). This creates the risk that parties will simply agree to contracts without having read or understood them, leading to significant legal liabilities for both parties and a lack of sufficient protection for data subjects. The chapter examines how parties should arrange their contracts to provide the best possible chance of complying with data protection law, focusing on how controllers can use technological and other non-contractual solutions to compliment such agreements—while still respecting each party's autonomy and freedoms.

Mark Fenwick and Erik P. M. Vermeulen conclude by returning to the broader implications of these developments for the future of the legal profession. Two interconnected arguments are introduced. First, the ongoing "digital revolution"—the expansion of Legal Tech—will continue to disrupt legal work as it has traditionally operated. Several aspects of this disruption, many of which are discussed in multiple chapters, are outlined. Second, in contrast to previous technological revolutions, the "deployment" of disruptive innovation in the context of the digital revolution seems unlikely to be primarily "state-led." Instead, new technologies will be deployed by a coalition of diverse private actors (entrepreneurs, technologists, consultants, and other professionals) working in collaboration. Crucial amongst these actors will be the lawyer of the future operating as "transaction engineer." The chapter outlines this transaction engineer function and its importance in the deployment of emerging digital technologies and for the future of the legal profession.

References

Asharaf S, Adarsh S (2017) Decentralized computing using blockchain technologies and smart contracts: emerging research and opportunities. Information Science Reference (IGI Global), Hershey

Blank S (2017) Why lawyers don't run startups. https://thinkgrowth.org/why-lawyers-dont-run-startups-25c5e0c877ed. Accessed 10 Sept 2018

Bues M-M, Matthaei E (2017) LegalTech on the rise: technology changes legal work behaviors, but does not replace its profession. In: Jacob K, Schindler D, Strathausen R (eds) Liquid legal: transforming legal into a business savvy, information enabled and performance driven industry. Springer, Cham

Creative Commons (n.d.) About the licenses. http://creativecommons.org/licenses/. Accessed 10 Sept 2018

Cummins T (2016) Can contracts really change? IACCM/Commitment Matters Blog, 2 March. https://www2.iaccm.com/resources/?id=9147. Accessed 10 Sept 2018

Drescher D (2017) Blockchain basics: a non-technical introduction in 25 steps. Springer, New York

Haapio H (2006) Business success and problem prevention through proactive contracting. In: Wahlgren P (ed) A Proactive approach. Scandinavian studies in law, vol 49. Stockholm Institute for Scandinavian Law, Stockholm. http://www.scandinavianlaw.se/pdf/49-9.pdf. Accessed 10 Sept 2018

Haapio H (2013) Next generation contracts: a paradigm shift. Lexpert Ltd., Helsinki

Haapio H, Passera S (in press) Contracts as interfaces: exploring visual representation patterns in contract design. In: Katz MJ, Dolin RA, Bommarito M (eds) Legal informatics. Cambridge University Press, Cambridge

Hagan M (n.d.) Law by design. http://www.lawbydesign.co. Accessed 10 Sept 2018

Hazard J, Haapio H (2017) Wise contracts: smart contracts that work for people and machines. In: Schweighofer E et al (eds) Trends and communities of legal informatics. Proceedings of the 20th international legal informatics symposium IRIS 2017. Österreichische Computer Gesellschaft. http://books@ocg.at, Wien

Howarth D (2013) Law as engineering—thinking about what lawyers do. Edward Elgar, Cheltenham

Huang P (2015) A dissection of bitcoin. Lulu.com, s. l.

Kosba A et al (2015) Hawk: the blockchain model of cryptography and privacy-preserving smart contracts. https://www.weusecoins.com/as-sets/pdf/library/Hawk%20%20The%20Blockchain%20Model%20of%20Cryptography%20and%20Privacy-Preserving%20Smart%20Contracts.pdf. Accessed 10 Oct 2017

Kost de Sevres (2016) The blockchain revolution, smart contracts and financial transactions. https://www.dlapiper.com/en/uk/insights/publications/2016/04/the-blockchain-revolution/. Accessed 10 Oct 2017

LeDA/Legal Design Alliance (n.d.) https://www.legaldesignalliance.org. Accessed 10 Sept 2018

Linthicum D (2016) Linking up blockchain and cloud. https://www.cloudtp.com/doppler/linking-blockchain-cloud/. Accessed 20 Nov 2017

Lipshaw J-M (2018) The persistence of 'dumb' contracts. Suffolk University Law School Research Paper No. 18–11, 25 June, last revised 6 Sep (Stanford Journal of Blockchain Law & Policy, 2019, Forthcoming). https://ssrn.com/abstract=3202484. Accessed 10 Sept 2018

Morabito V (2017) Business innovation through blockchain: the B^3 perspective. Springer, Cham

Mougayar W (2015) Understanding the blockchain: we must be prepared for the blockchain's promise to become a new development environment. https://www.oreilly.com/ideas/understanding-the-blockchain. Accessed 16 May 2017

Prusty N (2017) Building blockchain projects: develop real-time practical DApps using Ethereum and JavaScript. Packt Publishing, Birmingham

Siedel G, Haapio H (2011) Proactive law for managers: a hidden source of competitive advantage. Gower, Farnham

Swan M (2015) Blockchain: blueprint for a new economy, 1st edn. O'Reilly, Sebastopol (CA)

Stark J (2016) How close are smart contracts to impacting real-world Law? http://www.coindesk.com/blockchain-smarts-contracts-real-world-law/. Accessed 16 May 2016

Szabo N (1997a) Contracts with bearer. http://szabo.best.vwh.net/bearer_contracts.html. Accessed 17 Oct 2017

Szabo N (1997b) The idea of smart contracts. http://szabo.best.vwh.net/smart_con-tracts_idea.html. Accessed 17 Oct 2017

The Economist (2015a) The great chain of being sure about things. http://www.economist.com/briefing/21677228-technology-behind-bitcoin-lets-people-who-do-not-know-or-trust-each-other-build-dependable. Accessed 15 Oct 2017

The Economist (2015b) Bitcoin: the next big thing. http://www.economist.com/news/special-report/21650295-or-it-next-big-thing. Accessed 15 May 2016

Tomas P (2017) Cryptocurrency 101: a beginners guide. Pronoun

Walch A (2018) Open-source operational risk: should public blockchains serve as financial market infrastructures? In: Lee D, Deng R (eds) Handbook of blockchain, digital finance, and inclusion, vol 3. Academic Press, London

Waller R, Haapio H, Passera S (2017) Contract simplification: the why and the how. Contract Excell J (July 24). http://journal.iaccm.com/contracting-excellence-journal/contract-simplification-the-why-and-the-how. Accessed 10 Sept 2018

Wattenhofer R (2016) The science of the blockchain. Inverted Forest Publishing, s. l.

Weber I et al (2016) Untrusted business process monitoring and execution using blockchain. In: La Rosa M, Loos P, Pastor O (eds) Business process management, 14th international conference, BPM 2016, Rio de Janeiro, Brazil, September 18–22, 2016, proceedings. Springer, Cham

Williams D (2017) Cryptocurrency compendium: a reference for cryptocurrencies. Lulu.com

Smart Contract This! An Assessment of the Contractual Landscape and the Herculean Challenges it Currently Presents for "Self-executing" Contracts

Rory Unsworth

Abstract The widespread use of "self-executing" contracts is now only a question of time. For certain standard contract types with simple and well understood provisions, little international variation, no intermediation and short execution periods, that time is now as the change is already happening (examples are digital rights management and various banking applications.). It is the other more complex, more entrenched, and less agile sectors of the global economy which are the focus of this paper. Here there will be hurdles to overcome and more time needed for implementation—it will be a difficult task. The arrival of this new technology presents important questions about the future of contracting, as well as about traditional legal practice within both legal departments and law firms, calling for a new quality of cooperation between business and their lawyers. Given that the natural reaction to change is resistance, that companies are having ever-greater challenges navigating international regulation and that as a result legal department within companies tend to exert a strong influence out of line with the number of employees they include, the power of institutional resistance to delay adoption of the change will be considerable. This chapter will seek to add a dose of realism to the techno-optimists in the late adolescence of the 21st century for whom the change is so far advanced it is practically finished. In this chapter it is largely assumed that readers understand how Distributed Ledger Technology works, and the principal focus will be on the contractual challenges standing in the way of the implementation of "self-executing contracts," to which it will also offer some solutions. The original idea contained in this chapter is to embark on a well-planned Digital Contract Optimization journey, supported by new technologies, as a means to manage various risks associated with algorithmically driven processes. This chapter will address the question of the institutional legal mindset as a potential delaying factor and will present a Darwinian argument to explain that change is inevitable and will be radical in terms of the new demands on lawyers.

Keywords Smart contracts · Law · Legal practice · Technology

R. Unsworth (✉)
Swiss Re, Head Contracts Centre and Smart Contracts Counsel, Zurich, Switzerland
e-mail: rory_unsworth@swissre.com

© Springer Nature Singapore Pte Ltd. 2019
M. Corrales et al. (eds.), *Legal Tech, Smart Contracts and Blockchain*,
Perspectives in Law, Business and Innovation,
https://doi.org/10.1007/978-981-13-6086-2_2

1   Introduction

This chapter deals with "self-executing," or "autonomous" contracts. This includes not just Smart Contracts, but also hybrid Smart Contracts,[1] or Ricardian forms.[2] These are relatively recent technologies[3] turning a Distributed Ledger Technology (abbreviated to "DLT," of which the best-known examples are Blockchain and Corda)[4] into a contract execution system by embedding transactional protocols and orders which respond to the happening of certain data events (or "States").

This technology is innovative and modern, but paradoxically, mainstream contracting practices have gone the other way—more deeply into complexity and obscurantism. Whilst technology has evolved with more or less the speed predicted by George Moore in the 1960s,[5] the legal and contracting framework of many branches of commerce has not. The format of complex commercial contracts remains as it was 30 years ago—formatted like a book, with long, impenetrable texts which are frequently subject to litigation in Courts. The chapter of this book *Successful Contracts: Integrating Design and Technology* by Barton et al., suggests sensible approaches for the creation of "Successful Contracts"—nevertheless, the fact remains that complex commercial contracts in their current form are the opposite—they are "Unsuccessful Contracts." This chapter suggests that to all intents and purposes the current entities are encrypted. Decrypting these entities *en masse* is nothing less than a Herculean task requiring time, perseverance, dedication and multidisciplinary skills and expertise to unlock their secrets.

This chapter considers the process by which the two—the shining technology and the dusty old contracting practices—will converge over time. It suggests a way for the meaning of existing contracts to be decrypted—a process which is referred to as "Digital Contract Optimization" and which is compared to the civilizing tasks that Hercules was set by his cousin, enemy and sponsor, Eurystheus.

To better illustrate the challenges that will be encountered during the convergence, the focus is kept specifically and deliberately on more complex contracting segments (usually Business to Business arrangements) such as infrastructural projects or commercial lines insurance. Many of the examples will come from insurance because this is a popular paradigm of complex contracting, and a sector well-known to the author. This chapter utilizes simpler and more standard contract forms—which are generally easier to turn into smarter contracts—merely to compare and contrast with the more complex contracting segments.

---

[1] Norton Rose (2017), p. 21.

[2] Grigg (2015).

[3] Smart Contracts were first proposed in the 1990s by Nick Szabo and first utilized on an industrial scale in 2008 with the arrival of Bitcoin—for the original academic paper on this topic, see Szabo (1997). Ricardian contracts were proposed in 1996 by Ian Grigg, see Grigg (2004).

[4] See, e.g., White Paper from Corda entitled *Corda, An Introduction*, Brown et al. (2016).

[5] Moore (1965), p. 3.

For some, the complex contracting segment is not the sweet-spot of self-executing contracts at all, and some critics believe it is not even worth attempting such convergence. The argument in this chapter is that it is both possible and worth doing, but that there are civilizing tasks which will have to be carried out proactively, the first if not the most important being to find intra- and inter-organizational agreement on what precisely the contracts are supposed to mean in their current state, let alone in digital form.

Existing contract forms for such complex segments are extremely influential and create change inertia. It is simply not possible to rip up all the existing contracts and start again from scratch utilizing simple, well-illustrated documents easily translated into code—in complex segments, existing contracts are the mandatory starting point of any drive towards self-executing contracts. A strategic approach will be required, like the one which gave rise to the adoption of Incoterms.[6]

This chapter proposes strategies to deal with that uncertainty as to meaning, and that institutional change inertia by taking a proactive portfolio approach. It underlines some of the pitfalls that will be encountered along the way, but also reassures that a conscious effort fully to (re)understand existing books of business and to re-engineer the contract assessment process around new tools is a standalone benefit, with or without a final apotheosis on the Mount Olympus of fully self-executing contracts on a DLT.

As it was for Hercules, so it will be for the present generation of contracting demi-gods. Looking back after the tribulations, it may not always be entirely clear why it was specifically the Lernaean Hydra that had to be slaughtered, nor why it is Hippolyta's belt rather than any other belt in the world which the sponsor wanted in his hands. What we do know is that when all the tasks are completed, the aggregate effect will be to make the world of contracting a safer and better place for sustainable commerce and cooperation to thrive.

The title of this chapter, therefore, is both a challenge and a call to arms. This chapter focuses on process rather than generic DLT topics such as security and privacy, or Smart Contract risks including validity, judicial interpretation, signature, or bugs in coding. Other sources cover these issues perfectly well.[7]

2 Self-executing Contracts—How They Work

2.1 Smart Contracts

As the best-known example of a self-executing contract is a so-called "Smart Contract," we will start there.

---

[6]Incoterms are standard terms for Commerce published by the International Chamber of Commerce. They have been around since the 1930s, and their usage took many years to become standard.

[7]See, e.g., Fulbright (2016). In terms of the vision behind DLT and its potential benefits, see B3i (2018).

A Smart Contract is not a written contract on paper of the traditional kind, nor is it simply an online contract. It is described as "smart" because it can do more than both of these paradigms, in the same way that a "smart phone" can do more than just making calls. It takes the form of computer code on a Distributed Ledger Technology (which can be a Blockchain but can also be another type of DLT such as Corda)[8] and *executes itself* upon receipt of electronic data inputs. It effects an action on a DLT in a manner comparable to a formula in the cell of an Excel spreadsheet—it adjusts itself or transfers payment or other assets, monitors stock levels, or effects other actions automatically because that is what it is programmed to do.

Contracts have been concluded online for many years. Indeed, a large proportion of all shares in the US are traded through automated systems. With a Smart Contract the key enhancement is self-execution through the *combination* of its ability to react to "online" data triggers, *and* the access of the Smart Contract to the value itself. It is the combination of Smart Contracts and DLT that leads people refer to Blockchain as "the Internet of Value"[9] or "the World-Wide Ledger."[10] It is also this combination which makes "Smart Contracts" the most transformative Blockchain application at time of writing, since they allow a new standard of trading—disintermediated, safe, efficient, and without a central point of potential failure.

To understand this better we need to compare the working of a Smart Contract with that of an online contract. The typical Internet contract describes in words on an Internet form (usually, integrating a set of long form General Conditions) what will happen but does not have access to the value which will satisfy the trade. If, say, an online book retailer fails to deliver a textbook which has been ordered, it will be for the purchaser to enforce any recourse by taking the next step, such as triggering a complaint procedure or claiming a refund or compensation through a special email address. Usually, this will be prescribed in the boilerplate General Conditions which the purchaser has to click-and-accept before the sale/purchase contract is concluded. After that, it is for the book seller to trigger the payment from its bank account (on a separate ledger kept by the bank), or to issue a refundable credit note to the buyer.

The Smart Contract goes further than that customary online paradigm. Not only does it *define* the next step, it *executes* it by re-ordering the textbook from the next supplier, and if necessary transferring value captured on the DLT from seller to buyer to represent a time penalty against the book seller. Access to this value is granted to the Smart Contract because it sits within a DLT which captures that value. Incidentally, it is not that the Smart Contract needs to be embedded on the same DLT as the value to be transferred, it just needs a command function over it.

---

[8]Corda is a Blockchain technology for business which provides the infrastructure for various well-known Blockchain Consortia such as the banking consortium R3 and the insurance industry initiative B3i. Further details can be found at: https://www.corda.net. Accessed 20 August 2018.

[9]See, e.g., Deloitte (2017a, b) publication *The Internet of Value-Exchange*. Available at: https://www2.deloitte.com/content/dam/Deloitte/uk/Documents/Innovation/deloitte-uk-internet-of-value-exchange.pdf. Accessed 20 Sept 2018.

[10]Tapscott and Tapscott (2016), p. 75.

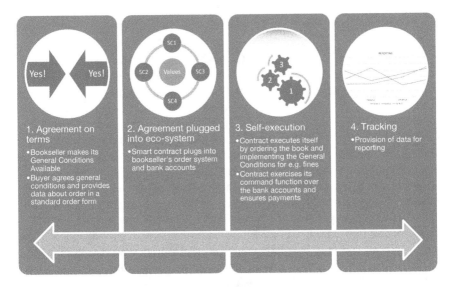

Fig. 1 Simple smart contract transactional process. *Source* Author

The visual below seeks to illustrate the enhancement to the transactional process provided by a Smart Contract approach (Fig. 1).

With this kind of approach, the amount of human intervention after contract conclusion will be more limited than ever before. For good or bad the need to assert rights post-closure will be reduced. The computer code will not contain human concepts such as largesse or opportunism. It will not be guilty of holding onto funds that should be handed over, nor will it waive rights of recovery because it cannot be bothered to enforce them, or (more consciously) because it will be too expensive to enforce, or because it wants to conserve the relationship between the parties. The computer will simply do what it has been programmed to do at the outset—funds will be transferred from one party to another on the Distributed Ledger, and other remedies will be triggered.

Naturally, the data inputs triggering contractual actions need to be trusted by both parties and agreed at the outset. Examples of such sources will include official registers capable of providing electronic messages, the Internet (including the Internet of Things), and other business networks, and they will need to be joined to the DLT by connectors known as "Oracles," which will amongst other things exercise the level of human oversight required.

Some governance may be introduced across business networks by foundation-type organisations, similar to the International Standardization Organization (ISO), to ensure minimum standards, and a common "language" and approach.

2.2 Smarter Contracts

In his foundational paper on Smart Contracts, computer scientist Nick Szabo[11] described them quite narrowly—as entirely automated processes. His best-known comparison is to a vending machine which delivers its bottle of soft drink after receiving a coin, and without human intervention. This purist notion fits well with the simplest transactions (e.g., transfer of Bitcoins from one owner to another on the Blockchain ledger) but cannot work for every aspect of more complex contracts, which is why the rest of this chapter describes self-executing contracts more broadly, either as "self-executing contracts," or as "smarter contracts." "Smarter contracts" are not claimed to be better than Smart Contracts, they are just intended to designate a broader category of technology types, which would include Smart Contracts as fully automated entities as per the original description by Nick Szabo, but also "hybrid" or "split" models (the latter to include Ricardian forms[12]). The "hybrid" model allows human intervention, and broader consequences of a triggering data point beyond simply payment—it may be that the input triggers a message to an Oracle to become involved and to take and record a decision.

The "split" model is based on the notion that the long-form natural language contract retains its place and its importance, but that key elements of it are "translated" into data points that trigger Smart Contract mechanisms. This is possible as long as:

  i. There is a clear precedence between the long-form contract and the mechanisms effected by the Smart Contract aspects;
 ii. The two mechanisms work together harmoniously, and;
iii. There is some kind of Errors & Omissions clause prescribing what will happen in the event of disharmony between the two arrangements.

In that sense, unlike with pure Smart Contracts, "smarter contracts" do not mean that humans disappear from the process—for complex contracts this will be neither possible to achieve, nor desirable. A useful comparison is between fully autonomous cars—where there is no need for a human driver—and semi-autonomous cars such as those of the current generation, where a human driver is prompted to take over at certain key moments. "Smarter contracts" reduce principally the amount of human administration, not necessarily the amount of human oversight or judgment.

This kind of hybridization is happening quite naturally in more complex contract segments. By way of example, various DLT-based Flight Delay Insurance products have been developed in the last 3 years, and each has a set of boilerplate General Conditions in natural language which has precedence over the automated mechanism.[13] This is a typical "split" model. When an insured party sets up a new contract with such a company it is mandatory to click "Agree General Conditions" before the contract can be accepted, just as in the existing Internet world. There are experts who

---

[11] Szabo (1997).

[12] Grigg (2004).

[13] For example, separate products are on offer from the Atlas Company (which offers the Etherisk platform https://fdd.etherisc.com); AXA; Chubb (in partnership with Swiss Re) and Ergo.

describe the effect of a transaction triggered by a Smart Contract as irrevocable,[14] but with "smarter contracts" this is an option within the set-up, not a pre-requisite. As in the Flight Delay Insurance products referred to above, off-chain appeals are still allowed, and a bug in the code will not stop the insured being able to recover off-ledger under the General Conditions, nor will it necessarily stop recovery in the other direction. The nature of these products remains insurance, not code.

In addition to Flight Delay Insurance, such contracts are already used in loan and related credit agreements, stock and other asset trading contracts, and commercial letters of credit. These are simpler contracting segments, and we will now examine the factors promoting ease of smarter contracting in such segments, in order to then understand the special factors of complexity in the complex segment.

3   Why Creating a New Book of Smarter Contracts Is Easier

Any business in the privileged position of selling non-negotiable contracts, or of creating "new books of business" will find it easier to transition to smarter contracts. In definitional terms, by a "new book of business" in this case is meant:

  i.   A new business;
 ii.   A new product;
iii.   A new client segment;
 iv.   A new client in a Business-to-Consumer ("B2C") context.

In the context of our online book seller, the sale of books to consumers is easy to transition to a DLT. In the current state of contracting, that "online retailer" has its customer ordering process online, but it may still conclude some or all of its supply-side contracts in the traditional "off-line" manner. Its online operation can easily be transformed into DLT-based smarter contracts because each order is a new contract (requiring acceptance of current General Conditions), and the seller has the power to determine the terms of its sale to the consumer. A book buyer will not care, nor necessarily even notice that its next order for a textbook is driven by a smarter contract on a DLT. The form she needs to fill out does not need to change in look and feel, as the same data points will be required as before. Designers[15] are skilled at making new forms with the same Graphic User Interface as old forms to ensure a smooth user transition. Our book buyer may have to note a change to the General Conditions to cover the installation of the smarter contract approach, but as usual she

---

[14] See, e.g., Fulbright (2017) in their report *Arbitrating Smart Contract Disputes* state: "Irrevocable: once initiated, the outcomes for which a Smart Contract is encoded to perform cannot typically be stopped (unless an outcome depends on an unmet condition)." They do however agree that Smart Contracts lie on a spectrum, including "a hybrid or split model e.g., a contract in code incorporating by reference the terms of a natural language master agreement"; and "a natural language contract with some encoded performance e.g., the payment mechanism."

[15] The key role of designers in the new contracting landscape is covered in the Chapter of this book *Successful Contracts: Integrating Design and Technology* by Barton et al.

will probably just tick what she is expected to (without necessarily reading) and move on. The placement process will match her expectations, and she will be positively surprised if she receives a credit for her next purchase if the textbook arrives one week later than agreed.

In contrast, it will be harder for the online bookseller to transfer into that format its existing and continuing supply-side (Business-to-Business, or "B2B") contracts, whose wording will have been negotiated, and will therefore come with a legacy complexity which is dealt with in the next section.

In the same way, if a start-up bank or a start-up retail insurance company decides to set up its processing platform based on smarter contracts, the new customer will not notice because there is no precedent between itself and the financial institution. As it is a Business-to-Consumer business model (or "B2C") the consumer (new account holder or new insured) will in any event be expecting to have to accept standard Terms and Conditions and will be prepared to share certain information about herself in a standard form provided (essentially, imposed) by the selling institution. The order or placement process will be designed in line with the consumer's expectations, which are relatively few in number, and quite adaptable prior to the establishment of a normalized relationship.

The party driving creation of the new book of contracts (the seller) will be able to analyze its new product offering and the means of its provision. It will assess the data it needs from the new client, create the smarter contract clauses and essentially drive dissemination of the new offering quite comfortably and with high compatibility with its requirements for an efficient DLT. In short, it will be in control.

4 Why Transforming an Existing Book of Contracts into Smarter Contracts Is Harder, But Still Desirable

4.1 Difficulty

Some commentators wonder whether the complex contracting segment is actually a fit for smarter contracts at all.[16] This chapter coheres with the views expressed in the chapter of this book *Successful Contracts: Integrating Design and Technology* by Barton et al. Namely, that leveraging smarter contracting in this segment is possible, and that collaborative approaches will indeed be found to ease the way, if the business case is strong enough. Section 4.2 ("Desirability") covers the business case. This section examines the high-level, or foundational factors contributing to the difficulty.

---

[16]See Cap Gemini (2016). Their paper *Smart Contracts in Financial Services: Getting from Hype to Reality*, suggest that firms should consider whether they really need Smart Contracts in cases where terms are not simple and standard.

For most established companies seeking to ramp up adoption of smarter contracts and to capture the benefits of such new infrastructure, value in their businesses is trapped in existing contracts. Some of those contracts have lasted or been renewed for many years. Many of the individual contracts in the portfolio have been changed over time by means of addenda or endorsements which will make it more challenging to read the documentation to establish the real-time contractual position which prevails on every topic at the point of transfer to the DLT. In addition, where the contractual mechanisms are complex and contextual, a clause used in one context or subject to one applicable law can have a very different impact to the same clause used in a different context. Particularly for global institutions (e.g., companies) contracting under hundreds of applicable laws, the challenge of running an expert network to understand how a particular clause works in every situation is considerable.

Even if a business can manage to translate all the existing clauses from the legacy book into smarter contract clauses reflecting the net contractual position (i.e., after application of amendments), the existing contracts may change again next year and create a requirement for more translation, and an ever-growing collection of coded clauses. The existing book is a living book, continuously shape-shifting, whereas the creation of a new book on a DLT involves form-filling, drop-down menus and radio buttons precisely to limit the changes that can be made to the data structure. The contract in such cases is already made of structured data at the outset, whereas traditional contracts are unstructured.

The expectations prevailing in such existing (and more complex) contractual relationships constrain the parties within a matrix of terms and conditions which they—as well as other stakeholders such as regulators—have become used to over time, even though the original authors of the individual clauses, or textual blocks, may be long gone. Applying a literal-minded, contract-by-contract method, and translating every clause, it could take many decades to on-board large books of business.

Rendering legal text in current complex contracts into computational logic will be a fundamental change to the nature or style of an agreement. In such cases, the parties naturally want to know what has changed—or preferably that nothing has changed. If anything has changed, the parties will want to know whether the balance of value in the contract has changed in one direction or another. If so, the party receiving less value than before will normally wish to vary the price. It may even be that both parties wish to vary the price in their favor in order to share the savings in transactional costs. In order to establish the value of any contract changes that have been made in the transition to smarter contracts, the parties would need to apply the following steps:

i. "Translate" the contract clauses into coded clauses;

ii. Agree that new "translation" including the new data sources and metrics by which the contract will be triggered and, finally evaluated;

iii. Adjust the price if necessary to consider any changes made in the act of translation and to fairly distribute the savings captured by the efficiencies created by the smarter contract.

In Step 1 above (translating the clauses from its book of contracts), each party would again go through an internal alignment on meaning and in that process no doubt discovers certain consequences of existing long-form clauses which it had not intended when it agreed them. It would then take an effort highly comparable to a full renegotiation of the terms whilst the performance of the contract runs on uninterrupted. For professionals on the working level, it is like changing the wheels on a moving train. For senior management, it is like learning afresh about the true construction of the train you are travelling in. These are things that no one wants to do, or to think about, as they travel from A to B.

One of the key factors of this difficulty is often the sheer size of the book. In "The Truth About Blockchain,"[17] Marco Iansiti and Karin R. Lakhani make a useful comparison between the adoption of DLT and the adoption of the Internet Protocol Suite (aka TCP/IP)[18] in the development of email and the Internet. They posit that "two dimensions affect how a foundational technology and its use cases evolve. The first is novelty—the degree to which an application is new to the world...the second dimension is complexity, represented by the level of ecosystem coordination involved—the number and diversity of parties that need to work together to produce value with the technology." In the following section, techniques will be proposed to prepare complex contracts for the DLT, and a closer examination of the individual challenges will be covered in Sect. 6. For the time being, the key take-away point is that in most existing business sectors currently utilizing complex contract forms, the novelty of self-executing contracts is undeniable, and the complexity involved in the transformation from status quo is large.

4.2 Desirability

Based on a survey of their corporate members (numbering 12,000 at the time of the survey, now 50,000 globally), the International Association of Contracts and Commercial Management (IACCM) estimates that the current pitfalls of contracting lead to value erosion of 9% or more[19] across commercial sectors. Not all of the pitfalls identified by the IACCM can be resolved by self-executing contracts, but even half the total—4.5%—translates to huge numbers in dollar terms when applied to the size of the business enshrined in more complex contracts. This makes self-executing contracts in these sectors (which include energy, petrochemicals, shipping, real estate, public utilities, infrastructure and commercial insurance) just as desirable as in the simpler sectors. By way of just a few examples:

---

[17]Iansiti and Lakhani (2017).

[18]TCP/IP stands for Transmission Control Protocol/Internet Protocol. It is the set of protocols upon which two or more computers can communicate within a network on the Internet. It was developed to standardize Internet exchanges following an original idea by Vint Cerf and Bob Kahn and is now adopted as a networking standard.

[19]See Cummins (2016) slide 8.

i. Santander stated in 2015 that Smart Contracting could reduce banks' infrastructure costs attributable to cross-border payments, securities trading and regulatory compliance by between \$15–20 billion per annum[20];

ii. A 2017 study of investment banks by Accenture[21] led to the conclusion that 27% of the cost base could be saved;

iii. Almost half the total P&C insurance premiums in the US come from more complex Commercial lines,[22] which are nearly always brokered[23] and therefore subject to broking fees which could be reduced through self-executing contracts. IBIS World estimated that in 2017 the size of the global insurance industry broker revenues was in excess of USD600bn.[24]

In any event, the size of these sectors is clearly very significant, as are the potential savings, including opportunities for disintermediation, both from outside and from within organizations.[25]

Other than pure transaction costs, the "push" factors[26] include excess documentation requiring reading at each step of the lifecycle; a manual claims process; regulatory and legal checks; slow settlement times; high exposure to Cyber risk as documents are exchanged via email or other unsecured mechanisms. On this last point, the existence of self-executing contracts on the DLT means that—assuming an appropriate governance structure and coding—transaction security is much higher than in standard online commerce. Immutability and trust are central promises of DLT, which are enforced by means of cryptography with an appropriate level of complexity set by the network for itself.

Paul Meeusen, CEO of B3i, has an interesting image which helps to visualize the scale of the benefit.

'Imagine,' he says, 'that a market for goods or services is like an urban traffic system. At the moment we spend time and emotional energy waiting for traffic lights and sitting at a Stop sign for the flow of traffic to allow us to move forward. We are forever stopping and starting, and occasionally bumping into each other or being caught speeding. Travel times are extended and it can be frustrating, particularly on hot days or when we are stressed about other things. In a future where cars are autonomous and communicate with each others' operating systems without human intervention, all this will be a thing of the past. In the

---

[20] Santander (2015).

[21] See Accenture's 2017 report. Available at: https://www.accenture.com/t20171108T095421Z_ _w__/sa-en/_acnmedia/Accenture/Conversion-Assets/DotCom/Documents/Global/PDF/ Consulting/Accenture-Banking-on-Blockchain.pdf#zoom=50. Accessed 23 July 2018.

[22] Insurance Information Institute (2016) Facts and Statistics; Commercial Lines. https://www.iii. org/fact-statistic/facts-statistics-commercial-lines. Accessed 11 July 2018.

[23] Swiss Re Sigma (2017), pp. 17, 19.

[24] IBIS World Report (2017) *Global Insurance Brokers & Agencies—Global Market Research Report*.

[25] Principally in the line of fire for disintermediation from such processes through the impact of smarter contracts are: Internal Contract Administrators and claims handlers; Brokers; Agents; Banks; Lawyers; Bailiffs.

[26] A "push" factor is the real management problem needing to be solved, see further Susskind (1990), p. 115.

same way such stop-start is a feature of the current contract landscape. I personally am looking forward to the time when contracts also will be autonomous, and will communicate with each others' computational logic in a way that reduces operational risk and brings other benefits such as improved accumulation control.'[27]

To quote the World Economic Forum[28]: "Good use cases must solve real problems for organizations. Great use cases solve real problems at a cost that is significantly lower than the benefits the adoption brings." There is clearly a great business case for self-executing contracts in the complex contracting segment. In comparison to the simpler contracting segment it will be more expensive to arrange and to implement, and there are various risks along the way. It will be costly, and it will take time, but a careful approach and good preparation will lead to gains which far outweigh the cost. The following section suggests how to prepare appropriately for the implementation.

5 Cleansing the Augean Stables: The Need for Digital Contract Optimization to Prepare Existing Books of Contracts for Smarter Contracting

As explained above, "Smart Contract That!" is easier to say than it is to do, particularly for large books of existing contracts coming from various drafting sources and showing factors of complexity. Time and evolution have sculpted contracts which are inherently complex and non-digital, in the way that time and evolution have produced jellyfish which inherently belong in salt water. When you take a jellyfish out of water it loses its shape and its abilities and dies within an hour. Naturally, time and design can allow that jellyfish to evolve, and to develop amphibian qualities. Where design is accidental, that time can amount to millions of years. The accelerating factor in the evolution would be deliberate re-design by genetic engineers and biologists.[29] In the case of complex contracts, that deliberate re-design will hereafter be called a Digital Contract Optimization.

This point is so central to this chapter that—even at the risk of mixing metaphors—it merits a second comparison, this time with the atonement myth of Hercules.[30] As a punishment for a crime committed in a moment of literal madness, the tale has him spending 12 years of his life serving his worthless, capricious and ungrateful sponsor in the execution of random tasks selected purely for their risk profiles (the more likely to result in death, the better). Constant innovation was required to deliver the tasks—his method and his tools were all for him to design, to

---

[27]Interview conducted between Paul Meeusen and the author on 21 August 2018.

[28]World Economic Forum (2018), p. 4.

[29]Techniques exist to accomplish this, such as targeted gene flow, see Andrew Trounson of the University of Melbourne in Science Matters. Available at: https://pursuit.unimelb.edu.au/articles/speeding-natural-selection-in-the-name-of-conservation. Accessed 28 May 2018.

[30]The best available rendering of the full story is in *Bibliotheca* of Pseudo-Apollodorus (1st or 2nd century AD), 2.4.1.2 and following.

find or to source. To make matters worse, Hercules had difficult annual performance appraisals requiring him to bring proof of execution (often very dangerous and very heavy animals carried alive and snarling from far-away lands) and from the second task onwards, he had no direct access to his sponsor, who spoke to him only through an intermediary[31] who could give no insights into strategy or task selection. As if these difficult working conditions were not enough, when a weary Hercules reported back after the last planned task (the 10th), the sponsor increased the requirement to 12, which makes it arguably the first recorded example of "scope creep."[32]

The tasks selected came with quite varied challenges. The most common relied on physical strength or speed, but the Augean Stables challenge tested his ability to withstand humiliation, as well as his skills in cooperation, planning and execution (he had a single day in which to accomplish the task). It is also the only challenge that ended up involving him in litigation.

Travelling across the Peloponnese, Hercules found the stables he was to clean covered in 30 years' worth of cow dung. The stock was immortal, thousands-strong, with a tremendous collective appetite, and digestive systems still in divine working order, meaning that more dung was continuously being produced within the confines of the stables. Poor Hercules. He had contributed nothing to the mess, but it fell to him to clean it up, and he was provided with neither the tools nor resources for the work. In the end, he diverted two rivers and completed the work on time and on budget!

In order to move to smarter contracts, the current generation of lawyers, legal engineers or contract experts will first need to clean the Augean Stables of current practices. In this case, the mess also consists of COWDUNG, though not the same type which Hercules was faced with. In this very specific 21st century case it consists of COWDUNG in the form posited by Professor Conrad Hal Waddington.[33] A geneticist and popular scientist,[34] he used the rough acronym COWDUNG for what he referred to as the Conventional Wisdom of the Dominant Group—essentially, the type of group-think that prevents progress in thinking. As pointed out by Helena Haapio[35] the COWDUNG in the case of contracts is that it is appropriate and useful for the documents to be presented in the way they currently are. In cleaning the COWDUNG of contracting, the smell may be better than it was for Hercules, but there is an additional layer of difficulty which he did not have, namely those with an ambition to clean the stables of contracting will not be able to move out the metaphorical bovines—the business is generally good and needs to be recorded and

---

[31] The most favorable tradition for Hercules has Eurystheus hiding in a clay pot during these feedback sessions, safely out of reach.

[32] Scope Creep is a feature of many projects, whereby a small change in the initial plan leads to a need to extend the deliverables, and the newly extended deliverables then give rise to another small change in the initial plan, etc.

[33] See Waddington (1977).

[34] "Popular scientists" are experts in teaching and communication who help to socialise and popularise certain branches of science for a broad public—a very famous example being Prof. Stephen Hawking.

[35] See Haapio (2013).

notarized in contractual form. The approach will require an extra layer of agility and lateral thinking. Given that the author of this chapter has himself contributed to the mess as a contract architect and drafter of 15 years, he wishes at least to provide our future contracting demi-gods with some tools and a possible plan, in the form of a proposal for Digital Contract Optimization.

5.1   What Is Digital Contract Optimization?

Digital Contract Optimization is defined as a process to prepare a book of contracts currently in unstructured form (written documents) for a digitally enhanced treatment in the origination and execution phase. The state of the art at the time of writing suggests that "digitally enhanced treatment in the origination and execution phase" should ultimately involve processing via DLT and self-executing contracts. This chapter accepts this prevailing view, and assumes that to be the case, despite the fact that most Digital Contract Optimization journeys will take a number of years, and that the digital world changes rapidly.

In order to complete the journey, both the contractual entity (single contracts) as well as the collection of contractual entities (the book), will need to be fully understood and catalogued by the book owner on an extremely granular level. At that point, a business can truly say the portfolio is understood on a portfolio level.

Naturally, the portfolio aspects add a layer of complexity but there are certain key improvements which can be captured on the route to Digital Contract Optimization, such as:

i. Creating more objectivity by being able to improve comparison of one contract with another in terms of mechanisms, but also in terms of quality (and, potentially, value);

ii. Automating what can be automated but leaving the business person in charge, supported by subject matter experts;

iii. Disintermediating the knowledge trapped in contracts and making it more accessible to the book owner;

iv. Turning unstructured data in contracts into structured data, without necessarily touching the unstructured contract, or changing it.

In its 2016 report into Distributed Ledger Technology in the Financial Services Industry, the World Economic Forum remarked that DLT is not a panacea[36]; instead, the report states that DLT should be viewed as one of many technologies that will form the foundation of next-generation financial services infrastructure. Some of the other technologies are mentioned in this section, and their purpose is to prepare the contract for a fully digital treatment.

---

[36]World Economic Forum (2016).

5.2 Benefits of a Digital Contract Optimization: Resolving Inefficiencies, Eliminating Blind Spots

As explained above, a key benefit of a Digital Contract Optimization is that it unlocks the door to the efficiencies of the DLT. It is not, however, the only benefit. Other benefits include the enhancement of governance, of consistency and the deployment of expert resources in an efficient manner. There is also the opportunity to clear up blind spots (unnoticed disagreements) between the parties which arise as a logical result of existing processes.

Traditional pre-contract review and drafting paradigms assume each contract to be a unique object. The motivation for the review/drafting process comes from a fear of leakage. Most lawyers or contract reviewers hold two principal concerns motivating careful attention:

i. That the contract will breach internal company guidelines. This is the fear of the internal contract deity—usually senior management or the Audit department;
ii. That the contract will "end up in court," i.e., be insufficiently contract certain, cause disagreement between the parties and need resolution before a tribunal. The external contract deity—the ultimate contract deity—is the judge or the arbitration panel, before whom there will be a final reckoning if anything goes seriously wrong.

During the pre-inception negotiation, the drafter/reviewer attempts to placate those deities by applying 3 main approaches:

i.   Negotiation;
ii. Drafting clarity;
iii. "Clever" wording.

"Negotiation" means calling out proposed terms or conditions which are problematic for the reviewer, for example because they breach company guidelines, or they are contrary to the instructions which the reviewer received from the business. It is an engaged response to disagreement.

"Drafting clarity" takes the form of challenges to anything that is unclear, in order to make it clearer, and more contract certain.

"Clever" or "lazy" wording" is used as an alternative to drafting clarity where the reviewer wishes to avoid frank negotiation or is otherwise disengaged. It is used where the reviewer wishes to change the suggested wording to position their business in a favorable light before the "contract deities" but are running out of time or out of patience with each other or have some other reason for creating or allowing intransparency. It is a disengaged yet fully understandable response to disagreement. The contract architects are under pressure from their business customer to drive the business (i.e., to move towards deal execution, or to promote the relationship) whilst staying within company guidelines; and they are under pressure to adapt to the alternative requirements (for content and phrasing) from the counterparty. Unfortunately, "clever" wording may be clever in the short term—it can help move the contract towards conclusion—but over the long term it is far from "clever," as it builds up layers of unobserved disagreement. In short, it creates blind spots. "Lazy" wording is a short-term short-cut which can create additional work further down the line.

Following contract conclusion, most organizations apply a limited sample-based portfolio review approach. In the best of cases this is carried out by an independent party such as Audit, but generally speaking that process just checks the top risks. In addition, auditors are not usually contract experts, do not always understand the implications an applicable law may have on meaning, and are constrained by time and method. Generally, they look with limited subject matter expertise at anomalies in processes and patterns across the book. This is not a process likely to uncover or resolve blind spots.

In short, the contract governance cycle is capable of significant improvement. The result of the current review cycle described above is a patchwork of clause wordings across a book of business. The challenge of "unpicking" that patchwork—of clustering the mechanisms and detecting the exceptions—is considerable and can only be achieved by Digital Contract Optimization.

It will take a while for DLT infrastructure to become the norm and to replace existing systems in established companies. As that development takes place, the contracts experts in the company should not wait to prepare the company's contracts—they should act proactively by putting them through a Digital Contract Optimization journey, which itself has a high inherent value.

5.3   What a Digital Contract Optimization Might Look Like

A Digital Contract Optimization journey can in theory be completed without any new technology beyond an organization's current tools and platforms. Without any constraints on the availability of time and people, a book of contracts can be prepared for DLT and smarter contracting with nothing more than an electronic spreadsheet of the standard kind. Our current obsession with technology sometimes leads us to forget that the principal asset in data management and exploitation is the human will. In the 19th century, Matthew Fontaine Maury was able to produce extremely sophisticated maps of the seas utilizing only a paper ledger, some non-digital data points provided in paper form by mariners, and a team whose (human) members he referred to as "computers."[37]

Nevertheless, given that the advantages of the final objective are considerable, and given the availability on the market of increasingly sophisticated Optical Character Recognition, language processing, machine learning, semantic and even Artificial Intelligence tools, it is likely that where budgets allow, a Digital Contract Optimiza-

---

[37]Maury's findings are carefully documented in his book "The Physical Geography of the Sea and its Meteorology." His data driven, but non-digital methodology is explained by Chester B. Hearne in his book "Tracks in the Sea," International Marine/McGraw-Hill (2002).

tion journey will include some of these tools. This certainly is one of the assumptions made in giving the following example of what a Digital Contract Optimization journey might look like in terms of process steps:

i. *Clause Extraction*: Clauses are the DNA of contracts. As DNA is the carrier of genetic information, so clauses are the carriers of contractual information. Some seem rather anodyne, and unlikely to generate insights. Many, however, create performance patterns of their own. Without knowing what clauses are contained within the book, it will be hard to make experience correlations or to do many of the steps described below. Clause extraction can of course be done manually, and there are organizations which can help with manual extraction. However, there are techniques to do this using computers, and some off-the-shelf tools already existing to support this task[38];

ii. *Clause Clustering*: Clustering the clauses by theme is an important step in extracting meaning from the corpus. A good high-level taxonomy will allow an understanding of typical contract composition, and of the types of clauses which could be turned into smarter contract clauses;

iii. *Importance Assessment and Expert Allocation*: Not each theme in the taxonomy will be as important in the area of activity (commercial or otherwise) under consideration; not all functions of contracts will need to be executed with smarter contracts, even where that would be possible. A weighting or scoring system, on the right level of granularity can give a good guide to the relative importance of each theme from a risk perspective and/or from the automation opportunity inherent to the topic. On that basis, the available expert resources can be distributed towards the more important themes;

iv. *Quality and Scope Assessment*: Once the key clauses have been identified, quality assessment is needed—a quality scoring system can be used, or a clustering by mechanism, or (even better) by both quality scoring and mechanism. Usually, organisations will already have views on this topic, but may or may not have recorded them in a digitally optimized format, and their view may be quite high-level instead of registered on clause level;

v. *Book Investigation and Benchmark Creation*: Once the existence and the profile (risk, mechanism) of the clauses in the portfolio is known, following the above steps, that knowledge can be leveraged, and can start to give insights. Using very established text mining techniques[39] or tools, the book can be investigated for clauses and answer useful questions such as: in which contracts are which clauses contained? What are the trending clauses and the disappearing clauses? Adding a points system to the data mix, it is also possible to answer the question: What is the average wording quality of my book of business from a terms

---

[38] Analytical systems such as KM Standards (https://kmstandards.com), RAVN (https://www.ravn.co.uk), and Seal Software (https://www.seal-software.com/) can be used for clause extraction.

[39] Smith-Waterman is one of many well-established algorithms, available without fee and first posited in 1981. See Smith and Waterman (1981).

and conditions perspective, and how does each contract benchmark to that average?[40];

vi. *Automated Contract Review*: Benefiting now from an encyclopaedic collection of clauses and some insights into real-life standards, a contracting party can move on to investigate new incoming contracts in a more or less automated manner. What they will need for this is a text mining tool applying fuzzy logic[41] coupled potentially with a semantic layer. The only elements remaining to investigate by experts as new contracts come in will be new clauses which have never been seen before by the company, and contracts bearing little relationship from a content perspective with contracts already within their book of business. In that way, expert reviews will become more consistent, less time consuming (i.e., more efficient) and quicker to turn around (enhancing so-called speed to market). The incoming contracts can also be compared against the average quality of a contract in the subject portfolio, and if necessary a surcharge imposed for broader or more disadvantageous wordings. Longer term, the method for this automated contract review will change, as the adoption of Smart Contract clauses and the standardization opportunities it affords will allow boilerplate to be *referenced* in the contract rather than *included*;

vii. *Reap Benefits with Self-executing Clauses and Other Advantages*: With a catalogued collection of clauses, assessed for quality or triaged by mechanism, and a clear framework to assess the quality of a contract made up of known clauses and unknown clauses, the Digital Contract Optimization process is ready to feed into its final state: self-executing contract clauses. The mechanisms capable of being reflected in smarter contract clauses can be identified and listed in a Unified Contract Language and the most appropriate smarter contract clauses selected and agreed or co-created by the parties in the manner suggested in the chapter of this book *Successful Contracts: Integrating Design and Technology* by Barton et al. Naturally, various follow-on advantages are additionally available, such as drafting tools and template creation (inductively utilising available clauses and knowledge of quality) in order to guide future consistency and standardization.

The starting point will differ from one organization to the next. In the most extreme case, the organization will not even have digitalized its contracts yet, still maintaining a paper-based approach. In that case an initial digitalization process will be required to allow Optical Character Recognition. In other cases, an organization may have completed one or more steps outlined above, or may have a final target which is different from self-executing contracts on DLT. Another variable is that an organization may employ the services of a vendor offering a different Digital Contract Optimization journey than the one described above. There is not a single way to cleanse the Augean Stables.

---

[40]One example of such an exercise can be seen in Swiss Re's Sigma (2018), p. 16.

[41]For "Fuzzy Logic," see Stanford Encyclopedia of Philosophy, Bryant University, 2006-07-23.

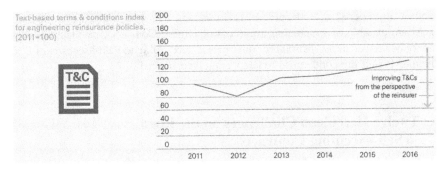

Fig. 2 Extract from Swiss Re's index of terms and conditions 2011–2016. *Source* Swiss Re (2018). *Note* The line shows the aggregate index of the overall standard of terms and conditions in a sample of over 1000 engineering reinsurance treaties for North American risks in which Swiss Re participated. The index is constructed from a count of around 30 key Swiss Re contract clauses where the latter are weighted by their risk characteristics, as judged by reinsurance experts

What is certain is that for the owners of complex books of business, a fresh look at the clauses and the clause patterns in their book will be needed, in addition to a clear view on what is a good versus a bad contract wording, before they can enjoy the benefits of smarter contracts. And along the way, they will be able to revolutionize the way they deploy resources in the expert review process (Fig. 2).

5.4   The Potential of Semantic Computing or AI as Tools in Digital Contract Optimization

The explanation in Sect. 5.3 above may surprise some readers who will have noted that the process described above is not a purely semantic, Artificial Intelligence or other machine-driven solution. Expectations have been raised by technological developments many will have heard of.[42] Those expectations are now high, and a common assumption is that it should be relatively simple to throw some semantic intelligence at a book of contracts and sit back while the machine does the work of understanding the portfolio and learning as it goes. In fact, this assumption is based on a misunderstanding of the features of a complex, non-standard book of contracts (see Sect. 6.1.1 below), as well as a misunderstanding of the continuing need for

---

[42]Back in 2011 a schoolboy, Nick D'Alosio, created the Summly app to summarize documents, utilising advanced Natural Language Processing. The App was bought by Yahoo and turned into News Digest, see Sam Shead in Business Insider UK, 23 June 2017. Available at: https://www.businessinsider.nl/yahoo-has-shut-down-nick-daloisios-news-digest-app-2017-6/? international=true&r=UK. Accessed 12 July 2018. In the meantime, the promise of semantic computing has been amplified in significant marketing campaigns by companies like IBM, whose Watson is a well-known product in this space.

people (i.e., experts), after the process is completed.[43] In short, whilst semantic tools or AI are capable of *supporting* a process of Digital Contract Optimization, they cannot be viewed as a *substitute* for the process. According to Paul Meeusen of B3i: "Human beings are condemned to keep using their brains!"

6   Twelve Herculean Challenges on the Road to Self-executing Contracts

One of Hercules's challenges was that he never knew where he was on his journey. His lack of direct access to his sponsor, as well as the autocratic and capricious personality of the latter, meant that he frequently lost heart and wondered whether he would ever be finished. 12 years is a long time to stay focused! The risk posed by disorientation became most evident during his second task, which was to kill the Hydra. This many-headed creature had only one mortal head, but whenever he cut off one of its immortal heads, it grew back in double. As well as speed and accuracy, therefore, the hidden snag of this challenge was keeping track of the heads he cut off so that by a process of deduction he could find its central weakness and finish it off.

The rise of self-executing contracts is inevitable due to the strength of the business case. One of the challenges today's contracting demi-gods will be faced with is the despair trap, which could risk pushing them back towards lazy old contracting practices. To keep well oriented, therefore, we need to list the various tough, but manageable challenges which established businesses will encounter on their journey of Digital Contract Optimization and tick them off as we go. To help the reader keep better track of these challenges as they are dealt with, they are mapped out as follows:

i.   *General Challenges*: challenges of a general nature;
ii. *Internal Challenges*: challenges within organizational structures (e.g., companies, governments);
iii. *External Challenges*: challenges between contracting counterparties, or within industries or eco-systems;
iv. *Expert Mindset*: challenges facing individual experts, or colleges of individual experts, whose importance is clearly greater in the more complex contracting segments.

A Venn diagram of the 12 challenges covered in the following section is set out below, for ease of navigation through this section (Fig. 3).

---

[43]On this topic, Rodney Brooks, an eminent robotics expert and digital visionary is already predicting a re-calibration of popular expectations around the actual societal impacts of these technologies over time (see his blog entitled "My Dated Predictions" from 1 January 2018. Available at: https://www.rodneybrooks.com/my-dated-predictions/). Accessed 30 September 2018. See also his paper for the MIT Technology Review from 6 October 2017 entitled "The Seven Deadly Sins of AI Predictions." Available at: https://www.technologyreview.com/s/609048/the-seven-deadly-sins-of-ai-predictions/. Accessed 30 September 2018.

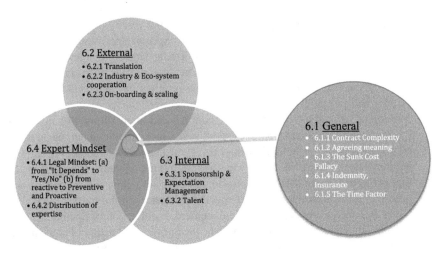

Fig. 3 Factors of complexity in the drive towards digital contract optimization in complex contract segments. *Source* Author

6.1 General

6.1.1 Contract Complexity

This chapter is focused on complex non-standard contracts. The individual drivers of that complexity are worth a detour however, as they inform the solutions. These drivers are listed below:

i. *Writing Style*: The language in these contracts is complex because it tends to include terms of art, long sentences, buy-backs and antiquated language. David Mellinkoff memorably called this approach to language "Contagious verbosity."[44] To make matters worse, sometimes this will be "clever" language,[45] where the complexity is expressly designed to hide the true meaning, or "lazy" language where the counterparty knowingly fails to challenge a provision which is unclear or ambiguous. Whereas university professors have for years had student results as one of their own key performance indicators, there is no neutral body which can evaluate the writing style of legal consultants, or the justification of including certain terms in the contract, or not;

ii. *Document Length*: A longer document has more provisions to account for, and usually a higher level of textual and clause interdependencies;

---

[44] Mellinkoff (1963), pp. 404 et seq.

[45] Clauses written in "clever language" are designed to hide their meaning as much as to reveal it. Semantic computing is about training computers to understand like a human does, and we cannot currently expect computers to decrypt language where there is a deliberate ambiguity with which human readers would struggle.

iii. *Document Structure*: Complex contracts come in a variety of structures. They are often composed of different layers such as Special Conditions and General Conditions, Master Agreements, Terms of Trade, Side Agreements, Endorsements, Amendments and Addenda. The net contractual position prevailing between the parties at any particular time requires an understanding of the priority and interrelationship of those documents;

iv. *Document Language(s)*: Whilst large national and international organizations (governments, agencies) tend to conduct business in an official language, large companies operating in multiple markets often have books of business in different languages. Where an industry has a predominant language (whether or not that is English) an individual contract can be set out with a side-by-side translation, or have embedded, market-specific references in the market language. Given the need to render the whole document or collection of documents into the unified language of smarter contracts, the multilingual nature of some of the contracts in the book will prove a challenge involving a greater need for collaboration between experts from different markets as well as natural language translators[46];

v. *Relationship Complexity*: Given the number of services and relationships required in the complex contract segment, individual contracts often inter-relate beyond simple questions of off-set amongst the parties. One example is a global insurance program where a large corporate group having multiple entities in different jurisdictions buys a Master Policy for the parent company with related Local Policies issued to each entity to suit their legal entity requirements and local regulatory and tax requirements. The limits and coverage of the Master Policy relate to the limits and coverage of the Local Policies, meaning that each Local Policy has a direct impact on the Master Policy, and an indirect impact on the other Local Policies. A lack of data standardization and integration makes management of such programs challenging, and most brokers advertize a service aimed at simply reviewing such Global Insurance Programs to ensure intra-program coherence;

vi. *Complex Embedded Mechanisms*: One such mechanism is indemnity which is worth its own explanation, set out in Sect. 6.1.4 below;

vii. *Applicable Laws*: Contracts are written subject to multiple laws and customs, which have an impact on meaning. A single clause can have many different outcomes depending on the law applicable to it. This is a factor exacerbating all the other challenges referred to above.

The aggregation of these existing factors creates a complexity which make these contracts poor instruments of communication both between the parties to the contract. The difficulty is amplified where the ambition is to "train" machines to implement them. Said machines must be coded accurately by non-expert humans to correctly reflect the real meaning of the language. The risk of distortion during the translation process is proportional to the amount of complexity which has been allowed to creep

---

[46]Note also that even the most advanced semantic tools have a lexicon which is frequently biased towards English, and often has weaknesses for some, or all other languages.

into the book over time, in the way that the level of mess in the Augean Stables was a factor of the size of the herd and the years of neglect.

6.1.2 Agreeing Meaning in a Contextualist World

This challenge is paradoxical, given that a contract is by definition an agreement. The challenge is one of contractual certainty. When the parties initially enter into the contract, they mostly believe they know what they have agreed upon in all necessary detail. Yet during the effective period, contract interpretation remains a very common—if not the most common—source of commercial litigation.[47]

Contract complexity (including unclear language) is a frequent cause of disagreement as to meaning, and the challenge it poses to smarter contracting is dealt with above. Another key driver for misalignment between the parties post-close is contextualism in contracts, which is worth a detour as it also informs the later passage on Translation (see Sect. 6.2.1).

There are two opposite approaches to contract interpretation: a *textualist* and a *contextualist* approach. In a textualist approach, the general principle is that the external contract deities (judge or tribunal) cannot consider anything outside of the four corners of the contract, for instance representations made during the negotiation about certain aspects of contract scope or performance. Such an approach suggests that the contract is a bespoke agreement between legally sophisticated parties who would have included all language they needed to include to cater for all future contingencies. In a contextualist approach, the contract deities are obliged to take relevant circumstances into account, beyond the written agreement.

Typically, the US approach to business contracts is more textualist in nature than that applied either under other Common Law systems, or by legal systems based on Civil Law traditions. As a direct consequence of this different approach, US commercial contracts tend to be the longer documents,[48] containing extensive recitations of applicable law and definitions sections to ensure that every base is covered, and to minimize the risk of a Court having to opine on gaps. As part of that approach of completeness, US contracts frequently include Entire Agreement clauses to impose a textualist approach as part of the contractual foundation. Such a clause—generally considered boilerplate—can read: "The terms herein contained comprise the whole contract between the Parties and may only be changed in writing, signed by or on behalf of both Parties."[49]

---

[47]There is no definitive international study, hence my diffidence. However, I rely for my statement on the "chorus effect" found in the literature. Gilson et al. (2013a, b) have brought together some sources. They cite sources.

[48]Lundmark (2001), pp. 121–131.

[49]A light adaptation on a clause used in the US Insurance market and published by the BRMA clauses committee.

Whilst a textualist versus contextualist approach seems nicely binary and therefore compatible with smarter contracting, there are several important factors which mean that it is not possible to apply in a binary manner, and that no overarching approach can be adopted for coding purposes:

i. Entire Agreement clauses have different meanings in different applicable legal systems[50];
ii. Such clauses, despite being generally regarded as boilerplate, do depend on wording and can be limited in effect so as not to exclude for example implied terms,[51] liability for misrepresentation or other applicable conventions[52];
iii. Such clauses do not prevent parties adducing evidence of the meaning of the contract content (in the event that the contract terms are unclear);
iv. Where Entire Agreement clauses are missing, or the law does not impose a completely textualist approach by some other means, custom or usage really could create an important context to the arrangement which a translator would have to take into account each time. In some ways, contracts where context is important can be considered incomplete.[53] This means that unlike other professional translators, those who translate the entities into smarter contracts will need to understand the sector well enough from a legal point of view to add any parts which are missing. They can either decide to include the missing provisions in their digital translation of the contract, or to focus the self-executing parts on the mechanisms which are not impacted by context.

The general tendency is towards a textualist approach and away from a contextualist approach[54] though, at the time of writing, context does remain important and some thought needs to be given to this topic during the smarter contracting process.

At the outset of a Digital Contract Optimization process, issues like complexity and context lie latent in the contracts to be translated. Organizations or industries intending to transfer their counterparty contracts fully or partially into smarter contracts should not underestimate the challenge of overcoming those latent disagreements. Clauses will undergo scrutiny by parties less familiar with the originally intended context, and the new rules require that a contract clause can only deliver a yes/no answer.

Agreement on meaning will be easier where there are no claims depending on the outcome or interpretation of the difference of opinion. In such cases, if agreement is not reached then the clause can be labelled "faulty"—this is typically what happens in Open Source software development. Clauses labelled that way are simply avoided

---

[50]See, e.g., Bjørnstad (2007) where the author compares the application of the concept under Norwegian and American juridictions.

[51]*ExxonMobil Sales and Supply Corporation v Texaco Limited* (2003) EWHC 1964 (Comm).

[52]In the UK, *Akenhead J in Mears Ltd v Shoreline Housing Partnership Ltd* (2015) EWHC 1396 (TTC) cited the equitable doctrine of Estoppel to prevent literal application of an Entire Agreement clause.

[53]See, e.g., Hart and Moore (1988).

[54]Cordero-Moss (2011), p. 1.

in future—an approach akin to Charles Darwin's description of natural selection.[55] For clauses which are already contentious or would require reimbursements in terms of the way they have been applied in the past, practical ways will have to be found to reach a mediated decision if matters are to avoid going to Regulators, Arbitrators or to the Courts. Any DLT consortia will be well advised to offer pre-on-boarding mediation services as part of their governance structures, and to have close relationships with trade associations who can provide guidance or support decision-making around contentious topics.

6.1.3   The Sunk Cost Fallacy

This challenge goes hand-in-hand with contractual complexity—indeed, it is a consequence of it, stemming from the recesses of our human psychology. The fallacy of Sunk Costs is our "greater tendency to commit to an endeavor after a prior investment of time, money, or effort."[56] Like Belgian lace makers, generations of lawyers have—often in good faith, and by lamplight—spent hours twisting the language to fit the circumstances, and business people have spent much money paying them to do this. Complex legal prose may now be out of fashion but it is still hard to throw away. However, if we are indeed to digitalize clauses, they will need to be re-written with a different, more modern mindset which must involve being prepared to throw away the old. Many will do this with mixed feelings, despite the huge potential upside of doing so—all the research suggests that dealing with Sunk Costs provokes deep emotions,[57] which may come out in the form of objections and attempts to delay the process by all those who were involved in the process which gave rise to the initial investment.

6.1.4   Indemnities, Insurance Products

Indemnities are direct obligations responding to payments made, or losses suffered by the parties being indemnified. The types of event triggering an indemnity are specified in the contract, but the action(s) needed to compensate the innocent party are largely situational. There is usually a financial cap on the indemnity, partly to enable the defaulting party to obtain appropriate insurance. If the purpose of an indemnity is compensation, often taking the form of payment of the counterparty's remediation costs, a self-executing contract must know how much the counterparty's costs are before it can trigger payment of the correct amount from the defaulting party to the innocent party. Often this will depend how much the innocent party decides to spend on the various elements of mitigation, defense and settlement. Most applicable laws require a "reasonable" approach by the party to be indemnified

---

[55]Darwin (1872).

[56]Arkes and Blumer (1985), p. 124.

[57]Coleman (2010).

which cannot use the opportunity to divest itself of the responsibility to control expenditure just because another party will finally pick up the bill. There is a need for a secondary trust mechanism, which adds an extra layer to the process embedded on the DLT. Unlike ownership of a Bitcoin (you either own it or you do not own it) the duty of reasonableness is "soft" in nature. The secondary trust mechanism can be as supervised or as unsupervised as the parties agree to make it, but there must be one agreed between the parties. A totally supervised approach would be an off-line inter-parties agreement on a case-by-case basis, with the intervention of an Oracle where there is disagreement. A totally unsupervised approach would be an automatic agreement based purely on the claim of the counterparty, with or without a subsequent right to review for reasonableness. Other procedures can be agreed where possible, such as benchmarks to industry or market losses.

This need for a separate agreement as to the secondary trust protocol will be particularly felt in Property and Casualty insurance where the entities are, generally speaking, pure products of indemnity.[58] Insurance compensates the policyholder or beneficiary for actual material or economic loss up to the policy limit. The traditional insurance product currently meets the secondary trust obligation by requiring the insured claiming against the insurer to provide proof of loss. It also usually imposes an obligation to recover where third parties share responsibility for the loss (via a mechanism known as "subrogation"). In the motor insurance industry, where the various professional parties (insurers, parts suppliers etc.) already exist in a loose eco-system and can be brought under a single DLT, this should be possible as a formalization of an existing network. In other branches these third parties can easily be off-chain, meaning that the final amount of compensation which the smarter contract should pay, or reimburse (in the case of overpayment) has a dependency on a potentially unrelated, offline action (the recovery against the third party).

Technologists turning their eyes on insurance often focus on new so-called parametric insurance such as flood insurance linked to Met Office data feeds, or Flight Delay insurance to prove that the Blockchain can quickly work for insurance. Such conclusions are tempting but misleading, as these products are highly simplified forms of insurance, missing two of the key complicating factors typical of mainstream insurance contracting:

i. Proof of loss: they are built precisely to be triggered by reliable external data;
ii. Pre-contract disclosure during the submission process.

The point is that such products are a tiny (if growing) part of the insurance eco-system, and that indemnity remains an issue to overcome, requiring appropriate trust mechanisms to be built into each contractual arrangement, or into the governance of the Distributed Ledger in question.

---

[58]Life insurance may be easier to bring onto a DLT given its tendency to pay fixed amounts in lump sums.

6.1.5   The Time Factor

Time is a factor of complexity for any eco-system aspiring to create smarter contracts. The main reason is that data sources are in flux. Smarter contracts rely on data inputs to trigger actions or transactions. In DLT parlance, the smarter contract is informed about the "state" of a condition. The data triggering the action or transaction comes from a certain source. Essentially, what happens if that source itself changes? If DLT is revolutionizing the way data is stored, then many of the data sources we currently rely on will themselves change over time. Time therefore becomes its own challenge. Given that the complex contracting segment tends to record longer-term relationships (selling a book can be done in seconds whereas Project Finance contracts can last decades), it will require close monitoring, adjustment for equivalency, etc.

The time factor will weigh most heavily on actions or transactions subject to multiple conditions simultaneously. In shipping reinsurance, for example, a payment to an insurance company to indemnify that company for a claim made by the owner of goods lost at sea should only be made if:

  i. The initial owner ("the Owner") still owns the goods at the time of delivery; and
  ii. The goods are in fact lost at sea, and;
  iii. The Owner is not under economic sanctions, and;
  iv. The Owner has not breached any aspect of the insurance policy (e.g., has paid premium), and;
  v. The insurance company has not breached any aspect of the reinsurance contract (e.g., has paid premium), and;
  vi. The insurance company is not under economic sanctions.

The means by which any one of these six states is recorded may change over time as existing recording infrastructure changes.

The more complex an arrangement becomes by dint of the time factor, the less automatic and the more supervised that arrangement needs to be.

6.2   External Factors

6.2.1   Translation and Adaptation

Accurate translation is extremely important generally in contracting,[59] but it will be crucial in the journey towards smarter contracts.

---

[59] St. Jerome is the patron saint of translators, as much known for a famous mistake as for his incredible achievements. Of Illyrian stock, he studied Latin as a secondary language and was the first to translate the Bible into Latin directly from the Hebrew original. In that sense he is a key figure in the spread of Christianity around the world. His mistake was a simple one—he mistook the word for radiance for the word for horn, and wrongly described Moses as having horns when he came down from meeting God on Mount Sinai. This is merely one example of a translation error. Naturally, it did nothing to reduce anti-Semitic prejudice around the Roman empire—in that sense, it set a precedent for the high potential cost of translation errors.

Catford[60] defines translation as "the replacement of textual material in one language (SL) by equivalent textual material in another language (TL)." SL stands for Source Language and TL for Target Language. In the complex non-standard contract segment, SL is a mixture of legalese and deal specific terms whereas TL is a coded mechanism with parameters (embedded variables and execution triggers).

Eugene Nida (1964) distinguishes between formal equivalence and functional equivalence. Formal equivalence is a translation matching form *and* content between TL and SL; functional equivalence is creating the same *effect* on the target reader. In this case there are a number of target readers (including the Distributed Ledger itself) but formal equivalence is not required or desirable in this translation process, only functional equivalence. In addition, it will be impossible, unnecessary and even undesirable to achieve full functional equivalence between SL in words and TL in computational logic for all clause types, particularly ones which deal with scope or which contain an element of subjectivity (e.g., indemnities, or any clause requiring "best efforts").

Both the parties and their stakeholders (e.g., regulators) will have to be comfortable with the idea that:

i. The act of translation will bring changes to the initially described mechanisms, however subtle—it will be a fine balance between translation and adaptation;
ii. Those changes may bring a degree of simplification and standardization through rewording and paraphrasing.

Where the parties apply a "split" model of "smarter contract," there will have to be a dynamic approach allowing both interpretation and if necessary changes to that long-form contract to achieve the originally intended meaning. It is likely that we will see the rise of pre-bind arbitrations to drive agreement on equivalence. It will be essential that stakeholders, particularly Sponsors—who can approve any deviations—remain available during the translation and adaptation process, and the graphic below illustrates the degree of involvement which will be required (Fig. 4).

Assuming also that large organizations decide to on-board their contracts to a DLT or multiple large organizations decide to on-board to a DLT at the same time as part of a consortium, the sheer number of clauses to be translated at the same time could be huge. This challenge will not only require large numbers of translators all at once, it will also most likely create a need to compromise on meaning, to allow adaptations, and thereby to drive over time towards more standard clauses.

In the business context also, translation errors can be serious and hugely costly. Over 200 translation errors were made when South Korea decided to do an internal translation job of the South Korea-EU Trade Agreement, leading to significant delay in implementation and billions of dollars in lost trade: Kim Tae-gyu, *EU-Korea Free Trade Pact Lost in Translation* in the Korea Times 03.08.2011. And the famous Canadian dispute (Rogers Communications of Toronto v Bell Aliant) worth CAD1 m about a single comma leaves us in no doubt that good translation is key and bad translation is costly. The same will be true of the translation process of contract clauses into self-executing clauses, once original meaning and intention is agreed.

[60] Catford (1965), p. 20.

Fig. 4 Stakeholder involvement in the translation/adaptation process to self-executing contracts. *Source* Author. No copyright asserted

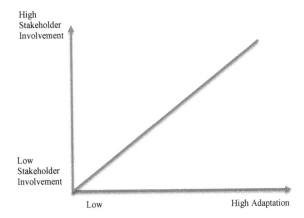

By going through their own internal Digital Contract Optimization journey before consortia and associations start to form, organizations can learn to:

i. Flex the translation muscle (including identifying experts to support the translators);
ii. Ready their expert base for the flexibility required to harmonize complex contracts, as part of that translation process (Change Management);
iii. Cluster clauses which, whilst expressed differently, create a similar mechanism, thus reducing the number of smarter contract clauses needed on the journey from SL to TL;
iv. Build-in the user interface so that TL does not end up being totally incomprehensible to all but the machine and the IT experts[61];
v. Prioritize, i.e., to confirm their understanding and those of their agents and employees as to which clauses they can and cannot compromise on.

6.2.2 Industry and Eco-system Cooperation

The main benefit of DLT—on which self-executing contracts live—is interconnectivity. An entity can gain something in efficiency and governance by having its internal data and standards on a private DLT, but the gain becomes important when organizations can communicate with each other on shared business-focused platforms, be they public or private. The gain becomes a game-changer if an entire market can adopt the same approach. The actors in any market will choose how to adapt to this

---

[61] A more sophisticated version would come with the possibility to translate the Smart Contract mechanism back into text, so as to avoid creating a Black Box of the kind referred to later in this chapter. This latter step would provide opportunities to cluster the original natural language clauses (SL) into a more neutral unique contract language. This build-on opportunity is discussed in greater detail in the Chapter of this book *Successful Contracts: Integrating Design and Technology* by Barton et al.

opportunity according to their context. As Gibson, Sabel and Scott point out,[62] "the choices are driven centrally by the thickness of the relevant market—the number of actors who see themselves as facing similar circumstance—and the uncertainty related to that market...When markets are thinking in the same way, and many actors face similar changes in their dealings and stand to benefit from concerted responses to them, the affected parties often will institutionalize their innovative contract forms and terms through collective action."

At time of writing, DLT is indeed driving various industry joint ventures and consortia—particularly in the Financial Services Industry,[63] Health Care[64] and Logistics.[65] Collaboration opportunities for organizing smarter contracting in a coordinated manner can therefore be seized by the players in a market. More than 40 consortia have been formed and are at various stages of development, from exploration to daily usage. According to research by Deloitte,[66] "Among executives knowledgeable about Blockchain technology, 18% already participate in a consortium, 45% are likely to join one, and 14% are considering forming one." In other words, the movement towards consortia is accelerating.

Cooperation will yield tremendous benefits. At the moment, each smarter contract is created individually. While a few developers share code, there is currently no consensus, no standard, presumably a lot of mistakes being made, and much duplication as individual developers solve the same problem over and over. For existing companies seeking to collaborate with each other there is a need for standardization so that each company does not have to solve the same problem every time it uploads a new contract to the DLT.

The need for cooperation is clear, but there are certain latent challenges to smooth cooperation which are worth mentioning at this point:

i. *Leadership*: Not all companies in the complex contracting segment are familiar with contract decryption tools to organize a Digital Contract Optimization, and some have not even started thinking about its relevance to smarter contracts. The same applies to the provision of smarter contract clauses. Where one party within the association knows how to do this, will they be prepared to share their knowledge to bring all the members to the same level despite the fact that it may currently be giving them a competitive advantage in the off-chain market?;

ii. *Sharing Data*: To create a shared language of smarter contract clauses it will be necessary to share the original clauses, or—trickier—to find a way of building a smarter clause library without sharing original clauses. Given the fact that often the industries are highly competitive, and differentiated terms can be applied to individual partners, there may be an initial reluctance to share proprietary information. Once those clauses start to be rendered into code, it will again be necessary to share the computer code to allow them to be clustered by meaning

---

[62] Gilson et al. (2013a, b), p. 1 (introduction).

[63] See, e.g., R3, Fundchain and B3i.

[64] See, e.g., Hashed Health Consortium, Healthcare Blockchain Consortium.

[65] See, e.g., BiTA, Trade Lens, the latter between Maersk and IBM.

[66] Deloitte (2017a, b).

and thereafter harmonized and standardized. At time of writing there are promising developments in this direction from the CommonAccord project, based on cooperative models and information sharing[67]—a kind of Github for Smart Contract clauses. For this kind of initiative to really take off, more competitors will have to share more data[68];

iii. *Governance*: Into the consortium's own governance model will have to be integrated governance around smarter contracting, based on a minimum standard of governance, but with enough flexibility to allow more rules if individual players wish to apply these within cooperative sub-clusters. Good governance is likely to convince competitor companies to overcome their concern about working together to drive smarter contracting. In addition, it is likely to convince Courts and Regulators, where they do become involved, that scope for abuse of one participant by another is limited, and that intervention can be kept to a minimum.

iv. *Expertise*: With the move to smarter contracts, the experts currently performing tasks around the contract in individual companies may anticipate job-losses from the creation of tech-driven synergies. This may create a "brain-drain" which may in turn delay implementation. For that reason, it will be important to take some of those experts away from the member companies and into the consortia themselves.

6.2.3   On-boarding and Scaling: The Need for Smart Contract Analysts

As explained above, hundreds or thousands of contracts will need to be on-boarded in order to move out of a Proof of Concept phase, and into productive usage, to capture the efficiency and other benefits. This need for prompt action will require coordinated acts of translation and adaptation. As eco-systems move away from one-off on-boarding initiatives to a stable "business-as-usual" usage of their DLTs to conclude and manage new and renewing contracts, the deal table will need an extra seat for the Smart Contract Analyst. This person is an enabler more than a gate-keeper, and will help to guide the parties towards more standard contractual mechanisms which will be easier to code and therefore less costly. In the build-up period prior to the production, publication and registration of all self-executing contract clauses, the intensity of the period *after* contract conclusion will be no less

---

[67]For further details about the CommonAccord prose objects, see Hazard and Haapio (2017).

[68]James Hazard of CommonAccord believes this will be a significant impediment at small scale, but not at big scale. In correspondence with the author he states: "There are actors and communities who have an interest in making terms clearer. There are model document projects, market-makers, trade groups, etc., and sometimes there are intermediaries or groups of end-users who organize to benefit from clarity upstream in the supply chain…There is obvious public interest in improving the flow of information, and work by many organizations, including a model Data Sharing Agreement by Chatham House." Naturally, such cooperative models can inspire the cooperative approaches needed to achieve DLT objectives, but in highly competitive markets with strong vigilance around anti-trust principles, the basic cooperative frameworks do not always exist and will need to be cultivated.

than *during the negotiation*, as the Analysts seek to ensure the translation/adaptation of as many clauses as possible into self-executing mechanisms and—crucially—to agree to the translation/adaptation. Over time, there will be an increasing number of standard smarter contract clauses which the parties will agree to accept as a surrogate for the actual clauses. The cost of contracting is likely to shift from the end to the beginning.

6.3   Internal Factors

6.3.1   Sponsorship and Expectation Management

With banks setting up DLTs and leveraging consortia arrangements with impressive speed, the expectations are currently high. It would however be a mistake to assume that within the complex contracting segments we are now within easy reach of workable and fully scaled distributed ledgers with effective smarter contracting. In the real world, the time taken to create and scale complex tasks is so well-known that it has its own "law," called Hofstadter's law. That "law" states: "It always takes longer than you expect, even when you take into account Hofstadter's law."[69]

There are a number of granular factors which business sponsors will need to be aware of to ensure the right level of patience with the project owners:

i. *The Nature of DLT*: Many see DLT as a disruptive technology, whereas it is in fact foundational—it can create new infrastructure for commerce and society upon which disruptive technologies (including self-executing contracting) could be built, but it will take a while to do so. The efficiency savings which Sponsors want to achieve will only come after a significant period of investment in creating the new distribution channels, and there will be a need to reconcile the operational departments of organisations and their strategic counterparts to reach a harmonized and sensible investment approach over the longer term. A useful comparison is with the spread of Internet protocols TCP/IP. These went from single use to complete overhaul of the economic system but took about 30 years to do so. DLT will still take many years to realize its full potential. Steady sponsorship will be required over the business lives of many CEOs, as well as an agility and a readiness to view their role and the boundaries of their enterprise differently[70];

---

[69] Hofstadter (1999), p. 152.

[70] The Tapscotts (in their book, *Blockchain Revolution*) have an excellent chapter on this topic, entitled "Rearchitecting the Firm: The Core and the Edges." Their view is that corporate culture and retention and collection of big data will remain core activities but that other activities over which CEOs used to have direct control through employee relationships can move further from core through the flexibility of Blockchain contracting and control mechanisms.

ii. *Level of Contract Certainty Prevailing in the Complex Segments*: This is a significant and hard-to-admit challenge which is dealt with in more detail at Sect. 6.1.2 above;

iii. *The Need for Digital Contract Optimization*: The types of distributed ledgers banks have built to date generally focus on payment systems, where each payment is triggered by a human. The need for complex smarter contracts in such arrangements is limited, and the underlying product or its delivery does not change. This will not be the case in complex contracting segments, where the point is less about executing the payment, and more about agreeing the payable, and where Digital Contract Optimization will be required before on-boarding to smarter contracts. Managing Sponsor expectations about the timing of adoption of smarter contracts will therefore include managing their expectations around the current limits of AI or semantic, and their inability to avoid a Digital Contract Optimization;

iv. *The Nature of the Change*: The principal change in the move to smarter contracts is not technological, rather it is organisational. The way experts work together around the contract will need to change, as will the way in which companies reach agreements amongst themselves. For example, the traditional separations between contracting and claims teams will become blurred, giving rise to potential restructuring of the sponsors' teams and organisations.

Whilst many potential sponsors (e.g., CEOs or CFOs of large companies, Government ministers) recognize the value behind the vision, many will inevitably go through cycles of (dis)trust in the new solutions.[71] In order to manage this appropriately, Project Managers will have to rise to the challenge of Sponsor Management. This means obtaining fully informed consent by explaining the difficulties above to CEOs and reminding Sponsors frequently of that consent as trust cycles rise and fall.

6.3.2 Talent

To many concerned about the future of employment, smarter contracts are about automation and automation is a threat. The author of this chapter believes that self-executing contracts will enhance the impact of experts and allow new capabilities, rather than replacing them. In actual fact, existing enterprises have a problem of talent which in the author's view will create additional employment needs, certainly in the short term. Companies in business-related DLT ventures do not have a glut of smarter contract coders,[72] but there are other gaps which they will have to address as well. These gaps are mainly caused by the fact that people currently working around contracts are being asked to take a contract-by-contract approach, as opposed to a

---

[71] See Kronblad and Haapio (2018).

[72] Universities such as Oxford, MIT, Stanford, and Cornell have dedicated research groups focused on smarter contracts and DLT, and some of them have also begun to offer courses in this field. We can still however talk of a trickle of talent high up the mountain rather than a glut of fresh water in the lake below.

portfolio approach. This is because most managers do not see alternatives and are stuck in old ways of thinking. There are very few people out there who can organize a portfolio or the clauses in a portfolio, stepping away from the individual contract entities.

There are several existing or new professions where extra talent will be required including:

i. Business Analysts and Data Modellers;
ii. Project Managers;
iii. Smart Contract Translators;
iv. Digital Contract Optimization Architects;
v. Semantic Computing, AI and Machine Learning Experts.

Last but not least, companies will need existing talent to be future ready and may need to support them on this journey. This will involve trying to explain the possible future state, and the role of existing talent in those scenarios. It will also involve transparently admitting that the future may look different, and that there is an element of uncertainty along the journey, as well as potential opportunities. As such, a Change Management[73] strategy will be key.

6.4 Expert Mindset

6.4.1 Legal Mindset: From "It Depends" to "Yes/No"

There is an old joke about lawyers which goes like this: A young lawyer rings up in response to a job advertisement for an "armless lawyer" and asks why this disability is so important to the potential employer. "Well," says the business leader. "I am sick of hearing "On the one hand…on the other hand…".

Whilst this kind of hedging is often an honest response, and there may be more than one answer to any question, there is also an element of personal risk-management which creeps in at times, when lawyers talk to their customers. There are good governance reasons for a legal function to keep its independence from the business. In the contracting arena, there is a genuine uncertainty factor caused by the contextual nature of current contracting as well as the reliance on courts and tribunals for final decisions. In crude management language, the lawyer is admitting that the final decision—about contract interpretation or any other topic—will be "beyond their pay-grade." Whilst the client wants certainty, it would be both risky (from a liability perspective) and presumptuous (from a behavioral perspective) of the lawyer to predict what the final outcome will, in fact, be.

In the world of smarter contracts, however, there will be:

---

[73]Change Management means essentially having a robust plan to drive the change. PROSCI, the organization behind the ADKAR change model, define Change Management as "the process, tools and techniques to manage the people side of change to achieve a required business outcome." See Prosci (2018) (ed).

i.   Reduced reliance on governments to build the permission framework for a business segment;
ii. More freedom from courts and tribunals in validating actions and decisions within the framework;
iii. A need for a digital "yes/no" response—not necessarily to pay an amount of money, but to create a triage and management system marked by efficiency;
iv. Joint risk-taking and a need for lawyers to have skin in the game.

To stay relevant, lawyers need to be ready to support these requirements,[74] and to recognize the difference between risk identification and mitigation action recommendation. It is therefore appropriate to call for an entirely new mindset from legal and contracting departments within companies, and more sparing uses of phrases like "that's up to the business."

6.4.2   Legal Mindset: From Reactive to Proactive and Preventive

Professor Richard Susskind was among the first legal scholars to pay attention to what he in his book "The Future of Law," first published in 1996, called "the paradox of reactive legal service."[75] Throughout the book, the author talks about "the latent legal market," which calls for embracing techniques of proactivity. He states:

> Legal systems of the information society will evolve rapidly under the considerable influence of ever more powerful information technologies…Legal risks will be managed in advance of problems occurring so dispute pre-emption rather than dispute resolution will be the order of the day. Our law will thus become far more fully integrated with our domestic, social and business lives. [76]

One of the most powerful information technologies at time of writing is DLT and each DLT eco-system comes with its own legal and governance system. The paradigm of DLT is uninterrupted service, and proactivity is key to ensure the continuity of any system. Where the contract condition triggers the payment, as opposed to triggering a manual assessment of whether a payment is required, the element of finality is greater, if not absolute. For that reason, protections need to be integrated up-front, proactively, rather than on the back-end.

In addition to adapting their support to the business generally, lawyers engaged in contracts will have to anticipate potential issues by:

i.   Setting up governance structures to manage new eco-systems;
ii. Training algorithms via machine learning;
iii. Advising on the meaning of legalese and contract conditions;
iv. Supporting the creation of crawlers to find exceptions and issues.

---

[74] For the potential of lawyers to use their gatekeeper role to actively hinder the process, see Kronblad and Haapio (2018).

[75] Susskind (1998).

[76] Susskind (1998), pp. 23–27.

Due to their familiarity with the products, lawyers are well positioned to drive Digital Contract Optimization processes but will lose that opportunity if they do not act in a manner that is preventive[77] and proactive.

6.4.3 Distribution of Expertise

Lawyers are the experts singled out for special attention above. Naturally, they are not the only experts involved in the contract who must be brought along on a Digital Contract Optimization journey, towards self-executing contracts.

Organizations or consortia seeking to leverage the maximum benefit from smarter contract will no doubt seek to automate as much of the contract's mechanisms as possible, and the type and origin of the expertise required for each contract mechanism may be different.

A complex commercial contract has many different classes of terms:

i. Commercial;
ii. Legal/boilerplate;
iii. Compliance;
iv. IT (particularly for data management issues);
v. Payment; etc.

Frequently, the knowledge of these different classes of terms is owned by different functions within an organization.[78] The Author has previously argued that the means for an organization to overcome the knowledge silos is by creating a cooperative expert culture described by Müge Cöteli as "Flexpertise."[79]

In defeating the Amazons in his successful bid to capture Hippolyta's belt, Hercules also had to team up with an army of others, and to learn the art of military organization and battle planning—his raw strength was not up to the task, as the knowledge of lawyers will only be one part of the professional firepower required. The illustration below shows how the Digital Contract Optimization Architect can gather the team of multiple experts needed to drive a Digital Contract Optimization process, and to drive adoption of self-executing contracts on the DLT (Fig. 5).

Note that at time of writing, the central role is still available to lawyers, but that like other expert groups such as management accountants, they will have to make a pitch for the business and prove their competence over time.

---

[77]For Preventive Law see, e.g., Brown (1950, 1955, 1972, 1986). A National Center for Preventive Law (NCPL) was established in his honor and acts as a knowledge network for Preventive Law. For its application to legal practice, see "www.preventivelawyer.org." For Proactive Law see "Quality Improvement through Proactive Contracting: Contracts are too important to be left to lawyers!", a conference paper presented by Helena Haapio at the Annual Quality Congress of the American Society for Quality (ASQ) held in Philadelphia in 1998. The paper was later expanded to an article entitled "Preventive Lawyering in International Sales: Using Contract Reviews to Integrate Preventive Law, Risk Management, and Quality" published in the Winter 1997/1998 issue of the Preventive Law Reporter.

[78]See Haapio (2013).

[79]See Unsworth (2016).

Fig. 5 New "Flexpert" alignment around the digital contract optimization architect. *Source* Unsworth (2016). No copyright asserted

7   Risks

Undertaking the Herculean challenges listed in Sect. 6 comes with a number of risks. These relate particularly to the new transparency which a move to digital "smarter contracts" entails. Organizations need to be aware of them in designing the transition.

7.1   Unravelling Existing "Agreements"/Waking Sleeping Dogs

Like people, markets rely on assumptions about the reality of the world in which they exist. When a fundamental assumption proves incorrect, this leads to a moment of market disruption.[80]

As explained above, the following assumptions are not safe:

i. That the parties to complex contracts really know what their contracts mean, and;

---

[80]Until the late 1980s, for example, the Lloyd's insurance market relied on the assumption that when the vast majority of companies reinsured their risks, they knew what they were reinsuring. It relied on a second, related assumption: that the vast majority of companies taking on risk in return for premium knew what risk they were taking on. The Lloyd's "spiral" effect meant that assumption was increasingly incorrect, with less and less transparency for both risk transferor and transferee each time the risk was recycled in the market. When companies slowly realized that they had taken through the back-door risks which they had let out of the front door, they realized that all along they had not been aware of their actual risk position. The resulting market disruption was disastrous for many. For further details, see, e.g., Bain (1999).

ii. That the parties agree on the meaning of every aspect of their contracts with their
     counterparties.

In fact, there is likely to be a significant increase in litigation in the medium term
as the translation process gets underway. Covert disagreements—hidden until now
because of the continued solvency of the parties and the win-win nature of the shared
profits, the ongoing relationship, and the ambiguous language—will come to light as
clever drafting and other less contentious language is gradually shoe-horned into the
yes/no answers required in smarter contracts. As always, most disagreements will be
capable of settlement and compromise, but others will trigger litigation particularly
where they affect past claims and settlements, and require financial adjustment, with
one party paying to settle unnoticed debts. The existing paper contracts will come
under greater judicial scrutiny, relationships may be affected and the commercial
courts will have a busy few years unless DLT consortia can support by setting up
dispute resolution processes of their own.

7.2   New Black Boxes

Most business people, and most senior managers are not experts in computer coding.
When there is an issue on a contract written in natural language, the business can
get hold of the text and try to understand it for themselves. This approach will be
more difficult if the clause is only in code. Much has been made in this chapter of the
need for translation services. Professional translators are trained to render the Source
Language (SL) into the Target Language (TL) in ways that communicate appropriately to the target audience. One of the skills they are taught is simplification of
expression, because they are professional translators. Coders on the other hand tend
to have strong mathematical and programming skills, as well as a pride in their ability
to handle complexity. Unlike translators, they are not generally experts in communication. The risk then is that by seeking to be free of the existing intermediaries
such as administrators, lawyers and brokers, organizations become reliant on new
intermediaries (coders) or lose a proper ability to understand their agreements in the
event that the new intermediary is no longer willing, available, or able to translate.
Almost worse than this, an organization can simultaneously disengage all its people
and all its experts by creating new Black Boxes which people on the working level
simply don't trust or perceive as "evil robots."
     A Digital Contract Optimization journey is proposed as an appropriate means of
Change Management, as it keeps the experts fully involved in the process and gives
them the transparency they need to remain engaged. As semantic computing is itself
a "Black Box" for most business people, it will be necessary to weigh its possible
usage and benefits against the Change Management aspects.

7.3 Other Risks

Naturally, there are many other risks which are general to any attempt to change the way contracting is done. These are not central to the Digital Contract Optimization process described in this chapter, but a good summary in the smarter contract context can be found in law firm Norton Rose's paper entitled "Smart Contracts: Coding the Fine Print."[81]

8 Need for Change in the Legal Industry

Above we covered the mindset change which individual lawyers will have to go through in order to serve their clients in the new DLT world. Naturally the legal industry will also have to change to adapt to the new needs and challenges.

8.1 Legal Education: From Fixed Mindset to Growth Mindset

The important notion of "Mindset" was the product of research by Carol Dweck, a Stanford Psychologist.[82] Trapped in a fixed mindset, people believe their basic qualities, like their intelligence or their ability to argue and persuade, are fixed and immutable. Their working life is spent recording and leveraging their intelligence or abilities instead of developing them. A lawyer trapped in a fixed mindset will often state "I am a lawyer" in answer to a challenge of logic, as if that in itself improves the quality of the argument. People blessed with a growth mindset tend to believe in the concept of constant development, and to be more able to capture the benefits provided by the expertise of others in their own development. Legal education is currently based on reinforcing a fixed mindset.[83] It is just this mindset which could delay implementation of smarter contracts, given the need for continued learning for the lawyers, and the new importance coders and other experts will have in digitalizing legal obligations. Roles and responsibilities will become more blurred than before and legal education will have to support fledgling lawyers in dealing with this additional ambiguity.

It is possible to change mindset, but it is not easy. A fixed mindset can be comfortable. In our context, the thought "I know what is in my contracts" allows the holder of a fixed mindset to sleep at night. The thought "I know the law, coders know coding" allows lawyers to reassure themselves that they will benefit from full employment

---

[81] Fulbright (2016).

[82] Dweck (2007).

[83] See, e.g., generally, Sperling and Shapcott (2012), where the authors review mindset research more generally then proceed to examine its application to law schools. The paper contains recommendations for the creation of a feedback culture in law schools. See also Adams-Schoen (2014).

throughout their careers and are irreplaceable. It also allows them to represent their clients with confidence.

In order to train mindset there should be a greater variety of modules at law school, including statistics and logic, systems development, and basic explanations of modern computing techniques such as Artificial Intelligence, Text Mining, Distributed Ledgers etc. As well as encouraging a Growth Mindset, a more modern legal education would need greater emphasis on ethics, technology and the arts as a means of stimulating the imagination and encouraging acts of co-creation. This will be required in order to *create* new and appropriate governance structures around DLT rather than simply *critiquing* proposals from others and reviewing them for risk.

8.2 Delivery Models

Currently, lawyers mostly have inflexible delivery models based on the deployment of associates and partners who are charged by the hour. They are able to charge additional success fees in litigation, but in other spheres of the law this approach is not applied, and the fee structure provides no interest vested[84] in the outcome. For the larger firms with more financial strength to invest in technologies, the amounts charged per hour can be very high. Given the huge initial time investment required to transfer the first batch of complex contracts into self-executing form, it will not be economical to involve law firms unless there is innovation of their business models. At present time, there are some developments in that direction,[85] but more will have to follow if law firms are to have a significant involvement in the adoption phase of the technology.

8.3 Resistance to Change

Coming from a fixed mindset, lawyers may find ways of delaying the development of smarter contracts, utilizing any number of arguments around risk and feasibility. In technological innovation, people tend to talk of a "fail-fast" culture, whereas for a lawyer the notion of failure is anathema. Lawyers have another weapon, as they

---

[84]For Vested Contracts, see Vitasek et al. (2010).

[85]See, e.g., Allen & Overy LLP, with a stated ambition to become the world's foremost technology law firm, currently charges over GBP1'000 per hour for a senior partner. In 2014 they completed a survey of large firms which led to the publication "Unbundling a market: The appetite for new legal services models." The results led to them creating new delivery models to enable growing needs, such as for Contract Lawyers (being defined as "self-employed, independent lawyers engaged for short periods or a fixed term to provide flexible project support or fill an absentee position") and Document Review Services (being defined as "Outsourced organizations that review high volumes of legal documents at a lower cost, sometimes by non-legally trained individuals;often used in litigation or due diligence").

are incumbents in the drafting space—there is no one else, they will argue, who can properly certify the translations and adaptations of the clauses they drafted, as the latter are turned into smarter contracts. At this point in time, theorists such as the Author are claiming that the smarter contract technologies will work in the complex contracting segment, but it must be admitted that they are neither proved on a significant scale, nor positively and consciously trusted at this point in time. Along that journey there will be important legal issues at stake such as the liability related to self-executing contracts which trigger a result not intended by one or more of the parties. Such cases will inevitably arise and will provide arguments for lawyers to leverage in order to feed people's natural resistance to change.[86]

If fear can be the weapon, loss of income is clearly the motive. Here we can speak of lost fees and reduced income. Once the smarter contract is in place, and the process less mediated, the skills required to read and understand complex grammar and awkward negations in human language will reduce.

8.4 Renaissance Lawyers

In a 1990 paper on Artificial Intelligence and Law, Richard Susskind[87] made prescient comments about the deployment of AI that apply equally well to the Smart Contract/smarter contract technology. He identified six obstacles to implementation, the first of which he named as the lack of knowledge engineers, being experts both in the law and in the digital space. Temperamentally and educationally, lawyers tend to prefer to occupy the shades of grey in specialist areas which they are then paid to interpret in hedged terms. Turning those shades into black and white, which is the starting point in computational logic, requires a different stance.

Not enough has changed since the 1990s, and the situation described by Susskind persists to this day, with a significant lack of tech savvy lawyers on the market.

Tech capability is just one of the requirements for lawyers who wish to be involved in the exciting initiatives described in this chapter. Given the difficulty of analysing the complex world which their predecessors have done so much to create, mathematical logic has a new relevance to the practice of law beyond simply drawing up a correct set of partnership accounts, with particular emphasis on statistics and logic. Other areas of interest for lawyers are touched upon in Sect. 8.1, and the call is for lawyers with multiple interests and skills ("Renaissance Lawyers") to replace today's specialists to cement their relevance in today's new landscape.

---

[86]In any change process there is a tendency to idolize the status prior to the change, and to elide the problem statement—the fact that self-driving cars have an impressive safety record compared to human drivers does not stop people calling for bans on algorithms when Tesla or Uber cars have their rare crashes.

[87]See further Susskind (1990), p. 115.

9 Conclusion

Since the second industrial revolution, complex legal contracts have evolved into an eco-system characterized by:

- High business value;
- Heavy intermediation (including lawyer presence);
- High levels of manuscripting in contracts;
- Lengthy contracts with many passages simply not understandable to someone without years of legal studies, and/or who is not privy to the deal;
- Intense pre-contract negotiation for advantage on an entity basis;
- Low technology;
- Little standardization.

With the move towards smarter contracts the eco-system will change considerably. Over a number of years, we will see the impact of this new eco-system on the contracts themselves. This impact will most likely be characterized by:

- Greater industry collaboration;
- Greater cross-disciplinary collaboration;
- Greater efficiency in execution;
- Improved presentation of the human language contracts, with more optionality of presentation.

Other changes will also be witnessed further down the evolutionary path, including:

- A change in legal mindset and training;
- Simpler language, relating better to the real world;
- Reduced wording ambiguity;
- More standardization.

The move towards self-executing contracts in segments currently recorded in complex non-standard contracts is a true change of eco-system. As such, the effects will take a while to notice. There will likely be a period of modest hybridization and then contracts will become increasingly automated.

To end this chapter with a strong visual, it will be as if Charles Darwin, arriving on the Galapagos Islands, had decided to move the entire animal population he found there to another island. Little change would be visible to the biologist's naked eye in the first few years of the new evolutionary cycle. After the first or second generation, however, the entire flora and fauna would have changed in highly perceptible ways, as the new environment affects the new inhabitants, and vice versa. This chapter has highlighted some of the challenges which the current "fauna"—complex business contracts in high-value segments, and their expert carers—will encounter as they adapt to their new eco-system. Getting there will be extremely hard,—it will be a truly Herculean task, with a need for lateral thinking, speed and courage. There will be many challenges including around people, cooperation, sponsorship and client relationships. A Digital Contract Optimization is proposed as a key proactive step for preparing the journey, and I hope that the legal community can seize the chance to drive this, and to re-deploy their skills towards enhancements in the real world, instead of risking their own alienation. The ideal outcome would be for lawyers three generations from now to read this chapter and be less enlightened by the solutions presented, than they are puzzled and amused by the description it contains of the legal and contracting practices still prevailing in the second decade of the 21st century!

Acknowledgements This chapter is dedicated to the memory of the late Thomas Tschopp, an innovative computer scientist who helped me work through many of the challenges encountered during my first Digital Contract Optimization. Thanks to Helena Haapio for honoring me with the commission to write this—her trust in others and her collaborative spirit make her a true Flexpert; to Müge Cöteli, who kindly proof-read the manuscript but, more importantly, broadened and modernized my legal horizons, introduced me to this theme and stimulated me with creative ideas and encouragement during the writing process; to Paul Meeusen, Gerhard Lohmann and John Carolin, CEO, Chairman and CFO respectively of B3i for allowing me privileged access to a pioneering DLT Consortium in a complex segment, the former providing a very close reading of this chapter, and some telling insights, examples and clarifications; to Tim Cummins and Sally Hughes and their team at the IACCM for inspiring me over the years with their rare ability to nourish thousands of minds, starting with just a handful of bread and a basket of fish.

References

Adams-Schoen S-J (2014) Of old dogs and new tricks—can law schools really fix students' fixed mindsets? Leg Writ J Legal Writ Inst 19(3); Touro Law Center Legal Studies Research Paper Series No. 15-20. http://works.bepress.com/sarah_adams-schoen/1/. Accessed 21 July 2018

Allen & Overy (2014) Unbundling a market: the appetite for new legal services models. http://www.allenovery.com/SiteCollectionDocuments/Unbundling_a_market.PDF. Accessed 18 July 2018

Arkes H, Blumer C (1985) The psychology of sunk cost. Org Behav Hum Decis Process 35:124–140

B3i (2018) The B3i way. https://b3i.tech/single-news-reader/the-b3i-way-with-paul-meeusen.html. Accessed 18 Aug 2018

Brown R, Carlyle J, Grigg I, Hearn M (2016) Corda, An introduction. https://docs.corda.net/_static/corda-introductory-whitepaper.pdf. Accessed 11 August 2018

Bain A-D (1999) Insurance spirals and the London Market, University of Glasgow in The Geneva Papers on risk and insurance, issues and practice. Issues Risk Manag Insurance 24(2):228–242

Bjørnstad H-W (2007) "Entire agreement clauses," in English translation. https://www.jus.uio.no/ifp/english/research/projects/anglo/essays/bjornstad_abstract.pdf. Accessed 18 July 2018

Cap Gemini (2016) Smart contracts in financial services: getting from hype to reality. https://www.capgemini.com/consulting-de/wp-content/uploads/sites/32/2017/08/smart_contracts_paper_long_0.pdf. Accessed 16 July 2018

Catford J (1965) A linguistic theory of translation. Oxford University Press, London

Coleman M-D (2010) Sunk cost, emotion and commitment to education. Curr Psychol 346. https://doi.org/10.1007/s12144-010-9094-6. Accessed 14 July 2018

Cordero-Moss G (2011) International commercial contracts and the applicable law. Cambridge University Press, pp 1–6

Cummins T (2016) Commercial agility and creativity through contract simplification. In: Presentation at first international conference on contract simplification, Rüschlikon, 29 March 2016. http://media.swissre.com/documents/Presentation_Tim_Cummins.pdf. Accessed 24 July 2018

Darwin C (1872) The origin of the species, 6th edn

Deloitte (2017) The Internet of value exchange. https://www2.deloitte.com/content/dam/Deloitte/uk/Documents/Innovation/deloitte-uk-internet-of-value-exchange.pdf. Accessed 16 July 2018

Deloitte (2017) Banding together for blockchain: does it make sense for your company to join a blockchain consortium? https://www2.deloitte.com/insights/us/en/focus/signals-for-strategists/emergence-of-blockchain-consortia.html. Accessed 16 July 2018

Dweck C-S (2007) Mindset: the new psychology of success, updated edition. Ballantine Books, New York

Gilson R-J, Sabel C-F, Scott R-E (2013) Text and context: contract interpretation as contract design. Cornell L Rev 100(23). https://scholarship.law.cornell.edu/clr/vol100/iss1/1. Accessed 28 July 2018

Gilson R-J, Sabel C-F, Scott R-E (2013) Contract and innovation: the limited role of generalist courts in the evolution of novel contractual forms. NYU Law Rev 88(1). http://www.nyulawreview.org/sites/default/files/pdf/NYULawReview-88-1-Gilson-Sabel-Scott.pdf. Accessed 21 July 2018

Grigg I (2015) On the intersection of Ricardian and smart contracts. http://iang.org/papers/intersection_ricardian_smart.html#ref_Szabo. Accessed 24 July 2018

Grigg I (2004) The Ricardian contract. In: Proceedings of the first IEEE international workshop on electronic contracting, pp 25–31

Haapio H (2013) Next generation contracts: a paradigm shift. Lexpert, Helsinki

Hart O, Moore J (1988) incomplete contracts and renegotiation. Econometrica 56(4):755–785

Hazard J, Haapio H (2017) Wise contracts: smart contracts that work for people and machines. In: Schweighofer et al (eds) Trends and communities of legal informatics. Proceedings of the 20th international legal informatics symposium IRIS 2017. Österreichische Computer Gesellschaft/books@ocg.at, Wien

Hofstadter D (1999) Gödel, Escher, Bach: An eternal golden braid, 20th anniversary ed. New York

Iansiti M, Lakhani K-R (2017) The truth about blockchain. Harvard Business Review. https://hbr.org/2017/01/the-truth-about-blockchain. Accessed 29 July 2018

Insurance Information Institute (2016) Facts and statistics; commercial lines. https://www.iii.org/fact-statistic/facts-statistics-commercial-lines. Accessed 11 July 2018

Kronblad C, Haapio H (2018) Smart contracts—not so smart legal professionals? In: Schweighofer E et al (eds) Data protection/LegalTech. Proceedings of the 21th international legal informatics symposium IRIS 2018. Editions Weblaw, Bern 2018 and in Jusletter IT

Lundmark T (2001) Verbose contracts. Am J Comp Law 49(1):121–131

Maury M-F (1855) The physical geography of the sea and its meteorology, in a re-publication by Forgotten Books in 2012, London

Mellinkof D (1963) The language of the law. Little Brown & Company, Boston

Moore G (1965) Cramming more components onto integrated circuits. Electronics 38(8)

Norton Rose Fulbright (2016) Smart contracts—coding the fine print. http://www.nortonrosefulbright.com/files/smart-contracts-137872.pdf. Accessed 11 June 2018

Norton Rose Fulbright (2017) arbitrating smart contract disputes from international arbitration report, pp 21–24. http://www.nortonrosefulbright.com/knowledge/publications/157162/arbitrating-smart-contract-disputes. Accessed 11 June 2018

Nida E (1964) Toward a science of translating. EJ Brill, Leiden

Prosci (2018) An introduction to change management. https://www.prosci.com/resources/articles/what-is-change-management. Accessed 5 August 2018

Pseudo-Appolodorus (1st or 2nd Century AD) Bibliotheca of Pseudo-Apollodorus. Translated by Sir James George Frazer. Loeb Classical Library Volumes 121 & 122. Harvard University Press, London

Santander Bank (2015) The Fintech 2.0 paper: rebooting financial services. http://santanderinnoventures.com/wp-content/uploads/2015/06/The-Fintech-2-0-Paper.pdf. Accessed 20 July 2018

Smith T-F, Waterman M-S (1981) Identification of common molecular subsequences. J Mol Biol 147:195–197

Sperling C, Shapcott S (2012) Fixing students' fixed mindsets: paving the way for meaningful assessment. Leg Writ 18(39):1–48

Susskind R-E (1990) Artificial intelligence, expert systems and law. Denning Law J 5(1):105–116

Susskind R-E (1998) The future of law. Facing the challenges of information technology, revised paperback edition. Oxford University Press, New York

Swiss Re (2017) The China growth engine steams ahead. In: World Insurance in 2016. Sigma 03/2017:17–19

Swiss Re (2018) Constructing the future: recent developments in engineering insurance. http://media.swissre.com/documents/sigma2_2018_en.pdf. Accessed 12 July 2018

Szabo N (1997) Formalizing and securing relationships on public networks. First Monday 2(9). http://firstmonday.org/ojs/index.php/fm/article/view/548/469-publisher=First. Accessed 24 Sept 2018

Tapscott D, Tapscott A (2016) Blockchain revolution. Penguin Random House, London

Trounson A (2018) Speeding natural selection in the name of conservation. https://pursuit.unimelb.edu.au/articles/speeding-natural-selection-in-the-name-of-conservation. Accessed 14 June 2018

Unsworth R (2016) "Meet the Flexperts!" How to bring in expert contributions around the contract in support of commercial interests. J Strateg Contract Negot 1–18

Vitasek K, Ledyard M, Manrodt K (2010) Vested outsourcing, 2nd edn: Five rules that will transform outsourcing. Palgrave MacMillan, New York

Waddington C-H (1977) Tools for thought. Paladin, St. Albans

World Economic Forum (2016) The future of financial infrastructure: an ambitious look at how blockchain can reshape financial services, White Paper, Aug 2016. http://www3.weforum.org/docs/WEF_The_future_of_financial_infrastructure.pdf. Accessed 1 Aug 2018

World Economic Forum (2018) Blockchain—beyond the hype, White Paper. http://www3.weforum.org/docs/48423_Whether_Blockchain_WP.pdf. Accessed 2 June 2018

Successful Contracts: Integrating Design and Technology

Thomas D. Barton, Helena Haapio, Stefania Passera and James G. Hazard

Abstract Commercial contracts are sometimes ruefully described as "documents written by lawyers, for lawyers," artifacts of a negotiated exchange wrapped tightly in pages of clauses intended to insulate the agreement against litigation attacks. Yet this verbal padding decreases accessibility, functionality, and efficiency. Reforms to the classic forms and mentality surrounding contracting have recently been proposed, several of which look to insights and methods outside the legal system. This chapter describes two branches of those efforts: information design and computer codification. Considered separately, each could be helpful. When combined, however, and especially when employed using the values and goals of Proactive/Preventive Law, these methods can enhance communication, participation, and usefulness across the entire life-cycle of contracting: assessment of needs, gathering background resources, negotiation, commitment, implementation/monitoring, adjustment, and sometimes dispute resolution. Although challenging to integrate, better design and codification re-conceptualize contracting as a process for gathering and sharing information toward generating value and managing human and business enterprise.

Keywords Simplification · Codification · Design · Legal information design · Legal technology · Contract automation · Smart contracts · Proactive/preventive law

T. D. Barton (✉)
California Western School of Law, San Diego, CA, USA
e-mail: tbarton@cwsl.edu

H. Haapio
University of Vaasa, Vaasa, Finland

S. Passera
Legal Tech Lab, Helsinki University, Helsinki, Finland

J. G. Hazard
CommonAccord.org, Sacramento, CA, USA

© Springer Nature Singapore Pte Ltd. 2019
M. Corrales et al. (eds.), *Legal Tech, Smart Contracts and Blockchain*,
Perspectives in Law, Business and Innovation,
https://doi.org/10.1007/978-981-13-6086-2_3

1   Introduction

Recent innovations in contracting reflect collaborations by lawyers—especially Proactive/Preventive Law-oriented (PPL) lawyers[1]—with non-legal professionals. Lawyers have paired with information designers to pioneer *legal information design*, including stronger uses of visualization and simplification techniques,[2] and with software engineers and other information technology specialists to develop examples of *legal automation* and *legal technology*, including coded prose and self-executing Smart Contracts.[3] The co-authors of this chapter represent such a team and have contributed to several of those efforts.[4]

These ventures among lawyers, designers, and computer coders are ongoing and immensely promising, both in research and in practice. To date, however, many designer and computer-technology collaborations have proceeded independently of one another, in part because the work is still exploratory and in part because the two groups have not developed a common vocabulary for methods or goals.[5] Responding to the growing length and complexity of commercial contracts,[6] information designers employ simplified language, usable information architectures, thoughtful layouts, charts, graphs, or other images to render prose and data appealing, functional, and above all comprehensible to humans. Technologists, by contrast, write code to make contracts comprehensible to machines in order to accelerate, scale up, standardize, or automate contract operations. Lawyers may participate in either the design or the digital worlds, but many cling tenaciously to conventional legal schema and language that are expected to ensure the enforceability and desired legal interpretation of their contracts.

---

[1]The term "Preventive Law" was coined by Louis M. Brown in his book Preventive Law (1950). Preventive Law promotes the idea that lawyers should engage with clients as advisors and planners, rather than solely as advocates, with a view to preventing legal problems. "Proactive Law" was developed by Helena Haapio and others to emphasize positive goal-seeking methods: "ways to use the law to create value, strengthen relationships and manage risk" (Nordic School of Proactive Law (n.d.)); and lawyers' role as designers helping clients achieve objectives and succeed (Haapio 2006). See, generally, Barton (2009), pp. 1–26; Berger-Walliser (2012); Siedel and Haapio (2011).

[2]Passera et al. (2013); Waller et al. (2016), (2017); Haapio and Passera (2013); Keating and Baasch Andersen (2016); Plewe and de Rooy (2016).

[3]Hazard and Haapio (2017); Clack et al. (2016a, b); The Linux Foundation (2015).

[4]Stefania Passera devised and undertakes Legal Design Jams, workshops in which information designers, graphic artists, and lawyers work together to simplify, redesign, and visualize existing contracts and policies; together with Helena Haapio she advances contract redesign and simplification in conjunction with the International Association for Contract and Commercial Management (IACCM), and elsewhere; and James G. Hazard founded and directs CommonAccord.com, which collects, develops, and shares ideas and templates for contract codification.

[5]Examples of fine integrative work, however, include Rossi and Palmirani (2017); Mabey (2018); Passera (2018a, c), and Hagan (2016b). Margaret Hagan's innovative website http://legaltechdesign.com makes ongoing contributions.

[6]Passera (2017); Waller et al. (2016), (2017).

Following this introduction, Sect. 2 reviews the design initiatives of visualization and simplification, plus fast-unfolding developments in computer codification and "smart" contracting. It then imagines how contracting might be understood differently, if design and drafting efforts were integrated with code at every stage of the contracting life cycle and also permeated with the values and mentality of PPL.[7] Section 3 details possible ways of harnessing potential emergent properties of design/data integration: (1) broadened and deepened communication and relationships among lawyers and clients, and within and across implementing organizations; (2) more balanced, objective standards in the substance of economic exchange; (3) stronger capabilities to cope with the increasing complexity and geographic reach of global business; and (4) significant efficiency gains and business benefits. The chapter concludes optimistically, with a vision toward transcending long-perceived dilemmas about contract language and goals.

2 Simplification, Visualization, and Codification

2.1 Contracts as Documents Written by Lawyers for Lawyers

Many traditional contracts can be described as documents "written *by* lawyers *for* lawyers,"[8] a phrase that sums up an unfortunate conflation of rich economic and interpersonal activity into a professionally isolated artifact. From humbler beginnings documenting simple transactions of a largely agrarian economy, contracts gradually ossified into lengthy, inaccessible prose dominated by the goal of ensuring certainty—and victory—when challenged in court. Three intertwined, essential contracting relationships—the economic, legal, and personal—gradually separated, and eventually were dominated by legal ideas and language. The results were less linguistically friendly, and arguably less useful, documents that deflected attention from the ongoing planning, implementation, and governance aspects of the exchange.

Over the years PPL researchers and practitioners, together with principals at the International Association for Contract and Commercial Management (IACCM) have proposed a variety of reforms to restore a better balance among these three relationships, with the aim of advancing business goals, enhancing mutual value, and averting commercial disputes. This chapter, envisioning an integration of design and digitalization throughout the life cycle of the contracting process, extends that tradition. The systemic thinking inherent to PPL identifies methods by which business, law, design, and coding can be successfully combined. From a PPL perspective, each of these four realms potentially contributes to the knowledge and trust underpinning consensual enterprise: business provides the factual and economic context along with strategic choices and direction; design advances comprehensibility and ease of use;

---

[7]Haapio and Barton (2017); Berger-Walliser et al. (2017); Barton (2016); Barton et al. (2013), (2016).
[8]Berger-Walliser et al. (2011), p. 56.

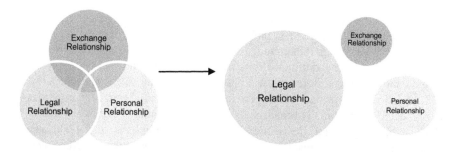

Fig. 1 Detachment and legal domination of contracting relationships. *Source* Thomas D. Barton. 2015 © Used with permission

technology supplies the flexibility and scale of searchable, re-combinable data and operations; and the law cements normative as well as exchange expectations (Fig. 1).

Our call for stronger integration of contracting relationships is timely. The fast-moving trend toward codified or Smart Contracts opens new opportunities, but also new risks. Humans may no longer understand whether and when they are creating legally binding contracts, or they may not understand their rights and obligations under their contracts. Law infused with technology may create systems in which users—business people, consumers, employees, or others needing to create or implement those contracts—have only a marginal role on operations dominated by experts: software developers, lawyers, or both. Consciously or not, such superficially "smart" systems are comprised of complex internal workings that are inaccessible by the users.[9] Users become dependent on experts to translate their needs into an input for which the system is designed, and the system might neglect or devalue concerns that do not fit readily into pre-formed technical or legal concepts. This kind of "smart," in our view, is not wise.[10]

Our work envisions a system which is not only smart, but also wise: one that provides a user-friendly interface for business people and lawyers to deal with the contracting process and its outcomes. Such a system and tools can (and should) be built on smart technology, yet the system should seem simple, intuitive, and clear. A user-friendly interface should hide the complexity, simplifying and improving the user experience of the system. Navigating the system should be simple. Our goal is to use technology and legal thinking to create a user-friendly interface. Figure 2 shows our vision of such a system which, despite being genuinely "smart" at the back, seems simple at the front.[11]

In our view, the classical conception of contracts as "documents written by lawyers, for lawyers" is expanded in several ways: (1) "Documents" becomes transfigured into modules of information that can be aggregated and retrieved by individ-

---

[9]Barton et al. (2015), p. 18, citing Lessig (2001), pp. 26–34.

[10]For Smart Contracts as opposed to wise contracts, see Hazard and Haapio (2017).

[11]"Be simple on the front, and smart at the back" is principle 5 in Hagan (2016a); we are indebted to her for this generative and felicitous phrase.

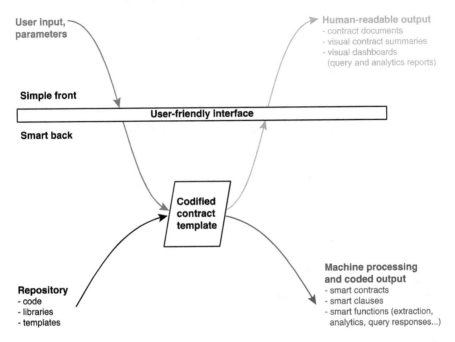

Fig. 2 A model for wise contracts: bringing together simplicity "at the front" and smartness "at the back" through user-friendly Interfaces. *Source* Stefania Passera. 2018 © Used with permission

ual user query; (2) "written" becomes supplemented by visualization, hyperlinks, or videos as well as computer code; (3) "by lawyers" becomes a group of builders that include users, information designers, and coders; and (4) "for lawyers" becomes a broad set of potential users, both humans and machines, each of which interfaces differently with the agreement across its life-cycle. When these innovations are aggregated, as explained in the sections below, a broader contracting path is revealed that is both more functional and more efficient.

2.2 Simplification and Visualization: Contracts as More Than Documents, Shaped by More Than Lawyers

The visualization innovation began by questioning the assumption that contracts are necessarily "written" or "documents." Colette R. Brunschwig published a path breaking exploration of multisensory law, expressing legal ideas visually and auditorily.[12] Design-minded lawyers and information designers followed, attracted to the

---

[12]Brunschwig (2011). For the origins of legal visualization (Rechtsvisualisierung), see also her doctoral dissertation, Brunschwig (2001), which includes a large collection of historical images of legal norms (Rechtsnormbilder).

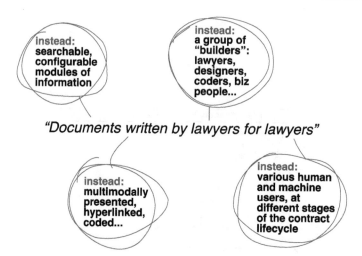

Fig. 3 The paradigm shift from traditional contracts to wise contracts requires challenging the assumptions about what contracts are and who creates contracts, for whom, and how. *Source* Stefania Passera. 2018 © Used with permission

enterprise of representing contracts or regulations visually—typically to simplify or supplement the texts of legal documents rather than to displace them. At least partially, they challenged not only the traditional notion of contract as "written" or "legal documents," but also the idea that contracts could effectively be drafted only by lawyers. Their involvement with contracts has shown tremendous potential (Fig. 3).

But what do we mean by visualization? A variety of approaches differing in style, basic assumptions, and goals have emerged.[13] Some look at visualization techniques and visual thinking as tools for transactional lawyers to envision, plan, and audit their work—as well as communicating with their clients in a clearer and more effective manner.[14] Others, envisioning a future where contracts are created and managed digitally, have explored the idea of visual interfaces and interactive platforms to support the processes of goal-alignment, negotiations, and deal-making.[15] Others still have focused on the design of the contract document itself rather than on facilitating

---

[13] Visualization may deal with data, information, or knowledge, and so can be divided into three different fields: *data* visualization, *information* visualization, and *knowledge* visualization. The first two are mainly about computer-assisted exploration and visualization of large volumes of data, while knowledge visualization is about supporting the creation, application and communication of knowledge and insights. See, e.g., Haapio (2013), p. 12, with references; see also Infogineering: Surviving and Thriving in the Age of Information Overload (n.d.).

[14] See, e.g., Mahler (2013); Haapio (2013); Conboy (2014); Mitchell (2016).

[15] See, e.g., Plewe (2013).

its creation process, addressing the comprehension challenges faced by business-to-business contract users,[16] consumers and laypeople,[17] and vulnerable workers.[18]

Despite the differences, these approaches are often similar in terms of the reasons to adopt visualization. The aims of visualization can be summarized along these common recurring themes, as follows[19]:

i. Supporting comprehension

- by clarifying what written language does not manage to explain fully;
- making the logic and structure of the documents more visible;
- supporting evidence, analysis, explanation, and reasoning in complex settings; and
- providing an alternative access structure to the contents, especially to the non-experts working with the document.

ii. Improving perceptions and relationships among contractual parties

- by reframing contracts as managerial tools designed to achieve specific strategic goals;
- signaling trustworthiness and a willingness to put effort into transparent communication;
- establishing a more personal, direct, and less threatening tone of voice; and
- consequently, engaging stakeholders who have been alienated by the conventional look and feel of contracts.

iii. Supporting cross-professional, inter- and intra-firm collaboration

- by helping the parties articulate and clarify tacit assumptions, and align expectations;
- giving overview and insight into complex terms and operational processes, facilitating goal-alignment, coordination and collaboration; and
- overcoming language, professional and cultural barriers in communication.

Research into the communicative effects of graphical information has started to yield empirical and conceptual results. Empirical quantitative studies suggest that simplified or visualized materials (an example appears in Fig. 4) lead to enhanced comprehension and a more positive user experience[20]—which may in turn lead to better engagement and compliance with contractual information.

---

[16]Passera (2015); Passera et al. (2017); Waller et al. (2016).

[17]Kay (2010); Kay and Terry (2010). For using comics to communicate contract cancellation, see Botes (2017a); for visual communication as a legal-ethical tool for informed consent in research, see Botes (2017b).

[18]Robert de Rooy shares his story on how he developed and created the world's first Comic Contract for this purpose at https://creative-contracts.com/our-story/. See also Vitasek (2017), (2018); Haapio et al. (2017).

[19]This categorization is based on Passera et al. (2013) and Passera (2017).

[20]Passera (2015), (2018b); Passera et al. (2017); Mamula and Hagel (2015); Botes (2017a).

7. Pets

- Outside of your apartment you must keep pets **on the leash** and they **should not disturb** other tenants
- It is strictly forbidden to take cats and dogs out at the **yard, children's playground** or its immediate **vicinity**
- Pets must not make **dirty** the building or outdoor areas of the housing company
- It is forbidden to **keep or wash** pets in **common facilities**

8. Safety and prevention

1. Use of dishwashers and washing machines

- The Tenant is responsible for the **use, supervision and possible problems** that occur with any equipment/machines that **they or the previous tenant** has installed
- Washing machines and dishwashers should always be **installed by a professional**
- The **water supply tap** must always be **turned off** after using the machine and a safety bin should be installed under the dish washer
- If a washing machine/dishwasher tap cannot be found in the apartment, it means that using one **is not allowed**
- In order to use washing machines and dishwashers the Tenant must have a **home insurance**

2. Fire

- When using doors which are to be kept locked, including fire doors, be sure that they **remain locked** after you for safety reasons
- It is forbidden to **barbecue, light up torches** or practise any other kind of activity on the balconies/terraces that may increase the **risk of a fire**
- **Mopeds** and similar items must not be stored in the basement/other indoor facilities **unless fuel is completely drained**

Fig. 4 An excerpt from a tenancy agreement which employs companion icons, bulleted lists, separation lines and boldface to improve information findability. *Source* Stefania Passera. 2013 © Used with permission

Simplified and visualized materials can also help to overcome other sorts of barriers: cultural resistance or mistrust of the content of legal documents. One qualitative case study is the Aurora project, an oil sands venture on British Columbia lands controlled by Aboriginal Peoples. Requests for proposals and related contract documents were viewed with suspicion among the Aboriginals, blocking progress on the project. The Aurora team of contracts, information design, language, and cultural specialists set out to create intelligible, useful, and collaborative documents that would develop mutually respectful relationships.[21] Their success is an important reminder of how the exchange, legal, and personal relationships of contracts can reinforce one another if pursued in an integrative way.

A second case study describes how CartaFirm (a pseudonym) employed visualizations in the sales of operation and maintenance outsourcing services (Fig. 5).[22] Visualizations were used to help the parties coordinate and collaborate effectively across three knowledge gaps (between professional communities, between firms, and between contracting phases), which were caused by the complexity of the deal, the need for integrating cross-professional expertise and input, and the length of negotiations.

---

[21]Waller et al. (2016). Gary Crag, one of the co-authors of Waller et al. (2016), won the IACCM Contracting Excellence Award 2017 in the Social Benefit category for his work in this project, transforming the bidding and contracting process and document design. The judges applauded this initiative in social inclusion; see IACCM (2017).

[22]Passera et al. (2016).

CartaFirm SERVICE SCOPE MAP

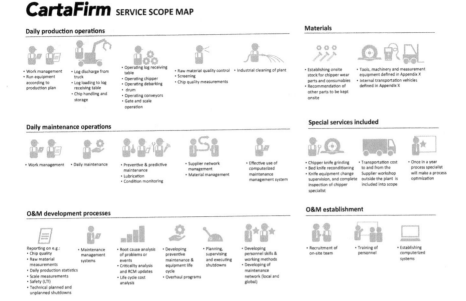

Fig. 5 Example of service scope map used to envision outsourcing service modules during negotiations. The map was also attached to the agreement, as part of the appendix describing contract scope in detail. *Source* Stefania Passera 2014 © Used with permission

Enhanced comprehension can be especially important for persons with disabilities,[23] or those who are illiterate. A remarkable example of using visualization to empower vulnerable contract parties are the comic book contracts developed by South African lawyer Robert de Rooy.[24] Faced with the challenge of developing labor agreements among rural and domestic workers with limited educations and in a multilingual context (South Africa recognizes eleven official languages), de Rooy paired with visual artists to create contracts based in comic-book style narratives. The results (a sample is depicted in Fig. 6) were gratifying and achieved the goal of effectively informing the workforce of their tasks, rights, and duties, with broad acceptance of the agreement and generally stronger trust within the workplace.

These examples illustrate the various possibilities of using visualizations within the contract lifecycle. They may exist not only as comprehension aids *in* contracts or within explanatory documents and resources *about* contracts (e.g., a contract

---

[23] Brunschwig (2011).

[24] Vitasek (2017), (2018); Dirk (2016). For this project, De Rooy won the IACCM Innovation Award (Program of Visionary Change). Comic Contracts have literally made the news, first in South Africa and later in other countries. See, e.g., Robert de Rooy's Creative Contracts Blog at https://creative-contracts.com/blog/ and Vitasek (2017), (2018). A Google search with "comic contracts" brings more than 2,900 results. See also Haapio et al. (2016), (2017); Plewe and de Rooy (2016). Comic contracts have also been employed effectively with literate audiences, in NDA and employment contracts, by Keating and Baasch Andersen (2016). See also Aurecon (2018).

Comic Contract - Clemengold Fruit Picker Agreement - Copyright: Robert de Rooy

Fig. 6 Example of comic contracts. *Source* Robert De Rooy. 2015 © Used with permission

guide),[25] but they may be used *for* contracting (e.g., as tools, canvases, and interfaces facilitating contract planning, negotiation, and creation) or *as* contracts (e.g., comic contracts constituting the actual, legally binding contract document).[26]

2.3 Computer Codification and Smart Contracts: Contracts not just Written and not for Lawyers Alone

As explained above, information designers have collaborated with lawyers to enhance the "prose" of traditional contracts. Through simplification and visualization techniques, they have added functionality to contracts through enhanced comprehensibility. Recently, computer experts similarly have been adding potential functionality to traditional contracts, but rather than enhancing the prose with design solutions, they are expressing it in computer code.

The advantages of making any contract machine-readable could be enormous—financially, organizationally, and relationally. Realizing these potential gains requires provable efficiency gains and genuine personnel engagement with the tools that make such gains possible.[27] Yet examples of each are not hard to imagine. Some promised undertakings—like payments—could be self-executing (a feature typically used to distinguish Smart Contracts) upon software-verified satisfaction of specified contractual conditions. Self-executing provisions offer obvious and dramatic efficiency gains, but more modest code can enhance a broad range of human activity. Coded provisions can supply a wealth of immediately available, flexibly configurable information to assist in human problem solving. Virtually any parameter embedded within contract coding can be automatically updated and rendered into human-readable for-

---

[25]Barton et al. (2013).

[26]Haapio et al. (2016).

[27]See Unsworth (2018).

mats as real-world events unfold. With the growing use of the Internet of Things, for example, the loading, transport, and delivery of goods can be tracked automatically. Potential problems can be flagged instantly, the managers alerted to a risk, and fallback options made immediately visible before the risk escalates. The coding may even prevent the problem from arising. Text instructions for implementing various tasks under an agreement can be sent automatically at the appropriate time, to the appropriate person, within an organization. Once coded, this enhanced contract implementation requires little or no additional investment of time or money. Finally, even after their completion, coded contracts could continue to contribute. The code provides an electronic record of operations that can facilitate ongoing refinement throughout a business. Data detailing past transactions generate historical information that can be readily mined, aggregated, and analyzed in response to diverse queries throughout an organization.

As implied above, not all undertakings of a contract are likely (or wise) to be made self-executing, even where the technology may permit it. Some aspects of a contract may require stronger human oversight and flexibility. Karen E.C. Levy sounds a cautious note about self-executing clauses: "The technology of Smart Contracts neglects the fact that people use contracts as social resources to manage their relations. The inflexibility that they introduce, by design, might short-circuit a number of social uses to which law is routinely put."[28] Such non-legally required social practices surrounding contract include, she says, "the inclusion of facially unenforceable terms, the inclusion of purposefully underspecified terms, and willful non-enforcement of enforceable terms."[29]

Levy's thoughtful analysis underscores what has been well known for decades: business people prefer to remain flexible and will often negotiate contract adjustments even in the face of a clear breach, rather than engage in courtroom battles that may be financially and relationally costly.[30] Nonetheless, the efficiency gains of universal recognition and touchless execution are clear, so that even partial contract automation is advantageous. Contract operations can be self-executing—occurring automatically—without taking the further step of being "self-enforcing," like the difficult-to-reverse step of forfeiting a deposit through a Blockchain transfer. Only slightly less visible than the efficiency advantages to codified contracts are the easier and better communications between contract makers and contract implementers, and the potentially enhanced trust among contracting parties that may flow from employing reliable, transparent, automated operations inside a Smart Contract.

Beyond generating stronger productivity and business relationships for individual users, coded contracts may offer important social fairness gains. That possibility underpins the efforts of co-author James Hazard, founder and director of CommonAccord.org. Once any bit of legal prose is expressed digitally, it can be posted to the Internet. Then, like a Wikipedia entry, it can be viewed, rated, refined, and ultimately standardized through community consensus as a fair and balanced provision.

---

[28]Levy (2017).

[29]Levy (2017).

[30]Macaulay (1963); Hadfield and Bozovic (2016).

CommonAccord.org is just such an open source collaboration initiative, dedicated to codifying contract prose. The goal is to generate modules or larger templates of codified prose ("prose objects") that can be readily incorporated into a larger agreement, ready for automation and execution as Smart Contracts when bound to the contract's parameters (i.e., the specified terms and conditions of a particular transaction).

CommonAccord's prose objects would be machine-readable in the soft sense that the machine would know them to be standard components, and therefore share equivalent meaning with other uses of the component. Prose objects can also be paired with computer code that implements aspects of the prose, making them directly actionable by machines. This is similar to the relationship of an app and its terms of use—with code both enacting and limiting user interaction with the app. The differences are that prose objects are more granular, but also broader by being publicly sourced.[31] Importantly, each prose object would be open to transparent community comments, rating, and iterative refinement. The prose objects could also include graphics, and suggestions from users and information designers about their human level comprehensibility. Over time, the prose objects or larger templates would become "codified" in two senses: first, iteratively standardized by a community; and second, handled with the efficiency of computer code. Users who adopted them as templates for a particular transaction could be better assured of a fair, evenly balanced provision than resorting to the boiler-plate originally generated within a law firm representing only one party to a transaction.[32]

The use of codified contracts is illustrated in Fig. 7. The CommonAccord template is represented by the "Contract template." This contains human-level prose and visualizations, with certain "parameters" or deal terms left to be filled in as input by the parties to an individual transaction. Underneath the prose is a code version of some aspects of the agreement. Once the parameters are completed by the parties along with an electronic signature object, a legally enforceable agreement has been created whose human-readable terms may be rendered visible at any time. Furthermore, the underlying code can also trigger any embedded "Smart Contract" self-execution when matching conditions are met.

Creating machine-readable contracts has another possible use that can contribute to standardization and fairness assurances. Once digitized, fully completed contracts may be uploaded and archived in databases. There, they may be mined analytically in various ways, generating transparent information about transacting practices. Easy availability of most-common practices can be helpful to ensure that contract negotiations proceed within at least conventional boundaries. Such "Big Data" possibilities are the basis of work done by Kingsley Martin at KM Standards.com, for instance, by mining the SEC EDGAR contract collection.[33] Further, existing contract lifecycle management systems come with interactive and collaborative tools and application

---

[31]The description below is simplified. Further technical details about the CommonAccord prose objects may be found in Hazard and Haapio (2017), building on the work of Clack et al. (2016a, b).

[32]Lee and Barton (2015).

[33]KMStandards.com; see also kReveal at http://kreveal.com: "We read contracts...kReveal turns contract data into a business asset by connecting it to key business processes. We inform companies

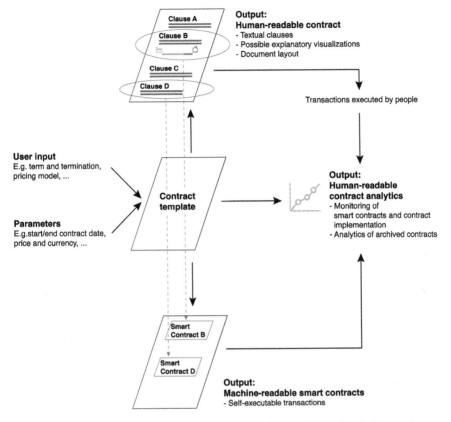

Fig. 7 Using a codified prose Template. *Source* Stefania Passera. 2018 © Used with permission

programming interfaces (APIs). Our envisioned system can talk to existing APIs and have an API of its own, allowing limited outside program access to specific sets of features and requests for data so as to interact with the rest of the codified world.

2.4 Emergent Properties of Integrating Design with Data

Considered separately, the sections above demonstrate the tremendous advantages of bringing information design and computer codification into contracting. When we imagine the two brought together, however, the strengths of each are augmented.

The successful coordination of design + data cannot be taken for granted, because at first blush their methods may appear antagonistic. Information design connotes expensive personal interactions and customized agreements supplemented with

about everything inside their contracts by performing full-service, legacy contract analysis that is accurate and fast."

digestible graphics and images; it often requires bespoke tailoring, based on specific data and contexts for communication. The digital approach, in contrast, seeks scale and replication. It harnesses computer-based processing of information to achieve stronger productivity at dramatically lowered cost—but only through limiting human touches. On a practical level, therefore, does design fight code? Actually, we believe that reconciling these two approaches is not only possible, but perhaps crucial to the success of *each* innovation.

Taken alone, either innovation may fail. Design may be too costly and codification may be too obscure. But together, they may achieve synergies that attract use and investment in each. If all design projects are exclusive and non-replicable, the enterprise may be viewed as a luxury that is too costly for most contracts. Digitalization, however, may provide much-needed economies of scale to information design. Reciprocally, however, most users cannot comprehend or use code directly, and the best software will fail to attract users or investors if it does not include easily used, flexible interfaces. Information design may be crucial to the development of codification. Good design and good code reinforce one another, a concept that has served Apple extraordinarily well.

In sum, designers and coders must collaborate closely and well. It bears noting, however, that the business people or lawyers—other elements in our envisioned integrated system of contracting—cannot be left behind. For a contract to capture its business and legal objectives, it must ensure the successful completion of the project by providing clarity about the parties' roles and responsibilities, scope, and goals. It must also be legally sound: that is, it must summon the state as a binding force, and be clear in its express terms as well as the impact of underlying default provisions, which are dependent on the applicable law. If this is somehow jeopardized by a design or digital proposal, then the risks of using the innovation will likely outweigh its advantages. Enforceability remains a valid reason for making contracts, even though contracting parties are distinctly hesitant to resort to the formalities of the law for enforcement.[34] Absent enforceability, the best innovations will wither, at least in the context of contracts.

As explained above, moving beyond understanding contracts solely as documents written by and for lawyers reveals the potential roles for designers and coders in building contracts. Furthermore, it reveals contracting as a process as well as product. The section below details how each stage in the life-cycle of that contracting process requires information or background data, upon which operations or decisions are based. The section also describes how each of the four builder groups can help to supply that information. By focusing on the information and decision-making required to advance toward the next step in the life-cycle of contracting, we can see how design and codification may combine to supply the scale and integration needed for contemporary contracting.

---

[34]Macaulay (1963).

3 Elements of the Contracting Process: Builders, Users, Layers, and Stages

3.1 Summary of System Elements

Building a system—like that of the contracting process—requires (a) identifying its elements; (b) specifying the functional interactions among those elements, especially as they change with context; and (c) creating some means of measuring the system's performance.

The sections above have suggested the constituent elements of a stronger contracting process, and underscored the need for integration among those elements. By focusing on the life-cycle of contracting, the functional interactions of those elements can be better understood. Finally, those interactions begin to suggest metrics for evaluating the performance of a contracting process. Our contracting system is relatively complex, so it first will be summarized, and then elaborated.

In sum, the elements of our system consist of:

i. **"Builders"**

   a. business people;
   b. lawyers;
   c. designers; and
   d. digitizers.

ii. **"Users"**

   a. humans—users of both the *process* (contracting through digital tools) and its *output* (human-readable contracts);
   b. business users in non-adversarial settings (e.g., managers, in-house counsel, …)
   c. court users in adversarial settings (e.g., judges, arbitrators, litigating lawyers, …); and
   d. computers—users of the machine-readable output.

iii. **"Layers" of information**

   a. a background repository of available codified contract templates, clauses, visualization libraries, and searchable, big data libraries of past contracts;
   b. a human-readable output, in the format of modular contract documents and contract analytics, with automated summaries and visuals, where appropriate; and
   c. Smart Contracts or smart clauses.

iv. **"Stages" in the life-cycle of the contracting process**

    a. assessment of needs;

    b. gathering background resources;

    c. negotiation;

    d. commitments and conditions;

    e. implementation; and

    f. adjustment or dispute resolution as needed.

These elements interact to facilitate the gathering, sharing, and processing of information so that contracting parties or computers can make informed decisions or appropriate operations at each stage of the contracting process. Each decision should be agreeable, feasible, and balanced. The quality of information supplied is measured by attributes like: relevant, appropriate, comprehensible; searchable; and well archived. These metrics are not easily quantified, but that makes them no less real or important to contract users.

3.2 Builders and Users

As suggested, four types of professionals must come together if the contract innovation aspirations of any one group are to be fully met: business, legal or contract professionals, designers, and coders. Collectively, these are the builders of our envisioned contracting process and tools. Rather than relying on their expertise to create bespoke contracts, the builders employ their expertise "upstream," creating a framework for systems that are both simple at the front and smart at the back.

i. Building a *simple front* means, for instance:

    a. codifying and standardizing contract clauses and templates, along with related design patterns, style guides, or design systems;

    b. making contract content machine-readable, so that it can be self-implemented as Smart Contracts and is compatible with Blockchain, where appropriate;

    c. enabling input and output in user-preferred languages and formats, which may include not only text and images, but also voice, visuals, and audiovisuals;

    d. ensuring that all user choices and actions are financially and legally sound, while being presented in a simple manner.

ii. Building a *smart back* on the other hand involves:

    a. designing graphic user interfaces and user flows that make it easy and intuitive to interact with the system, make the right decisions, create and retrieve relevant information;

b. creating libraries of clauses in clear, consistent, plain language, libraries of well-designed and highly readable contract document layouts, together with libraries of visual design patterns[35] to be used in connection with contracts; these may be merged into libraries of style guides[36] and design systems[37]; and

c. creating contract monitoring and analytics dashboards that reflect the actual information needs of users and provide them with insights to accomplish their business goals.

Each professional group will help to serve two distinct categories of users within the contracting process: humans and computers (Fig. 8). Firstly, *human users*: on one hand, we have a variety of individuals, teams, or organizations with roles, rights or duties under the agreement. These are the end users of the *contract*, like business buyers/sellers, service providers, delivery team members, project or contract managers, or consumers. On the other hand, we have business management and personnel, mainly non-lawyers, as well as lawyers and judges, the end users of the *system* through which contracts are made, interpreted, and enforced. Secondly, *computers-as-users*: machines must be able to read aspects of the contract in order to record choices, data, or events pertaining to the agreement, or to perform operations automatically (Smart Contract features).

Each user category is defined by a distinct "language" (for lack of a better term) used within the category to interface with contracts. Among human users, business personnel interface with the contract through common vernacular, supplemented by any technical language pertinent to the actual substance of the underlying economic exchange. Lawyers and judges, instead, interface with the contract by measuring particular contract language against background contract rules, so as to interpret the meaning, enforceability, and possible legal liability for breach of the agreement. Finally, computers interface with contracts through code, i.e., their machine-readable languages.

For contracting to communicate effectively among all of the important user groups, each category of user should be supplied information in the particular language or format demanded by that user. For that reason, information in the system should be supplied in different layers, as considered below.

---

[35] For design patterns in the context of contracts and legal documents, see Haapio and Passera (in press); Waller et al. (2016); Haapio and Hagan (2016). For a Contract Design Pattern Library and a collection of further Legal Design patterns, see Legal Design Pattern Libraries (n.d.).

[36] See, e.g., Adobe Legal Department Style Guide (n.d.).

[37] A design system is a collection of design standards, documentation, and principles, along with a toolkit of reusable user interface patterns and code components that can be assembled together to build different applications and achieve those standards. See, e.g., Rutherford (n.d.) and Lambert (2018).

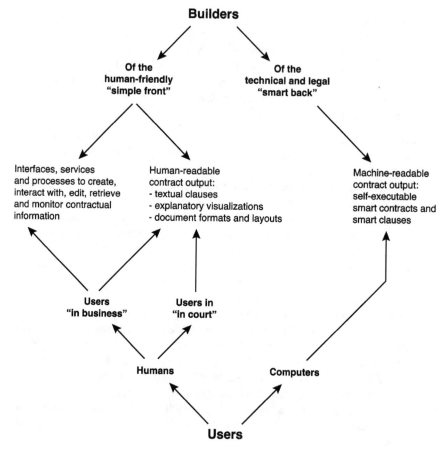

Fig. 8 The builders employ their differing expertise to create a system that meets the needs of diverse users. *Source* Stefania Passera. 2018 © Used with permission

3.3 Information Layers

Since each category of users needs contractual information for different purposes and processes it in different ways, contracts must be expressed in different languages and formats, and then modularized. To accomplish that we rely on the basic information design principle of "layering."[38] Layering, simply put, is presenting different aspects of information in alternative formats to suit diverse needs.

We can identify at least three distinct layers in our contracting system:

3.4 A "Background Repository" Layer

The background repository layer is comprised of codified contract templates, clause libraries (gathered by an organization like CommonAccord.org) and future visual design pattern and design system libraries, plus accumulated past contracts in a repository that can be analyzed to uncover prevailing best practices and trends.

As shown in Fig. 7, the codified template would be the gateway to contract creation, acting as the interchange layer from which human-readable and machine-readable versions of the contract are generated. Users can access, edit and tailor the contract template through an interface, ideally as simple as a questionnaire or a setup wizard. Through the interface, users can provide case-specific input and set up the relevant parameters of their transaction, focusing only on the deal-specific and practical aspects of the deal. Legal and technical expertise run in the back of the interface, guiding the user through meaningful choices and allowing only legally, technically and business sound choices in first place—since these choices have been modeled on the basis of the expertise and mental models of experts.

3.4.1 The "Human-Readable Contract" Layer

The human-readable contract layer is one of the outputs of the contract creation process, and it encodes the particular commitments and conditions of a contract in prose, presented in well-designed, highly readable layouts, and possibly accompanied by explanatory visualizations and diagrams. The purpose of this layer is to augment contract functionality by supplying users with relevant content on demand, in formats suited for their tasks—from an easy snapshot of what must be done to implement an agreement, to the underlying conditions that limit commitments.

---

[38]Layering is used in the context of document design so that it can be read first at a summary level that gives an overall understanding, with additional information available if needed for expert readers. A similar concept is expressed in the field of data visualization by Shneiderman's "visual information-seeking mantra" (1996)—*Overview first, zoom and filter, then details-on-demand.* For examples in contract-related documents, see, Waller et al. (2016); Haapio and Passera (in press); Haapio and Hagan (2016). Creative Commons licenses offer a well-known example of a three-layer design: the Legal Code layer; the Commons Deed layer (also known as the "human readable" version of the license) summarizing and expressing some of the most important terms and conditions and working as a user-friendly interface to the Legal Code beneath; and the machine-readable layer, which recognizes that software plays an important role in the creation, copying, discovery, and distribution of works in a format that software systems can understand. See Creative Commons (n.d.). For examples of layering in the context of privacy communication, see Mabey (2018); Passera (2018c) and "Layered Notice" in the Privacy Design Pattern Library (n.d.).

The text can be presented both as static documents and as dynamic information in a contract analytics dashboard, which changes as the performance or conditions of the contract unfold. The static contract, too, can be represented differently for different users, for example legal experts, as compared to business people or lay consumers.

Static contract documents can be created based on user needs, in a highly modularized way: for instance, contract managers could request a business-oriented summary of the key terms of the agreements, in the format of a commercial term sheet, and those would suffice for most non-adversarial, business-as-usual scenarios of contract use. By simply clicking on the hyperlinks in the commercial term sheet, the manager could then "drill down" to other relevant details stored in contract appendices such as the scope of work, or the pricing and invoicing guide. If something starts to go wrong during implementation, the manager can query "what if?" clauses from the system that would not be otherwise needed (for instance Force Majeure or liquidated damages and other remedies for delayed or non-performance). In case of a dispute, lawyers and judges could simply print out the full contents of the agreement in order to interpret its meaning and decide on its enforcement.

Progress made in the real world toward completing these various promises or conditions can also be displayed as dynamic summaries and dashboards. The "analytics" view is created once the contract is machine-readable, and should be designed to be capable of communicating fully with ERP systems and the emerging Internet of Things. Visualizations such as swimlanes (Fig. 9) and timelines (Fig. 10), for instance, could be employed to communicate intuitively the duties of each party, together with any contractual conditions on those duties, possible deadlines, and the current status of implementation.[39] As events occur in the real world, the corresponding duty or condition in the swimlane could change color—perhaps from yellow to green signifying successful completion, or from yellow to red, alerting a contractual partner that a duty has been breached.

3.4.2 The "Machine-Readable Contract Layer"

The machine-readable contract layer should express the entire agreement in computer code, although not all portions will carry the same level of machine functionality. The machine-readable layer is also where the modularized nature of contract building is most readily seen and understood. By rendering the entire agreement in a searchable code language—even simple prose, tables, or accompanying visualization rendered in Word, Excel, or graphics software—this layer will carry at least minimal potentials for data-management, scalability, and archiving.

As a whole, the agreement should comply with the "Ricardian Contract" paradigm which posits the three parts of contracts necessary for full automation and legal enforceability: parameters, code and prose.[40] The parameters are the deal-specific

---

[39] Passera (2018b); Haapio and Passera (in press).

[40] Hazard and Haapio (2017), p. 425, citing Ian Grigg.

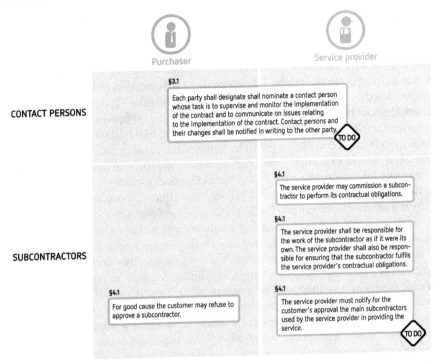

Fig. 9 Swimlanes depicting parties' obligations in a public procurement contract. *Source* Aalto University/Kuntaliitto ry. © 2013 Design: Stefania Passera. Used with permission

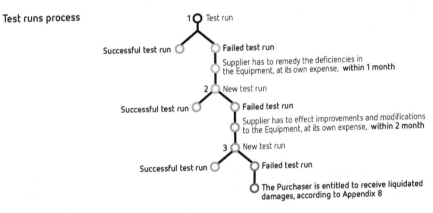

Fig. 10 Timeline depicting an equipment testing process. Depending on the success/failure of the testing, the timeline can show accurately the current status of the process. *Source* Stefania Passera. 2012 © Used with permission

terms and conditions of the specific agreement. They may be generated through one or more templates in the background repository acting like a set-up wizard and can be further supplemented by terms beyond those prompted in a repository template. What is to be *done* with the parameters are underlying human operations of manufacture, service-delivery, warranting, etc. These operations are described in the prose portions, supplemented by visualizations to assist in comprehension. The prose, as with the parameters, can be built up from modules and templates; other aspects of prose could be particular to the agreement. All the prose, however, will be digitized, to enable as much machine functionality as possible. Some of the ensuing coding will be left for individual human execution; other performances may be self-executing, requiring no ongoing human attention (so-called Smart Contract aspects).

Building on the work of Clack, Bakshi, and Braine,[41] two co-authors of this chapter have developed criteria for Smart Contract templates or modules: 1. Editing: Methods to create and edit smart legal agreements, including contract prose and parameters. 2. Transmission: Standard formats for storage, retrieval and transmission of smart legal contracts. 3. Stamping: Protocols for legally executing smart legal agreements (with or without signatures). 4. Binding: Methods to bind the parameters or deal points of a contract and its corresponding Smart Contract code to create a smart legal contract, i.e., a legally-enforceable Smart Contract. 5. Enforceability: Methods to make smart legal contracts available in forms acceptable to laws and regulations in the appropriate jurisdiction.[42] As suggested above, the purposes of rendering the entire agreement into machine-readable format is to enable flexibility in how the information is searched, aggregated, and viewed. Particular users may need a granular look at various parameters, or at the legal prose, or a dynamic picture of unfolding performance. Being machine-readable will also enable stronger data analysis of how this agreement fits in with others at the particular company or as compared with industry norms. Digitization of the templates or final agreement may enhance comprehension and usability at each stage of the contracting process, as described below.

3.5   Stages in the Contract Process

The life cycle of the contracting process, as illustrated in Fig. 11, consists of six stages: 1. Assessments of needs; 2. Gathering background resources about party interests, goals, and capabilities, together with market data about modal pricing, warranties, or other terms; 3. Negotiation of agreement among contracting parties; 4. Commitments for action and limiting conditions; 5. Implementation and monitoring; and, 6. Possible need for adjustments or dispute resolution.

Success at each stage requires the parties to gather information sufficient to make decisions. As generated by the builders, each layer should help provide this informa-

---

[41]Clack et al. (2016a, b).

[42]Hazard and Haapio (2017).

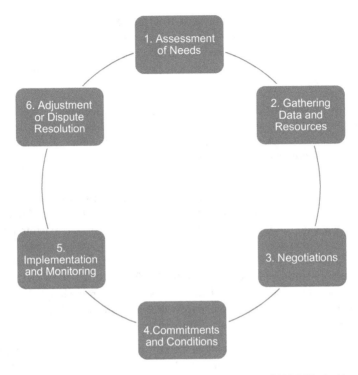

Fig. 11 Life-cycle of contracting process. *Source* Thomas D. Barton. 2018 © Used with permission

tion in ways that, ideally, are comprehensible; searchable; and well archived. Some users, like the judge, will play a far more important role on the "Dispute Resolution" stage; others, like business clients, will be primarily focused on "Implementation and Monitoring;" and business lawyers may access the system and help their customers during "Negotiations" and "Commitments and Conditions." Regardless, however, information should ideally be available in comprehensible, searchable, and well-archived ways to enable decision-making by that user, at that stage. This is a major synergy of combining information design with code: at each stage, information can be supplied to a particular user, possibly even specified into a particular format, to help discharge a particular function. Good design, combined with good code, vastly enhance the comprehensibility, and therefore the functionality, of the contract. Furthermore, as the implementation of the agreement proceeds, vital communications between the parties and real-world actions taken can be readily date-stamped and archived.

Stages 1–3. Traditionally, the first three stages of this process have used face-to-face interactions and negotiations between human actors. The digital tools and documents were mostly for communicating or memorializing information: email messages, spreadsheets, textual documents, slide sets, and so on. However, when we integrate coding and information design into the contracting process, digital tools can fully mediate human activities (at least, from the negotiation phase onwards). The design should guide the process step-by-step and ensure that all information regarding goal decisions are recorded and formalized in one system, which ideally is the same system (or can easily be integrated with the system) used to create pre-contract and contract documents and monitor their implementation.

The "Otto" online deal-design platform developed by Daniela Alina Plewe is an especially promising example highlighting these early stages. Otto is designed to permit users to reflect on, and adjust, goal hierarchies and values.[43] As explained in an article co-authored with comic-contract pioneer Robert de Rooy, Otto can be used efficiently to prepare for, and negotiate, strongly reflective agreements.[44]

Stage 4. The next stage, when commitments and conditions are created in the form of contracts, is where iterative, codified "prose object" solutions like CommonAccord start to appear. Traditionally, contracts are created through existing templates and language, which are endlessly tinkered with and copy-pasted to make contract document production more efficient. Recently, digital solutions such as contract document assembly software have been deployed to further standardize and accelerate the process of contract drafting.[45] Cloud-based solutions (from Google Docs to dedicated contract lifecycle management software) have been used to make contract editing and review more collaborative, transparent, and efficient.

Despite these trends, some problems persist that our proposed system attempts to address: 1. The prevalence of un-edited clause libraries that perpetuate clumsy or little-understood provisions; 2. The paucity of industry-accepted balanced standards that would decrease negotiation time; 3. Clauses that are available only in human-readable formats, not in a format that could be readily used to generate self-executing Smart Contracts; and, 4. Lack of integrated explanatory visualizations to aid in the comprehensibility of clauses, or even offer user guidance toward creating well-designed documents.

Stage 5. Implementing and Monitoring. The advantages of employing a coded contract would be abundant at the implementation stage. Every aspect of the agreement would be visible to any person within a contracting organization who has the right to access it. Those responsible for any commitment would be able to review the timing and performance criteria as needed. On the monitoring side, having a dynamic swimlane or timeline summary readily available to any person within an organization bearing responsibilities under the contract would be invaluable. The swimlane could also be supplemented with various links giving extended directions—perhaps in video formats—to assist performance. Further, e-mail prompts could be generated

---

[43] Plewe and de Rooy (2016).

[44] Plewe and de Rooy (2016).

[45] For a recent report on the current status of contract automation, see IACCM and Capgemini (2018). For the related Contract Software Comparison Tool, see http://software.iaccm.com; for a list of vendors, see http://software.iaccm.com/vendors. Using a search engine on the Internet for "contract automation" or "automated contract assembly" brings tens of thousands of results.

alerting particular persons about upcoming responsibilities or alerting people about commitments that are delayed. In sum, coding contracts paired with interfaces created through information design best practices could readily overcome the tendency of traditional contracts to be filed away and largely ignored once they have been signed. Providing helpful information at each stage of implementation would make the contract much more organic to the operations of a business—thereby realizing more of the potential functionality of contracts for the internal planning, quality control, and governance of a company.

Stage 6. Adjustment and Dispute Resolution. As suggested above, even if contracts could theoretically be fully automated, that may not be a wise or even efficient practice. Making contracts flexible in the face of changing financial or resource conditions is often desirable toward protecting long-term relationships. Contracts should be as smart as possible, but no smarter. A better course is to make many operations self-executing, but to permit the flexibility of adjustment. Coding contracts could assist in that by providing early warnings of delays in production or market changes. A coded contract could identify risks along various dimensions. If communicated early and transparently to both sides, preventive steps or less dramatic re-negotiation may be possible.

4 Conclusion

For many years, commercial contracts may have compromised readability, functionality, and potential innovation through their quixotic embrace of cut-and-paste legal verbiage. Armed with word processing software and a raft of templates and past agreements, contract drafters have produced longer, denser agreements in the hope of achieving more certainty and less legal risk. Simplicity may have been seen as risking ambiguity; accessibility may have been seen as losing control. These perceived dilemmas may never have been real. Yet the consequences of acting on these perceptions are all too evident: documents that are daunting to the personnel charged with their practical implementation, and that are bereft of communications that would advance strategic assessment. Adding pages is far easier than comprehending and interpreting them; but in the end, overburdening the reader is counterproductive.

Advances in the techniques of information design and modularized codification, as summarized in the body of this chapter, are fast eliminating whatever tensions may once have existed between the readability and usability of a contract and its legal defensibility. Information Age software, with their abilities to generate diagrams, charts, graphs, icons, and easy formatting—and then share and even execute that information almost seamlessly among linked computers—has gone far toward transcending the perceived dilemmas about contract language and goals. Modern contracts need not be comprehensible exclusively by lawyers in order to be reliable; and contracts that are accessible among many potential users need not be uncontrollable.

This chapter offers a vision of contracts through the conjoined lens of better design and embedded code. Its emerging contours advance contract drafting beyond the cottage industry of individual law offices, toward open-sourced, iteratively refined, modularized prose objects sensibly designed in layers that provide ongoing information in formats and sophistication that respond to the queries of diverse users. Where designers, digitizers, lawyers, and business people join forces, a contract that is "simple at the front, smart at the back" is achievable, scalable, and valuable.

References

Adobe Legal Department Style Guide (n.d.) https://files.acrobat.com/a/preview/049e2224-211f-4efa-b236-2a91ee9c1463. Accessed 25 June 2018

Aurecon (2018) Australia's first visual employment contracts launched. 5 May. https://www.aurecongroup.com/about/latest-news/2018/may/visual-employment-contract. Accessed 25 June 2018

Barton T-D (2009) Preventive law and problem solving: lawyering for the future. Vandeplas Publishing, Lake Mary

Barton T-D (2016) Re-designing law and lawyering for the information age. Notre Dame J Law Ethics Public Policy 30:101–134

Barton T-D, Berger-Walliser G, Haapio H (2013) Visualization: seeing contracts for what they are, and what they could become. J Law Bus Ethics 19:47–63

Barton T-D, Berger-Walliser G, Haapio H (2016) Contracting for innovation and innovating contracts: an overview and introduction to the special issue. J Strateg Contract Negot 2(1–2):3-9 https://doi.org/10.1177/2055563616677162. Accessed 4 Jul 2018

Barton T, Haapio H, Borisova T (2015) Flexibility and stability in contracts. Lapland Law Rev (2):8–28 http://urn.fi/URN:ISBN:978-952-484-799-5, http://www.ulapland.fi/InEnglish/Units/Faculty-of-Law/Research/Lapland-Law-Review/Issues/Issue-2,-2015. Accessed 18 June 2018

Berger-Walliser G (2012) The past and future of proactive law: an overview of the development of the proactive law movement. In: Berger-Walliser G, Ostergaard K (eds) Proactive law in a business environment. DJOF Publishing, Copenhagen

Berger-Walliser G, Barton T-D, Haapio H (2017) From visualization to legal design: a collaborative and creative process. Am Bus Law J 54(2):347–392

Berger-Walliser G, Bird R-C, Haapio H (2011) Promoting business success through contract visualization. J Law Bus Ethics 17:55–75

Botes W-M (2017a) Using comics to communicate contract cancellation. Comics Grid J Comics Scholarsh 7(1):1–21

Botes W-M (2017b) Visual communication as a legal-ethical tool for informed consent in genome research involving the San community of South Africa. Doctoral thesis, University of South Africa, 15 Nov 2017

Brown L-M (1950) Preventive law. Prentice-Hall, New York

Brunschwig C-R (2001) Visualisierung von rechtsnormen – legal design. (Doctoral dissertation). Zürcher Studien zur Rechtsgeschichte, 45. Rechtswissenschaftliche Fakultät d. Universität Zürich. Schulthess Juristische Medien, Zurich

Brunschwig C-R (2011) Multisensory law and legal informatics—a comparison of how these legal disciplines relate to visual law. Jusletter IT, 22 February. http://jusletter-it.weblaw.ch/en/issues/2011/104/article_324.html. Accessed 4 Jul 2018

Clack C-D, Bakshi V-A, Braine L (2016a) Smart contract templates: essential requirements and design options. Version v2, 15 December. https://arxiv.org/abs/1612.04496. Accessed 4 Jul 2018

Clack C-D, Bakshi V-A, Braine L (2016b) Smart contract templates: foundations, design landscape and research directions. Version v2, 3 August. https://arxiv.org/abs/1608.00771. Accessed 4 Jul 2017

Conboy K (2014) Diagramming transactions: some modest proposals and a few suggested rules. Tenn J Bus Law 16(1):91–108 http://trace.tennessee.edu/transactions/vol16/iss1/5. Accessed 4 July 2018

Creative Commons (n.d.) About the Licenses https://creativecommons.org/licenses. Accessed 25 June 2018

Dirk N (2016) Comic Contracts to keep employers honest. IOL, 14 July. http://www.iol.co.za/capetimes/comic-contracts-to-keep-employers-honest-2045555. Accessed 4 Jul 2018

Haapio H (2006) Introduction to proactive law: a business lawyer's view. In: Wahlgren P (ed) A proactive approach. scandinavian studies in law, vol 49. Stockholm Institute for Scandinavian Law, Stockholm

Haapio H (2013) Next generation contracts. Doctoral dissertation, University of Vaasa. Lexpert Ltd, Helsinki

Haapio H, Barton T-D (2017) Business-friendly contracting: how simplification and visualization can help bring it to practice. In: Jacob K, Schindler D, Strathausen R (eds) Liquid legal—transforming legal into a business savvy, information enabled and performance driven industry. Springer, Cham

Haapio H, Hagan M (2016) Design patterns for contracts. In: Schweighofer E, Kummer F, Hötzendorfer W, Borges G (eds) Networks. In: Proceedings of the 19th international legal informatics symposium IRIS 2016. Österreichische Computer Gesellschaft OCG/ books@ocg.at, Wien

Haapio H, Passera S (2013) Visual law: what lawyers need to learn from information designers. VoxPopuLII Blog post, May 15. Cornell University Law School http://blog.law.cornell.edu/voxpop/2013/05/15/visual-law-what-lawyers-need-to-learn-from-information-designers/. Accessed 4 Jul 2018

Haapio H, Passera S (in press) Contracts as interfaces: exploring visual representation patterns in contract design. In: Katz D-M, Bommarito M, Dolin R (eds) Legal informatics. Cambridge University Press

Haapio H, Plewe D-A, de Rooy R (2016) Next Generation deal design: comics and visual platforms for contracting. In: Schweighofer E et al (eds) Networks. In: Proceedings of the 19th international legal informatics symposium IRIS 2016, Österreichische Computer Gesellschaft OCG/books@ocg.at, Wien

Haapio H, Plewe D-A, de Rooy R (2017) Contract continuum: from text to images, comics and code. In: Schweighofer E et al (eds) Trends and communities of legal informatics. In: Proceedings of the 20th international legal informatics symposium IRIS 2017. Österreichische Computer Gesellschaft/books@ocg.at, Wien

Hadfield G-K (2016) Bozovic I (2016) Scaffolding: using formal contracts to build informal relations to support innovation. Wis Law Rev 5:981–1032

Hagan M (2016a) 6 core principles for good legal design. Legal design and innovation (Stanford Legal Design Lab's Medium publication), 7 November. https://medium.com/legal-design-and-innovation/6-core-principles-for-good-legal-design-1cde6aba866. Accessed 25 June 2018

Hagan M (2016b) User-centered privacy communication design. In: Proceedings of the symposium on usable privacy and security (SOUPS) 2016, Denver, Colorado, 22–24 June 2016 SSRN: https://ssrn.com/abstract=2981075. Accessed 14 Jul 2018

Hazard J, Haapio H (2017) Wise contracts: smart contract that work for people and machines. In: Schweighofer E et al (eds) Trends and communities of legal informatics. In: Proceedings of the 20th international legal informatics symposium IRIS 2017. Österreichische Computer Gesellschaft/ books@ocg.at, Wien

IACCM (2017) Contracting excellence awards demonstrate outstanding contributions. Contract Excell J, 30 May. http://journal.iaccm.com/contracting-excellence-journal/contract-excellence-awards-demonstrate-outstanding-contributions. Accessed 4 Jul 2018

IACCM Capgemini (2018) IACCM-Capgemini automation report. 15 May, https://www.iaccm.com/resources/?id=10162. Accessed 25 June 2018

Infogineering: Surviving and Thriving in the Age of Information Overload (n.d.) The differences between data, information, and knowledge. http://www.infogineering.net/data-information-knowledge.htm. Accessed 12 Jul 2018

Kay M (2010) Techniques and heuristics for improving the visual design of software agreements (Master thesis). University of Waterloo, Waterloo

Kay M, Terry M (2010) Textured agreements: re-envisioning electronic consent. In: Proceedings of the sixth symposium on usable privacy and security. ACM, New York

Keating A, Baasch Andersen C (2016) A graphic contract—taking visualisation in contracting a step further. J Strateg Contract Negot 2(1–2):10–18

Lambert Z (2018) Intro to design systems. 9 April. https://medium.com/@Zacksfunkyfresh/intro-to-design-systems-a983a60fbbaf. Accessed 25 June 2018

Lee N, Barton T-D (2015) Contract flexibility through trademarks: "Branded" intellectual property licensing practices. Lapland Law Rev (2):247–279. http://www.ulapland.fi/InEnglish/Units/Faculty-of-Law/Research/Lapland-Law-Review/Issues/Issue-2,-2015). Accessed 18 June 2018

Legal Design Pattern Libraries (n.d.) http://www.legaltechdesign.com/communication-design/legal-design-pattern-libraries. Accessed 25 June 2018

Lessig L (2001) The future of ideas: the fate of the commons in a connected world. Random House, New York

Levy K-E-C (2017) Book-smart, not street-smart: blockchain-based smart contracts and the social workings of law. Engag Sci Technol Soc 3:1–15

Mabey R (2018) Privacy by design: building a privacy policy people actually want to read. Juro blog/Better legal design, 2 May. https://blog.juro.com/2018/05/02/privacy-by-design-building-a-privacy-policy-people-actually-want-to-read. Accessed 25 June 2018

Macaulay S (1963) Non-contractual relations in business: a preliminary study. Am Sociol Rev 28(1):55–67 http://www.law.wisc.edu/facstaff/macaulay/papers/non-contractual.pdf. Accessed 4 Jul 2018

Mahler T (2013) A graphical user interface for legal texts? In: Svantesson D-J-B, Greenstein S (eds) Nordic yearbook of law and informatics 2010–2012—Internationalisation of law in the digital information society. Ex Tuto Publishing, Copenhagen

Mamula T, Hagel U (2015) The design of commercial conditions—layout, visualization, language. In: Schweighofer E, Kummer F, Hötzendorfer W (eds) Co-operation. In: Proceedings of the 18th international legal informatics symposium IRIS 2015 Österreichische Computer Gesellschaft, Wien

Mitchell J-A (2016) Picturing corporate practice. West Academic Publishing, St. Paul (MN)

Nordic school of proactive law. http://www.juridicum.su.se/proactivelaw/main. Accessed 19 June 2018

Passera S (2015) Beyond the wall of text: how information design can make contracts user-friendly. In: Marcus A (ed.) Design, user experience, and usability: users and interactions. Lecture Notes in Computer Science. Springer International Publishing, Cham

Passera S (2017) Beyond the wall of contract text—visualizing contracts to foster understanding and collaboration within and across organizations. Aalto University publication series, Doctoral Dissertations 134/2017. https://aaltodoc.aalto.fi/handle/123456789/27292. Accessed 4 Jul 2018

Passera S (2018a) Bringing legal design and legal tech to contracts. Stefania Passera/personal blog, 28 March.https://stefaniapassera.com/blog/ https://stefaniapassera.com/2018/03/28/legaldesign-and-legaltech-to-contracts. Accessed 25 June 2018

Passera S (2018b) Flowcharts, swimlanes, and timelines—alternatives to prose in communicating legal-bureaucratic instructions to civil servants. J Bus Tech Commun 32(2):229–272

Passera S (2018c) Why the time has come for design thinking and visualisation in legal documents. Juro blog, 10 May. https://blog.juro.com/2018/05/10/why-the-time-has-come-for-design-thinking-and-visualization-in-legal-documents. Accessed 25 June 2018

Passera S, Haapio H, Barton T-D (2013) Innovating contract practices: merging contract design with information design. In: Chittenden J (ed) Proceedings of the 2013 IACCM academic forum. International Association for Contract and Commercial Management, Ridgefield (CT). http://www.iaccm.com/resources/?id=4958. Accessed 4 Jul 2018

Passera S, Smedlund A, Liinasuo M (2016) Exploring contract visualization: clarification and framing strategies to shape collaborative business relationships. J Strateg Contract Negot 2(1–2):69–100

Passera S, Kankaanranta A, Louhiala-Salminen L (2017) Diagrams in contracts: Fostering understanding in global business communication. IEEE Trans Prof Commun 60(2):118–146

Plewe D-A (2013) A visual interface for deal making. In: O'Grady M-J et al (eds) Evolving ambient intelligence. AmI 2013. Communications in computer and information science, vol 413. Springer, Cham

Plewe D-A, de Rooy R (2016) Integrative deal-design—cascading from goal-hierarchies to negotiations and contracting. J Strateg Contract Negot 2(12):19–33

Privacy Design Pattern Library (n.d.) http://www.legaltechdesign.com/communication-design/legal-design-pattern-libraries/privacy-design-pattern-library. Accessed 25 June 2018

Rossi A, Palmirani M (2017) A visualization approach for adaptive consent in the European data protection framework. In: CeDEM 2017: proceedings of the 7th international conference for E-democracy and open government, Krems

Rutherford Z (n.d.) Design systems vs. pattern libraries vs. style guides—what's the difference? Studio by UXPin blog. https://www.uxpin.com/studio/blog/design-systems-vs-pattern-libraries-vs-style-guides-whats-difference. Accessed 25 June 2018

Shneiderman B (1996) The eyes have it: a task by data type taxonomy for information visualizations. In: Proceedings of the IEEE symposium on visual languages. IEEE Computer Society Press, Los Alamitos

Siedel G, Haapio H (2011) Proactive law for managers: a hidden source of competitive advantage. Gower, Farnham

The Linux Foundation (2015) Linux foundation unites industry leaders to advance blockchain technology https://www.linuxfoundation.org/press-release/linux-foundation-unites-industry-leaders-to-advance-blockchain-technology/#.WZ8FmCiG. Accessed 26 June 2018

Unsworth R (forthcoming, 2018 in this Volume) Smart contract this! An assessment of the contractual landscape and the challenges it currently presents for digital contract optimisation

Vitasek K (2017) Comic contracts: a novel approach to contract clarity and accessibility. Forbes, 14 February. http://tinyurl.com/hcfdtna. Accessed 25 June 2018

Vitasek K (2018) Plain language contracts on the rise. Forbes, 19 March. https://tinyurl.com/ydcrb8j9. Accessed 25 June 2018

Waller R et al (2016) Cooperation through clarity: designing simplified contracts. J Strateg Contract Negot 2(1–2):48–68

Waller R, Haapio H, Passera S (2017) Contract simplification: the why and the how. Contract Excell J, 24 July. https://journal.iaccm.com/contracting-excellence-journal/contract-simplification-the-why-and-the-how. Accessed 19 June 2018

Exploding the Fine Print: Designing Visual, Interactive, Consumer-Centric Contracts and Disclosures

Margaret Hagan

Abstract In this chapter, we present new models for the presentation of contracting terms and interactions, based on user research and design work into consumer contracts. As more contracts become machine-readable, there is an open question of how people will actually interact with these computable contracts, so that they can effectively, efficiently, and meaningfully use them. At Stanford Legal Design Lab we went through several human-centered design cycles to generate new contract designs, gather qualitative feedback about them, and then propose guiding insights and new conceptual models for better consumer-facing legal communications. This initial study led to key principles, models, and patterns that demonstrate how consumer contracts can be more comprehensible, engaging, and effective. Following on this qualitative design research, we then conducted more structured, qualitative evaluations of the new contract interface models that we had designed. We did a comparative study of how users engaged with and used different interface models to determine which ones were most effective. Effectiveness is judged on several criteria: the ability to engage the attention and actions of the user, the ability to help the user comprehend the content that it is communicating, and the ability to help the user make a decision that fits with his or her own preferences and needs. This study can serve all those interested in improving disclosures, terms of service, privacy policies, and various other forms of business-to-consumer contracts. It provides empirical research on new models for communicating complex terms and conditions to lay people. It bridges the literature of contract design for improved usability and outcomes, behavioral economics' concern for choice engines and decision making, legal scholarship on the effectiveness of disclosure as a regulatory mechanism, and HCI research on how best to engage users and help them navigate systems.

Keywords Legal design · Consumer contracts · Design patterns · Computable contracts · Communication design

M. Hagan (✉)
Legal Design Lab, Stanford University, Stanford, CA, USA
e-mail: mdhagan@stanford.edu

© Springer Nature Singapore Pte Ltd. 2019
M. Corrales et al. (eds.), *Legal Tech, Smart Contracts and Blockchain*,
Perspectives in Law, Business and Innovation,
https://doi.org/10.1007/978-981-13-6086-2_4

1 Introduction

People face contracts throughout their daily lives—when getting a credit card, renting a car, downloading an app, or attending a sports game. Consumer contracts pervade everyday life for most people. The problem is that these contracts are not often user-friendly. They can be difficult to read, understand, or act upon.[1]

Contracts as legal documents can be more user-centered and technologically-enabled. The value of a user-centered contract is that it would be easier to comprehend and use, especially for non-lawyers. The value of a technologically-enabled contract is that it would allow its users, authors, and regulators to better interact with its content and to explore and enact the rules that it embodies in its text.

The current status quo of legal contracts has not risen to these two standards. Most contracts are not created to be user-centered or to be technology-enabled.[2] But an agenda is being set, in literature and experiments, that envisions a new era of legal contracting. In this near term, contracts would become more comprehensible, usable, and interactive experiences. This chapter considers this new frontier of user-centered, technology-enabled contracts, with particular reference to consumer contracts—those agreements drafted by corporate organizations, which they intend lay customers to agree to, so as to govern the organization-person relationship. The chapter ties together two strands of literature: one that focuses on better designing contracts for increased usability, and another focused on computable contracts, which imagines how to increase the types of interaction and automation within a contract.

By bringing these two areas of literature together, we can expand the notion of what a user-centered contract is. In addition to the use of visuals to make it easier to approach and comprehend the agreement, we can also consider the possible tools and interactions that can be built upon the contract to transform how various stakeholders can use it. This two-track approach can increase the effectiveness and applicability of a conversation around computable contracts, going from a discussion about what might be possible in terms of technology to talking specifically about what would be the most usable and useful types of interactions and presentations of a computable contract.

This chapter presents findings from design research work at Stanford University's Legal Design Lab, where the lab team is exploring what user-centered computable contracts could be. The goal of this work has been to bring abstract concepts around computable contracts to implementation, and to scope how computable contracts might be made into usable, user-friendly tools—particularly for lay consumers dealing with contracts presented to them by businesses. The Legal Design Lab's classes and workshops have generated several new models for how contracts can be pre-

---

[1] See generally studies of the difficulty of reading consumer contracts and policies, including McDonald and Cranor (2008), McDonald (2009), Ben-Shahar and Chilton (2016).

[2] The literature on contract design and policy design proposes some new alternatives to the standard, de facto Legal Design, and in so doing demonstrate how the de facto designs fail to engage or inform people. See Passera et al. (2013), Passera and Haapio (2013), Ayres and Schwartz (2014), Passera (2012).

sented to lay users, and how users can interact with them in technology-enabled ways. This chapter documents these models and presents a preliminary evaluation of them. These models can be used to guide future development and contracting, and also can be tested in real-world contexts more fully, to determine what is most valuable for consumers.

1.1 Research Question, Output, and Audience

Our guiding research question is: "*In what ways do people prefer to read and interact with the terms of a legal policy or contract?*" Our hypothesis is that if we make contracts more visual and more interactive, we can improve (1) people's willingness to engage with legal information, and (2) their comprehension of the information and their ability to apply it to their situations. We are careful to recognize the many complications of this central question. There are different user types, so some people's preferences may vary wildly from others. There are also different types of contracts and contracting contexts that may shift preferences.

But given these complications, our research aims to identify key principles, patterns, and guiding insights that can inform the development of near-future computable contract presentations. As greater priority is given to remaking how contracts look and behave, this chapter lays out guidance for the lawyers, technologists, and designers who craft this next generation of contracts. It is also useful knowledge for policymakers, arbiters, and regulators, who are interested in how to evaluate contracts' usability and effectiveness.

1.2 Methodology and Initial Findings

To carry out this research, we used a Research Through Design approach. We used exploratory design workshops, with interdisciplinary participants, to take various consumer contract experiences and use the design process to generate new models of interactive, user-friendly, and powerful contracts (or applications on top of contracts). The design sessions produced early-stage prototypes of new computable contract tools, which could then be evaluated by target users, experts, and other stakeholders. These workshops' prototypes set an agenda of what types of computable contract tools might be developed, and then produced some initial evaluation of which tools are most worthwhile.

To supplement this exploratory design research, we conducted a wider survey of people using Amazon Mechanical Turk to inquire further into what kinds of computable contract tools they might find the most valuable, if any. Their responses further set priorities and principles to guide future computable contract tool development. This wider sample of potential users of computable contracts unveiled a diversity of viewpoints about the types of interfaces and tools people might prefer, as well as some of the fundamental principles that apply to most people's expectations and evaluation of contract tools.

From this work, we identified some key design patterns and requirements to guide future work on usable computable contracts. These findings include key user requirements and mental models around computable contracts. People, in our testing of new models, displayed a distinct lack of engagement with consumer contracts, often based on low self-confidence, a feeling that contracts are not meant to be read, and a preference for more peer-based and natural modes to learn about the terms of an engagement. Our research also uncovered some modes of contract presentation that might lead to more engagement. These include lightweight (not too quantitative) visual presentations, interactive chatbots or human-to-human chat, calculators and strategy-makers, and consistently structured term displays. These initial findings can drive future work on creating computable contracts and human-centered interfaces that will encourage more use and comprehension.

1.3 Chapter Structure

The chapter proceeds as follows. Sections 2 and 3 review the literature on user-centered contract design and computable, smart, tech-enabled contracts. This review identifies the key principles, insights, and agenda items that scholars have identified for the future of contracts.

Section 4 describes the exploratory workshops and user testing at the Legal Design Lab to define what the more usable experiences, interfaces, and interactions might be. It presents the emergent framework of models that have emerged from the Lab's recent workshops and courses in redesigning consumer contracts, with early-stage conceptual models and principles for how legal information can be presented to lay people so that they are more comprehensible, meaningful, and actionable.

Section 5 presents survey results in which different models were proposed to a large sample of respondents in order to understand what they value and prefer in terms of computable contract experiences. The chapter concludes with a discussion of next steps for further design, development, and research of a new generation of contracts.

2 Literature on User-Centered Computable Contracts

There is a growing body of literature in law, social science, design, and computer science fields that has set an agenda for what the future of contracts could be. This includes discussion of both what kinds of user-centered tools could be provided along with contracts, and how contracts themselves can be structured to be computable to increase the efficiency and transparency of understanding and using them. The concept of computable contracts, which intersects the fields of human-computer interaction, contract law, computer science, and behavior economics, holds vast promise in improving how contracts can be better used and understood—especially by ordinary consumers. Although the field of research is young, many scholars from these fields have researched and hypothesized different ways that a computable contract scheme, which differs from the de facto way of contracting via natural language, can meaningfully improve both the transparency of contractual terms and the level of agency and choice that can be exercised on these transactions.

These various scholars and practitioners have forwarded a vision of how a new era of contracts could emerge, and what benefits it would have for consumers. The scholars have also begun to document initial efforts to devise computable contracts, visual contracts, and other forms of contracts that allow for more interactivity and usability.

The work on proactive lawyering focuses on the importance of better contract visual design and interaction design.[3] The study of user-centered computable contracts links into a lively discussion among legal scholars about how to promote efficiency, better outcomes, and more user-centered approaches to creating legal contracts. In the past several years, several leading contracts and business legal scholars have pointed to the need for more modularity and patterning of the component parts of contracts. This call resulted from the problem with the current state of contract design and usability, both for corporate and consumer contracts. In regards to consumer contracts, the need for user-friendly contracts is particularly acute, though with promising opportunities for new models. Even as it becomes easier for companies to present terms of contracts online using new formats, companies are offering more voluminous amounts of terms in their contracts that are not readable and not comprehensible to the people for whom the contracts are intended.[4]

2.1 The Call for Usable, Visual Contracts

Many legal scholars call for more usable, interactive tools to make sense of contracts, including more visual design sensibility. Erik Gerding proposes that lawyers adopt a design-driven approach to their work in creating contracts by using Christopher Alexander's concept of a pattern language.[5] He suggests that just as computer scientists and architects use standardized modules—termed as patterns—to solve similar problems in different scenarios, lawyers can formalize contract patterns to solve recurring legal problems.

Stefania Passera, Helena Haapio and Thomas D. Barton similarly advocate for considering the legal contract as a design instrument that many actors—many of them not lawyers—will have to use, understand, and implement in their own workflows.[6]

---

[3]See Berger-Walliser et al. (2011), Salo and Haapio (n.d.), Fraser and Roberge (2016).

[4]Moringiello (2014), p. 276.

[5]Gerding (2013).

[6]Passera et al. (2013).

They argue for the need for greater contract usability, so that the terms can be more intuitively and efficiently acted upon by businesspeople and used to develop good workflows and relationships.[7] They identify promising ways to make the contract more user-centered by using information design principles, like spacious composition, use of plain language, use of graphs, tables, flowcharts and other visuals, and clearer navigation, to present terms in more meaningful and comprehensible ways.

2.2   *Imagining a New Generation of Tech-Enabled Consumer Contracts*

Contract scholars have defined a need for technology-enabled contracts that would be more comprehensible and actionable for lay people. Legal scholars concerned with business-to-consumer contracts call for "sci-fi solutions to contracts of adhesion"—in which laypeople must sign on to a business' contract terms in order to use the business' product or service. Even if the person does not have a choice in what these terms are, scholars like Gerding want to see user-centered technology that can make contracts more intelligible to laypeople, and to surface the terms that are more likely to be of importance to the users.[8]

Scott Peppet envisions a tool in which users can scan consumer contracts when they are about to purchase a product in a store and be shown user-friendly, media-rich explanations of what these contracts contain and what real-life consequences they might have for a consumer.[9] He predicts that as more information and ubiquitous connectivity spread, more tools will emerge that allow for consumers to sort through possible companies to buy things from and make more well-informed and strategic decisions about the contracts they might agree to.[10]

Kenneth Adams, a lawyer and blogger on contract design, has deployed visual design principles around the use of font, composition, and hierarchy to create a core of document design guidelines for more usable contracts.[11] He also proposes the design of new software that would allow for users to interact and navigate contracts more easily. For instance, Adams proposes that contracts might be best read in an electronic two-window interface.[12] One window would show the contract clauses you are reading, while the second window displays the definition section that gives more depth to the important terms included in the clause. He sees this as preferable to a pop-up window, which would be awkward to be clicking open and closed while reading through the contract.

---

[7]Passera et al. (2013).

[8]Gerding (2013).

[9]Peppet (2012).

[10]Peppet (2012).

[11]Adams (2011, 2012).

[12]Adams (2011, 2012).

Ryan Calo proposes a contract interface that is more visceral and interactive. In relation to privacy disclosures, Calo proposes that notices might harness more senses and experiential factors to compel more attention.[13] Privacy scholars have mapped out many of these other auditory, sensory, visual, and other channels that could be harnessed to promote better awareness of policy terms.[14] Florian Schaub, Rebecca Balebako, Adam L. Durity, and Lorrie Faith Cranor propose that those creating consumer contracts (in their case, privacy policies and terms and conditions) think of the "design space" in which their communications exist. This includes understanding the potential of smartphones, applications, the Internet of Things, and new emerging displays and channels for communication. Lawyers and the designers who work with them can create notices that employ different techniques around timing, channels, modalities, and controls in order to be more effective and engaging.[15]

2.3 Making Contracts More Modular and Machine-Readable

The call for more user-friendly contracts accompanies increasing scholarship around contracts that are drafted with a recognition of their similarity to computer code—being modular, clearly defined, and systematically logical. George Triantis highlights the efficiencies and innovation-drivers that come from more modular, systematic approaches to contract design.[16] The contracts scholar Henry Smith explicitly draws the link between contracts and computer code.[17] Alexey Lisachenko even more explicitly proposes that contracts and other legal rules are forms of computer code.[18] Contracting expert Kenneth Adams similarly proposes that contract terms and computer code are directly analogous. The words used by lawyers to compose a contract are meant to establish rules that guide how the contracting parties will act towards each other and to set methods to enforce this prescribed conduct.[19]

This conversation has begun to turn to how contracts could be made more technologically capable. Recent scholarship has proposed a new era of computable contracts that would be machine-readable and easily automated. Harry Surden introduces the term "computable contracts" to refer to how contracting parties express their terms and conditions in structured, computer-readable data formats.[20] Rather than expressing contracts in natural (human) language, if certain terms are expressed as highly structured data, then computers can process automatically what the contract's con-

---

[13]Calo (2013).

[14]Schaub (2015).

[15]Schaub (2015), pp. 6–7.

[16]Triantis (2013).

[17]Smith (2006).

[18]Lisachenko (2012).

[19]Padula (2014).

[20]Surden (2012).

ditions are and whether the parties have conformed with them.[21] This provides an advantage over current technology tools that lawyers use to scan natural-language contracts to analyze what patterns and trends appear in the contracts. This natural-language processing approach, commonly used in litigation e-discovery tools, may speed up the analysis of large volumes of contracts, but it does not allow the machine to easily, clearly identify and extract the contract terms and parties.[22] Computable contracts can improve efficiency, transparency, and technical automation of the contracting process.

Surden does not expect that all parts of a contract can be rendered computable rather than expressed with natural language, and he also limits what type of contracts should be considered ripe for being made computable.[23] Contracts that are straightforward, without significant complexity, abstraction, or uncertainty, would be more amenable to being encoded in precisely defined, highly structured machine-readable format.[24] Then it is possible to encode the terms and conditions the contract contains and assess whether the actual behavior of the parties is in conformance with them.[25]

Mark Flood and Oliver Goodenough, with the Office of Financial Research in the U.S. Treasury Department, explore how financial contracts can be defined in computational terms, with terms around selling, due dates, and payments made into "events" that then trigger consequences.[26] With this approach, a financial agreement can be created to run automatically. If it is encoded into formal computational models, then it can also be subject to automated assessments about whether it is internally coherent, and whether it is missing necessary terms to deal with the events and triggers it intends to resolve. Flood and Goodenough conducted a pilot experiment, encoding a simple financial contract for a loan in formal computational terms, to show how it is possible to render contracts in machine-readable rather than natural-language expressions.

Legal scholarship on contracts has begun to explore the potential for a more user-centered approach to making contracts more effective instruments, as well as how introducing technology-oriented approaches—particularly with contracts expressed in computable manners rather than natural language—can create more transparent, structured, and efficient instruments. These two areas of contract literature have not yet been effectively brought together to explore how the near future of computable contracts could be made real and how these new technology-enabled contracts could actually be used by lawyers, businesspeople, and lay people in ways that give them value. In other fields—primarily behavioral economics and computer science—more research has been devoted to what this marriage of user-centered and technology-enabled contracts may produce and how it can be implemented.

---

[21] Surden (2012), pp. 634–635.

[22] Surden (2012), p. 646.

[23] Surden (2012), p. 640.

[24] Surden (2012), pp. 636–637.

[25] Surden (2012), p. 658.

[26] Flood and Goodenough (2015).

2.4 Behavioral Economists' Choice Engines as One Model

User-centered computable contracts also relate to the discussion in behavioral economics and computer science about the need for more personalized, data-driven tools to help people make smart decisions. This scholarship emerged out of a dissatisfaction with simple designs meant to help consumers understand and make smart decisions when faced with complex choices. These inadequate simple designs include using Plain English words rather than legal jargon, or using tables and images to convey information. These presentations were an attempt to make legal fine print more comprehensible, but they did not show demonstrable success in improving consumers' comprehension and decision-making.[27]

Instead, behavioral economists advocate for a more complex, interactive design to help consumers navigate complex terms and conditions. Thaler and Tucker have proposed the concept of "choice engine," in which legal rules, government policies, and Big Data are combined to create a tool that helps a person make a choice.[28] They extol the choice engine as the new standard for serving consumers as they choose among offerings, so they can understand and act upon the information typically buried in contracts and disclosures. Shankar argues that "choice engines will kill search" in the next few years, because people want a smaller, curated set of options, and they want more expert support in making a choice.[29] The need for choice engines derives from consumers' apparent inability to make efficient, strategic choices when presented with all the options in a marketplace.

Joel Gurin and Beth Noveck predict a future in which more information about companies' offerings and policies will be made usable to consumers through smart choice engines, to allow people to quickly compare offerings and find the best fit for their needs.[30] Richard H. Thaler and Will Tucker similarly see that there is a new era of "smart disclosure" in which governments facilitate (or require) companies to disclose contract terms for their products and services in a standard, machine-readable format, and then an ecosystem of entrepreneurs build comparison tools and reasoning engines on top of this data to help consumers make smarter choices.[31] The hypothesis from behavioral economists is that as more information about companies and their offerings is presented in more engaging ways to consumers, consumers will demand more such information, and will reward those companies that both provide more of this information and that have better practices and offerings, and punish those that do neither.[32] It should result in a more competitive marketplace for consumer-friendly terms.

An initial crop of these choice engines has appeared online, provided both by private companies who have scraped data about companies' practices from their sites

---

[27]Thaler and Tucker (2013).

[28]Thaler and Tucker (2013).

[29]Shankar (2015).

[30]Gurin and Noveck (2013), p. 183.

[31]Thaler and Tucker (2013).

[32]Gurin and Noveck (2013), p. 192.

and from consumers' reported experiences, and by government agencies, who are able to use mandated disclosures from companies. Some of these choice engines include WhistleOut's cell phone plans comparisons,[33] NerdWallet's comparison of credit cards and rewards plans,[34] apps to use credit cards for maximum rewards,[35] the U.S. Department of Education's College Navigator site to decide how best to finance college education and choose the best college options,[36] the Consumer Finance Protection Bureau's mortgage tools,[37] and the healthcare comparison tools from Healthcare.gov and Medicare.gov.

This new generation of tools has been released only recently. There has yet to be definitive studies about whether they improve comprehension of complex systems and choices, and whether they improve the quality of decision-making. The proliferation of these comparisons and choice tools bodes a future of more such tools, the need for higher quality and interrelated data to feed into them, and the need for a vision of the future, more ambitious versions of these tools.

3 Others' Insights and Existing Models

In addition to our workshops and class brainstorms, we also did a competitive analysis of the current world of tools that aim to provide smart navigation on top of complex legal documents. This analysis gave us a first round of "design insights" that can help with the exploratory definitions of what people want from a user-friendly computable contract, and what modes of interaction might hold the most promise.

The Healthcare.gov redesign team, who worked on improving the health insurance marketplace website after its poor initial roll-out, did user research to determine the various types of users that need to be served by a government service.[38] The design research team made a schematic, dividing the core user types into four quadrants. The vectors dividing the quadrants are how much the person trusts/distrusts the "system" or the "government" and how much detail the person wants in order to make a smart decision.[39] The graph presents four quadrants, each with a unique persona. There is the *Passenger*, who trusts the system and wants few details, preferring to delegate. The *Apprentice* trusts the system but wants more details, to understand what is going on. The *Manager* trusts the system less, but wants few details—they still want to have oversight and the ability to make sure the system is working for them. And the *Engineer* has low trust in the system and wants more details—essentially preferring

---

[33] See WhistleOut (2018).

[34] See NerdWallet (2018).

[35] See AwardMe (n.d.), Walla (n.d.).

[36] See National Center for Education Statistics (n.d.).

[37] See for example, its mortgage interest rate comparison tool. Consumer Financial Protection Bureau (n.d.).

[38] Valberg (2014).

[39] Mullen (2015).

to do a thorough job in understanding the dynamics of the decision and to do the work themselves to make a wise choice. The design groups also did research into other languages' and cultures' personas and how these personas differed in their preferences for receiving information.[40]

Beyond design understandings of users' preferences, academic research also presents a range of better ways of presenting legal terms and conditions that current disclosures and consumer contracts, presented by businesses to laypeople, attempt to communicate. A common proposed intervention for improving legal communications is to change the nature of the language used, to make it more plain language that can be understood by people. The Plain Language movement pushes lawyers, courts, and government agents to present information in straightforward text.[41] The goal is text that has shorter sentences, is a more basic reading level, and is without jargon. There are federal plain language guidelines that the U.S. government released in 2011,[42] as have other governments (like in Australia and Canada).[43]

As Passera points out, the use of plain language may be a step forward from complex text as the mode of communication, but even with more plain language these documents still can be difficult to operationalize. As she observes, though, these documents aim to regulate behavior, telling people what to do, but they "are presented as statements rather than as instructions: this leads to misunderstandings" because the readers must figure out how to interpret and apply them.[44]

Another track of proposed legal communication intervention is about combining changes to the plain language and the *visual composition* of the text-based contract. Omri Ben-Shahar and Adam Chilton created a new privacy disclosure that had more headings, bullet-point lists, short sentences, and white space, but otherwise was a standard text-based list of terms.[45] They created this new design in order to run experiments to evaluate new privacy disclosures, to see if they could improve user comprehension of legal communications, or if they could affect users' ability to act strategically, as compared to a more paragraph-based text disclosure.[46] Other new visual compositions include Passera and Haapio's creation of visually-enhanced business contracts[47] that may include *images or other illustrations* of the terms at issue.[48] Many contract professionals and designers have invested in combinations of visuals to better present contract terms.[49]

---

[40]Salazar and Bergstrom (2014).

[41]Balmford (2018).

[42]See Plain Language (n.d.).

[43]Passera (2018).

[44]Passera (2018).

[45]Ben-Shahar and Chilton (2016).

[46]Passera (2018).

[47]Passera and Happio (2013).

[48]See Passera (2018) for more of such designs.

[49]Some articles present reviews of these new design styles. See Haapio et al. (2016), Brunschwig (2014), Mitchell (2015).

Icons, a standard visual illustration of a particular term or topic, have been particularly popular in privacy disclosures.[50] Tables of information are another common pattern. Federal regulators and the design consultants, Kleinmann Group, who work with them, have drafted model disclosures. This drafting has included new legal communication design for privacy and financial product terms.[51] The interface they have regularly proposed over the past two decades has been the *executive summary table*. It is a standardized composition, with rows of the same categories across all companies and disclosures. In the columns, each company lists out its specific terms. It summarizes the contents of the contract, and it is standardized for easier comparison and to reinforce how to read the terms. It is like a Nutrition Label, but it has no ranking or percentage. Rather, its central hypothesis is that disclosures that are laid out in standard, clear compositions create increased consumer literacy that crosses over communications and that increases the likelihood of engagement.

Diagrams, including charts, timelines, and flowcharts, have been found to be functional and effective in conveying a procedure. Diagrams are particularly good at laying out sequences of actions and comparisons of different paths. Flowcharts are often proposed to help people make decisions or follow complex pathways so they can see the factors or tasks in a step-by-step manner. As Passera notes, diagrams are largely absent from most legal and governmental communications. Her study of a diagrammatic presentation of procurement terms and conditions show that diagrams improve comprehension accuracy and answering speed, and that they attract more users to engage with the terms.[52] These new diagrams included swimlane tables to show how different stakeholders would interact with these terms; flowcharts to show how various courses of action would proceed; and timelines to demonstrate possible scenarios that might play out.[53]

Aside from these visual mechanisms, a few other types of communication designs have been proposed or provisionally used as ways to improve the usability of contracts. These designs include learning games, like Zynga's privacy policy communication PrivacyVille, which is a quiz game of privacy terms that follows a staged step-by-step walkthrough of the privacy terms.[54] Another emerging mechanism is the contract follow-up, with a company (like Facebook) sending a notification for a person to check in on the terms of their service despite there being no change to them.[55] Other proposals have been for user-facing evaluation tools that let people scan, analyze, and check contracts against each other, or against given standards.[56]

---

[50]These icon examples include the Privicons, the Know Privacy Icons, and the Mozilla Privacy Icons. Aza Raskin, a designer at Mozilla, led a small group to create standardized icons for representing common data practices. Each icon had variations, depending on if the company and policy allowed a practice, prohibited it, or had some third way.

[51]See Kleimann Communication Group (2009, 2013).

[52]Passera (2018).

[53]Passera (2018).

[54]Rao (2011).

[55]Facebook Help Center (n.d.).

[56]See work from the Usable Privacy Project network, including Zimmeck (2017), Liu (2014), McDonald and Cranor (2008).

4   Design Experiments to Understand Future Computable Contracts

The team of students, fellows, and partners at the Stanford Legal Design Lab has been running a series of design experiments to understand what new computable contract user experiences will and should be. Between 2014 and 2017, the Lab team conducted exploratory interviews, envisionment workshops, and qualitative testing to identify guiding design principles for computable contracts. This design work helped us to assess (1) key use cases for computable contracts, (2) values and needs people have regarding computable contracts, and (3) specific interfaces, experiences, and visual design requirements that best engage people with a computable contract tool.

Our use case research concerns what types of contracts laypeople might be most interested in interacting with, as inspired by the literature's proposals of choice or reasoning engines, visualization mechanisms, or other computable contract tools. Our team chose several different types of consumer contracts that people commonly interact with, including health care insurance policies, privacy policy terms, and credit card and investment product terms and conditions. We also considered, but did not pursue, other common use cases like credit card terms and reward programs, intellectual property policies of universities towards students and staff, and mobile phone carrier contracts with consumers.

Our exploratory design work aimed to see if the promise of a computable, contracts-based, user-facing tool was indeed desired by people—and what forms it could take to be most attractive and assistive. With our work, we were inquiring into whether user interfaces to computable contracts would help users to understand these contracts before they sign them, as they compare them with comparable businesses' contract offerings, and after they sign them, to know more effectively what their rights and obligations are.

4.1   Design Research with Privacy and Financial Terms

The team ran a series of three classes at Stanford Law School, to explore the potential for new models of consumer contracts. These three classes were Get Smart: Making Complex Information User-Friendly in Spring 2014; Consumer Contracts: Legal Design Lab in Autumn 2015; and Exploding the Fine Print in Spring 2016.[57] These classes each had a similar structure: the teams of students, partners, and teachers worked in workshop studio mode, using a human-centered design approach to remaking how legal information is presented to consumers. The classes generated and evaluated new concepts for how computable contracts could be made to help

---

[57] For class information, see Stanford Law School (n.d.).

people understand terms, choose whether they agree with them, and make decisions based on them.

Each class considered a different variation of consumer-facing contracts and policies. In the first class, Get Smart, the focus was on financial and privacy-related terms that a consumer might see when using a banking or investment application. In the second class, Consumer Contracts, the focus was on privacy policies and statements made by mobile technology companies to consumers of their hardware and software. The challenge presented to teams was how to redesign these policies so that more users of technology would read, understand, and use these policies to make smarter decisions about their data privacy. In the third class, Exploding the Fine Print, the design work focused on the terms that mutual funds and other investment products offer to potential consumers who are deciding how to invest their money. In this class, we partnered with the U.S. financial regulator FINRA. The challenge from their perspective is how to set standards and requirements for companies' disclosure of their contract terms in ways that will encourage more consumer engagement, understanding, and protection.

4.2 The Process of Design Work

With these different use cases, the teams were given a similar challenge: how do we make consumer-facing contracts and terms of service more approachable, comprehensible, and actionable? The teams were also given the literature and examples from the literature, calling for more intelligent, computable, and interactive contract experiences. Each of the classes had small teams of students, working with professional designers, interview laypeople, propose new models for consumer contracts, and test and refine them with stakeholders and with subject matter experts. The three classes on consumer contract design aimed at producing new conceptual models for how laypeople could interact with contracts to make them of higher value and use. The user research, brainstorms, and vetted ideas, brought together, constitute a short-list of promising new ways to interface computable contracts to the public.

We used a Research Through Design methodology. This involves adapting the human-centered design process to be used to create better knowledge about what both the needs and possible solutions might be.[58] This is an empirical method, but in a qualitative, generative way. It does not involve large numbers of participants or quantitative or statistical analysis of their behavior. Rather, it focuses on deep, qualitative interviews, testing sessions, and design work to give a thorough understanding of the users' motives, needs, and preferences. This work can help a team to craft better interventions that can then be tested rigorously and at a much larger scale. The method has eight steps.

---

[58]Zimmerman et al. (2007).

  i. *Landscape the Challenge*: Consultation with lawyers, managers, and business people about their interest in the contract, what they have tried before, how they are regulated, and what their interests are;

 ii. *Early Generation*: Creation of initial concept designs—thoughts about what a new contract could be—and rendering them into images and posters that describe the proposed new intervention;

iii. *Focus on Specific People*: Decision about use cases, types of users to focus on initially, so as not to be overly broad in our work;

 iv. *Research rounds*: Holding of short interviews with target users, for around 30 min, to hear their current thoughts about this contract experience, and what they do, don't do, focus on, etc.—what they want to get out of it;

  v. *2nd Generation*: Creation of second round of concept designs, creating around 15 possible new documents, experiences, and services to test;

 vi. *Ideabook Evaluation and Priority Sort*: Distribution of the "ideabook" out to stakeholders and target users, for their ranking and thoughts;

vii. *Design Insights*: Incorporation of feedback to create some finalized "design deliverables" that detail not just the proposals, but also the insights, requirements, preferences, journeys, etc.;

viii. *3rd Generation*: Refinement of the prototypes into versions that are more highly detailed, and closer to a final product, that can then be distributed as possible models for new contract design.

From this generative user research and design work, the process can then move to a more controlled experiment that has more deliberate, quantitative testing of well-developed new interventions. This process allows for ambitious experimentation with what is possible in new interactions with contracts, going beyond the standard presentations and expectations that consumers have when dealing with terms and conditions. It is driven by the needs, preferences, and mental models of the people themselves, rather than the status quo of how companies typically craft and present contracts.

4.3 The User Journey Through a Contract

In our three class' design sessions, we mapped out the user experience that people had with consumer contracts. A central design insight that we took away was that there is an arc of a person's experience with a contract, and at various points of this arc there are distinct needs and functions for a computable contract tool. We observed the contract not as a single document, but as a thing that is woven into a series of interactions and decisions that the person makes. As the contract user decides whether to use a product or service, as she determines her relationship to the company on the other side of the contract, and as she chooses how to behave, we observed the contract's influence on these various "touchpoints" between the consumer, the company, and the product or service being contracted about.

This mapping helped us to identify distinct points at which a computable contract tool might be relevant by thinking about it in the context of what needs, decisions, and functions it might support for the person. The phases for the consumer contract journey were the following:

 i.   Education/learning about the field;
 ii. Deciding on a strategy;
 iii. Making the agreement and having a "honeymoon" phase of contentment and accomplishment, and;
 iv. Carrying on and checking to see if the decision and contract is "normal," if anything is going wrong, if a condition springs into action, and if anything needs to be clarified.

From this mapping of the user's experience of a contract journey, our team identified different types of computable contract tools for different points of the journey. There can be a variety of tools or interfaces, or multiple stages for a single one, depending on what the user's "job to be done" is. Our group laid out multiple types of tools that could fit the different user tasks, drawing from our earlier competitive analysis and our own brainstorm (Fig. 1 and Table 1).

Fig. 1 The phases of a consumer's interaction with a consumer contract

Table 1 Possible computable contract tools for distinct functions and moments

Task phase of the user	Type of computable contract tool or interface
Learning and Orientation about the domain area to get an initial understanding of an unfamiliar topic	Overview of what the contract is User personas to choose from Bird's eye maps of terms Learning/training modules In-person events and education Pathway guides, games
Decision-Making about what options are available, what best suits them	Cross-contracts comparison Contract analyzer/flagger Scenario spinner Good visual design of paper Social/crowd analysis of what is normal
Signing Moment when the user actually agrees, purchases, or otherwise makes a choice about what to do	Reminder, summary Customized visual representation
Honeymoon, right after the agreement has been made, and the user starts to see what they've done, and might have buyer's remorse	Cooling off changing window
Long Haul of the relationship between the person and the company or the product/service, which is governed by the agreement	Ongoing checkup that periodically takes the user through a small questionnaire or presents the statistics/outcomes of the choices Reminder emails of what the terms are and how to change them
Issue Arises, when the user is seeking to resolve a question or problem, and is trying to figure out what rule applies, what actions he or she can take, and what outcome he or she can get	Q-and-A query tool, like a chatbot Scenario spinner
Condition Springs, when a thing happens that changes how the agreement applies to the parties	Reminder email that informs what happened and what the effect will be

4.4 Priorities, Values, and Hooks for the User

Our qualitative design work uncovered several streams of insights about people's relationships with consumer contracts that can guide future design work. These insights derived particularly from user research with Millennials with college educations based in the United States (though coming from many different backgrounds). They come from the three class' interviews and focus groups with Bay Area, California professionals, students, and recruits from Craigslist.

An overwhelming response we heard from our design research was that contracts are not engaging and likely never will be—because of, in part, their presentation. The nature of the contracts and disclosures signal that, in the words of one participant, *"they're not for me."* Laypeople will hardly ever (or never) click to look at the fine print or other contract terms. They will not choose to peruse, or even glance at, the policy document, the contract, or the paragraphs of legal communications. The respondents think that terms (as they are currently communicated) are for regulators and other lawyers. They do not consider themselves the target audience for this communication. It is "for lawyers, from lawyers." Accordingly, they don't engage with the communication. They don't think it is speaking to them or that it is worth their attention. Put simply, they think "disclosures are not for me."

Another theme was a *lack of self-confidence* in being wise in regards to these contracts and the decisions entailed within them. The participants did not feel that they knew enough about legal and financial matters to make wise decisions. That didn't lead them to read legal communications from companies, though. Rather, it made them reach out to other sources, like family, friends, blogs, YouTube videos, and online forums, in order to build their knowledge. This lack of confidence was not necessarily grounded in truth, either. When one team tested focus group members using Finra's Investor Quiz to assess their knowledge about investing, the participants scored well, though they doubted their own knowledge and ability. This lack of confidence made them cautious about making investments and more likely to reach out to social networks and third-party authorities to guide them in their behavior. It did not lead to their engagement with fine print or other mandatory disclosures.

Many people in our focus groups reported that they wish they had a "trusted advisor" who would explain the contracts and their implications to them. When asked for examples of who this advisor might be, they referenced a parent, a knowledgeable friend, or the collective of their online social networks. Others mentioned banks, universities, or employers and said that they would trust what these institutions, with which they had long-term relations, had to recommend to them for investments. Another possible source of trusted advisors existed online, in the form of experts who blogged, wrote articles, created comparison tools, or provided media-based guides to smart investment.

One of the most surprising findings from our focus group interviews was that users had a strong *hunger for in-depth, complex information* about how their potential contracts will work, what the drawbacks and advantages of different terms are, and how they should evaluate different options. This hunger does not translate into engagement with disclosures. Among several of our participants, this manifested as extensive Internet searches and reading for third-party neutral information. The participants did not necessarily discriminate about where they read information based on source, but rather read voraciously from blogs, public forums, magazines and newspapers, and YouTube. Their strategy was to consume as much conversation and advice about a topic—especially around others' strategies and stories—and then to sift through the information looking for common themes. Essentially, these types of users reasoned that they are smart Internet searchers, consumers, and sifters, so they relied upon these skills to provide them guidance enough to understand investing.

They *did not consider companies' contract terms or disclosures* as part of the reading they would do in their information search or as a final thing to check before making their investment choice. This is a paradox that our research and development aimed to tackle: how do we engage users with the content of the legal communications when they are hungry for this kind of information but don't find the legal communications (at least in their current design and context) worth looking at? They do not see terms and conditions, policies, or footnote disclosures as speaking to them—so what kind of presentation would make them tune in?

Another insight was that *graphs and charts often undermined* the communication in a contract or disclosure. Many of our participants, particularly those who were "rookie" in a given topic, were put off by communications that included charts and graphs—such as about the financial performance of investment products. Our participants did not find these visuals legible. Rather, they indicated it took too much mental effort and background research to understand what these types of visuals were actually communicating, and how they should affect their decision-making. Complex representations of data and performance were off-putting, as they were seemingly only legible to experts.

4.5 Design Models that Have Emerged

These classes, though tackling different types of consumer contracts (privacy policies and terms and conditions around financial investment products), arrived at very similar insights about what laypeople want from contracts, how they want to interact with them, and what types of technology-based tools would be valuable to them. These findings then led to a shortlist of concept models with promise that could guide development of websites, apps, and other tools that can make computable contracts useful to laypeople.

   i. *Question-and-Answer Tool*: in which the user submits a query to the tool and the tool responds with a short summary answer that refers back to specific contract provisions. It might be in a chatbot form;
  ii. *Strategy Calculator*: in which the user can enter details of possible scenarios into the calculator, which then will use the modeled contract terms to compute what outcomes the user can expect to occur;
 iii. *The Personal Assistant*: that sends reminders, prescriptive advice, and warnings to a user based on contract terms and comparisons across different contracts. This type of tool collects the user's preferences, as well as crowdsourced preferences and standards, and then alerts the user when the contracts he or she signs are in violation of personal preferences or the general standard, or when the company on the other side of the contract changes the terms or issues a recall or warning about it;
  iv. *Comparator*: that lays out the various options and key features regarding each one in a format that lets the user easily compare these features against each other. It is a table or a matrix, that the person could reorganize;
   v. *Social Signaller*: that displays what other people have done and valued with the contract, indicating what similar peers have found important and what they've done in response;
  vi. *Warning Labels*: that put the most important cautions and priorities onto the contract, highlighting only the most dangerous risks of it;

vii. *The Nutrition Label*: which displays all the most important information contained in the contract, in a standardized way across them, and that allows for consistent comparison across different products;

viii. *Roadmap and Step-by-Step Tour*: which gives a clear overview of what is inside, like a cover page with more visuals that sets it up as a process. This type of tool takes a person through a contract in a staged, interactive journey. The user can go through terms one at a time (one per screen or staged in another way, where the focus is on a single term) or through groups of terms that are relevant to each other. Rather than facing an entire document of terms at once, the user has a more guided and focus experience;

ix. *Dashboard*: that lets the user see the key things about the contracts, and that lets the user express his or her preference on any option that he or she has. Rather than a take-it-or-leave-it document, users can see options to to tweak. A dashboard tool gives the user both oversight of the terms that the contract contains and options and actions the user can take in regards to this contract. If it is before the contract has been agreed to, the user can flag, opt-out, or express a question about a term through the dashboard;

x. *Follow the Role Models*: in which people understand the contract through the perspective of a persona that they identify with. They take on what this person (fictional or real) has determined matters about the contract, and then can possibly also follow the actions or recommendations that this role model has designated. These personas explain the contract through human stories.

These various models of user-facing tools are not exclusive. There is the possibility of a suite of computable contract user tools, or sequences of them, at different points in a user's journey through a given contract relationship. Most of these proposed tools depend on drawing data from current contracts and disclosures in an intelligent way. Either each contract would be hand-coded to be structured and computable, or many similar contracts would be structured in standard ways. With this basic premise, then the data of the contract could be drawn into these interactive displays and tools for the users to engage with.

5 Survey Evaluation of Insights and Concepts

During our exploratory phase, we relied on qualitative, small-scale, in-depth feedback through interviews and focus groups to review these models and to provide direction for future iterations of them. Afterwards, we went through a wider round of feedback. We had the various concepts for user-friendly computable contracts reviewed by hundreds of people through Mechanical Turk, and we had a group of expert design professionals review them as well. The goal with these two rounds of evaluation was to further critique and define which new models of contracts have the most promise.

In Summer 2016, we ran a study to assess laypeople's interest in having various interfaces and tools on top of their legal contracts. Our team presented various hypothetical options for a consumer contract's representation to laypeople and asked them to rate what they would find most useful. For the study, we used a health insurance policy as the example consumer contract. In this instance, we prepared respondents to reflect on their own experience in choosing among health insurance offerings and looking at their policies. We also gave them a sample use case so that they would be replying to our queries with a consistent purpose and story across the study. We asked 125 respondents,[59] recruited via Amazon Mechanical Turk, to give feedback about different mechanisms that might affect their relationship and use of consumer contracts with the health insurance policies. We also asked them to reflect on their needs regarding these contracts and their preferences for what kind of tools they would like to have in order to make sense of them.

All participants were technology-literate, by virtue of responding to a request for online survey participation and completing the digital survey within a reasonable time. The majority made between $30,000 and $70,000 per year. Most had a four-year college degree, with some master's degrees and 2-year college degrees. Most were between 26 and 54 years old. There was a fairly even gender representation.

The survey had three main sections. First, we confirmed that the participant had experience with this type of consumer contract, around health insurance policies, and asked about their past experience in reasoning or strategizing around the contract. Second, we asked them their main concerns, needs, and identification with needs statements around the contract—to see if they fit with our exploratory work's propositions about how people interact with contracts and what they need to do with it at different touchpoints. Third, we proposed different types of tools and interfaces, derived from our exploratory work, and asked about their preferences for where a contracting tool should focus and for their reactions to our concept proposals.

The survey design was to understand if the interviews and focus group insights represented a larger population, and to have a wider public feedback session for the ideas and insights we had derived during the design classes. The survey results confirmed that most people felt low confidence in their ability to navigate consumer contracts around health insurance policies. They had long lists of questions about the terms—especially about the precise nature of what was covered and protected under the contract, how to operationalize it if they needed to make use of the terms, or how to compare one policy against another in regards to specific scenarios. Though many had positive assessments of the company on the other side of the contract, they felt incapable of making sense of the policy's terms to take care of their health insurance planning and needs.

The respondents' current strategies to make sense of health insurance policies and consumer contracts were most commonly Internet searches (129 people did this); customer service phone calls (109 people); looking at the text itself of the policy (89 people); and talking to a spouse (63 people), family network (60 people), or friend network (44 people). Below most of these strategies was a tool that the insurance

---

[59]Some participants dropped out of the survey midway, so though we had 125 participants who completed most of the survey, we had a total of 190 participants who began the survey.

company itself provides on its website or app (55 people). Only 6 people said they had ever used an app on their phone to deal with the policies.

Over 70% of respondents (92 people out of 124) said that they would download a tool from the insurance company itself that would let them ask questions about the policy and that would tell them more usable explanations. There is a hunger for this tool, and the respondents were not particularly concerned if it came from the company or from a "neutral" third-party. Several participants noted that they would rather the tool come from the company, so it would be more likely that the information would be accurate and particular. Participants valued a tool for the possible speed and comprehension it would offer. As one representative respondent said, "policies are extremely long and can be difficult for an average person to understand. Having an app that would answer questions and break information down into manageable bites would be useful" (Participant 6). They also valued convenience, to be able to have a consistent and mobile place to look at the contract policy, inquire about it, and get responses about it while dealing with the policy at the doctor's office, at the pharmacy, or in transit (Participant 32). Those who didn't want the tool were mostly concerned about privacy and security, or about the company misusing their information to change prices or quality of service.

The survey sought to understand if a tool (that would provide the functionality and interactions of a computable contract to a person) would be of higher value than other current strategies. The survey asked participants to rank tool-based strategies against other common ones. It asked them to rate each strategy on how likely they would be to use each of the six different modes, on a scale of 1–7, with 1 being very unlikely and 7 being very likely. The strategies, from most popular to least are as follows.

i. A tool that the insurance company provides on its website or app: 5.36 mean, standard deviation of 1.52;
ii. A tool made by a neutral third party (not your insurance company, hospital, or doctor) on a website or app: 4.68 mean, standard deviation of 1.76;
iii. A tool the hospital/doctor provides on its website or app: 4.46 mean, standard deviation of 1.59;
iv. Searching the Internet for different sites and media that explain the policy: 4.26 mean, standard deviation of 1.80;
v. Hearing other people's experiences on a forum: 4.03 mean, standard deviation of 1.79;
vi. Talking with friends or family: 3.66 mean, standard deviation of 1.59.

After inquiring about general interest in a tool, the survey then asked what the best way for this tool to communicate the policy would be. This question was meant to priority sort possible new interfaces and to find which would be most attractive (at the very highest, most abstract versions of the concepts). We asked them to react to some of our more experimental models, as well as some more traditional status quo mechanisms for making legal communication easier to understand. For the use case of a health insurance policy, participants could choose one (or none) of the six design patterns for contract presentation. The ranked list of most preferred to least is as follows:

i.   Live person for you to talk to (35 respondents chose this as the best way);
ii. Calculator, you enter your specific details into and get a custom answer back (33 chose this as best);
iii. Question and answer chat bot, like Siri (21 chose this as best);
iv. Short video explanations (16 chose this as best);
v.   A Frequently Asked Questions page (13 chose this as best);
vi. A forum of people talking about their experiences (7 people chose this as best).

The remainder of respondents chose none of the six proposed concept designs. Other proposals, that participants recommended as more preferable, included a "searchable interface of providers and services" that would let people compare terms across different companies offering contracts. This harkens to the "choice engines" mentioned in the literature review. The reasoning behind these rankings included qualitative values and requirements like:

i.   *Reliability and Quality*: The number one factor of interest was the need to get correct information that a person could act on clearly. This interest, though, pushed some to choose chatbots because "people are not perfect…I think the chat-robot is smarter and more reliable" (P23) whereas others would not trust automated tools to deliver this quality—only a live person would be trusted for some;

ii. *Accountability*: The choice of a live person is "to have someone that will be accountable if wrong information is given" (P3);

iii. *Speed*: The goal is to have "instant information" no matter the channel—texting, voice phone line, otherwise—that can clarify murky terms (P2). This means that a calculator or other automated response is preferable because it would cut down on the "legwork trying to find what you need" (P7). People wanted to "cut through a bunch of nonsense [so they didn't have to] waste more time than [they] need to find the information [they] want to find";

iv. *Retention*: The choice of video is preferable because "seeing it visually helps me retain the info[rmation] better" (P4);

v.   *Specificity and Depth*: Even if automated responses would serve "other people," many people said they wanted to chat with a real, live person so they could get in-depth, detailed scenario-based information. People doubted that "one size fits all" information would work for their particular, extenuating circumstances (P13);

vi. *Multi-Functionality*: Many people chose the chatbot assuming that it could serve them at many different points in their contract journey because, ideally, it "could do a combination of tasks that could fulfill the role of a calculator, faq, forum, and other information sources" at different points (P15);

vii. *Ego and Social Interactions*: A final factor was an interest in preserving one's own sense of reputation while asking potentially "stupid" questions. This desire to ask lots of questions "without feeling dumb about asking the questions" pushed people to choose an automated bot or calculator over a human (P25). Others explicitly referenced shyness and that they "don't want to talk to people if [they] don't have to" (P30).

5.1 Design Insights for Future Computable Contract Tools

The survey, in combination with our earlier exploratory work, points to some guiding insights that can guide future development of user-facing consumer contract tools, harnessing computable contracts' power. These include distinct user types, overall principles, and guiding insights. There are distinct principles that are near universal among recipients, while on other factors there are vectors along which different user types can be located.

Vector 1: Visuals Versus Numbers Versus Text. Participants, when explaining why they preferred one type of strategy or tool over another, declared their preferences for different types of information as the most trustworthy and useful. When attempting to understand and apply contracts, there were themes of "give me the cold hard numbers" (P44) to help analyze exactly how these terms will apply in dollar amounts or time amounts. Or, others wanted to visually retain information and preferred multimedia and illustration modes. Some people preferred the full contract text, so that they could see all the details for themselves.

Vector 2: Expert Source Versus Peer Source. Another notable divide among participants was whether they trusted their peers—meaning people they knew directly, like spouses, families, and friends, and even those they did not know but learned about online—over experts. Experts could mean people who work for the companies offering the contracts or other paid professionals. Many people, at least within the survey population, prefer to seek out stories from peers to find how to deal with the contract and make sense of its terms.

Vector 3: Automated Versus Human as Highest Quality Information. There was a clear split among people who preferred automated tools versus live human support. One participant summed up the former with the comment, "I trust math more than people" (P19). Another participant contended, on the other side, "No automated junk" (P20). There was not a clear trend of one group over another. Participants had one of these two distinct opinions about which would be smoothest, quickest, and most reliable—automated bots and calculators, or chatting with a customer service representative. The survey did not investigate what the underlying variables contributing to higher trust of bots versus humans were—but the divide was distinct, and clearly worth making a primary design factor in future usable computable contracts.

Vector 4: No Sharing of Personal Info Versus Take My Personal Info and Make Sense of It. This final vector pointed to differing concerns over privacy when interacting with online tools. Of the minority of people who did not want to download or use a consumer contract tool, most of them cited data privacy concerns as a reason that they would resist using it. They were concerned how the information they would share when using the tool might harm them in the relationship with the company, or how it might be sensitive and subject to a data breach. Most people did not express this concern and would use a tool if it offered them a more efficient contract experience, but about one-fifth of the survey respondents resisted using a tool out of privacy concern.

Our work also confirmed many of the persona types that previous research by the U.S. government, around Healthcare.gov, had found when considering how laypeople interact with complex systems information. Expanding upon their four user archetypes of the Passenger, the Apprentice, the Manager, and the Engineer, we found the following archetypes:

i. *The "What Would My Parent/Role Model Do"*: the person who wants to find a trusted authority, like a parent, an employer, a university, or even a bank who can tell them what to do—and whom they trust enough to delegate the decision to;

ii. *The "Semi-DIY/Light-Researcher"*: the person who has an interest in understanding the dynamics at play in the contract and the wider system, but who does not have the confidence or the time to fully engage with the decision. This person will do some preliminary conversations, browsing of the Internet, and skimming of the contract—and then will go with their hunches based on this light research;

iii. *The "Proto-Lawyer"*: the person who wants to dive into all the fine print, understand the references, and explore the data to ensure that they are fully in control of the decision and making the best choice for their situation;

iv. *The "CEO"*: the person who is ready to delegate, who is looking for a third party to do the research for them, and who then wants to see a high-level menu of options so they can make the final decision and give the sign off.

5.2 Do People Want Computable Contract Tools?

Generally, participants said they would want an application to use to make sense of the policy. A definite theme was that such a tool would be useful as a way to "converse with the contract." The tool ideally would help a person make sense of the policy and its terms, so that they could operationalize it in their life.

That said, in their explanations about why they would or would not use such a tool, participants put forward many conditions that qualified whether they would in fact engage with such a tool. Even if they rated the idea of a computable contract application as potentially a good idea, participants noted that they would not certainly use such a tool. For many, they would only use such an application if it met quality criteria. Namely, the application must demonstrate itself to be convenient, to be simple to understand, and to be capable of resolving a problem. The respondents had expectations that a tool must meet these qualifications, or else they would not use it, or would not even bother to visit or download it.

Another set of respondents declared that even if they would download or browse around a tool to help navigate the contract, they doubted they would use it in a meaningful way. There were various themes of reasons for this view. Some respondents declared that they are so exhausted with contracts, policies, and fine print already, that even an application that says it would simplify the experience is still too taxing. Contract exhaustion would include a computable contract tool. Several respondents explained they wouldn't download an application because they did not trust that it would be useful or easy to use. Previous experiences with policy tools or interfaces have not proven themselves to be valuable, and so they have a low estimation of future such tools. Finally, some respondents would not use a contract application because they do not like apps generally, and would prefer not to have a tech-based tool at all.

5.3 Guiding Principles for Computable Contract Interface Design

From the study, some more general principles and insights emerged to guide future design work. These apply to most of the respondents, regardless of where they sit on the vectors and user types outlined above.

  i. *Make it efficient*: No matter which presentation mode users chose, they tended to choose it because they assume it will be the quickest way to get the correct piece of information they are seeking out. Efficiency and speed are central priorities. A contract tool is the most preferable when it gets the user to the desired outcome as quickly as possible;
 ii. *Make it specific, reckon with my uniqueness*: Another priority by which respondents judged various contracting tools was how capable it would be in dealing with the unique set of issues in a given situation. A tool is more valuable if it can take in these specific details, make sense of them, and apply the terms to the specifics;
iii. *Make it simple*: A major factor by which respondents judged the presentation modes was by how easy to understand they assumed the presentation would be. Respondents expressed their preferences for jargon-free communication of information. They want to comprehend the contract in familiar terms, and a tool should support this;
 iv. *Make it reliably smart and comprehensive*: A key factor was the quality of the information and logic that the tool would employ. A presentation is only as good as the intelligence of the information presented within it;
  v. *Address social anxiety and contracts*: People find value in chatbots and automated tools on top of contracts because these experiences allow them to ask questions that would feel too awkward to ask a person. Several respondents

expressed a preference for a chatbot to alleviate their feeling of being dumb, or of being shy, when faced with the prospect of talking to a live person about the contract;

vi. *Multiple, redundant presentation modes*: Several respondents expressed resentment over having to choose just one way to interact with their contract. They wanted to be able to use various methods, in order to see which would give them the best service, and to use them in concert with each other;

vii. *Direct connection to contracting party*: One of our questions was about what actor should be the creator, maintainer, and 'sponsor' of a computable contract application. We had hypothesized that people would prefer a neutral third party as the tool sponsor, so as to be more of an impartial, trustworthy source. This hypothesis relied on a consumer's wariness of a tool sponsored by the other party to the contract, out of concern that the other party might bias the tool in their own favor, against the consumer. Most people, however, selected that they would prefer the tool to be authored and sponsored by the other party to the contract, not a third party. They wanted the offeror of the terms, the insurance company, to be directly involved so that the information would be higher quality and they could hold them accountable to this information.

6 Conclusion

The field of user-centered computable contracts is nascent, but with great promise. If legal agreements can effectively be encoded into machine-readable standards, it can introduce a new era of transparency, efficiency, and engagement with the legal terms that govern people's relationships with each other. Particularly for laypeople, who must agree to hundreds of contracts in order to use products and services, but for whom it is difficult to understand or act upon the legal fine print, computable contracts could offer a more intuitive, meaningful, and proactive way to make sense of contracts. Our initial efforts have shown that it is possible to model legal rules and contractual relationships into declarative code, which can then serve as the foundation for reasoning engines and other user-facing tools.

This chapter provides early stage research on new models for communicating complex contracts to laypeople. It bridges the literature of contract design for improved usability and computability, behavioral economics' concern for choice engines and decision making, and computer science research on how best to encode natural-language agreements into machine-readable code. The research presents results from our exploratory design and technological work, about how new user-friendly, computable consumer contracts can be created. It presents our initial designs of better ways to present legal terms and conditions and our efforts to encode legal contracts into computable logic and data.

This work opens up an important new track in human-computer interaction research. Bringing legal and behavioral economics scholarship into the conversation with computing and design, there is great value in making the complexities of business-to-consumer legal contracts more navigable, more consumer-friendly, and more valuable. There are many more studies that can be conducted to establish how best to technologically create computable contracts, and what new product, service, and information design make them most usable to laypeople.

References

Adams K (2011) Adding document-design bling to contracts? Dec 1. http://www.adamsdrafting.com/adding-document-design-bling-to-contracts/. Accessed 28 Aug 2018

Adams K (2012) So a corporate seal can be relevant! June 26 http://www.adamsdrafting.com/so-a-corporate-seal-can-be-relevant/. Accessed 28 Aug 2018

AwardMe (n.d.). http://awardmeapp.com. Accessed 30 Aug 2018

Ayres I, Schwartz A (2014) The no-reading problem in consumer contract law. Stanf Law Rev 66:545–610

Balmford C (n.d.) Plain language: beyond a movement. In: Plain language action and information network. https://www.plainlanguage.gov/resources/articles/beyond-a-movement. Accessed 6 July 2018

Ben-Shahar O, Chilton A (2016) Simplification of privacy disclosures: an experimental test. University of Chicago Coase-Sandor Institute for Law & Economics. https://doi.org/10.2139/ssrn.2711474

Berger-Walliser G, Bird R-C, Haapio H (2011) Promoting business success through contract visualization. J Law Bus Ethics 17:55–76

Brunschwig C-R (2014) On visual law: visual legal communication practices and their scholarly exploration. In: Schweihofer E et al (eds) Zeichen und zauber des rechts: festschrift für friedrich lachmayer. Editions Weblaw, Bern

Calo MR (2013) Against notice skepticism in privacy (and elsewhere). Notre Dame Law Rev 87(3):1027–1072

Consumer Financial Protection Bureau (n.d.) Explore interest rates. http://www.consumerfinance.gov/owning-a-home/explore-rates. Accessed 30 Aug 2018

Facebook Help Center (n.d.) What's privacy checkup and how can I find it? https://www.facebook.com/help/443357099140264. Accessed 29 July 2018

Flood M-D, Goodenough OR (2015) Contract as automaton: the computational representation of financial agreements. SSRN Electron J https://doi.org/10.2139/ssrn.2538224

Fraser V, Roberge J (2016) Legal design lawyering: rebooting legal business model with design thinking. Pepperdine Disp Resolut Law J 16:303–316

Gerding E-F (2013) Contract as pattern language. Washington Law Rev 88:1323–1356

Gurin J, Noveck B-S (2013) Corporations and transparency: improving consumer markets and increasing public accountability. In: Bowles N, Hamilton J-T, Levy D-A (eds) Transparency in politics and the media: accountability and open government. I.B.Tauris & Co. Ltd, London

Haapio H, Plewe D-A, de Rooy R (2016) Next generation deal design: comics and visual platforms for contracting. In: Netzwerke T, Internationalen rechtsinformatik symposions (IRIS). books@ocg.at, Salzburg

Kleimann Communication Group, Inc. (2013) Know before you owe: post-proposal consumer testing of the Spanish and refinance integrated TILA-RESPA disclosures. https://files.consumerfinance.gov/f/201311_cfpb_report_tila-respa_testing-spanish-refinancing.pdf. Accessed 30 Aug 2018

Kleimann Communication Group, Inc. (2009) Web-based financial privacy notice: final summary findings report. https://www.ftc.gov/system/files/documents/reports/model-form-rule-research-report-creating-web-based-model-form/model_form_rule_research_report_on_creating_a_web-based_model_form.pdf. Accessed 30 Aug 2018

Lisachenko A-V (2012) Law as a programming language. Rev Central East Eur Law 37:115–124

Liu F et al (2014) A step towards usable privacy policy: automatic alignment of privacy statements. Carnegie Mellon University School of Computer Science. http://www.cs.ucf.edu/~feiliu/papers/COLING_2014.pdf. Accessed 30 Aug 2018

McDonald A-M et al (2009) A comparative study of online privacy policies and formats. In: Goldberg I, Atallah M-J (eds) Privacy enhancing technologies. PETS, 2009. Lecture notes in computer science, vol 5672. Springer, Berlin

McDonald A-M, Cranor L-F (2008) The cost of reading privacy policies. J Law Policy Inf Soc 4(3):543–568

Mitchell J-A (2015) Putting some product into work-product: corporate lawyers learning from designers. Berkeley Bus Law J 12(1):1–44

Moringiello J-M (2014) Notice, assent and form in a 140 character world. Southwestern Law Rev 44:275–284

Mullen E (2015) Healthcare.gov: helping millions gain coverage. http://www.edmullen.com/all/healthcaregov. Accessed 5 July 2018

National Center for Education Studies (n.d.) College navigator. https://nces.ed.gov/collegenavigator. Accessed 30 Aug 2018

Nerdwallet (2018) Compare rewards credit cards for good credit. https://www.nerdwallet.com/rewards-credit-cards. Accessed 30 Aug 2018

Padula D (2014) Bringing innovation to the tradition of contract drafting: an interview with Ken Adams. Scholastia, 22 Sept. https://blog.scholasticahq.com/post/bringing-innovation-to-the-tradition-of-contract-drafting-an-interview-with-ken-adams. Accessed 27 July 2018

Passera S (2018) Flowcharts, swimlanes, and timelines: alternatives to prose in communicating legal–bureaucratic instructions to civil servants. J Bus Tech Commun 32(2):229–272

Passera S (2012) Enhancing contract usability and user experience through visualization – an experimental evalution. In: Proceedings of the 16th international conference on information visualisation (IV). IEEE, Montpellier

Passera S, Haapio H (2013) Transforming contracts from legal rules to user-centered communication tools: a human-information interaction challenge. Commun Des Q 1(3):38–45

Passera S, Haapio H, Barton T-D (2013) Innovating contract practices: merging contract design with information design. In: Chittenden J (ed) Proceedings of the IACCM academic forum. International Association for Contract and Commercial Management, Ridgefield

Peppet SR (2012) Freedom of contract in an augmented reality: the case of consumer contracts. Univ Calif Los Angeles Law Rev 59(11):676–745

Plain Language (n.d.) Federal plain language guidelines. https://www.plainlanguage.gov/guidelines. Accessed 30 Aug 2018

Rao L (2011) Zynga combines privacy education, gaming and rewards with PrivacyVille. TechCrunch, 7 July. https://techcrunch.com/2011/07/07/zynga-combines-privacy-education-gaming-and-rewards-with-privacyville. Accessed 29 July 2018

Salazar S-I, Bergstrom J-R (2014) Spanish language personas: informing the design of healthcare websites. User Experience, Sept. http://uxpamagazine.org/spanish-language-personas. Accessed 30 Aug 2018

Salo M, Haapio H (n.d.) Making good business decisions – the business judgment rule as a tool for better decision making 1–53

Schaub F et al (2015) A design space for effective privacy notices. In: Eleventh symposium on usable privacy and security (SOUPS). USENIX Association, Ottawa

Shankar S-V (2015) The death of search and the rise of choice engines. Big data made simple, 14 May. http://bigdata-madesimple.com/the-death-of-search-and-the-rise-of-choice-engines. Accessed 30 Aug 2018

Smith H-E (2006) Modularity in contracts: boilerplate and information flow. Mich Law Rev 104:1175–1222

Stanford Law School (n.d.) Courses. https://law.stanford.edu/education/courses. Accessed 30 Aug 2018

Surden H (2012) Computable contracts. Univ Calif Davis Law Rev 46:629–700

Thaler R-H, Tucker W (2013) Smarter information, smarter consumers. Harvard Bus Rev 91:44–54

Triantis G (2013) Improving contract quality: modularity, technology, and innovation in contract design. Stanf J Law Bus Fin 18(2):177–214

Valberg C (2014) How healthcare.gov taught America to finally care about design. Wired, 10 Oct. https://www.wired.com/2014/10/big-design-awakening-healthcare-gov. Accessed 30 Aug 2018

Walla (n.d.), https://www.walla.by. Accessed 30 Aug 2018

WhistleOut (2018) Compare the best cell phone plans. https://www.aurecongroup.com/about/latest-news/2018/may/visual-employment-contract. Accessed 30 Aug 2018

Zimmeck S et al (2017) Automated analysis of privacy requirements for mobile apps. In: Proceedings network and distributed system security symposium. NDSS, San Diego, 3066(132):286–296

Zimmerman J, Forlizzi J, Evenson S (2007) Research through design as a method for interaction design research in HCI. In: Proceedings of the SIGCHI conference on human factors in computing systems. ACM, San Jose

Beyond Digital Inventions—Diffusion of Technology and Organizational Capabilities to Change

Charlotta Kronblad and Johanna E. Pregmark

Abstract Digitalization is currently creating numerous opportunities for value creation in intellectual industries. In the legal industry however, the vast majority of law firms have remained the same without responding to the rising opportunities. The reluctance in the mainstream legal industry to adopt new digital technologies has created a duality to the field (with legal tech enthusiasts on one side and traditional sceptics on the other). This chapter explores why and discusses the connection between industrial diffusion and capabilities to change residing in individual firms. We relate digitalization to technological shifts in the past and explore the specific challenges and barriers for a digital transformation among law firms. We find that most law firms neither have the technological capabilities nor the economical motivation to change, why digitalization has, instead, become a source of fear. However, in order to seize digital opportunities and adapt to the constantly, and rapidly, changing environment, law firms need to overcome this fear and develop organizational capabilities to change. We conclude that for a true industrial transformation—beyond digital inventions—we cannot only focus on the presence of new technologies but we also need to address the diffusion of them.

Keywords Digitalization · Legal industry transformation · Diffusion · Barriers for change · Dynamic capabilities

1 Introduction

We currently live in a time of fast advances in digital technology that is affecting all areas of the economy.[1] Digitalization entails the use of several new technologies that combined constitute a more profound shift than ever before—which will most likely

---

[1] Kagermann (2015), pp. 23–45.

C. Kronblad (✉) · J. E. Pregmark
Department of Technology Management and Economics, Chalmers University of Technology, Gothenburg, Sweden
e-mail: chakro@chalmers.se

© Springer Nature Singapore Pte Ltd. 2019
M. Corrales et al. (eds.), *Legal Tech, Smart Contracts and Blockchain*,
Perspectives in Law, Business and Innovation,
https://doi.org/10.1007/978-981-13-6086-2_5

challenge the core and identity of some of the organizations that we have today.[2] The pace of change is faster and the leaps are more radical than before.[3] Organizations of today must therefore constantly renew themselves under changed conditions.

Digitalization was first experienced within manufacturing industries where the digitalization of production process resulted in machines replacing workers for repetitive mechanical tasks. Brynjolfsson & McAfee termed this the *First Machine Age*. Following recent advances in technology, we are currently facing the *Second Machine Age* where also intellectual work is being replaced by digital tools and technologies.[4] This is posing new threats to intellectual industries, but also brings new opportunities for them to change their resource mix accordingly, and combine the use of man and machines to more efficiently complete different tasks demanding different intelligences.[5] For instance, the rapid development in artificial intelligence poses particular challenges to the human intense service production in intellectual industries, where an increasing amount of the work can potentially be conducted by machines. However, simultaneously as digitalization threatens the current way of work, artificial intelligence (AI) also creates a particular potential in industries where value is created from intellectual capital.[6] When intelligence can be created artificially, and the technology behind this development constantly improves—there is huge potential to scale, to cut costs and to improve speed and quality: in essence creating new value. To capture this value, however, and to build profitable and sustainable businesses, firms also need to adapt their business models (including, for instance, the resource—mix, value offering, pricing models and organizational forms) to accommodate the changed context.[7] Thus, digitalization is not only about innovation and introduction of new technology, but also about the successful implementation and diffusion of that technology.

The legal industry is often used as an example of an intellectual industry where value is produced mainly by the knowledge intensive input of professionals. In this setting, digital technology enables a transformation of work processes and service delivery but also challenges business models and organizational forms.[8] Digitalization promotes standardization, automation and re-use and introduces new information and communication technology that enables knowledge to be bundled, packaged and provided to the market in new ways.[9] More recently, the development in technologies such as Blockchain and AI bring immense opportunities, which is addressed in other chapters in this present book. Despite this new potential for value creation in law firms, however, it is primarily legal tech firms that have picked it up. The implementation of new technologies within traditional firms remain at a slow pace.

---

[2]See, e.g., generally, Pasmore (2015); see, e.g., generally, Pasmore (2018).

[3]Reeves and Deimler (2011), pp. 134–141.

[4]Brynjolfsson and McAfee (2014), pp. 14–37.

[5]Huang and Rust (2018), pp. 155–172.

[6]Barrett et al. (2015), pp. 135–154.

[7]Teece (2018), pp. 40–49.

[8]Brescia (2015), pp. 203–222; and, generally, Susskind and Susskind (2015).

[9]Christensen et al. (2013), pp. 106–114.

As a result, a divided industry has emerged where the mainstream part has yet to commence the digital journey. Following, the emerging firms within legal tech (that have effectively invented or adopted new technologies) challenges the traditional firms and their associated business models, why digitalization is met by fear and resistance. To overcome this, and for an industrial diffusion of digital technologies, law firms need to develop organizational capabilities to change.

This chapter departs in the challenges connected to the diffusion of digital technologies in the legal industry and aims to explore what makes digitalization of the legal industry differ from the digital transformation of other industries, and what capabilities are needed in law firms to transform to respond to the changing environment.

Where our previous research has discussed how digitalization changes legal industry characteristics,[10] how digitalization affects the media industry[11] and how firms can create capabilities to change,[12] this chapter attempts to combine our insights and further explore why digitalization within law firms has been such a challenge, as well as how law firms can create the necessary capabilities to change. In result, this chapter contributes to our current understanding of the challenges connected to the digitalization of intellectual industries and shows that capabilities for change are necessary, at individual—as well as organizational—and industry-levels, for a successful diffusion of contemporary digital technologies.

This chapter is organized in four sections. Following this introduction, we move into the theoretical frame. Here we present different perspectives on industrial change and explain the specific characteristics of law firms. In the subsequent section we use these perspectives to discuss what digitalization entails for the legal industry and explain why digitalization has divided the field (with legal tech enthusiasts on one side and traditional law firms on the other). Finally, we conclude our discussion and point out directions for future studies.

2 Theoretical Frame of Reference

In this section, we provide a brief overview of three different perspectives that are interesting to explore in order to understand the difficulties for the legal industry to adapt to a new digital world. First, we outline some key elements of previous technological shifts. Second, we briefly discuss the literature on barriers and enablers for organizational change and third, we draw upon knowledge about the specific characteristics of the legal industry. Figure 1 describes how we see that these theoretical areas could contribute to the discussion about the topic in this chapter.

---

[10]Kronblad (2017), p. 16193.

[11]Fredberg and Pregmark (2016), pp. 185–219.

[12]Pregmark (2016), pp. 26–27.

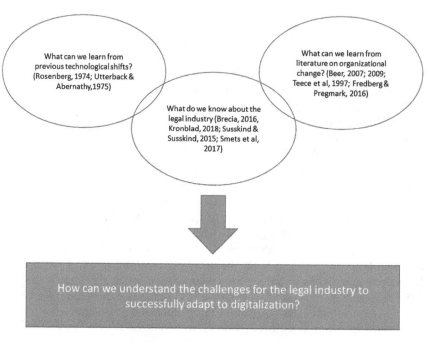

Fig. 1 Theoretical framing of the chapter

2.1 What We Can Learn from Previous Technological Shifts

2.1.1 Technological Cycles: Inventions, Innovations and Diffusion

Modern society is built on technological development where individual inventions build upon each other. Contemporary technological advancement stems from the accumulation of scientific knowledge of the past, and to solve the complex challenges of modern society continuous technological improvement is regarded as crucial.[13] Thus, for our future societal development it is critical that we continue to innovate.

The individual acts of inventions are the starting points for technological cycles.[14] When an invention is introduced to the market, or is used within an industry, the term innovation is instead used. Innovation marks the second stage of the technological cycle and refers to the initial market or industrial application of the invention. This stage is followed by the stage of diffusion, where the technology gains a larger social acceptance. These three stages of the technological cycles are illustrated in Fig. 2.

Through the history of technology; inventions and the early development of technology has been particularly emphasized. For instance, we tend to emphasize the importance of inventive minds and individual creativity among the inventors as the

---

[13]David (2007), pp. 91–114.

[14]Bernstein (2010), pp. 2257–2312.

Fig. 2 The technological cycle of industrial transformation

source of societal development.[15] This is evident in the example of the Wright brothers and the development of flight technology, the example of Edison and the light bulb,[16] or the more recent example of Steve Jobs and the iPhone. Thus, the inventors, as well as the actors that introduce new technologies to the market, are celebrated and used as symbols for social progress.

However, for an invention to take root in society, diffusion is imperative. Without diffusion of the new technology; without spreading the knowledge and the practical applications of that technology, it is hard to base an industry upon it.[17] If a technology does not become widely used and accepted, it will have less value for society at large. Thus, diffusion of technology is crucial to realize the value of a new technology. Despite the importance of the stage of diffusion, this part of industrial transformation has often been overlooked. Both legislative and economical actors tend to focus their attention and efforts on earlier stages, which can, instead, frustrate the progression of the development.[18] For instance, it is common that legislators create regulation that promotes invention or innovation (such as patent legislation that protects the inventor and seeks to create incentives for inventions) but that neglect subsequent issues; in how to promote the social adoption and dissemination of that innovation. Furthermore, even when diffusion of technology has been discussed, the emphasis has traditionally been on the inventor side of the equation, rather than on the receiving end,[19] but in order for true transformation and full-scale realization of the value brought forward by digital technologies there is a need to look at the demand side; where industry acceptance of technologies and social adoption plays a crucial role. Thus, we need to address the third stage of the technological cycle further, especially in regard to the contemporary challenges in digitalization, where there is not just one, but a bundle of technologies being simultaneously introduced.

Previous literature has to a large extent been focused on the adoption of a single technology or invention.[20] In that setting, it made sense to focus on the diffusion of one single technology. Such discussions have tended to focus on the communication and distribution capabilities on the inventor side and perceived utility and access on the receiving end. Some contemporary authors,[21] however, describe the current

---

[15]Crouch (1992), pp. 80–92.

[16]Carlson and Gorman (1992), pp. 48–79.

[17]Rosenberg (1974), pp. 90–108.

[18]Bernstein (2010), pp. 2257–2312.

[19]See, e.g., generally, Rogers (1962).

[20]Rosenberg (1974), pp. 90–108; See, e.g., generally, Rogers (1962).

[21]See, e.g., generally, Pasmore (2015); Johansen (2017), pp. 1–27.

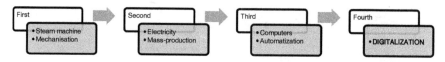

Fig. 3 Industrial revolutions

technological advances in digitalization as drivers for a more profound shift than ever before challenging organizations' core and identity. Moreover, digitalization does not only introduce new technologies but also represent a new line of thinking in regard to how individual, firms and organizations co-exist; for instance through the emerging network based world and the impact of the sharing economy.[22] Hence, the technological advances represent more of a social shift; where people, organizations and societies adapt their way of living and behaving and where organizations not only need to implement new technologies but also need to respond to the changed social context. Thus, we cannot explain the current development in digitalization only by looking at the diffusion of individual inventions or following individual technological cycles. We cannot solely talk about the diffusion of one invention but we need to address digitalization as an industrial shift where numerous technologies are introduced simultaneously bringing immence effects to society at large. Also, an industry's structure, attractiveness and crucial capabilities, may vary over time why different strategies may be suitable for the different phases.[23]

2.1.2 Digitalization as an Industrial Shift

Digitalization as an industrial shift, is often referred to as 4.0 (a term derived from a German initiative to digitalize its industry, that has inspired other nations to contribute similarly to the digital development of their industries).[24] Over a time-line, digitalization relates to the previous industrial shifts as the fourth major shift following the introduction of the steam machine; which introduced mechanical processes in manufacturing, electricity; enabling mass-production, and computers; enabling automatization.[25] In essence, these major shifts are often labeled as revolutions due to their ability in totally changing the industrial characteristics of their times with widespread impacts to society and to the progression of technological development moving forward (see Fig. 3).

Compared to previous industrial shifts, however, we need to regard the current shift in its contemporary context. Where prior technological shifts were dependent on mobility (of people and companies) for the diffusion of the inventions,[26] the

---

[22]Johansen (2017), pp. 1–27; See, generally, Pasmore (2015).

[23]Utterback and Abernathy (1975), pp. 639–656.

[24]Kagermann (2015), pp. 23–45.

[25]See, e.g., generally, Schwab (2017).

[26]Seely (2003), pp. 7–48.

digital economy provides means of immediate and global transfer and spread of technology. Thus, the speed of change and interaction is much faster today why the effects of digitalization will be faster and have a broader reach, which also means that firms today need to be more responsive to changes. Thus, being able to respond to contextual changes in technology can be a source of competitive advantage for firms. However, as we will explain below, there are certain challenges connected to this ability.

2.1.3 Digitalization and the Transformation of Related Industries

As mentioned in the introduction of this chapter, digitalization carries a particular potential to disrupt industries that base their value on intellectual capital. When these intellectual industries do not have to reside on human capital to create value but can resort to structural and technological capital, it is evident that firms need to change their resource mix, the way and organization of work, and how they bring, and price, their deliverables to the market. We have already seen such shift in the media industry, where actors such as Netflix, adhering to new technologies and business models have changed the dominant form of entertainment consumption in contemporary societies. We can see a similar shift in the newspaper industry. Though newspapers have been on the Internet since the mid-1990s,[27] it was not until the introduction of mobile media that the very core of newspaper production was threatened.[28] Hence, with introduction of mobile media, the role and identity of journalism was in question and digitalization was no more just a mean for process improvements and extended outreach. Many newspapers have had a long history of market dominance, stable business model and a tightly aligned systems to deliver profit over time. Following, they have not had any tradition in innovation and renewal. These capabilities seem to be crucial, however, to survive the digitalization of this industry.[29] Today, many newspapers and media houses still struggle, stuck in their business models based on physical papers, while competing with new companies such as Facebook and Google for attention.

Beside the purely intellectual industries, we have also already experienced a similar digital shift in other professional service industries; such as the medical profession,[30] where it is now common to get medical advice through an app, and where it can even be considered negligent of doctors not to use artificial intelligence as a source of expertise in diagnostics. We similarly experience a profound shift in banking and financing. A recent article in the Harvard Business Review, for example, argued that what the Blockchain will entail for the financial system, will be comparable to what the Internet did to media.[31] Stressing that a new digital financial system is emerg-

---

[27] See, e.g., generally, Fredberg (2003).

[28] Ihlström et al. (2008), pp. 29–57.

[29] Fredberg and Pregmark (2016), pp. 212–214.

[30] Patel et al. (2009), pp. 5–17.

[31] See, e.g., generally, Ito et al. (2017).

ing, that builds on new digital currencies and new patterns of behavior relating to investments, loans and payments.

Above these shift in intellectual industries, we have also experienced a contemporary shift in service industries that base their value creation on physical artifacts, building on the network economy. One example of this is in personal transportation. Here it is not the means of transportation; the car, that has changed (yet) but how we use it. Uber is an example of an actor that creates new patterns of behavior, bringing suppliers and buyers together on a digital platform. A similar trend is experienced within hospitality, where the currently largest provider of accommodation; Airbnb, do not own any physical property, but is merely providing a platform connecting supply and demand.[32] These firms are capturing the rising opportunities in the network economy by occupying positions on the customer interface. Similar examples can be found in retailing where the Internet market is booming and where the retailers do no longer have to carry inventory. With these examples from other industries we are not only targeting a discussion of particular inventions and their underlying technologies, but we direct our attention to the importance on those inventions and technologies when being diffused into society; creating new ways of consumption, behavior and even thinking.

It is clear that we can learn a lot from the history of technology, about how new technology and innovations spread.[33] However, if we are to believe the contemporary literature, that the shift we are currently encountering is more profound than ever,[34] it is appropriate to learn also from contemporary examples by looking at the effects of the digital transformation in related industries. Moreover, when new technology represents a shift rather than the just the introduction of a new tool or process, the traditional way of looking at technology adoption[35] seems not to be enough. In order to understand the full complexity of the digitalization process we need to go beyond traditional research components of looking at technology diffusion such as economic variables, and barriers and enablers and instead acknowledge that we are standing before a social shift, why we need emphasize micro-level components such as reluctance to change based on fear and regard how these play into dynamic capabilities and the development of organizational systems and structures.

---

[32]See, e.g., generally, Goodwin (2015).

[33]Rosenberg (1974), pp. 90–108; see, e.g., generally, Rogers (1962).

[34]See, e.g., generally, Pasmore (2015); see, e.g., generally, Johansen (2017).

[35]See, e.g., generally, Rogers (1962); Rosenberg (1974), pp. 90–108.

2.2 What We Can Learn from the Literature on Organizational Change

2.2.1 Why Change Is Hard and What Is Needed to Overcome the Challenges

Many established organizations find it hard to survive technological shifts.[36] Successful change often require substantial transformation—not only changing parts of a system.[37] Following, the success of an organization often depend on a tight alignment,[38] where strategy, structure, culture and processes have developed into a system that is designed to be efficient.[39] Technological advances naturally put pressure on radical changes to take place and often require entire systems to adapt accordingly. Therefore, when we regard digitalization as a shift, firms cannot solely implement selected technology but the digitalization process should fundamentally transform the entire business model. Thus, we cannot only study the emergence of new technologies and how these are implemented, but need to understand if and how this implementation demands for more radical changes in business models, organizational structures and strategy. To understand this transformation process, we need to understand the barriers for such change.

Various authors have discussed barriers for change in terms of resistance and fear.[40] Other authors have focused on capabilities needed to cope with radical change and renewal.[41] The change literature about technological shifts is vast and includes a number of important areas; for instance leadership[42] organizational design,[43] ambidexterity,[44] and system change.[45] In this chapter, we try to understand why law firms resist change and focus on the social process of change, where emotions, fear and needs play an important part as well as capabilities for change. We focus these factors since our previous research regarding intellectual industries points towards these factors as interesting to investigate.[46] Also, since law firm value is mainly built upon the intellectual input of individual lawyers, the business logic of a law firm is highly aligned with the logic of its individual lawyers,[47] why understanding their emotional reaction to changes becomes particularly relevant.

---

[36]See, e.g., generally, Christensen (1997).

[37]Beer (2009), pp. 223–230.

[38]See, e.g., generally, Pasmore (2015); Beer (2009), pp. 19–25; see, e.g., generally, Galbraith (2014).

[39]See, e.g., generally, Galbraith (2014).

[40]See, e.g., Beer (2007); see, e.g., generally, Pasmore (2015); Fredberg and Pregmark (2016).

[41]Teece et al. (1997), pp. 509–533; Teece (2018), pp. 40–49; Huy (2005), pp. 3–37; Pregmark (2016), pp. 26–27.

[42]Eisenbach et al. (1999), pp. 80–89.

[43]See, e.g., generally, Galbraith (2014).

[44]Tushman and O'Reilly (1996), pp. 10–30; Smith et al. (2010), pp. 468–461.

[45]See, e.g., generally, Pasmore (2015); see, e.g., generally, Beer (2009).

[46]Pregmark (2016), pp. 15–30; Kronblad (2018), p. 18075.

[47]Kronblad (2018), p. 18075.

Below we first present perspectives targeting the resistance to change. This is followed by a presentation on the capabilities that we consider necessary in order for firms to succeed.

2.2.2 Resistance to Change

According to Trader-Leigh,[48] social change processes can expect to encounter resistance. That is particularly true in change situations where organizational and individual values are threatened. The factors underlying the resistance are, to a large extent, related to emotional aspects such as fear of losing status or their sense of security and professional expertise.[49] Beer[50] summarizes the fear of losses in three categories; loss involving relationships, rewards and identity. This is to a large extent consistent with the findings of Rock,[51] who discusses how factors like certainty, status and autonomy guide emotions and behavior and Mabin et al.,[52] who stresses factors such as fear of the unknown, fear of losing control and loss of face as contributing to resistance.

Pasmore[53] discusses a situation where many organizations realize that new business models are emerging. To successfully leverage these new business models, they need to change the way they operate. However, organizations and their leaders often put up walls that inhibit them from creating the right prerequisites for change:

i.   The old model is still working (to some extent);
ii. Power is aligned with the existing model;
iii. There is no proof that a new model would work.

These three walls need to be teared down in order for change to succeed (see Fig. 4).

The notion of organizational resistance towards change is of course not new, but rather something that has been taken for granted for decades when discussing barriers and prerequisites for change[54]; As put by Lawrence:

> The key to the problem is to understand the true nature of resistance. Actually, what employees resist is usually not technical change but social change – the change in their human relationships that generally accompanies technical change.[55]

---

[48] Trader-Leigh (2002), pp. 138–155.

[49] Trader-Leigh (2002), pp. 138–155.

[50] See, e.g., generally, Beer (2007).

[51] Rock (2008), pp. 44–52.

[52] Mabin et al. (2001), pp. 168–191.

[53] See, e.g., generally, Pasmore (2015); see, e.g., generally, Pasmore (2018).

[54] See, e.g., generally, Coch and French (1948); see, generally, Lawrence (1969); see, generally, Cawsey (2012).

[55] Lawrence (1969), p. 6.

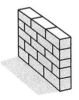

The old model is still working:
There is still revenue being
generated.

Power is aligned with the current model
The new model is a threat to people who
have won playing the old game and want
to continue.

There's no proof
In the beginning, no one can say for
certain that the new model will work.

Fig. 4 Barriers for adapting the organization (modified from Pasmore 2018)

2.2.3 Capabilities to Change

Various authors have discussed the necessary organizational capabilities for succeeding through radical shifts connected to technological advances.[56] These are often referred to as "dynamic capabilities." The term "dynamic capability" was defined by Teece et al. as "the firm's ability to integrate, build, and reconfigure internal and external competences to address rapidly changing environments."[57] This puts emphasis on an organization's ability to achieve new and innovative forms of competitive advantage. They proposed three dynamic capabilities:

   i. The ability to learn quickly and to build new strategic assets;
  ii. The integration of these new strategic assets, into company processes;
 iii. The transformation or reuse of existing assets.

Over time different authors have proposed modified or new dynamic capabilities as important. According to Beer,[58] rapid changes in the environment demands both innovation in the organizational design and development of dynamic capability—here described as "the capacity of the organization to reinvent itself over and over again."[59] Beer stresses the importance of a continuously ongoing dialogue where the leaders can learn from the whole system. Huy[60] suggests that renewal, which he discusses as more radical change, demands a specific set of organizational capabilities, related to, for example, commitment, learning and creativity. These capabilities are connected to positive emotions and aspirations.[61] These positive emotions and organizational capabilities are best evoked in a space of trust and absence of fear.[62] What kind of social dynamics that facilitates dynamic capabilities has also been

---

[56]Teece et al. (1997), pp. 40–49; Teece (2018), pp. 509–533; Eisenhardt and Martin (2000), pp. 1105–1122.

[57]Teece et al. (1997), pp. 509–533.

[58]Beer (2013), pp. 27–33.

[59]Beer (2013), p. 32.

[60]Huy (1999), pp. 325–345; Huy (2005), pp. 3–37.

[61]Huy (1999), pp. 325–345; Huy (2005), pp. 3–37; see, e.g., generally, Amabile and Kramer (2011).

[62]Rock (2008), pp. 44–52; Heskett (2007), pp. 1–2.

investigated by Fainschmidt & Frasier.[63] Their study supports the idea that dynamic capabilities need to be underpinned by a social climate in an organization that is characterized by trust and strong interpersonal relationships. Adding to that, Fredberg & Pregmark[64] suggest that work with innovation and change is supported by a climate where there is no fear of mistakes. This could be said to be in contrast to other suggestions of motivations to change, such as urgency,[65] dissatisfaction[66] or what sometimes is referred to as a "burning platform." This potential contradiction is discussed in Pregmark.[67]

Today, some authors are discussing a need for new more urgent dynamic capabilities. The network-based world,[68] enabled by digital advances, that we work and live in today, put new demands on organizations to not only mobilize its own resources quickly, but to also orchestrate and reconfigure externally sourced competences.[69]

2.3 What We Know About Legal Industry Characteristics

2.3.1 The Specific Characteristics of the Legal Industry

While digitalization is affecting all industries, it cannot be understood the same way in all of them. In some industries innovation and transformation is more difficult than in others, and depending on the industrial context, it affects them in different ways. Rosenberg[70] argues that that the process of innovation is dynamic and must be understood in context where he for instance stresses that the economic motives behind innovation matters, as well as inherent complexity to the technology of the inventions.

In order to understand why traditional law firms have been reluctant to implement digital technologies, we need to understand why they function the way they do, and what motivates their current path of behavior. Here some explanation lies within the specific characteristics of legal services and the legal industry. Legal services are knowledge intensive, which means that the main capital for value creation is the human capital of the professionals at work.[71] Only a limited amount of other capital have been needed in law firms. Due to this distinctive characteristic of knowledge intensity most law firms have based their business models on the sale of specialized legal advice by the hour. This has created a context where law firms have enjoyed

---

[63] Fainschmidt and Frasier (2017), pp. 550–566.

[64] Fredberg and Pregmark (2016), pp. 185–219.

[65] See, e.g., generally, Kotter (2008).

[66] See, e.g., generally, Beckhard and Harris (1987).

[67] Pregmark (2016), pp. 28–30.

[68] See, e.g., generally, Pasmore (2015); see, e.g., generally, Johansen (2017).

[69] See, e.g., generally, Shuen (2008); Shuen and Sieber (2009), pp. 58–65.

[70] Rosenberg (1974), pp. 90–108.

[71] See, e.g., generally, Løwendahl (2009).

both high revenues and high profitability, being able to set the price of the hour themselves[72] mainly considering the cost of the human capital (and the potential profit to the partners). The knowledge intensity in the production of legal advice has, therefore, meant that there has not been any significant need for external capital in the industry, which has enabled firms to be organized as professional partnerships, where the lawyers not only work in the firms but also own and manage them.[73] Furthermore, in most jurisdictions it is professional associations of lawyers that regulate the market for legal services. This self-regulation means that lawyers create a monopoly on the sale of certain legal services. The professional associations have consequently been very influential in how law firms work; how they are organized and managed, and how the services are priced and delivered.[74] Thus, there are three distinctive characteristics that serve to explain why law firms today look and function the way they do; high knowledge intensity, low capital intensity and professionalization.[75]

As pointed out above, the most common organizational form in the legal industry is the professional partnership, where the hour has also been key in promotional assessments through the common management structure of up or out.[76] Picturing law firms (and the legal industry) using the shape of a triangle is indicative of this practice, where a few partners have numerous associates working for them, from various hierarchical positions at the "back office." After annual reviews associates either climb up the hierarchy toward partnership, or are incentivized to leave the firm. Today we see some variation to this practice, but it is still very common in legal practice.[77] This is illustrated in Fig. 5. Also, indicative to picturing the legal industry as a triangle; is the nature and composition of legal work within law firms. Here the top of the triangle represents the most complex legal work task that demand more experienced attention, and the base represent the main bulk of work that is more of a routine nature.

While the boundaries of the regulated markets for legal services differ across different jurisdictions, there is currently a global trend of deregulation in the area, which in effect have opened up parts of the markets also for unregulated actors.[78] This has been a prerequisite for the emerging field of legal tech.

---

[72]Levin and Tadelis (2005), pp. 131–171.

[73]See, e.g., generally, Maister (2003).

[74]Greenwood et al. (2002), pp. 58–80.

[75]von Nordenflycht (2010), pp. 155–174.

[76]Morris and Pinnington (1998), pp. 3–24.

[77]Kronblad (2018), p. 18075.

[78]Garoupa (2013), p. 77–86.

Fig. 5 The "triangular" shape of law firms and legal work

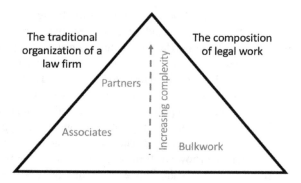

3 Understanding the Challenges for the Legal Industry to Adapt to Digitalization

3.1 Why Law Firms Do not Change: Economic Motives and Technological Complexity

Based on the realization that law firms have been very homogenous and that they have been both stable and extremely profitable over time, we can understand why, or rather why not, the legal professionals inhibiting these firms respond to external changes. In the current context, the majority of the actors holding power in this industry (regulators, owners, managers and workers) carry the same basic rationale for behavior, building into a strong logic that is institutionalized in all their business models and management practices; that they should just keep working the way they do.[79] As Pasmore[80] would put it, the power is aligned with the old model, that is still working, and there is limited proof that switching to a new model would work. Rosenberg[81] argued that there has to be an economical incentive for technological diffusion, and, in this case, the traditional firms have yet to experience such incentives.

Adding to this conserving effect is that the buyers of legal services are often past law firm lawyers that have been raised within traditional firms. In effect, they may not see the need for, or demand, technological implementation. This is a key explanation to the current duality of the field with traditional buyers and traditional sellers, on one side, and the buyers and providers of legal tech enabled products and services, on the other.

Moreover, for new technologies to root and to diffuse in an industry, Rosenberg[82] also stressed that the target population need to have sufficient understanding of the applicable technology and, here, the legal community face additional challenges;

---

[79] Kronblad (2018), p. 18075.

[80] See, e.g., generally, Pasmore (2015).

[81] Rosenberg (1974), pp. 90–108.

[82] Rosenberg (1974), pp. 90–108.

the homogenous community of traditional lawyers are not particularly interested or skilled in technology. Here the industry set up has also been highly influential; since regulations (by the professional associations) often prohibits external influences at both ownership and management levels. Consequently, the legal industry has been largely unaffected by other competencies but legal. This has also built a culture where only legal competence is considered valuable and where the individuals working at law firms are commonly divided under the labels "lawyers" or "non-lawyers". At a firm level, this means that the introduction of a new technology not only require a new pricing model or a new product offering, but that the entire business model needs to adjust. With that comes the need for changing the whole organizational system.[83] It could be hypothesized that the barriers for adapting the organization are harder to overcome in intellectual industries, in general, and the legal industry, in particular. In the legal industry, as discussed before, the power structure is created based on the success of the previous model. Traditionally, what has created the way to the top is not necessarily innovativeness and exploring new things. Hence, we can understand why the introduction of AI or Blockchain would be tricky for the traditional lawyer; the knowledge gap is too big and frankly; the cat is too fat. Current business models and organizational forms are not equipped in the right way to promote the implementation of new technologies. Current relationships, rewards and identity[84] are challenged by digitalization. The change process is thereby hindered by social considerations within the firms and there is a resistance and fear among individual traditional lawyers as of what such change would entail. It is not possible to fit digitalization in with the previous business model or organizational form. The established business models have conserving effects and the firms become locked into their current model and existing business relations.[85] When those in power in the industry support and drive the objectives of the dominant logic it is difficult for a contender to change them (however possibly they do not need to—as it may be possible for emergent legal tech firms to surpass the traditional firms and disrupt the industry from beneath).

Beyond Rosenberg's[86] argumentation that diffusion needs an economic motivation and the technological complexity must be acceptable to the target user, there also need to be a societal or cultural acceptance of the changes, and in the traditional part of the legal industry; these predispositions are simply not there. Especially not as long as "hour" is the basis for both value creation (from the input by human intellectual effort) and capture (from the common pricing models) in the industry. Thus, the dominant logic protecting status quo is stronger than in other industries, where there is often a wider spread among industry interests and a larger variation and appreciation of different competencies.[87]

---

[83]See, e.g., generally, Pasmore (2015); Beer (2009), pp. 9–13.

[84]See, e.g., generally, Beer (2007).

[85]See, e.g., generally, Chesbrough (2003) and Galbraith (2014).

[86]Rosenberg (1974), pp. 90–108.

[87]Kronblad (2018), p. 18075.

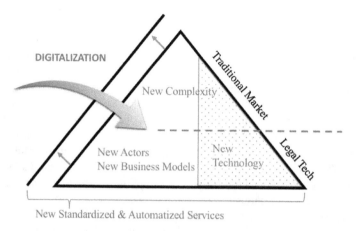

Fig. 6 The impact of digitalization on the market for legal services

3.2 The Impact of Digitalization and the Emergence of Legal Tech

However, despite the mainstream reluctance to change, it is indicative to our experiences, as well as to the authors of the other chapters in this book, that there is a prosperous emerging field of legal tech, where firms have invented and/or implemented digital technologies to legal services to create and capture value.

There is evidently huge potential for value creation from digital technologies, and there are firms willing, and able, to make the necessary investments in their attempt to realize this value. Here external investment can be necessary since other capital (but intellectual human capital) becomes integral parts of the value creation (for instance structural—or technological-capital).[88] This also brings an incentive for firms to work outside of the regulated market—to be able to attract such capital and to use other price models but hourly billing, that enable them to capture value also from the use of other capital but human. In effect, this has created a duality to the field where new, often unregulated, actors enter the industry and compete with different business models and organizational forms, following a different logic. Figure 6 illustrates the impact of digitalization in the legal industry and how it divides the field. In this figure the effects of new technology are indicated both for the traditional firms, where some of the associate work is already being replaced by the use of new technologies or tools[89] and for the legal tech firms. For legal tech firms, however, the use of technology in value creation does not represent a replacement of previous workers, but are instead a strategic choice in the resource mix (man/machine) given their business model and strategy for their invention or implementation of technology.

---

[88]Smets et al. (2017), pp. 203–239.

[89]Kronblad (2018), p. 18075.

Another effects of digitalization in the legal industry, indicated in Fig. 6, is that the total market is growing. This depends both on the increasing complexity that digitalization brings to the industry at large, and on the low-cost legal services that new technologies enable. For instance, on the top we can imagine the new legal (and ethical) issues arising when technology develops and introduces driverless cars; putting new focus on issues relating to responsibilities, we can imagine the increased number of legal matters involving infringements risks following the massive personal data collected on line, and we can imagine the complexity in designing legal structures for global e-commerce solutions within retail. An effect of this increase in complexity is that the market for legal services grows. Since this market growth is happening simultaneously as technology takes part of the associate work, and new actors taking part of the bulk business, the traditional firms are not exposed to any decreased demand, which in effect weakens the sense of urgency for their digital transformation. Urgency often being considered as a key driver of change.[90] As long as the market is growing, there is still good business opportunities for most law firms, and limited economic motives to change. However, also the lower end of the legal market has grown through the adoption of digital technologies for more repetitive or standardized legal bulk work being provided to the marked at low prices. Here digital technologies enable a larger scale of production at significantly lowered costs, which increases the market to encompass new buyers of legal services, that previously could not afford, or would prioritize, legal services. In this new market segment new legal products and services are developed with a user focus, that is previously unknown to the production of legal services. This is also what is often contributed to as the democratization of legal services; being increasingly accessible at affordable costs.

3.3 Digitalization of Intellectual Industries; Beyond Inventions

We argue that the current shift of digitalization that intellectual industries are going through, has more significant implications for these industries compared to, for instance, manufacturing—as it challenges the very core of the organizations, such as the business model, organizational structures and core capabilities.[91] As we have stressed before, technologies advancing artificial intelligence will be most disruptive in industries where human intelligence is the basis of the value creating service production. Following digitalization, we can also expect a shift in power dynamics, identity and relationships in the intellectual industries.[92] This is particularly important in understanding the slow diffusion process in these industries as these factors are often regarded, in the change literature, as key drivers for resisting change.[93]

---

[90] See, e.g., generally, Kotter (2008).

[91] See, e.g., generally, Pasmore (2015).

[92] Johansen (2017), pp. 1–27; see, e.g., generally, Pasmore (2015).

[93] See, e.g., generally, Beer (2007); Rock (2008), pp. 44–52; Mabin et al. (2001), pp. 168–191.

Hence, with the type of dramatic technological transition that we currently experience, resistance might come from social reasons and pressure on relationships, as already concluded by Lawrence.[94] From our different studies in the intellectual industries we have seen different levels of resistance and different renewal capabilities.[95] We hold that these differences stem from to what extent the representatives from the different industries perceive the shift as a social change that will affect their relationships, power or professional identity[96] in a negative way. Adding to that, the structural changes that might need to be made to leverage new business models and opportunities might be inhibited by barriers put up by social dynamics, as described by Pasmore.[97]

The barriers for an organization to change, as a result of interference with the social dynamics and relations, might be of special importance for the legal industry, where structures and culture are tied to parameters such as identity and power.

3.4 The Need for Dynamic Capabilities

As technology evolves, however, so do industry characteristics, products, and critical success factors. According to Utterback & Abernathy,[98] organizations without the right capabilities are going to be put out of business. Hence, an industry's structure, attractiveness and crucial capabilities, may vary over time suggesting different strategies for each phase.

This could be tied to a discussion around dynamic capabilities as the key for surviving technology shifts and transformation.[99] Teece et al.,[100] stresses the ability to learn quickly and to build new strategic assets, the integration of theses new assets into company processes as well as the transformation of existing assets. Huy[101] also discusses the capabilities for radical change and put emphasis on capabilities such as learning, commitment and creativity. Moreover, Huy as well as Pregmark[102] discuss that those capabilities are connected to a set of positive emotions, such as hope, openness and fun. Fainschmidt & Frasier[103] also shows that the social climate of trust is essential for dynamic capabilities and Fredberg & Pregmark[104] points towards a

---

[94]See, e.g., generally, Lawrence (1969).

[95]Fredberg and Pregmark (2016), pp. 185–219; Pregmark (2016), pp. 2–30; Kronblad (2018), p. 18075.

[96]See, e.g., generally, Beer (2007); Mabin et al. (2001), pp. 168–191.

[97]See, e.g., generally, Pasmore (2018).

[98]Utterback and Abernathy (1975), pp. 639–656.

[99]Teece et al. (1997), pp. 509–533; Beer (2013), pp. 30–33.

[100]Teece et al. (1997), pp. 509–533.

[101]Huy (1999), pp. 325–345.

[102]Pregmark (2016), pp. 10–30.

[103]Fainschmidt and Frasier (2017), pp. 550–566.

[104]Fredberg and Pregmark (2016), pp. 185–219.

need for a climate free from fear of failure. It could be discussed whether traditional law firms are characterized by such social climate. In an organizational system that is based on clear power structures and *up or out*-models it is easy to assume that openness, trust and safety is not necessarily key features. One could image a climate rather characterized by fear of failure than probing and innovating. This could be said to be in contrast with the capabilities discussed by Huy[105] and Pregmark.[106] Also, it could be hypothesized that it is contradicting a climate of trust,[107] where employees are not afraid of making mistakes.[108] Moreover, Beer[109] claims that to create and uphold dynamic capabilities the organization constantly need to learn from the whole system in dialogue. In the legal industry, such ongoing learning from the customer and learning from different employees with different educational background and skillsets is generally not in place.[110]

According to several authors, the technological shift that we encounter right now will eventually bring new, less hierarchical organizational forms and more network-based models of work.[111] This is also touched upon with regards to a possible need for a refined set of dynamic capabilities.[112] In a digitally enabled world, the ability to successfully work in a network, guided by a joint purpose rather than a strong hierarchy, is key. Moreover, in this new world, constantly reshaping the organization is necessary and the ability to mobilize organizational energy is critical.[113] It seems like this world remains, for the traditional law firms, a world of potential.

3.5 Practical Implications

It is high time that the legal industry digitalizes and for a successful digital transformation it is not enough that legal tech firms adopt a new technology or way of work, but the traditional law firms also need to change and implement new digital technologies and build successful business models and cultures around them. Based on our discussion, we recommend that law firms develop capabilities to change and that law firms:

i. Think about digitalization just as much as a social process as new technology and develop cultures that promote the implementation of technology;

---

[105] See, e.g., generally, Huy (2005).

[106] Pregmark (2016), pp. 10–30.

[107] Fainschmidt and Frasier (2017), pp. 550–566.

[108] Fredberg and Pregmark (2016), pp. 185–219.

[109] Beer (2013), pp. 27–33.

[110] Kronblad (2018), p. 18075.

[111] See, e.g., generally, Johansen (2017); see, e.g., generally, Pasmore (2015).

[112] See, e.g., generally, Shuen (2008); Shuen and Sieber (2009), pp. 58–65.

[113] See, e.g., generally, Johansen (2017).

ii. Use the new opportunities to increase client value, for instance by the means of more efficient communication, higher quality or new packeting or bundling of legal services;
iii. Create new business models to capture the value in the new technology;
iv. Address the potential in the network-based world—as law firms that find ways of building business models, organizations and capabilities to match these new opportunities might gain competitive advantages;
v. Consider new characteristics and capabilities when recruiting, to build the skill set of tomorrow—not only digital competence but also characteristics supporting renewal, change and innovation

4 Conclusion

As has been discussed in the other chapters of this book, recent years have provided us with new opportunities to use digital technologies to create value in the legal industry. However as pointed out in this chapter—while the technological inventions are here—they have yet to diffuse within the mainstream of the legal industry. In this chapter we have addressed the reason why, and can conclude that the key reason is that for traditional law firms' the implementation of digital technology simply have not made sense; the current business models are too profitable and the industry logic and rhetoric's are too pervasive. For a digital transition, the new technologies need to be implemented and accepted at a broad level, and this has been proved to be difficult in an industry where the mere business logic points the actors toward other paths of action.[114] There is a resistance for change that reside on a fear of changes in a social context; where relations, rewards and identity play in.[115] Traditional firms are reluctant to make a change that endanger the current relationships with clients, their monetary rewards and their professional identity. However, the question is how long traditional firms can hold on to this position. As numerous firms from the legal tech part of the field are realizing the value from digitalization, in developing new products and services, they are increasingly competing with traditional law firms; targeting the same markets, clients and work tasks. Therefore, we believe that a digital transformation is inevitable. Some mainstream legal industry actors are in fact beginning to see the potential in digitalization, realizing that if they do not jump on the opportunity to act, the legal tech firms will (and already have). Thus, for the future success of traditional law firms it is crucial that they swiftly adopt and develop dynamic capabilities to change. This will in effect make both them more profitable and will enable an industrial diffusion that would be beneficial to society at large, especially as a prime role of law firms is to enable other businesses to succeed in their endeavors. Higher quality output created in cheaper and more efficient ways therefore brings a potential to create value also in other industries. To do so however we need

---

[114]Kronblad (2018), p. 18075.
[115]See, e.g., generally, Beer (2007).

to understand the social processes that surfaces, such as resistance and fear[116] and build strategies to overcome them in order to accept and implement new technology and build new business models. A successful digitalization of the legal field demands for implementation and industry diffusion beyond technological inventions.

As we write this chapter in the summer of 2018, while being in the midst of the massive and complex digital transformation, it is only in retrospect that we will be able to understand the consequences of current developments. Thus, it is of great interest to continue to research the ongoing transformation of the intellectual industries. Because, while there is a general interest in the transformations of such industries, studies targeting the digitalization of these industries are rare.[117] We therefore suggest that more research goes into how digitalization affects the social aspects of intellectual industries in general, and the legal industry in particular. If dynamic capabilities are underpinned by a climate of trust,[118] it could be of interest to investigate how such a climate can be established in the legal industry. Moreover, it is yet to be discovered how a digitally enabled network-based world will affect how we organize and lead organizations.[119] We argue that this shift could be of special interest to explore for the legal industry. Today, the traditional law firm is far from network based. A network-based organization needs to be flat, guided by purpose and driven by energy.[120] Therefore, it might be of interest to follow the potential of a large transformation in the legal industry—for instance through case studies.

Furthermore, we find it particularly appropriate to apply an interdisciplinary approach in the future studies of this contemporary phenomenon. Such an approach strives to combine different streams of literature to enable a complete understanding of the digital development and associated challenges. In line with this argumentation, we would also like to thank the editors of this present book, that have invited us, as management scholars, to contribute to this volume with our insights from the implication of digitalization. Because if it is something that the history of technology teaches us; it is that from combining efforts and aligning the development in technology, science and law, that we can reach the positive advancement in society that we strive for.

References

Amabile T, Kramer S (2011) The progress principle: using small wins to ignite joy, engagement, and creativity at work. Harvard Business Review Press, Boston

Barrett M et al (2015) Service innovations in the digital age: key contributions and future directions. MIS Q 39(1):135–154

---

[116]See, e.g., generally, Beer (2007).

[117]Smets et al. (2017), pp. 203–239.

[118]Fainschmidt and Frasier (2017), pp. 550–566.

[119]See, e.g., generally, Johansen (2017); see, e.g., generally, Pasmore (2015).

[120]See, e.g., generally, Johansen (2017).

Beckhard R, Harris R-T (1987) Organizational transitions: managing complex change, 2nd edn. Addison-Wesley, Reading (MA)

Beer M (2007) Leading change. Harvard business school background note, 9-488-037, Rev. 2007

Beer M (2009) High commitment high performance: how to build a resilient organization for sustained advantage. John Wiley & Sons, San Fransisco (CA)

Beer M (2013) The strategic fitness process: a collaborative action research method for developing and understaning organizational prototypes and dynamic capabilities. J Organ Des 2(1):27–33

Bernstein G (2010) In the shadow of innovation. Cardozo Law Rev 31(6):2257–2312

Brescia R-H (2015) What we know and need to know about disruptive innovation. S C Law Rev 67:203–222

Brynjolfsson E, McAfee A (2014) The second machine age: work, progress, and prosperity in a time of brilliant technologies. WW Norton & Company, New York

Carlson B, Gorman M (1992) Bell, Edison and the telephone. In: Weber R (ed) Creativity in technology. Oxford University Press, New York (NY)

Cawsey T, Deszca G, Ingols C (2012) Organizational change: an action-oriented toolkit, 2nd edn. SAGE Publications, Thousand Oaks (CA)

Chesbrough H (2003) The logic of open innovation: managing intellectual property. California Manag Rev 45(3):33–58

Christensen C-M (1997) The innovators dilemma: when new technologies cause great firms to fail. Harvard Business School Press, Cambridge (MA)

Christensen C-M, Wang D, Van Bever D (2013) Consulting on the cusp of disruption. Harvard Bus Rev 91(10):06–114

Coch L, Jr French J-R-P (1948) Overcoming resistance to change. Hum Relat 1(4):51–532

Crouch T (1992) Why Wilbur and Orville. In: Weber R (ed) Inventive minds, creativity in technology. Oxford University Press, New York (NY)

David P (2007) Path dependence—a foundational concept for historical social science. Cliometrica 1(2):91–114

Eisenbach R, Watson K, Pillai R (1999) Transformational leadership in the context of organizational change. J Organ Change Manag 12(2):80–89

Eisenhardt K-M, Martin J-A (2000) Dynamic capabilities: what are they? Strateg Manag J 21(10/11):1105–1122

Fainschmidt S-M, Frazier L (2017) What facilitates dynamic capabilities? the role of organizational climate for trust. Long Range Plan 50(5):550–566

Fredberg T (2003) Interface strategies: internet and the business of large swedish daily newspapers. Göteborg: Department of Project Management, Chalmers University of Technology. Institute for Management of Innovation and Technology, Gothenburg

Fredberg T, Pregmark J (2016) Transformation in a tightly nested system: employing fast cycles of change. Res Organ Change Dev 24:185–219

Galbraith J-R (2014) Designing organizations: strategy, structure and process at the business unit and enterprise level, 3rd edn. Jossey-Bass, San Fransisco (CA)

Garoupa N (2013) Globalization and deregulation of legal services. Int Rev Law Econ 38(S): 77–86

Goodwin T (2015) The battle is for the customer interface, tech crunch. https://techcrunch.com/2015/03/03/in-the-age-of-disintermediation-the-battle-is-all-for-the-customer-interface/?guccounter=1. Accessed 20 July 2018

Greenwood R, Suddaby R, Hinings C-R (2002) Theorizing change: the role of professional associations in the transformation of institutionalized fields. Acad Manag J 45(1):58–80

Heskett J (2007) What is management's role in innovation, working knowledge. Harvard Business School https://hbswk.hbs.edu/item/what-is-managements-role-in-innovation# online publication, pp. 1–2. Accessed 11 Dec 2017

Huang M-H, Rust R-T (2018) Artificial intelligence in services. J Serv Res 21(2):155–172

Huy N-Q (1999) Emotional capability, emotional intelligence and radical change. Acad Manag Rev 24(2):325–345

Huy N-Q (2005) An emotion-based view of strategic renewal. Strateg Proc 22:3–37

Ihlström C et al (2008) Business models for m-services: exploring the e-newspaper case from a consumer view. J Electron Commer Organ 6(2):29–57

Ito J, Narula N, Ali R (2017) The blockchain will do to the financial system what the internet did to media. Harvard Business Review

Johansen B (2017) The new leadership literacies: thriving in a future of extreme disruption and distributed everything. Berrett-Koehler Publishers

Kagermann H (2015) Change through digitization—value creation in the age of industry 4.0. In: Albach H et al. (eds) Management of permanent change. Springer, Ipswich (MA)

Kotter J-P (2008) A sense of urgency. United States. Harvard Business School Publishing, Boston (MA)

Kronblad C (2017) Digitalization of the legal industry. In: Academy of management proceedings, vol 2017 (1), pp 16193

Kronblad C (2018) Managing digitalization—conflicting institutional logics within professional service firms. Acad Manag Glob Proc 2018(1):18075

Lawrence (1969) How to deal with resistance to change. Harvard Business Review 32(3). https://hbr.org/1969/01/how-to-deal-with-resistance-to-change. Accessed 25 Jul 2018

Levin J, Tadelis S (2005) Profit sharing and the role of professional partnership. Q J Econ, Oxford University Press 120(1): 131–171

Løwendahl B-R (2009) Strategic management of professional service firms. Copenhagen Business School Press

Mabin V-J, Forgeson S, Green L (2001) Harnessing resistance using the theory of constraints to assist change management. J Eur Ind Training 25(2/3/4): 168–191

Maister D-H (2003) Managing the professional service firm. Free Press, New York

Morris T, Pinnington A (1998) Promotion to partner in professional service firms. Hum Relat 51(1):3–24

Pasmore W (2015) Leading continuous change: navigating churn in the real world, (1st B edn). Berrett-Koehler Publishers, San Fransisco (CA)

Pasmore B (2018) Lecture note, seminar, the best way to understand the future of work is to design it. Chalmers University of Technology, May, 22nd, 2018

Patel V-L et al (2009) The coming of age of artificial intelligence in medicine. Artif Intell Med 46(1):5–17

Pregmark J (2016) Change models in need of renewal: building strategic practice to prevail in industry transitions. (Licentiate). Chalmers University, Gothenburg

Reeves M, Deimler M (2011) Adaptability: the new competitive advantage. Harvard Bus Rev 89(7/8):134–141

Rock D (2008) Scarf—a brain based model for collaborating with and influencing others. NeuroLeadership Journal 1:44–52

Rogers E (1962) Diffusion of innovations, 1st edn. Free Press of Glencoe, New York

Rosenberg (1974) Science, invention and economic growth. Econ J 84(333): 90–108

Schwab K (2017) The fourth industrial revolution. Crown Publishing, New York

Seely B (2003) Historical patterns in the scholarship of technology transfer. Comp Technol Transf Soc 1(1):7–48

Shuen A (2008) Web 2.0: a strategy guide: business thinking and strategies behind successful web 2.0 implementations. O'Reilly Media, Beijing

Shuen A, Sieber S (2009) Orchestrating the new dynamic capabilities. IESE Insight Rev 3:58–65

Smets M et al (2017) 25 years since "p2" taking stock and chartling the future of professional firms. J Prof Organ 4:203–239

Smith W-K, Bins A, Tushman M (2010) Complex business models: managing strategic paradoxes simultaneously. Long Range Plan 43:448–461

Susskind R, Susskind D (2015) The future of the professions. Oxford University Press, New York

Teece D-J (2018) Business models and dynamic capabilities. Long Range Plan 51(1):40–49

Teece D, Pisano G, Shuen A (1997) Dynamic capabilities and strategic management. Strateg Manag J 7:509–533

Trader-Leigh K-E (2002) Case study: identifying resistance in managing change. J Organ Change Manag 15(2):138–155

Tushman M-L, O'Reilly C-A (1996) Ambidextrous organizations: managing evolutionary and revolutionary change. Calif Manag Rev 38(4):8–30

Utterback J-M, Abernathy W-J (1975) A dynamic model of process and product innovation. Omega 3(6):639–656

von Nordenflycht A (2010) What is a professional service firm? toward a theory and taxonomy of knowledge-intensive firms. Acad Manag Rev 35(1):155–174

Contract Automation: Experiences from Dutch Legal Practice

Ivar Timmer

Abstract Organizations in legal practice, under pressure to do "more for less," are searching for ways to automate legal work, to improve efficiency of legal service delivery. Automated drafting of contracts (or: contract automation) is one of the areas where technology is—partly—replacing legal professionals. In Dutch legal practice, the number of organizations that are actively deploying contract automation is still relatively small, but growing. This chapter looks at experiences with contract automation of organizations from various sectors in Dutch legal practice. Contract automation can improve legal service delivery to consumers and SMEs, as well as contracting processes within organizations. Several organizations report positive results. However, successfully implementing contract automation, especially for internal use within organizations, is not simple. Tight budgets, resistance to change and poor integration with other software are some of the problems that organizations may encounter. Generally, human and organizational factors are often at least as important as the technological aspects. Successful implementation of contract automation requires design thinking, a proactive approach and process-oriented (legal) professionals. Regardless of these difficulties, the use of contract automation software in Dutch legal practice can be expected to increase, due to several factors. The number of organizations that are offering contracts (and other legal documents) online to SMEs and consumers has grown rapidly over the last years. Contract automation is not only offered to consumers and SMEs by commercial parties, but also by branch organizations, as a service to their members. Consumers and SMEs will become used to these self-help solutions for legal matters. Legal publishers are also increasing the offering of automated contracts and other legal documents. In addition, law firms and consultants are promoting the use of contract automation within client organizations. Finally, many corporate organizations are increasingly exchanging experiences on improving legal operations and the use

I. Timmer (✉)
Research Program Legal Management, Amsterdam University of Applied Sciences, Amsterdam, The Netherlands
e-mail: i.timmer@hva.nl

© Springer Nature Singapore Pte Ltd. 2019
M. Corrales et al. (eds.), *Legal Tech, Smart Contracts and Blockchain*,
Perspectives in Law, Business and Innovation,
https://doi.org/10.1007/978-981-13-6086-2_6

of Legal Tech, including contract automation. Eventually, increased use of contract automation may drive further harmonization of contracts within sectors and facilitate other technological applications, such as the automated analysis of contracts.

Keywords Contract automation · Expert systems · Legal Tech · Legal management · Legal operations

1   Introduction

Legal professionals perform many tasks that are difficult, or even impossible, to automate. Managing negotiations or conflicts, drafting new contract clauses for new business situations, or exercising wise judgment in situations where legal rules are unclear are but a few examples. However, large parts of the work of legal professionals consist, in essence, of managing and processing *information*. It is therefore clear that *information technology* can be useful to support, streamline, or even completely automate legal tasks. Organizations in legal practice, under pressure to do "more for less," are increasingly searching for ways to make use of technology. In his 2008 book *The End of Lawyers?*, Richard Susskind identified automated document assembly as one of ten disruptive technologies for the legal profession, because of its potential to greatly reduce the time expent by legal professionals on the drafting and production of documents.[1] Over ten years later, this chapter looks into practical experiences of organizations in Dutch legal practice with regard to the automation of a specific type of legal documents: contracts.

In the Netherlands, contract drafting certainly is one of the areas where, in various sectors of legal practice, substantial innovation through information technology is taking place. Several reasons may account for the fact that contract drafting is a favored area for innovation. First, contracts obviously play an important role in many areas of legal practice, from business-to-consumer transactions, government tenders, to, most notably, corporate legal practice. Secondly, contracts often have a repetitive character. For many organizations, it is common to close thousands of similar types of contracts every year, in which each individual contract has only a few variations. In addition, even contracts with a more bespoke character often have many elements in common with other contracts. Finally, from a technical point of view, drafting repetitive contracts is a relatively simple activity. It consists, for a substantial part, of choosing the right text blocks to fit the right situation. This activity can be supported by software that uses questionnaires to connect users' answers, via underlying decision trees and routings, to relevant text blocks. Not too long ago, advanced computer skills were necessary to construct this kind of questionnaires and decision trees and combine it with word processing. Nowadays, this has become

---

[1] Susskind (2008), p. 101.

much easier and within the reach of non-tech savvy legal professionals, due to the availability of—relatively—user-friendly software. It is self-evident that volume, repetitiveness and the availability of this software are important drivers to increase the pace of digitization and automation.

For this chapter, I have approached organizations from various sectors of Dutch legal practice that are actively involved in automating (parts of) their contract drafting processes. These organizations can be considered frontrunners, even though automation of contract drafting can hardly be called a new technology.[2] However, there are many organizations that have not undertaken any steps in this field, even when their contracting practices appear *prima facie* ideally suitable for automation. The overall view that emerges is therefore that, although Legal Tech has caught the attention of a broader legal public over the last years, (Dutch) legal practice is in the relatively early stages of digital transformation. Many sectors of legal practice are still conservative when it comes to implementing technology. Another important factor is that many legal departments or organizations only have limited budgets for innovation. Of course, genuine progress has been made with regard to certain aspects. Legal research and information retrieval, for example, have changed unrecognizably in a relatively short period of time, driven by the digitization of legal information by large legal publishers. However, many processes within legal departments or legal service providers are still based on ways of working that originated in a paper age.

Of course, the above does not imply that the automation of contract drafting (and other legal documents) is a must for every organization. The needs of a small legal department that mainly performs bespoke work, will be completely different from those of a large governmental organization or law firm. However, it seems fair to say that in the latter type of organizations one will almost always find documents for which automation may make sense. Ultimately, what makes sense for a particular organization should be decided at an organizational level, by the professionals most involved. Legal professionals therefore have an important role to play when it comes to successful innovation of legal processes through technology. To quote famous management scientist Peter Drucker on increasing the productivity of knowledge workers: "Continuing innovation has to be part of the work, the task and the responsibility of knowledge workers."[3]

---

[2] Susskind points to the article of Sprowl (1979) as the first publication on the subject of document automation in the legal sector.

[3] Drucker (1999), p. 84.

2 Methodology and Structure

The basis of this chapter is formed by a series of interviews.[4] In 2018, a total of 12 professionals and academics, working in the Netherlands, were interviewed, who were all in some way involved in automating contract drafting processes or had studied the automation of legal work from an academic perspective. They were working at a governmental organization, two corporate organizations,[5] one large and two medium-sized law firms, a legal advisory firm, an online "legal market place," two different software providers, a university and a legal publisher. Their organizations were using software from Thomson Reuters (ContractExpress) and SAP Ariba, as well as software from Dutch providers WeAgree, Berkeley Bridge, Juriblox and LegalThings. Some of these organizations are using the software to offer automated contract drafting online to clients. They sometimes combine this with offering the software as a service to other organizations, e.g., branch organizations, that are then offering contracts to their members or clients under their own label or brand, via a *Software As A Service* construction (SaaS). Legal departments of corporate organizations are using it in-house to improve legal service delivery to other departments. Others are using it as a part of consulting services, advising or implementing it in other organizations, from governmental organizations to SMEs or large corporate organizations.

The interviews were held under the condition that results would be anonymized, allowing respondents to speak freely about their experiences. Some of the quotes of respondents have, therefore, been modified slightly, to prevent identification. The results from the interviews were combined with previous experiences and results of earlier research on contract automation, expert systems and Legal Tech in general.[6] The table below provides an overview of the organizations, the manner in which they use contract automation and the target groups they aim to service with the contract automation.[7]

---

[4]Parts of the results, combined with other research, will also be used for the special issue "Law in algorithmic world" of Droit et Société (Université de Liège) for a contribution about the use and implications of rule-based expert systems in Dutch legal practice (expected: December 2019).

[5]A large technological company and a large media production company.

[6]This research has been conducted as part of the research program on Legal management, at the Amsterdam University of Applied Sciences (AUAS), one of the initiators of the Dutch Legal Tech Alliance, a collaboration between 11 UAS with an LL.B. program, to improve education in Legal Tech. I have also drawn from experiences of students, working in legal practice, in the course Legal service design, part of the master program in Legal management, which is linked to the research program.

[7]The table has been simplified slightly, but displays the most important manners of use and related target groups.

	Manner of use	Target group(s) of contract automation
Online legal marketplace	Offering online contracts through own website, as well as via websites of branch organizations	Consumers and SMEs
Legal advisory firm	Offering online contracts through own website, as well as via websites of branch organizations and other clients	Mainly SMEs
Law firms (mid-size and large) Law firm (small)	Using contract automation within the own firm and/or as part of their consulting services	Lawyers. In-house legal departments and/ or other professionals (e.g., sales procurement) within these organizations Offering contract automation to SME clients for use in-house
Legal publisher	Using contract automation to improve own products	All clients (mainly legal departments and law firms)
Corporate organizations	Using contract automation in-house to improve efficiency or in-house legal services	In-house counsel and non-legal professionals within the organization
Governmental organization	Using contract automation as a service to member organizations	Legal counsel and ICT and procurement professionals within member organizations

The first theme in the interview with the professionals working in legal practice was why and how the organization started with the automation of contract drafting. What were the specific reasons to start, how did the organization select its software and what were the expectations at the time? As a second theme, we discussed experiences using and implementing the software, including the integration of the software with other systems within the organization. As a third theme, I asked them whether automating (part of) the contracting process had had any personnel implications, such as a reduction in legal or other professionals, a need for different knowledge and skills of (legal) professionals working within the organization, or an increase or decrease in job satisfaction. Finally, we discussed future developments.

The structure of this chapter is as follows. First, to provide a broader context, some terminology with regards to contract automation will be explained, after which some historic background and an overview of the "state of digitization" of Dutch legal practice will be provided. After this, I will discuss the most important outcomes of the interviews, covering the themes above, split into different subjects and sections. Finally, I will draw some general conclusions, identify challenges and scenario's and some questions for future research.

3   Terminology, History and Digitization in Dutch Legal Practice

3.1   Terminology

The automation of contract drafting (contract automation) is, when viewed in the context of the age-old history of law, a relatively new phenomenon. Not surprisingly, the terminology around it has not yet crystallized. In this section, some of the terms used in discussions and literature on contract automation are discussed.

Contract automation can be looked at from a variety of perspectives. First of all, see the introduction, it can be considered a form of automated document assembly (also "document automation," "document assembly" or "automated document generation"). Some regard document automation as part of the broader concept of business process management *automation*.[8] Viewed from the perspective of legal departments within organizations, contract automation within organizations may indeed often be seen as a specific subset of this discipline. This is the case, because an organization will often really be trying to automate its contracting processes and policies, more than just speed up the drafting process of a specific contract. It will want the right (non-legal) professionals to be able to select, use and compose the right contract, by asking the right questions, preferably without the assistance of or review by the legal department. This whole process goes beyond the mere "legal craftsmanship" of drafting contracts, as contracting policies are directly linked to the (commercial) strategy and risk appetite of an organization. Automating this policy in a large and complex organization requires more than just the intelligent digital composition of text blocks, but demands, amongst other things, effective internal communication, training the professionals involved and continuously monitoring the use of the software. The software on the market often has features to support these process improvements, such as digital workflows and approvals.

Nevertheless, at the core of contract automation lies the use of technology to intelligently combine information to produce (complex) legal documents. It can therefore be viewed as a branch or application of *legal informatics*. Erdelez and O'Hare describe this field as follows:

> The American Library Association defines informatics as "the study of the structure and properties of information, as well as the application of technology to the organization, storage, retrieval, and dissemination of information." Legal informatics therefore, pertains to the application of informatics within the context of the legal environment and as such involves law-related organizations (e.g., law offices, courts, and law schools) and users of information.[9]

Within the field of legal informatics, systems for contract automation aimed at supporting non-legal professionals in drafting a contract could be characterized as *expert systems*: "computer programs which perform complex tasks at a level which is at or

---

[8]See, e.g., https://www.hotdocs.com/contract-automation.
[9]Erdelez and O'Hare (1997), p. 368.

near the level expected of a human expert."[10] Expert systems are traditionally seen as a branch of artificial intelligence, because they mimic a form of human intelligence. A system for contract automation could, more specifically, be characterized as a *rule-based legal expert system*. Rule-based expert systems are based on rules of logic, such as the modus ponens: if a conditional statement ("if p then q") is accepted, and the antecedent (p) holds, then the consequent (q) may be inferred.[11] These logical rules are often translated into decision trees. Expert systems have to be programmed by human specialists to deliver specific outcomes for specific scenarios, that have to be conceived beforehand by the programmers.[12]

One could be forgiven for raising an eyebrow over the characterization of an application that produces a relatively simple contract, such as a non-disclosure agreement (NDA), as an *expert system* and *artificial intelligence*, because the underlying decision tree or logical rule will have a low degree of complexity. However, there are still plenty of legal departments and law firms that draft relatively simple NDA's on a regular basis and a non-legal professional will certainly lack the expertise to draft a solid NDA from scratch. If a system for contract automation enables a non-legal professional (e.g., a sales or a research and development professional) to draft a NDA by answering some basic questions, the system performs the role of a human legal expert and could, strictly speaking, qualify as an expert system, albeit for a relatively simple expert task.

With regard to labeling it artificial intelligence (AI); this phenomenon has always been difficult to pin down in a definition. A common joke amongst experts is that things are called AI until the software actually starts working. In the recent past, things such as optical character recognition (transferring scanned typed or written documents into text) were considered AI. Nowadays, most will intuitively associate the term AI with more complex tasks or phenomenons, such as defeating world champions in Go[13] or self-driving cars. By way of illustration, natural language processing (NLP) is still an important branch of AI today. Probably, in 25 years or so, young children will consider a person very old, when told that he or she has witnessed the introduction of the first home assistants, such as Amazon's Echo, Apple's Siri and Google's assistant. It seems that defining AI has some resemblances with aiming at a moving target.

Of course, the answer to the question whether or not something is AI or an expert system, is not so interesting in itself. I do consider expert system a fairly useful term, simply because it describes the role a system for contract automation can fulfil within an organization. Some may want to reserve this term for systems that have a high degree of complexity, in which the system has digested a large amount of expert

---

[10]Tyree (1989).

[11]Branting (2017) uses the term logic-based, instead of rule-based, to distinguish from systems using data science techniques to assist in solving practical legal problems. For example, "robot-lawyer" ROSS, based on IBM's Watson, could be considered a system that is primarily data-centric (or: case-based), although it will, no doubt, use a variety of techniques.

[12]The relatively new phenomenon of Rule-based Machine Learning, in which machine learning is used to identify rules, is usually excluded from the field of "rule-based expert systems."

[13]See https://deepmind.com/blog/alphago-zero-learning-scratch/.

knowledge. They will prefer the term *decision support system* for systems with a lower degree of complexity. However, one could consider it equally valid for systems that perform relatively simple tasks, as long as the goal is to replace some form of (in-house) expert advice or support.[14] Within the context of this chapter, this will be the legal expertise needed to craft a professional contract on the basis of facts that the user provides, usually in response to certain questions. Of course, a real contract lawyer may often perform this job better, for example by ascertaining—through additional questioning or other forms of research—that the facts provided are indeed correct. To avoid any misunderstanding or controversy, I will simply use the term *contract automation software* (CAS). I do provide a brief history (and criticism) of legal expert systems and legal informatics in the next section, to promote a critical stance towards the automation of legal work.

Contract automation can be viewed as one of the first steps in the lifecycle of contracts.[15] Some also include the digital storage and management of contracts under the term contract automation, while others use the term contract management (CM) software for this. In this chapter, I focus on the drafting process and reserve the term contract automation exclusively for the automation of the *drafting* of contracts. An alternative term for this could be *contract assembly*, which I do not use, because I have found that some associate this term with assembling contracts using traditional word processing software. Needless to say, there is no right or wrong here, it is simply a matter of definition. A good advice is to start any discussion about the automation of any contracting process with an explanation of the terms used by the participants.

3.2 History

Attempts to automate the work of legal professionals go back several decades. Around the 1980s, with the rise of computer science, many universities established research groups in legal informatics and there was an active (inter)national network of researchers in the field of artificial intelligence and law. Several Dutch universities were very active in this field. Legal expert systems were at the center of attention, driven by the enthusiasm over expert systems in other fields.[16] The research evolved around solving complex legal problems, often for consumer problems (e.g., rent, social security). Reflecting the international situation, expectations of this—relatively—new area were high at Dutch legal faculties. Legal expert systems were generally expected to be able to improve quality, cost-effectiveness and/or accessibility of legal advice or decision-making and the climate for acquiring research funds was favorable. I remember, from my own time at university in the early nineties, debates about whether or not the computer would take over the role of the judge. The opinions

---

[14]Consequently, when a system for contract automation is used by experts themselves to support their own drafting processes, it is not an expert system, but simply a system to facilitate.

[15]See e.g. IACCM-CapGemini (2018).

[16]See e.g., Leonard-Barton and Sviokla (1988).

were, of course, strongly divided between tecnophiles and conservative lawyers, who dismissed the whole idea as preposterous. To illustrate the attitude towards technology of some legal professionals at the time: when I did an internship at the court of appeals at the time (in 1998), one of the judges refused to use a computer. He simply continued to use his typewriter, which was fully accepted. Today, most legal professionals acknowledge that technology can be a valuable tool, but many are still far from tech savvy. This is probably one of the reasons for the relatively slow pace of technological innovation within legal practice, as well as for the poor quality of many public debates around technology and law today. Debates on Legal Tech often end up discussing the same question as years ago: will technology be able to replace the judge or other legal professionals? This question may be interesting from a philosophical point of view, but we are still lightyears away from any scenario in which full replacement of the complex tasks that legal professionals perform will be possible. A more realistic question is therefore how technology can effectively support legal tasks and processes.

Returning to the developments in legal informatics at the time, constructing and successfully implementing working legal expert systems, with the aim of—almost—fully replacing legal professionals, proved difficult. As Leith described it:

> The primary reason why the expert systems project failed was that the ambitions were so difficult to achieve. What was being proposed was really the robotisation of lawyers - that their skills and knowledge could be easily formalised, and that as a process was at heart a quite simple operation - if you knew the rules, then you could give advice. This, unfortunately, proved wrong. This was a view which developed from the perceived success of early AI expert system programs, where the argument ran that if they worked in such complex domains as medicine or exploration, they should also work in the 'easier' field of law.[17]

Leith describes, as another flaw, that these expert systems departed from a over-simplistic view of law, equivalent with the views of Herbert Hart, in his famous book *The Concept of Law* (1961).

> However, what became clear to me through discussion with my new colleagues was why lawyers of the time were so keen on expert systems in law: they had been brought up in the context of a simplistic rule-oriented view of law of the sort promoted by Hart, and such a perspective neatly dovetailed with the approach used in rule based expert systems. In effect, there was a culture in law of denying the complexity of law. Those who teach in law schools today may be surprised that, 25 years or so ago, most law staff were not socio-legally or contextually inclined. They often taught part-time, did little research, and what research they did do was of the case-notes format. Hart, to this group, seemed perfectly fine in terms of legal philosophy.[18]

And he concludes:

> …any basic critical analysis of a system which is proposed as a 'working legal expert system' will quickly find that the system is not used, over promoted, and generally not much different from a list of boxes to tick.[19]

---

[17]Leith (2010).

[18]Leith (2010).

[19]Leith (2010).

In my view, an important part of Leith's criticism comes down to the fact that applying legal rules to complex cases is not a straightforward activity. Even legal rules that appear quite clear will, at a deeper level, always have a certain degree of vagueness or ambiguity, making it hard or impossible to fully capture this in a logical form. Applying a rule means either interpreting the rule, or interpreting the facts that have to be decided. Deciding on legal cases by applying legal rules therefore almost always implies some form of creating law, albeit on a microscale. The use of CAS in legal practice differs both in goals and complexity from the systems that were addressed by Leith's criticism. With regard to the *goals*: negotiating a contract can be extremely difficult, but the scope of contract automation is much smaller and only focuses on automating the drafting process. With regard to *complexity*, expert systems often have much higher ambitions than CAS. By way of illustration, researchers at the University of Amsterdam have recently built a modern expert system in the field of labor law.[20] It consists of over 800 interlinked questions and underlying decision trees. By comparison, most questionnaires for contracts do not exceed 30–40 questions. Nevertheless, Leith's short account does stimulate us to realize the complexity of automating legal work. This important nuance often appears to vanish in today's enthusiasm about the possibilities of Legal Tech.

As another reason for the failure of legal expert systems in the past, Leith points to the fact that the emphasis of the developers was, partly because of the underlying philosophy described above, very much on translating the legal rules into a working system, rather than on the needs of users of the system. Unsuccessful introductions of CAS in organizations can probably often be accredited to insufficient attention to users as well, as we shall see below. Leith's historic account mainly focuses on the British situation, but applies well to the Dutch situation. As a result of, amongst other things, the factors described by Leith, initial enthusiasm and research funding for legal expert systems quickly diminished. Scientific attention for legal informatics remained low for quite some time. On the wave of popular attention for Legal Tech, there appears to be a rejuvenation. However, most scientific attention currently seems directed towards data-centric or "case-based" techniques and the possibility of artificial argumentation and less towards "old-fashioned" rule-based techniques.

Lack of scientific attention aside, organizations in legal practice have certainly continued to develop expert systems and/or systems for decision support, as will be described in the next section.

Goodenough[21] describes the overall developments in technology for legal practice as a progression from Legal Tech 1.0, to 2.0 and 3.0. In his view, Legal Tech 1.0 is the first phase, which is for a large part based on the digitization of, formerly analog, legal information. This has enabled human professionals to search and work faster, without fundamentally changing legal work. In Goodenough's words: the system has pretty fully digested phase 1.0.

---

[20]Magontslag.nl.

[21]https://www.huffingtonpost.com/oliver-r-goodenough/legal-technology-30_b_6603658.html? guccounter=1.

In the second phase (Legal Tech 2.0) technology will actually replace humans. E-discovery practice, where machine learning approaches are replacing large parts of human document review, is a good example of an area where this second phase has arrived. In Goodenough's view, developing expert systems for contract automation is another area where automation may replace human work and legal practice moves beyond "mere digitization." Its potential lies not only within companies, moving legal work from the legal department to other departments, but also at the level of legal services for consumers, where it may empower those who can't (or won't) afford traditional legal advice.

Legal Tech 3.0, according to Goodenough, offers the prospect of more radical innovation, for example by statutes being written in (or at least being well-translatable to) computer code, allowing for the automation of legal processes on a larger scale. Although one could question the extent to which this is possible, it might be feasible for more formalistic areas of law (such as tax law). In many respects, Legal Tech 3.0 is probably still quite far away, but it is clear that more progress lies ahead. For now, as will be described in more detail in the next section, it seems fair to say that Dutch legal practice is in the process of the transformation from Legal Tech 1.0 to 2.0.

3.3 Digitization in Dutch Legal Practice: A Brief Overview

From a perspective of digitization, progress may have been slow, compared to other economic sectors, but the Dutch legal world has certainly changed over the last decades. The Netherlands is a small country, with little over 17 million inhabitants, and Dutch legal practice is consequently relatively small. By way of illustration, there are around 18,000 lawyers (members of the bar), around 12,000 legal professionals working for governmental organizations and around 5,000 legal professionals working for corporate or non-profit organizations.[22] It is estimated that around 100 Dutch corporate organizations have a legal department of more than ten legal professionals. For most of these corporate organizations, often very internationally oriented, English is the primary legal language. The Netherlands is home to a few large multinationals, such as Philips, ING, Shell, AkzoNobel and Ahold Delhaize. These have more sizeable legal departments (40 to >500 legal professionals worldwide), but are the exception.

As mentioned in the introduction, across all sectors of Dutch legal practice, legal research and information retrieval have been digitized almost completely; *Legal Tech* 1.0. As another manifestation of Legal Tech 1.0, virtually all corporate legal departments are working on digitizing their contract management processes,[23] to

---

[22]These figures represent the legal professionals who are physically working in the Netherlands. In the Dutch legal tradition, legal professionals working for governmental, corporate or non-profit organizations usually are not "lawyers" in the sense that they are members of the Dutch bar association.

[23]See Timmer (2016).

complete the transformation from paper to digital contracts. Unfortunately, from a perspective of taxpayer's money and the necessary transformation to complete digital litigation, in 2018 the Dutch judiciary paused an important "Legal Tech 1.0 project," aiming to digitize all forms of litigation. The project, which will continue in a different form and at a slower pace, may serve as a reminder of how difficult it is, in general, to digitize complex legal processes, especially in a conservative sector.

In a broad view, one could characterize the digitization of many other governmental processes as a manifestation of Legal Tech 2.0. In the Netherlands, especially in the domain of social security and environmental law (e.g., building permits), many governmental services of a legal nature have been digitized and automated. Not all of these innovations have been equally successful, but it is fair to say that many have increased both efficiency, speed and user-friendliness of governmental decision-making. The Dutch government is currently also very active in experimenting with Blockchain, to improve legal procedures and processes.[24]

As another sign of continuing digitization and the transformation to Legal Tech 2.0, providers of digital arbitration services have entered the Dutch legal market. The use of e-discovery software (or: software for technological assisted review), another Legal Tech 2.0 development, has increased in recent years. A few governmental organizations, regulators, law enforcement agencies, as well as some of the international tribunals in The Hague, were early adopters in the Netherlands. Law firms have been lagging behind with regard to this particular development, but are making efforts to catch up. In general, virtually all larger law firms and some mid-sized firms are currently investing in technological innovation, with contract drafting as an important area. While some of these firms are genuinely innovative, others still appear to struggle.

With regard to contract automation, as the main subject of this chapter, several alternative service providers have entered the Dutch consumer market. They provide online self-help contracts and other legal documents for consumers and small businesses. They often combine this with functioning as a online market place for law firms and notaries for customers that need more advice. In 2013, a large Dutch retailer entered into a partnership with some notary firms and launched an online notary service[25] for several standard documents (e.g., a basic will). Other examples are Overeenkomsten.nl,[26] Omnilegal[27] and Juriblox.[28] US provider Rocket lawyer[29] has also entered the Dutch market. In addition, legal publishers also offer automated legal contract templates to professional users for certain areas of law, such as mergers and acquisitions.[30]

---

[24] www.blockchainpilots.nl.

[25] notarisservice.hema.nl.

[26] Which in translation means: contracts.nl.

[27] https://omnilegal.nl/portfolio/omnilegal-doe-het-zelf-oplossing/.

[28] https://www.juriblox.nl/.

[29] https://www.rocketlawyer.com/nl/nl.

[30] https://www.wolterskluwer.nl/producten-diensten/juristen/tools-innovatie/smartdox.

For software that can be used as a "tool box" to automate contracts, on which this chapter focuses, the Netherlands has a few providers: WeAgree, Berkeley Bridge, LegalThings and the aforementioned Juriblox, which also offers their underlying software as a tool box. However, almost all major CAS applications, such as ContractExpress, HotDocs, Exari or NeotaLogic are used somewhere in the Netherlands.

From an international perspective, Dutch legal practice can probably be rated as fairly progressive when it comes to digitization. However, there are differences between and even within sectors, with some organizations lagging behind. To conclude, Legal Tech 1.0 has mostly arrived, Legal Tech 2.0 is on its way in many parts of legal practice, but Legal Tech 3.0 is still a scenario for the distant future.

4 Experiences with Contract Automation

4.1 Reasons for Starting with Contract Automation

As mentioned above, the first theme in the interviews with the professionals working in legal practice was why the organization started with contract automation. The respondents identified several benefits, that were often the same for comparable organizations. Many reasons came down to a desire to improve knowledge management by having a "single point of truth" instead of different templates circulating in the organization, increase speed of contract drafting processes, enable non-legal professionals to perform relatively simple legal tasks and to drive down costs and improve efficiency. The following quotes illustrate some of these reasons for the participating organizations.

The governmental organization (the association of Dutch municipalities) had introduced a contract generator (for ICT contracts) as a service to their member organizations.

> We see our 390 members having very similar problems and needs in this field. It makes sense to offer them this tool. We hope it will help them professionalize their ICT contracting practices.

The corporate organizations both identified as one of their primary goals to transfer simple legal work away from the legal department, to both save time for legal professionals, as well as improve in-house services to other departments.

> This simple work costed us quite some time and, to be honest, it was the least interesting legal work. However, you do want to have some control over it, because the amounts involved can be considerable and the organization could suffer serious risks if legal aspects are not handled properly.

> Because they don't have to run things by us anymore, it saves the other departments time and actually increases the 'popularity' of Legal.

The online legal market place, acting as a broker between consumers seeking legal advice and law firms, had recently started to use contract automation. It is offering "self-help" consumer contracts on their website, primarily as a marketing tool.

> Developing and maintaining this service may, in itself, not be economically viable, viewed from our specific business model. However, we think clients who use it will be interested in other services of our partners as well.

The law firms had, amongst themselves, broadly comparable reasons. One identified improving knowledge management as the most important reason.

> Using contract automation software introduces a single point of truth. Before, it was common to have different templates for the same contracts. Now, if we change a clause, it is automatically updated across all contracts.

Another mentioned speed as an important factor.

> We wanted to reduce the time to make a first draft. Traditional word processing software has its limitations for that.

Two respondents from law firms stressed the importance of using contract automation as a tool to improve in-house services within their clients' organizations.

> We help our clients improve their in-house services. With it, we are increasingly moving away from the traditional law firm model.

> I believe that charging for relatively simple and standard documents will be a thing of the past soon. We want to offer a full-service package to our SME-clients (small and medium-sized enterprises) with which they can organize their own internal legal affairs. We are no longer charging them to make one contract, but are help them professionalize their legal function.

The argument that increased speed or the possibility of self-help by clients conflicts with the traditional hourly rate model of law firms was discussed with most respondents, from different perspectives. Most agreed that this, in general, had delayed innovation in legal practice and continued to be a factor. However, all agreed that change had set in and that even more conservative law firms were moving towards more innovation and a change in business models. One of the respondents, with a background as a lawyer at a law firm, but now working for a large technological company, had expected in-house legal departments to be further on the innovation curve.

> When I switched from a major Dutch law firm, which I considered to be dinosaurs, to a corporate department a couple of years ago, I expected the corporate world to be a lot more proactive and focused on technological innovation. I must say, I was a bit disappointed, although it is easier to change things here than in a traditional law firm. Fortunately, the general climate is changing and moving towards more innovation.

4.2 Selecting the Software

With regard to the software on the market, a distinction can be made between software that is primarily designed for contract automation (such as ContractExpress,

WeAgree or Juriblox), or has broader decision support features (such as Berkely bridge or US Neota Logic), but can also be used for contracts.[31]

Most organizations had not followed an intensive selection procedure before acquiring the software, although most had compared a couple of providers.

> We didn't really have any experience at the time, so, to be honest, we found it hard to determine what we really needed. We finally relied on a recommendation from someone in our network.

One law firm had made a deliberate choice for software that allowed for broader applications than just contract automation.

> We like that the software is more generic and allows for more applications than 'plain' contract automation, such as more complex automated decision support with weighted factors. We use it for other types of processes as well. But for other organizations, simpler may be better. It all depends on your goals.

That, in most cases, there had been no intensive selection process may have been caused by the fact that all these organizations started early with contract automation. The market for contract automation software is still relatively inmature, but this was certainly the case when the interviewed organizations started, with the first respondent starting over ten years ago. Other research confirms that the market is still developing (IACCM-Cap Gemini 2018). There are various small and independent providers. Large legal publishers are more actively entering the market, of which the acquisition of Business Integrity (now ContractExpress) by Thomson Reuters in 2015 is an example. Many providers are currently trying to optimize the options of integrating their solutions with related software such as Salesforce. Conversely, providers of applications for enterprise resource management, procurement or contract management, such as SAP Ariba, have also developed modules for contract automation.

> At the time we decided on the software, this was basically a decision based on relations. Today, we would probably look closer at the possibilities of integration with other software. Contract drafting is just one step in a broader process and the process should be leading in selecting the software.

Almost all respondents acknowledged the integration with other software as a bottleneck, especially within large organizations.

> Sales and procurement use different software, attuned to their needs. Ideally, they would all use the same contract management software with an integrated assembly module, but that's not going to happen. Of course, it is technically possible to integrate the software we use now, but this can be costly and our budget is limited. It is the art of finding the best possible solution in situations that will always be imperfect.

---

[31] Of course, software such as Contract Express and WeAgree can also be used to create other legal documents, such as powers of attorney. However, the software is primarily designed for document automation, as opposed to the software of providers such as Berkeley Bridge and Neota Logic. The latter types could be characterized as "decision tree software," that can be used for various types of decision support, with document automation as an option.

In some interviews the difference between larger and smaller providers were discussed.

> Working with a smaller provider has advantages and disadvantages. Their service and ability to quickly make small changes or fix bugs are usually better – they are simply more agile-, but their budget for truly innovating the software is lower.

Most respondents indicated that there is a trend towards more attention for organizational and operational aspects of the legal function in organizations, with a strong focus on technology: the "new" field of "legal management" or "legal operations." To illustrate this trend, one could point at the foundation of the Corporate Legal Operations Consortium[32] in 2016 by some large US corporate departments, with the aim of sharing and developing knowledge and experience on optimizing the legal function. In the Netherlands, several networks facilitate and promote the exchange of experiences, such as the General Counsel Network Netherlands. It appears that legal departments within the corporate sector see themselves as having shared interests towards legal service providers and software providers, rather than seeing each other as competitors. This trend of increased attention for legal operations was strongly reflected within the respondents' organizations.

> We're looking at all the processes of the legal department, analyzing them and looking for ways to improve efficiency. Technology is almost always in the mix when we redesign it.

> We're learning from experiences in the field of legal operations, including contract automation, from other organizations in our international network.

As as result of this general trend, there are now more options for organizations to be assisted in selecting software and/or inform themselves about their options. Some large consultancy and technology firms have started "legal operations consultancy" or "Legal Tech consultancy."[33] In addition, there are websites that compare features of available legal software on the market.[34]

4.3 Selecting the Contracts

As a second theme in the interviews, we discussed experiences using and implementing the software, including good practices, challenges and pitfalls. The following sections cover several of the items, all strongly interrelated, discussed within this second theme.

---

[32] www.cloc.com.

[33] See, e.g., https://elevateservices.com/consulting/law-departments/ and https://www2.deloitte.com/global/en/pages/about-deloitte/articles/deloitte-legal-launches-legal-management-consulting.html.

[34] An example from the Netherlands is the (commercial) website www.it-kieswijzer.nl, or the tool developed by the International Association for Commercial and Contract Management and Capgemini, https://software.iaccm.com/. Some of the software providers used by the respondent's organizations can be found in the IT-Kieswijzer, none had yet been examined by the IACCM tool.

A first question was which contracts were selected for automation. The answers logically depended on the target groups. The organizations that had implemented CAS for use by consumers or SMEs simply had decided on the basis of their historic data and the contracts that were most used by their clients.

As we focus on consumers and our historical data tells us which problems our clients encounter most frequently, we have attuned the available contracts to those situations.

Of course, there are little differences between sectors, but for SME there is definitely a certain set of contracts that almost all of them will need. We now have around 15 of them programmed. With another round, we will have about 30. More will probably not be necessary. Keeping it manageable is also a factor.

We're providing services to business in the ICT sector. Unlike some other sectors of Dutch legal practice, that can be more informal, contracts are important for them. We know quite well what types of contracts they need, simply based on the services we provide them. Our software allows them to draft a professional contract, which we can review for them if desired. This is an option they often select.

Based on the interviews, as well as previous research, arguments may differ within corporate organizations. Sometimes CAS is used first for contracting processes in which speed is of the essence. CAS could then be an alternative for mandated advice or review by legal, especially in routine cases. Other arguments for selection may be a need for multiple users to work together on the same contract, which can be made easier by CAS. However, the overall view is that within most corporate organizations using CAS, only a few relatively simple contracts have been automated. The impression is that organizations are planning for more contracts to be automated. Respondents consider collaborating with other stakeholders (e.g., sales, procurement, research and development) of key importance for success.

Currently, the NDA is probably the overall champion in automation, as a relatively simple contract with high volume in many large corporate organizations.

We started with the NDA. We also have some straightforward licensing contracts. These are the types of contracts that you don't really want to spend a lot of time on, even though they can be important from financial or other perspectives.

Initially, years ago, we programmed all the standard templates that we have, basically as a service to our in-house lawyers. What we saw in practice, was that, over a period of time, they returned to using this only as a repository and were not using the questionnaires. In our current practice, the NDA is the only contract that is available for use outside the legal department. This may sound uneventful, but because we have a lot of them it saves us a lot of time and we consider it a true success. We are currently working to have our contracts for non-strategic procurement available for non-legal professionals, but we are integrating this into the software procurement uses.

The last remark holds an interesting observation, that was visible in the practice of other organizations. The use of CAS by legal professionals themselves, as a tool to speed up their own drafting process, appears relatively low and seems most successful when it allows for a lot of data-entry to be skipped, for example by using a link to a Customer Relationship Management (CRM) database, or other databases with relevant information.

> Our goal was to have all documents for standard transactions automated, such as the Standard Purchase Agreement and Loan to Market Agreement. These often involve a whole set of related documents with the same client data. Compiling the set requires a lot of data-entry. Automating them saves time in 'stupid work' and reduces the chance of mistakes.

Some of the respondents indicated that they did see potential in increasing the use CAS by legal professionals, for example by optimizing the use of all its features or tying it closer to contracting policies and processes.

> We are not really using the clause library now. Possibly, if we would make an effort and update it, it could save us time.

> If the software would more or less integrate our whole contracting playbook, that could help. Our contract lawyers cannot (and do not have to) memorize our whole contracting policy.

4.4 Decomposing and Reconstructing Contracts

Almost all respondents acknowledged that one of the important benefits of automating legal documents is that it is a unique chance to analyze and redesign contracts.

> It is an excellent opportunity to rethink the whole contract.

However, in doing so, there are quite a few challenges. Some contract templates may have been used for years, without anyone really attempting to change them. The nature of legal work probably stimulates this. When a contract has worked for years, lawyers may fear unforeseen consequences of changing it, even though they might admit that language, wording or design are not perfect. Additionally, legal professionals may consider "their" templates as "their" knowledge and might feel that sharing and redesigning it undermines their position. They may also see, in the words of one respondent, certain elements of practice as part of their professional identity and may therefore feel very strongly about certain clauses, customs or phrasings. Several respondents, especially those working with more conservative colleagues, indicated that this aspect was one of the most challenging parts of contract automation.

> To be honest, we didn't go as far as I would have liked. For some contracts, I was happy to have the 'old' version in there, simply to avoid more debate.

> I've seen grown men fight over whether or not definitions should be at the beginning or in an appendix. It's almost unbelievable sometimes…

Not every respondent experienced these kinds of difficulties. Some indicated that working with a relatively young team or in a relatively young business was probably a reason for not encountering much resistance.

> They simply took it as an interesting challenge and were enthusiastic.

Due to limited time, the exact manner in which contracts were redesigned was only briefly discussed in the interviews and could not be analyzed in depth. Nevertheless, an observation was that no respondent made explicit references to the relatively new field of *legal information design*. This approach departs from a thorough analysis of the needs of users of a contract and stimulates attention for language (for example, by avoiding "legalese") and using other methods and techniques, such as visualizations, to improve comprehensibility and user-friendliness of contracts. This observation concurs with previous findings that most organizations still have a fairly traditional approach to contracts, possibly for similar reasons as described above ("fear of change"), and/or because they are simply unaware of methods and techniques of legal information design. Still, some organizations were certainly making steps in improving their contracts. Several respondents indicated that, when redesigning, their main focus was on shortening the contracts and removing unnecessary clauses. The underlying argument was that a longer and more detailed contract can often trigger debate about relatively unimportant aspects, prolonging negotiations. One respondent emphasized the importance of the use of plain language instead of legalese.

> I think our strong point is that we dare to use plaiin language to describe things in our documents. Laywers are often afraid to do this, out of a fear of losing nuances.

4.5 Personnel Implications

As a fourth theme in the interviews, we discussed personnel aspects, such as implications for staffing and training. A first question concerned the technical skills necessary to be able to program the contracts and the training necessary for using the software. Respondents answered that the software was relatively user-friendly and could be learned to use at a basic to intermediate level in a few training sessions. Most did indicate that overall user-friendliness and "look and feel" of the software could be improved. There appeared to be only small differences between different providers.

Mastering more elaborate skills did not appear to be a problem either, and was done mainly through frequent use and practice, often with the help of the software provider. Maintaining learned skills was a bigger problem, as this requires periodically using the software: "*use it, or loose it.*" Some organizations had only one professional who programmed the contracts, with a few others who had some basic skills. They admitted that this created some organizational vulnerability.

Most of the respondents thought that programming the contracts should not have to be done by specialized legal professionals, although they deemed it good when these professionals had some basic skills, to understand the possibilities of the software. A paralegal or other support professional could do most of the work in practice.

> I think it's good when our lawyers know how the system works and possibly are capable to make some minor changes. They are responsible for the content, but do not have to be involved in every step. A support professional can manage the software. You need routine. He or she can then also monitor the use of the software, make monthly reports, etcetera.

Based on the interviews and previous research, most organizations view contract automation as something that can save the legal professionals time, leaving room for more strategic work. Still, it is not uncommon that legal professionals fear the consequences of automation.

> You can sometimes see them think: what is going to happen to my job?

Of course, fte reduction can be a goal of contract automation. One respondent specifically mentioned a reduction in fte for the legal department as an important goal.

> I do think we have too much lawyers. When all is digitized, I think we can do with less. Maybe a 20% reduction?

Apart from a reduction in fte, respondents indicated that contract automation and the overall move towards improving legal operations, required a different type of (legal) professional, in addition to more "classic legal professionals."

> We need more process-oriented legal professionals and more hybrid functions between legal and the business.

> We're now driving the project of contract automation, but I can definitely imagine that we will be positioning it within other departments, such as sales and procurement, with their own professionals doing the work. They will need to have a basis in law, but do not have to be highly specialized legal professionals. There should still be a dotted line between legal and these departments, but it does not have to be our responsibility.

4.6 Challenges and Pitfalls

In Sects. 4.1–4.5, some of the challenges that organizations face have already been discussed. In this section, some other, often related, challenges and pitfalls are discussed, mostly for the situations where CAS is implemented in corporate or governmental organizations. Most are tied to human and organizational factors. Inability to free time for innovation was often identified as a pitfall.

> I do sometimes feel that our organization is like the cavemen in the cartoon, pushing a cart with square wheels, claiming that they're too busy pushing the cart to switch to round wheels. It's hard to break out of the vicious circle.

> We had one support professional assigned to programming them and it was really hard for him to get the input from the experts. We all have extremely busy agendas. This slowed things down tremendously.

Almost all respondents mentioned or recognized the focus of many legal professionals on substantive issues, rather than on processes, as another factor that complicated innovation.

> Lawyers focus on legal issues, not on processes. They're not used to thinking that way and some don't really like it either. It's like the surgeon only wanting to operate.

The more general resistance to change by legal professionals, but also by professionals from other departments as well, was another common factor.

> You can duck it, as a contract lawyer. Some like sitting comfortably in their own space, pretending to be busy. Automation and innovation bring this to the surface. That's threatening.

> Lawyers are fond of their own templates and used to their own way of working. If you want them to use it, CAS has to be mandated or the only available option, or some will find a way around it.

The last remark links to the observation in Sect. 4.3 that the use of CAS by legal professionals themselves appears relatively low. With regard to other decision support systems, previous research has also provided indications that some legal professionals tend to work around these systems. Sometimes this may be because the software is not user-friendly enough. It could also be that users feel that the software does not do justice to their professional skills and feels too much like "ticking boxes," or that they feel checked and monitored. Another reason could be that they want the system to fail, out of fear of change or fear that they might lose their work. I do not have enough information to have a solid opinion and the cases I am referring to were very different. However, I believe that signals such as these, combined with the fact that the list of failed ICT projects is long, are reason enough to never underestimate the importance of a well-structured design and implementation process, that continually involves professionals and other stakeholders. The importance of keeping everyone on board while redesigning contracting processes was a recurring theme in the interviews.

> It's a change process. These are always complex. Never underestimate the psychological aspects.

The organizational structure is a relevant factor that can complicate this change process. Many branches and locations, as well as related differences in organizational cultures, will make implementing CAS more difficult. Finally, tight budgets and economic aspects were frequently mentioned as important complicating factors. Because the legal department is, in non-legal organizations, a support function and a cost center, it can sometimes be hard to present a business case for technological innovation.

> Management may see reducing the number of legal professionals as the main opportunity for saving money, while we want to use saved time to improve our services. Framing is important.

4.7 Future Developments

Discussing future developments, most respondents answered that they would continue to explore other possibilities of contract automation. The respondents working for the selected law firms saw it as an important part of a new and changed business model. All agreed that contract automation was in the early stages. With several respondents, I discussed possible further changes in the market. Most agreed that contract automation could be a driver for further harmonization of contracts in legal practice, with references to other countries being made. For example, documents from the Practical Law Company have a large market share in the UK. Especially for the consumer and SME market, most stated that there are no good reasons for a lot of different templates. They expected that the market would probably see more combinations of software and content ("semi-finished products," that users can attune to their needs) and more integrated solutions.

> A mid-sized company now has to use different types of software. Ideally they would use one solution that covers most or all of their legal needs and can be easily integrated with an ERM software. Things like: content, automation of documents, document lifecycle management, claims, monitoring and reporting. I believe that legal publishers could do more in this area.

The legal publisher, one of the leading publishers in the Dutch market, also identified contract automation as a driver towards more harmonization and an important part of their strategy.

> We are transforming from a publisher to a legal service provider. The automation of legal documents, for use by our customers in different contexts, is an important part of this transformation.

This respondent also pointed to an interesting side effect. Greater harmonization could eventually make automated analysis of contracts easier. Automated analysis was identified by more respondents as an interesting opportunity for the future, with the first steps already being taken. By way of illustration, Dutch software provider Juriblox recently introduced NDA Lynn[35]: an AI-application that analyzes NDA's and advises whether or not it is wise to sign it. A technical aspect is that these types of application function better once more data (and data that is more comparable) are available. It is therefore not a surprise that the NDA (high volume, few variations) is currently the first contract for which this type of analysis is introduced. Especially for contracts that have high volume, it is imaginable that AI could automatically analyze contract proposals from a counterparty and advise professionals whether or not this is in line with contract policy, without interference of the legal department. Availability of data is a bottleneck for this, especially for legal documents in the Dutch language. Comparability of data facilitates analysis and could therefore be helped by further harmonization of contracts and contract clauses, driven by legal publishers and/ or branch organizations.

> AI simply needs a lot of data to work well.

5   Conclusion

This Chapter has provided an overview of some experiences with contract automation within organizations from various sectors of Dutch legal practice. The organizations depicted in this chapter are frontrunners. Most Dutch organizations in legal practice are not yet using any form of contract automation. Nevertheless, the number of

---

[35]https://www.ndalynn.com/.

organizations that does is growing and the use of contract automation can be expected to increase, due to several factors.

First, the number of organizations that are offering contracts (and other legal documents) online to SMEs and consumers has grown rapidly over the last years. Contract automation is not only offered to consumers and SMEs by commercial parties, but also by branch organizations. It can be expected that consumers and SMEs will increasingly become used to using contract automation for legal matters. The market for contract automation software is still developing rapidly. Providers of ERM, procurement and contract management solutions are increasingly offering contract automation modules. Legal publishers are also increasing the offering of automated contracts and other legal documents, while progressive law firms and various consultants are promoting the use of contract automation within client organizations. Finally, many corporate organizations are are increasingly exchanging experiences on improving their legal operations and the use of Legal Tech, including contract automation.

Legal service providers (law firms, as well as alternative service providers) that offer contract automation directly to consumers and SMEs basically believe that a business model based on traditional delivery of these type of documents is not sustainable. They trust that the automated contracts and other legal documents they offer for relatively small fees will act as a stepping stone to other, more profitable and complex legal services. These types of providers are slowly disrupting the Dutch legal market. It will become increasingly difficult for legal service providers to have a business model that is based on "manually" delivering relatively standard legal documents.

Within (non-legal) organizations, CAS currently appears to be used most successfully for contracts with high volume, a repetitive character and relatively low complexity, such as NDA's, licensing contracts and contracts for non-strategic procurement. Use for more complex contracts exists, but appears less prevalent. In most cases, CAS enables other departments (e.g., sales, procurement, research and development) to draft their own contracts and reduces or eliminates the need for review by legal.

The use of CAS to speed up the drafting process of contracting professionals, as a sort of advanced word processing software, appears to be low. The reasons for this are unclear and the results may not be representative, considering the low number of respondents. However, a question is whether current CAS on the market is ideally suited for this purpose. Overall, respondents are fairly positive about the user-friendliness of the software when it comes to the way in which contracts can be programmed and the software can be used by non-legal professionals, although they do indicate there is room for improvement. However, it seems fair to assume that the needs of non-legal users using the software to draft contracts are different from the needs of specialized contracting professionals. This is an interesting theme for future research.

From an organizational point of view, deploying CAS to offer online contracts to external clients is relatively simple. Successfully implementing CAS within organizations is more difficult. This can be viewed as a complex change process, in which human and organizational factors are at least as important as technological aspects. Several complicating factors were identified. Legal departments often only have limited time and budgets for (technological) innovation. Legal professionals within organizations regularly demonstrate resistance to change and are primarily oriented towards substantive issues, rather than on processes. Furthermore, integration of contract automation software with other systems within the organization can prove to be complex or costly, especially when client departments (such as sales or procurement) use different software.

Regardless of these difficulties, the research indicates that contract automation—as well as the automation of other legal documents—can bring substantial benefits to organizations. It can move simple legal work away from legal departments, freeing time for more strategic legal work, or simply reducing the number of legal professionals, if desired. Increased speed and the possibility of self-help by other departments may also increase the "popularity" of legal. Another important benefit is that it facilitates monitoring and reporting on the contracting process.

Collaborating with other departments is essential for contract automation to work. Contract drafting is only one step in a process that will involve several departments and should be viewed in an integral manner. For successful implementation, a design thinking approach is necessary: thoroughly analyzing the process, identifying needs of the various users and stakeholders and modelling the process accordingly. Of course, in the complex world of organizations, perfection will be hard to attain and compromises will be inevitable. It may, for example, be wise for the legal department to use contract assembly options that procurement or sales software offers, even when these options may not be ideal.

With regard to the automation of the full contract life cycle, many organizations in legal practice are currently still struggling with effectively implementing software for other steps of the process, such as contract management and digital signatures. It seems fair to assume that it will become easier to integrate contract automation (or: Legal Tech 2.0) in organizations, when these Legal Tech 1.0 steps have been taken.

Currently, contract automation still has a fairly low-tech character, with mainly contracts of low complexity being automated. With the continuing digitization of contracting processes, more advanced use of technology may eventually become possible, such as the use of AI for automated analysis of contracts. However—be it Legal Tech 1.0, 2.0 or 3.0—an important overall conclusion can be that human and organizational factors will always be essential for technology to work.

Acknowledgements I thank all respondents for their input and inspiring conversations.

References

Branting L-K (2017) Data-centric and logic-based models for automated legal problem solving. Artif Intell Law 25(1):5–27

Drucker P-F (1999) Knowledge worker productivity: the biggest challenge. Calif Manag Rev 41(2):79–94

Erdelez S, O'Hare S (1997) Legal informatics: application of information technology in law. Ann Rev Inf Sci Technol 32:367–402

IACCM-Cap Gemini (2018) Automation report https://www.iaccm.com/resources/?id=10162. Accessed 20 Aug 2018

Leith P (2010) The rise and the fall of the legal expert system. Euro J Law Technol 1(1). http://ejlt.org/article/view/14/1. Accessed 8 Aug 2018

Leonard-Barton D, Sviokla J (1988), Putting expert systems to work. Harv Bus Rev https://hbr.org/1988/03/putting-expert-systems-to-work. Accessed 8 Aug 2018

Sprowl J-A (1979) Automating the Legal reasoning process: a computer that uses regulation and statutes to draft legal documents. Law Soc Inquiry J Am Bar Found 4(1):1–81

Susskind R (2008) The end of laywers. Oxford University Press, Oxford

Timmer I (2016) Changing roles of legal: on the impact of innovations on the role of legal professionals and legal departments in contracting practice. J Strat Contract Negot 2(1–2):34–47

Tyree A (1989) Expert systems in law. Prentice Hall, New York

Legal Automation: AI and Law Revisited

Cecilia Magnusson Sjöberg

Abstract This chapter is about legal automation understood broadly as the use of modern information and communication technology mainly without human intervention. The role of legal education serves as a platform for remarks about the need for IT-professionals to be somewhat in command of IT Law as well as for lawyers to grasp Legal Tech. Another focal point is digital resources management both within and outside the legal domain. The analysis concerns rights of access on the one hand and corresponding restrictions on the other. For instance, freedom of expression and information are limited by personal data protection, transparency by secrecy, open data by information security and re-use of public sector information (PSI) by intellectual property, etc. This legal landscape of contradictions is generally speaking why artificial intelligence (AI) comes into the picture as lever of legal system management. At the same time, it is important to remember that there have been attempts to automate law in a broad sense for decades, and that quite a few of the principle challenges concerning decision making systems are still valid. In response to the legal implications of today's AI developments and implemented applications a new legal entity—digital person—is introduced. The overall purpose is to acknowledge the need for a conceptual model for legal reasoning supplementing the well-established notions of "natural person" and "legal person." By way of such a legal innovation more adequate discussions about accountability and the rule of law can take place, e.g., when robots are to be programmed based on algorithms that intentionally are dynamic by way of machine learning. If such thoughts about new legal entities—here digital person—are set aside due to conventions and traditions there is no doubt a risk for inadequate assessments of responsibility, privacy infringements and the like.

Keywords Artificial intelligence (AI) · Digital person · GDPR · Legal automation · Digital resources management · Legal education

C. Magnusson Sjöberg (✉)
Faculty of Law, Stockholm University, Stockholm, Sweden
e-mail: cecilia.magnussonsjoberg@juridicum.su.se

© Springer Nature Singapore Pte Ltd. 2019
M. Corrales et al. (eds.), *Legal Tech, Smart Contracts and Blockchain*,
Perspectives in Law, Business and Innovation,
https://doi.org/10.1007/978-981-13-6086-2_7

1 Introduction

The scope of this chapter is intentionally broad. Legal automation is a research field in itself, primarily encompassing legal science and informatics.[1] Of particular interest is the interplay between law and computer science. The impact of information and communication technology (IT) on law and vice versa is thus a core aspect of this contribution. More precisely, the perspective is here distilled to legal implications of automation with a particular focus on artificial intelligence (AI).[2] The time span is wide, allowing for reflections on matters emerging some decades ago, as well as more recent trends, bearing in mind the rapid future-oriented development of the digital society.

The structure of the content is such that the role of legal education serves as a starting point for the analysis and discussion. One might have expected educational matters to be introduced at the end of the text, as a way forward. Here, they will instead serve as a road map for the analysis right from the beginning.[3] After this first section, Sect. 2 illustrates a potential AI application within digital resources management.[4] Section 3 includes a discussion on the legal entities commonly referred to as "natural persons" and "legal persons". The point is to introduce the concept of a "digital person" as a new legal entity. The overall purpose of this abstraction is to safeguard legal mechanisms needed primarily for trustworthy AI. Finally, a few concluding remarks are made (Sect. 5).

2 The Role of Legal Education

The impact of AI in society is noticeable not only in everyday life, but also within legal education.[5] Digitalization of society in general is of course not a feature being dealt with solely within academia. Other stakeholders are found among public agencies and private enterprises.

---

[1]Magnusson Sjöberg (1992); Wahlgren (1992). To illustrate the development over time, reference could be made to Bergin et al. (2018), pp. 14–18.

[2]For an introduction to AI today and in the future, see, e.g., (Thegmark 2017). A much more historical reference is Winston (1984).

[3]As a matter of fact, e-learning is yet another theme worthwhile to investigate. See, e.g., Carlson et al. (2017).

[4]Digital resources management should not be mistaken for digital rights management regarding intellectual property rights. The first may be described as a more generic concept, including, for instance, digital management of copyright.

[5]A basis for the discussion below is experience primarily from the Faculty of Law at Stockholm University where the course "Rättsinformatik" (Legal informatics) has been held regularly and has been mandatory for students since 1981. Similar developments, with elective courses, can be seen primarily in Norway, but also in other Nordic countries. There has been a strong incentive to mirror research in education in Belgium, Germany, the Netherlands, etc., for many years. Among the foreign activities, the so-called SubTech Conferences ought also to be mentioned: https://oigus.ut.ee/en/studies/subtech-conference-2018.

In response to the computerization that took place during the 1960s, law faculties around the world—to a varying extent—recognized IT Law as an emerging new legal discipline.[6] Some universities have over the years emphasized substantive law issues in terms of interpretation and application of legal rules and regulations in digital environments. Other institutions have concentrated on methodological aspects associated with legal system design, development, implementation and management. A critical success factor in this context has been to let the intersection of IT Law and legal system management be the focal point for both research and education. To give a brief illustration: creating a "legally safe" website for consumers might require not just understanding to what extent—if any—there is a formal need for a signature to conclude an agreement, but also knowing whether an electronic signature at a certain security level could meet that legal requirement. It should be noted that not only law students but also tech students could benefit from legal awareness in connection with digitalization.[7]

Given the rapid development of technology and the applications associated therewith, one may question whether there is any need for IT Law as a standalone subject. Considering that more traditional subjects are increasingly reclaiming (so to speak) the IT perspective as inherent to them, the question is certainly valid. This is occurring in areas such as contract law (e.g., so-called Smart Contracts), intellectual property (e.g., copyright to computer programs) and administrative procedural law (e.g., public records in electronic formats).[8] Time will tell, but experiences so far show that there is still a need for scholarly expertise with regard to quite a few fields of law. As a matter of fact, the lawyers of today can be surprisingly ignorant when it comes to new legal infrastructures regarding automatic data processing, electronic documentation, etc. Unfortunately, this applies not only to older generations, but also—somewhat surprisingly—to younger ones as well. For instance, business models referred to as Cloud Computing solutions may very well need an explanation in the classroom so as to avoid misunderstandings and illusions of transactions taking place in "outer space" without any hardware servers in a fixed geographical location.[9] To summarize, the answer to the first question in this section is that yes, there is still a need for substantive IT Law, but how long this will be the case remains uncertain.

Adding to the picture is the fact that there is, among practitioners, an intensifying quest for qualified in-house IT Law expertise to meet current client expectations. This is a solid trend and does not apply only to lawyering in commercial environments, but also to public sector undertakings, concerning for instance outsourcing activities. From a scholarly point of view this development is rewarding as a lever of more academic analyses and discussion concerning legal infrastructures. This

---

[6]See, e.g., Seipel (1977).

[7]See further Magnusson Sjöberg (2005a, b) (ed). A more recent publication is Magnusson Sjöberg (2018).

[8]Another theme is discussed by Cecilia Magnusson Sjöberg under the heading. The Swedish Administrative Procedure Act and Digitalisation in *50 years of Law and IT*. See Wahlgren (2018), pp. 309–320.

[9]To find out more about the legal implications of this business model see, e.g., Millard (2013) (ed).

applies in particular when it comes to automation, network communications and digital documentation.

In this context, it is important to note that some problem areas specifically call for legal attention with regard to both substantive IT Law and legal system management. The European Union (EU) 2016/679 General Data Protection Regulation (GDPR)[10] is the obvious example. In addition to common provisions concerning material and territorial scope, legal definitions, sanctions, etc., there are rules in the GDPR that necessitate methodological skills in order to meet the requirements on for instance "data protection by design and by default" (Article 25). Another example of how substantive IT Law interacts with the more methodologically oriented legal system management track concerns legal implications of information security. Current regulative approaches also comprise the so-called NIS Directive on security of network and information systems.[11] To conclude, it is not difficult to argue that legal system management or Legal Tech[12] has become increasingly important in today's society.

With reference to the wording of the chapter title, indicating that AI and law are to be revisited, it is time for some historical reflections. The very early development of computers and programming is not addressed here, but AI came to have a significant impact on the legal domain already in the mid-1980s. Generally speaking, the challenge in common law systems has been to find what could be referred to as "similar court cases"[13] in legal databases, whereas in civil law systems the ambitions were primarily to create normative decision support and complete decision-making systems. The latter were referred to as expert systems and were built on knowledge bases, inference mechanisms and knowledge engineers extracting (sometimes tacit) expertise from legal professionals.[14]

At that time, available data, software and hardware did not meet quantitative or qualitative needs, given the ambitions to develop well-functioning AI-based applications. In the Nordic countries, for instance, attempts were nevertheless made to develop so-called knowledge(-based) systems within areas such as social insurance, social security, study administration and taxation. The algorithms used at that evolutionary stage were, however, all conventional in their deterministic nature. Challenges mainly concerned issues of principle, such as whom, representing what organizational body, had the authority to transform law into computer programs. More precisely: how should the system deal with the open texture of law without leaving it up to the programmer to code vague and ambiguous rules and other legal sources. The seeming logic of a legal text could very well turn out to be based on vague

---

[10]Regulation (EU) 2016/679 of the European Parliament and of the Council of 27 April 2016 on the protection of natural persons with regard to the processing of personal data and on the free movement of such data, and repealing Directive 95/46/EC (General Data Protection Regulation).

[11]Directive (EU) 2016/1148 of the European Parliament and of the Council of 6 July 2016 concerning measures for a high common level of security of network and information systems across the Union.

[12]In this text, the term Legal Tech is used synonymously with legal system management, but denoting modern developments in particular.

[13]Brodda and Gimmie More (1990), pp. 251–270; see also Von der Lieth Gardner (1987).

[14]See, e.g., Susskind (1988); see also Lessig (1999).

criteria expressed in natural (human) language such as a right for citizens to have a "reasonable standard of living" or "specific" as opposed to "special" circumstances in a particular case, etc.[15] In practice, it all boiled down to a need for the transformation of a regulatory text into strict criteria for the purpose of computation. Needless to say, at that time, machine learning by way of dynamic algorithms was not on the agenda outside of lab environments.

In response to the current technological AI-centred development, including robots and IoT,[16] a shift of attention from core substantive IT Law to legal system management can be noted. This is not to say that IT Law is not important (see above), but there is no doubt that Legal Tech has a special role to play nowadays. This applies to AI being used within the legal domain itself when it comes to regulative decision-making, records management and communication. Legal Tech can also support and legalize AI applications in society as a whole. A purposeful understanding of Legal Tech thus ought to be two-fold.

3 The Potential of AI Applications

3.1 Setting the Scene

Information is a key asset in today's society. This implies a need for management in a variety of ways. In this context, effective law is a critical success factor. However, the legal toolbox is not easy to master, due to contradictory goals laid out in various legal frameworks. To put it simply, either the intention is that all information should be free or it is expected to be under some kind of control. This polarization is seen, for example, in the forces surrounding personal data processing, on the one hand, and open data movements, on the other. Given this background, a focal point of this text is to shed light on the legal landscape of contradictions within the context of digital resources management. A next step is to discuss a methodological approach that can meet expectations of modern digital governance encompassing both commercial markets and public administration. One important point is that AI might provide full or partial solutions in the quest for digital resources management.

Artificial intelligence is wide-ranging in both theory and practice and thus not easy to grasp, but nevertheless has the potential to play an important role in shaping the law. In response to the rapid development of technologies enabling automation based on advanced algorithms and high-tech digital settings, there is an increasing demand for better understanding of the potential of AI applications, not least from a legal point of view. This brief contribution thereto will be based on digital resources management, partially motivated by the fact that digital information supply has been regulated in a somewhat inconsistent way. This unfortunate regulatory state of affairs

---

[15]Sergot et al. (1985).

[16]Connected devices (sensors), commonly referred to as the Internet of Things.

will be touched upon in general terms below, bearing in mind the potential for AI applications.

Despite the attempt to use a holistic approach, the aim cannot, for several reasons, be completely comprehensive, but rather offer a few insights into current developments where AI calls for attention.

3.2 The Topic in Brief

The digital resources management concept is multifaceted, but this is not the place for an in-depth analysis. Suffice it to say that it encompasses critical infrastructures, in particular for data collection, processing, communication and documentation. Generally speaking, societal infrastructures can be of a hard or soft nature. Road networks and broadband networks are examples of hard infrastructures, whereas social and organizational ones are soft. Legal infrastructures of a soft nature refer to core components necessary for the functionality of a legal system (jurisdiction).

Infrastructures, as such, might not be relevant to study, but when certain perspectives are added, a more in-depth analyses can be performed based on, for example, economy, finance, technology, and, of course, law. Over the years, the impact of technology on legal infrastructures has been immense. Previously, lawyers handled data manually—now, information processing increasingly includes automated data processing. Legal paperwork is transformed into the management of electronic documents. Meetings that used to take place face-to-face are instead occurring over digital networks.

A major reason why it is important to investigate digital resources management from a legal perspective is evidently that law can both facilitate and hinder the potential of the digital market, comprising both public and private sector initiatives and activities. So, what is the problem? To put it rather bluntly, many fundamental legal frameworks governing the digital society are contradictory in both goal and scope. As already mentioned, one important example concerns data protection weighed against open data. This could be further illuminated by the interplay between the so-called Right to be Forgotten (Article 17 GDPR) on the one hand and a right to know based on a duty to remember on the other. Yet another ambiguity can be seen in ambitions emanating from a view of privacy by way of data protection as a means for a strong digital market.

A somewhat closer look at the overall purpose of the GDPR as regulated in its Article 1 reveals this two-fold objective divided into three major points:

1. This Regulation lays down rules relating to the protection of natural persons with regard to the processing of personal data and rules relating to the free movement of personal data;
2. This Regulation protects fundamental rights and freedoms of natural persons and in particular their right to the protection of personal data;

3. The free movement of personal data within the Union shall be neither restricted nor prohibited for reasons connected with the protection of natural persons with regard to the processing of personal data.

It is also important to keep in mind the overall goals of the EU's recent data protection reform, which could briefly be referred to in terms of enhanced data protection, improved harmonisation between member states, reduced bureaucracy, and better technical adaptation, and, last but not the least, improved adaptation to the digital single market.[17]

Furthermore, it is worth noting the ambition to set up a technically neutral regulatory framework. In spite of this approach, the GDPR undoubtedly contains references to today's digital society, not least when it comes to provisions concerning security of processing (Articles 32–34). The approach is present in Article 22, which captures all kinds of personal data processing based on automated decision-making, including profiling. The latter is defined in Article 4.4, reading as follows:

'Profiling' means any form of automated processing of personal data consisting of the use of personal data to evaluate certain personal aspects relating to a natural person, in particular to analyse or predict aspects concerning that natural person's performance at work, economic situation, health, personal preferences, interests, reliability, behaviour, location or movements.

The wording of Article 22 is somewhat complicated from a semantic perspective. Usually, it would be considered obvious that automated decision-making can take place without profiling, and vice versa: profiling can take place without automated decision-making. However, one interpretation of Article 22 could be to apply a much narrower scope, so that the provision would comprise only automated decision-making that includes profiling. This issue appears open to discussion.

From an AI perspective, matters become even more complicated with regard to the right of access by the data subject, and in particular Article 15.1 (h) (see also Article 12), which states that this right of access comprises:

The existence of automated decision-making, including profiling, referred to in Article 22 (1) and (4) and, at least in those cases, meaningful information about the logic involved, as well as the significance and the envisaged consequences of such processing for the data subject.

In particular, the requirement on information about the involved logic could develop into a Legal Tech challenge. Relatively simplistic AI-based applications would probably not be a severe obstacle to compliance, but more advanced machine learning with self-learning algorithms may complicate matters. In a digital setting where not even the system designer and/or programmer are in (complete) command of the code, the "black box syndrome" becomes a reality. Furthermore, it is not quite clear to what extent a data controller (Article 4.7) is obliged to explain underlying logic not only at a general level, but also with regard to a particular data subject. This makes it wise to keep legal developments under observation.

---

[17]See further the Commission's website: https://ec.europa.eu/commission/priorities/digital-single-market_en. Accessed 29 September 2018.

3.3 Overview of Substantive Law

The heading of this section is quite ambitious, but nevertheless accurate given the topic, bearing in mind that the mapping is not comprehensive. It is also important to emphasize that the overview serves the purpose of illustrating what is here labelled as a legal landscape of contradictions. The core concept is rights of access modified by corresponding restrictions (see Fig. 1).

To begin with, freedom of expression and information is a challenge to personal data protection and vice versa.[18] Furthermore, transparency gives rise to issues of how to balance needs for secrecy while aiming for openness, as well as the other way around. Open data need information security safeguards to a varying extent in order

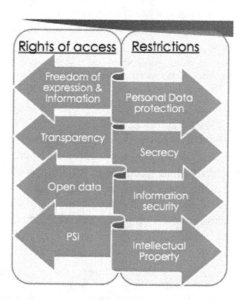

Fig. 1 Illustrating the legal landscape of contradictions

---

[18]The conflicting interests are addressed in Article 85 GDPR, under the heading Processing and freedom of expression and information: "Member States shall by law reconcile the right to the protection of personal data pursuant to this Regulation with the right to freedom of expression and information, including processing for journalistic purposes and the purposes of academic, artistic or literary expression." Another example of contradictions is related to processing and public access to official documents in Article 86: "Personal data in official documents held by a public authority or a public body or a private body for the performance of a task carried out in the public interest may be disclosed by the authority or body in accordance with Union or Member State law to which the public authority or body is subject in order to reconcile public access to official documents with the right to the protection of personal data pursuant to this Regulation." The provision might seem clear and concise but could very well turn out to be complicated to interpret and apply in practice. Principles of openness encompassing official documents including personal data vary considerably among member states. See, e.g., Lind et al. (2017).

to be reliable. Reuse of public sector information (PSI)[19] is limited by intellectual property rights, e.g., copyright.

Of particular interest at this point in the discussion is how the perspective of information security stands out as relevant in spite of traditionally being a non-legal area of expertise and of little importance to the legal domain. It appears as if a majority of core information security concepts could serve as a bridge not only between law and information technology, but also with regard to the rights and restrictions themselves. To give a brief example, the GDPR includes provisions on integrity and confidentiality among its general principles relating to processing of personal data (see, e.g., Article 5.1 (f)). This all boils down to interplay between (personal) data protection and information security, with the former being a means for information security and the latter being a condition for data protection from a privacy point of view. These kinds of interactions could be presented as illustrated in Fig. 2.

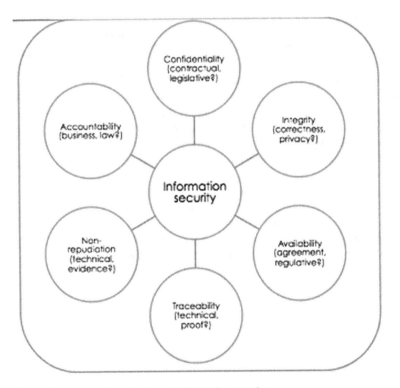

Fig. 2 Illustrating the legal implications of information security

---

[19]See further Proposal for a Directive of the European Parliament and of the Council on the re-use of public sector information (recast) COM/2018/234 final—2018/0111 (COD).

3.4 Methodological Approach

In order to deal with the contradictory legal landscape of digital resources management, there is a need for a holistic approach offering a broad scope for the weighing
of conflicting interests. This, in its turn, requires a combined multidisciplinary and
interdisciplinary approach, which will be commented on briefly below.

Within the area of data protection, it is, for instance, not enough to make separate assessments based only on public law, private law, tort law, etc. Instead, a
more in-depth analysis calls for an understanding of several areas such as administrative procedures (legal grounds), contracts (agreements between data controller
and data processor), and liabilities (administrative fines). Adding to the picture is
the internationalization of legal regimes and the important contributions of comparative approaches based on digital awareness. A sign of this is that legal scholars are
increasingly working across borders, as are practitioners.[20] To conclude, there are
several reasons for applying a multidisciplinary approach in the context of digital
resources management.

The demand for an interdisciplinary approach has its origin in the early understanding of the need to study law together with information technology (especially informatics) and vice versa. The discussion above about information security
reflected in data protection legislation is just one example hereof.

Furthermore, a holistic approach opens the possibility of allowing law to play
a more proactive role than the traditional reactive one, i.e., as a conflict-solving
mechanism when things have already gone wrong.[21] The proactive law perspective
will presumably be both supported and challenged by AI when it comes to legal
steering mechanisms. This new digital environment is, generally speaking, to be
found in the context of cognitive computing, based on data mining that could evolve
into self-learning algorithms. In terms of legal sources we are here faced with a new
kind of soft law, with the potential for AI-based law or, more specifically, algorithmic
law as a new legal discipline. Of course, this is a future-oriented way of reasoning,
but traditional doctrines of legal sources are questioned already in today's digitalised
society and more discussion is to be expected. Based on these reflections, the notion
of a digital person, as a new legal entity, will be investigated below.

4 Digital Person—A New Legal Entity?

This section will bring to the fore a question concerning a potential new legal entity
in the AI-based society—the digital person. The notion of a legal entity is to be
understood as a general concept established in a certain legal system that could
represent both obligations and benefits. Just to give an example, a so-called third

---

[20]Susskind (2017).

[21]For a presentation of the Nordic School of Proactive Law, see Magnusson Sjöberg (2006),
pp. 13–19.

party can be seen as a kind of legal entity that may turn out to be important in a legal situation, without formally being a party thereto.[22] This reasoning could similarly be applied to a creditor or debtor. The first condition refers to someone who is a claimant and the second to someone who is indebted. Of particular interest in this context is to what extent—if any—the long-since established system of "natural persons" and "legal persons" is dynamic enough to meet the requirements that the development and use of AI brings about.

Looking back through history, it is obvious that there was a time when no distinction was made between natural and legal persons. Expressed in another way: the conceptualizations we readily recognise today have not always existed. Legal conditions nowadays are characterized by legal rules and regulations directed towards individuals and/or organizations in various constellations. Of course, it is difficult, even impossible, to predict the future. Still, speculating about continued digitalization beyond what we experience in today's digital society does not seem very daring (see below). However, this is not the same as saying that we already know, for instance, what kinds of embodiments of advanced technologies into robots we will experience during the years to come. Much like our shift from an agricultural society to an industrial one, a shift to a modern information society, in which AI has become a force to reckon with, is now being experienced in large parts of the world. While this does not entail an immediate change of environment, the change is nevertheless remarkably quick. As already pointed out, a critical factor associated with this development is the occurrence and use of advanced (dynamic) self-learning algorithms, in particular in digital environments characterised by comparatively large amounts of data.

The major question here—whether there is a need for a new legal entity in the form of a digital person—cannot be answered easily. This kind of issue is so complex that an in-depth analysis would in principle require a whole range of academic dissertations, legislation, court decisions, agreements, etc. Nevertheless, now is the time to stretch the legal reasoning beyond the theoretical comfort zone. History is made in its passing, which is not always obvious to those who are part of it. Still, it is noticeable how digitalisation is currently increasing with regard to both quantity and quality.

In order to protect and also affirm a humanitarian perspective when machine solutions to a growing extent shape our private lives, working lives, administration, businesses, etc., the societal dialogue needs to expand towards new solutions. The hypothesis is, as already pointed out, that there is a need for some kind of analytical (conceptual) model—here based on a new legal entity—that could capture topical reasoning about AI and law. However, the approach is not based on the assumption that a new legal entity in the form of a digital person would solve all legally oriented questions related to AI applications. There are legal issues concerning accountability, intellectual property rights (copyright, patents, etc.), e-government and e-services for citizens and consumers, to mention just a few. Still, a well-balanced attempt to

---

[22] An example is the definition in Article 4.10: "'third party' means a natural or legal person, public authority, agency or body other than the data subject, controller, processor and persons who, under the direct authority of the controller or processor, are authorised to process personal data."

legitimize AI has the potential of resulting in law supporting technological developments for the good of the people, instead of instantly becoming an obstacle. Further research is vital.

With this in mind, the need emerges for a more purposeful model, one that could more aptly support a legal analysis of AI. This implies an understanding and acceptance of AI as an at least partly new phenomenon that fundamentally changes legal infrastructures. We will most probably be faced with for instance an "intelligent agent," which is described by Wikipedia as "an autonomous entity, which observes through sensors and acts upon an environment using actuators (i.e., it is an agent) and directs its activity towards achieving goals (i.e., it is "rational," as defined in economics)." A digital person should thus not be mistaken for a digital identity on the Internet. Furthermore, a digital person is not the same as a biological creature, although it can be noted that the traditional border between man and machine is becoming blurred as artificial components are inserted into human bodies in the form of implants and the like. A digital person is also not someone or something that can be defined as a kind of legal person such as a company or a firm.

In a discussion like this, one might reflect upon a situation where no legal actions at all are taken to uphold the rule of law. It is not difficult to see the risk that the concept "digital person" may never be introduced. What would be the outcome of AI without legislation associated with a new entity? From a legal point of view, it is possible to extract negative consequences at both a macro- and a micro-level. Generally speaking, a future dysfunctional state of law could easily emerge where legal safeguards are not only hampered by this lack, but worse, the very existence of law is threatened if there is no legal entity that can be held accountable for some actions. Well-established principles of openness and transparency would also be at risk. This becomes apparent when dynamic, i.e., self-learning, algorithms serve as a basis for automation of various kinds.

More specifically, staying passive, watching the AI-based society develop without human intervention and legal steering implies exposing individuals and organisations to a risk. Who will be held responsible when things go wrong and there is neither a natural person nor a legal system to blame? The mere existence of the "digital person" thus has the potential to serve a supportive function in future legal matters. There are many questions to be asked rather than answered at this stage and a few more will therefore be presented here as a kind of personal statement.

I am convinced that a combination of a scientific and everyday dialogue is most fruitful embracing such initiatives as addAI.org[23] under the banner "Liberty, equality

---

[23] The following presentation can be found on the website: http://www.addai.org. Accessed 29 Sept 2018.

"What will IT mean to be a human in the future? The Swedish based initiative addAI is collaboration between experts in academia, government and companies to discuss and explore the impact of smart algorithms and AI on society.

The initiative works on typical questions like:

1. Sociology: What is the best ways to interact with AI and how may it change the relations between humans?

2. Law: How much responsibility should AI have? AI and the rule of law?

and AI." And remember, law and lawyers might be perceived as boring, but lawyering could offer methods apt for facilitating human-centred AI. Supporting the introduction of a digital person to the same legal system that once accepted the notion of a legal person need not be more complicated than that.

At the same time, it is important to be aware that the concept of a digital person is not merely an addition to the vocabulary already comprising the concepts "natural person" and "legal person." Rather, it concerns a legal entity that under certain circumstances could be acknowledged to have a certain legal capacity with associated rights and obligations. This is especially interesting when it comes to executable power intended to have a decisive impact on legal actions in various digital environments.

As an exercise, the legal entity, i.e., the digital person, could alternatively be described as a constellation of algorithms, with certain ones representing the core identity. A feature of such a core identity would be the possibility to profile and specify its characteristics and functionalities given a certain purpose.

In order to evaluate whether a digital person governed by a certain algorithmic identity is functioning in accordance with the intention, traditional criteria related to ethics, law, trust, etc., would probably be sufficient to begin with. Methodologically, the aim would be to achieve what can be referred to as functional equivalence. This has been the predominant approach applied not least by lawmakers when trying to adjust legislation, model contracts, etc., that were drawn up long ago and need to be adjusted to the modern digital information society.

In the long run, one could envisage the lawmaker empowering digital persons with legal capacities with either a narrowing or a broadening scope. Certain legislation might even be self-generating. The traditional courts of justice and staffing with human judges might have an expiration date sooner than we think. Either way, legal professionals have reason to be alert when it comes to being in command of the legal implications that not least AI brings about. One thing is certain: there is no point in lawyers taking a stand of alienation in relation to AI. Instead, algorithms and associated automation should be seen as natural parts of a new legal era.

5 Conclusion

When it comes to information and communication technology, the role of education is fundamental and multifaceted. Substantive IT Law is one major field that should preferably interact with legal system management. Legal Tech—another label for the latter—can in turn be divided roughly into studies oriented towards the legal domain as such or towards addressing legal methodological issues in general, and in particular those that AI gives rise to. In this context, worries about the future legal profession appear to be valid, at least to a certain extent. Handling of massive

---

3. Business: What does a AI strategy mean for an organisation or a country?".

amounts of documents within a due diligence procedure is just one example of a likely feature of a future AI application.

It could therefore be argued that a new kind of advanced legal education is needed, acknowledging the impact of AI, and not clinging to technological neutrality in all legal assessments. This latter is unfortunately a characteristic of the old school of technological adaption. What we need is legal education where professors and students are open to learning about and understanding in particular the legal implications of algorithms in various digital environments.

This leads to yet another area for studies and research: information security. This field is indeed short on legal scholars and practitioners, in spite of issues of confidentiality, integrity and availability being critical success factors for trustworthy AI.

For a lawyer, it is not always easy to grasp the vocabulary of recently made technological achievements in this field, such as cognitive computing, neural networks, natural language processing, big data repositories, data mining,[24] machine learning, etc. What does stand out is, as already mentioned, AI-based algorithms that are dynamic in that they are self-learning and modified during the operation of an already implemented system. In such a digital environment, it is especially difficult to uphold the rule of law. How can we preserve openness and provide remedies when not even programmers can trace alterations to the applied code?

As discussed above, it is perhaps time to expand the concept of legal entities and introduce digital persons in addition to natural and legal ones. One reason, beyond the well-known legal safeguards of transparency, foreseeability, etc., would be to capture innovations such as digital intelligent agents.

Digital resources management is nowadays part of the legal profession both within the legal domain and externally covering other subjects. The weighing of interests with regard to contradictory substantive law requires up-to-date education and training. Furthermore, there is a need to broaden the methodological approach to include AI-based methods. The academic field of IT Law and Legal Tech offers a theoretical framework for these kinds of studies. To conclude, AI has a potential to improve digital resources management, but this requires legal education and a broad analysis of how a legal system is constructed. Finally, investigating the digital person as a new legal entity appears worthwhile.

References

Bergin Q-C, Terence, Tannok Q (2018) AI: changing rules for a changed world. Comput Law 14–18
Brodda B, Gimmie More OT (1990) A potential function in document retrieval systems? In: Seipel P (ed) From data protection to knowledge machines: the study of law and informatics, Boston
Carlson L, Magnusson Sjöberg C, Papadopoulou F (2017) The wired world of university teaching—legal challenges. Ex Tuto, Copenhagen

---

[24] See further, e.g., Colonna (2016).

Colonna L (2016) Legal implications of data mining: assessing the European union's data protection principles in light of the United States government's national intelligence data mining practices. Ragulka Press, Visby

Lessig L (1999) Code and other laws of cyberspace, 2nd edn. Basic Books, New York

Lind A-S, Reichel J, Österdahl I (2017) (eds) Transparency in the future: Swedish openness years. Ragulka Press, Visby

Magnusson Sjöberg C (1992) Rättsautomation: Särskilt om statsförvaltningens datorisering (Eng. Legal Automation: Computerisation of public agencies). Norstedts Juridik, Stockholm

Magnusson Sjöberg C (2005) (ed) IT law for IT professionals—an introduction. Studentlitteratur, Stockholm

Magnusson Sjöberg C (2005) (ed) Legal management of information systems: incorporating law in e-solutions. Studentlitteratur, Stockholm

Magnusson Sjöberg C (2006) Presentation of the nordic school of proactive law. Scandinavian studies in law, vol 49. A proactive approach. Institute for Scandinavian Law, Stockholm

Magnusson Sjöberg C (2018) The Swedish administrative procedure act and digitalisation, in 50 years of law and IT. In: Wahlgren P (ed) Scandinavian studies in law, vol 65. The Swedish Law and Informatics Research Institute 1968–2018, Stockholm. Institute for Scandinavian Law, Stockholm

Millard C (2013) (ed) Cloud computing law, Oxford University Press, Oxford

Seipel P (1977) Computing law: perspectives on a new legal discipline. Liber Förlag, Stockholm

Sergot M et al (1985) The British nationality act as a logic program. Department of Computing, Imperial College, London

Susskind R (1988) Expert systems in law: a jurisprudential inquiry. Oxford University Press, Oxford

Susskind R (2017) Tomorrow's lawyers, 2nd edn. Oxford University Press, Oxford

Thegmark M (2017) Life 3.0: being human in the age of artificial intelligence. Knopf Publishing Group, New York

Von der Lieth GA (1987) An artificial intelligence approach to legal reasoning. Massachusetts Institute of Technology, Cambridge

Wahlgren P (2018) In report Livet med AI (SSF-rapport nr 29) published by S23elsen för strategisk forskning. pp. 52–57

Wahlgren P (1992) Automation of legal reasoning: a study on artificial intelligence and law. Kluwer Law Series 11, Deventer-Boston

Winston P-H (1984) Artificial intelligence, 2nd edn. Addison-Wesley Publishing, Boston

Smart Contracts and Smart Disclosure: Coding a GDPR Compliance Framework

Marcelo Corrales, Paulius Jurčys and George Kousiouris

Abstract This chapter analyses some of the main legal requirements laid down in the new European General Data Protection Regulation (GDPR) with regard to hybrid Cloud Computing transformations. The GDPR imposes several restrictions on the storing, accessing, processing and transferring of personal data. This has generated some concerns with regard to its practicability and flexibility given the dynamic nature of the Internet. The current architecture and technical features of the Cloud do not allow adequate control for end-users. Therefore, in order for the Cloud adopters to be legally compliant, the design of Cloud Computing architectures should include additional automated capabilities and certain *nudging* techniques to promote better choices. This chapter explains how to fine tune and effectively embed these legal requirements at the earlier stages of the architectural design of the computer code. This automated process focuses on Smart Contracts and Service Level Agreements (SLAs) frameworks, which include selection tools that take an information schema and a pseudo-code that follows a programming logic to process information based on that schema. The pseudo-code is essentially the easiest way to write and design computer code, which can check automatically the legal compliance of the contractual framework. It contains a set of legal questions that have been specifically designed to urge Cloud providers to disclose relevant information and comply with the legal requirements established by the GDPR.

Keywords Smart contracts · European general data protection regulation (GDPR) · Smart disclosures · Nudges · Service level agreements (SLAs) · Unified modeling language (UML) · Pseudo-code

M. Corrales (✉)
Institute of European and American Studies, Academia Sinica, Taipei, Taiwan
e-mail: marcelo.corrales13@gmail.com

P. Jurčys
Nanomolar, Inc., California, CA, USA

G. Kousiouris
Department of Informatics and Telematics, Harokopio University of Athens, Athens, Greece

© Springer Nature Singapore Pte Ltd. 2019
M. Corrales et al. (eds.), *Legal Tech, Smart Contracts and Blockchain*,
Perspectives in Law, Business and Innovation,
https://doi.org/10.1007/978-981-13-6086-2_8

1   Introduction

Smart Contracts are self-executing and autonomous computer protocols that facilitate the performance and execution of agreements between two or more parties. The advantages of Smart Contracts are numerous. They can provide better security performance than traditional contract law and reduce transaction costs associated with the negotiation, verification and enforcement of agreements.[1]

They are encoded in such a way that the correct execution is guaranteed by the Blockchain.[2] The Blockchain is essentially a distributed ledger that can be configured to be accessible publicly or privately and the technology guarantees the transaction history.[3] This Blockchain-based Smart Contract technology allows the involved parties to transfer, receive and store value or information through a distributed peer-to-peer computer network.[4] Decisions are typically based on a majority vote while variations exist in which accessors of information may have only partial access to a selected subset of the data (permissioned Blockchains).[5]

In other words, each transaction is distributed across the entire network and is stored in a block only when the rest of the network approves the validity of the transaction. This process is based on past events taking into account the previous block.[6] Each block holds a unique fingerprint built on cryptographic hash code techniques similar to those used in the creation of digital certificates and electronic signatures to secure authentication.[7] Furthermore, a transaction history is maintained and can be accessed in order to check the sequence of events up to this point in time.

The main purpose of Smart Contracts is to automate obligations, which are held as "code." As Lawrence Lessig ably stated: "code is law."[8] Code is essentially the set of rules or instructions that structure the Internet. That is, the hardware and software applications that "make" the Internet architecture as it is.[9] Denise Carusso has also powerfully stated:

> It is still true today that software—written by a team of sleep-deprived programmers in some fusty cubicle—is the code that lays down the absolute law by which we live our lives. We are not free to change that code; our choice is to love it or leave it.[10]

One of the main challenges of Smart Contracts will be to embed the laws of the physical world into the digital code. The crucial question is how to translate

---

[1]Carnevale (2017), pp. 64–65; Wattenhofer (2016), p. 88.
[2]Kost de Sevres (2016); Wattenhofer (2016), p. 88.
[3]Wattenhofer (2016), p. 88; Swan (2015), p. 16.
[4]See, e.g., generally, Morabito (2017); Swan (2015).
[5]Varshney (2017).
[6]Kost de Sevres (2016).
[7]Mougayar (2015).
[8]Lessig (2006), p. 1.
[9]Post (2009), p. 129.
[10]Lessig (2001), p. 283.

these technical options into an agreement.[11] This is the reason why lawyers can (and should) learn how to code. Coding is essentially just a range of agnostic problem-solving techniques and tools.[12]

Thus, the best way to start coding is through "pseudo-code." Pseudo-code is the best way to write and design computer software *before* it is coded. In Myler's view, pseudo-code is "a simple, structured representation of a program sequence or algorithm that is not intended to be run on a machine."[13] In other words, it is the outline of a program without using any specific programming language.[14]

To put it another way, the pseudo-code describes how the designer would implement an algorithm without getting distracted by the syntactical language details.[15] It is essentially a generic text containing some keywords that provide specific instructions to write the programming language itself. This way the pseudo-code can then easily be translated into the specific source code[16] and thus implemented both in the preliminary and detailed architectural design stages.[17]

Smart Contracts could be developed on a pseudo-code based on "If" and "Then" statements. The aim of this chapter is, therefore, to present an example of a pseudo-code template, which includes the disclosure of relevant legal (and technical) information using *smart disclosures* as prime nudging techniques. This will prompt Cloud Computing providers to effect the necessary changes in their SLAs and underlying software in order to make the processing of personal data compliant with the new GDPR.[18]

This chapter is divided in 9 sections. After this introduction, Sect. 2 highlights some of the key components and changes proposed by the GDPR. Section 3 explains the new challenges of managing Smart Contract SLAs in Cloud Computing transformations. Section 4 adopts the behavioral law and economics approach to *nudge* and positively influence decision-making in Cloud Computing architectures. Section 5 focuses on *smart disclosures* as they are considered to be one of the most powerful nudging techniques. Section 6 follows Nudge Theory and proposes the implementation of embedded legal and technical questions in order to disclose relevant information as part of a Unified Modeling Language (UML) schema. Section 7 elaborates on the idea of a pseudo-code, which is also an integral component of the Smart Contract SLA framework. Section 8 presents a set of legal and technical questions—which

---

[11]Asharaf and Adarsh (2017), p. 50.

[12]Hogan (2017).

[13]Myler (1998), p. 37.

[14]Kamthane and Kamal (2012), pp. 79–80.

[15]Ford (2015), p. 163; ISRD Group (2007), p. 192; ITL Education Solutions (2006), p. 222.

[16]Brooks (1997), p. 27.

[17]Agarwal et al. (2010), p. 130.

[18]Regulation (EU) 2016/679 of the European Parliament and of the Council of 27 April 2016 on the protection of natural persons with regard to the processing of personal data and on the free movement of such data, and repealing Directive 95/46/EC (General Data Protection Regulation). While the Regulation entered into force on 24 May 2016, it shall apply to all EU Member States from 25 May 2018. See European Commission, Reform of EU Data Protection Rules. http://ec.europa.eu/justice/data-protection/reform/index_en.htm. Accessed 10 October 2016.

is necessary for the elaboration of the pseudo-code—and explains in detail the programming logic that have been carefully crafted to comply with the new provisions enshrined in the GDPR. Finally, Sect. 9 concludes.

2 Key Areas to Consider with Regard to the GDPR

The advent of Cloud Computing, Big Data and Internet of Things (IoT) poses great challenges concerning the processing of personal data especially in hybrid Cloud scenarios. This section presents some of the main legal requirements that need to be considered in light of the new GDPR. While the GDPR proscribes some new rights to create more transparency and empower data subjects, it has also sparked criticisms with regard to the increased burden and responsibilities imposed on data controllers and data processors.

Some of these limitations may fall foul of the current Big Data and IoT movement, in particular if one looks at this problem from a global perspective. This means that we need a whole new contractual framework. Therefore, one of the main objectives of this cis how to translate and effectively embed those new legal requirements (sometimes seen as constraints) in the computer code of Cloud architectures.

The GDPR was adopted on 27 April 2016 and after a two-year transition period it came into force on 25 May 2018. The GDPR replaced the previous European Data Protection Directive[19] and was designed to strengthen and unify data protection and privacy for all European Union (EU) citizens and to empower individuals by granting them more control and certainty over their data when using Internet services.[20]

The GDPR has been generally welcomed for updating some of the rules of the previous data protection regime. However, it has also created concerns among legal scholars and privacy associations. The most significant changes that triggered heated discussions, which deserve a closer attention in the context of this chapter can be summarized as follows:

i. *International Data Transfers*: The GDPR imposes more stringent rules for the transfer of personal data to third countries and international organizations outside the EU. This change was designed to ensure an adequate level of protection in a globally connected world[21];

ii. *Extra-Territorial Scope*: The GDPR expands its territorial scope of protection (extra-territorial applicability) to data controllers and processors established in the EU and *outside* of the EU territory with regard to the processing of personal data of European citizens[22];

---

[19]Directive 95/46/EC of the European Parliament and of the Council of 24 October 1995 on the protection of individuals with regard to the processing of personal data and on the free movement of such data.

[20]See, e.g., Mc Nealy and Flowers (2015), p. 199; Gjermundrød et al. (2016), p. 4.

[21]Article 46 GDPR; Voigt and von dem Bussche (2017), p. 120.

[22]See Article 4 (1) (c) of the GDPR; Svantesson (2013), p. 89; Hijmans (2016), p. 497.

iii. *Consent*: The GDPR strengthens the definition of consent, meaning that consent must be concise, unambiguous, clear and freely given. Companies will no longer be able to use long terms and conditions full of legalese[23];

iv. *Breach Notification*: Data breach notifications are mandatory. Data controllers must notify the breach immediately (within 72 h) to their supervisory authority, whereas data processors must report the breach to the controllers[24];

v. *Access Rights*: Data subjects have more rights to get access and control regarding their data. This allows them the right to request the data controller whether personal data concerning them is being processed, where and for what purpose[25];

vi. *Right to be Forgotten (data erasure)*: This right endows data subjects to have the controller delete their personal data and stop further processing and dissemination of data from third parties[26];

vii. *Data Portability*: The GDPR creates a new right to data portability. This right allows data subjects to receive their personal data concerning them—which they have previously submitted to the data controller—in a "structured, commonly used and machine-readable format," and to send those data to another controller[27];

viii. *Privacy by Design and by Default*: The Privacy by Design (PbD) approach was first introduced by the Information and Privacy Commissioner of Ontario,[28] and has existed as a general concept ever since. The PbD entails the notion of embedding privacy (and data protection) requirements directly into the architecture design of information technologies and related systems. However, the GDPR introduces, for the first time, the PbD (and Privacy by Default) as a legal obligation. Data controllers and processors must adopt this approach by default, making an explicit reference to "data minimization"[29] and the possible use of "pseudonymization."[30]

---

[23] See Recital 43, Article 7 (4) of the GDPR; Wisman (2017), p. 357.

[24] See Article 33 of the GDPR; Müthlein (2017), p. 78.

[25] See Articles. 12–14 of the GDPR; Quelle (2016), p. 143.

[26] See Article 17 of the GDPR; Sobkow (2016), p. 36.

[27] See Article 20 of the GDPR; see also Article 29 Data Protection Working Party, Guidelines on the right to data portability. Adopted on 13 December 2016. As last revised and adopted on 5 April 2017; see also Fosch Villaronga (2018), p. 232.

[28] Cavoukian (2015), pp. 293 et seq.; see also Information and Privacy Commissioner of Ontario, https://www.ipc.on.ca/. Accessed 10 October 2017.

[29] See Article 5 (1) (c) of the GDPR; Lynskey (2015), p. 206; Thouvenin (2017), p. 218.

[30] See Article 25 (1) of the GDPR; see also D'Acquisto et al. (2015); Voigt and von dem Bussche (2017), p. 62.

3 Smart SLAs in the Cloud

The Cloud is an emerging trend that can be broadly defined as "an architecture by which data and applications reside in cyberspace, allowing users to access them through any web connected device."[31] The Cloud changed the way services are managed today offering a variety of resources for businesses[32] and scientific institutions.[33] The main reason for this shift is that IT resources in the Cloud are no longer stored on end-user personal devices, but accessed through a distributed network.

The Cloud allows consumers to operate a broad gamut of applications ranging from email and web-based spreadsheet services to more robust and reliable business software.[34] It touches upon almost every corner of our society. Evidence of the ubiquitous nature of the Cloud abounds in our daily life activity during time spent on the Internet. The following are best examples of Cloud Computing services: webmail services such as Gmail or Yahoo; blogging or social networking sites such as Twitter, Facebook or LinkedIn; picture sharing platforms such as Instagram; or even rating sites such as Tripadvisor.[35]

The Cloud is, however, much more than this. It is an Internet-based computing network that provides services enabling individuals and companies to jointly access a shared pool of resources and information.[36] Its benefits have contributed to improve all aspects of the society. From a service provider perspective, the Cloud optimizes resources. From a customer standpoint, the Cloud reduces costs in terms of hardware, software and other services.[37]

The main problem is that these services have different SLAs tied to it and this is often the last thing a customer of Cloud services will review. SLAs are essentially contracts that resemble those outsourcing agreements, web hosting services[38] and application service agreements found on the Internet. They provide similar terms and conditions that the involved parties need to fulfill. The main difference is that in the traditional form of outsourcing agreements the customer deals directly with the service provider, knowing exactly the type of service and where the IT infrastructure is located.[39]

SLAs are legally binding contracts used to guarantee the quality of service (QoS) and fulfill the expectations between the parties at both organizational and operational levels. These include the appropriate sanctions and penalties if the services are not delivered according to the terms and conditions. Their structure is similar to software

---

[31]Horrigan (2008).

[32]Millham (2012), p. 2.

[33]Balasubramanyam (2013), p. 102.

[34]See, e.g., IBM Cloud Computing, Cisco Cloud Computing, Microsoft Azure, Rackspace and Amazon Web Services (AWS).

[35]Naughton and Dredge (2011).

[36]Moskowitz (2017), p. 59.

[37]Hossain (2013), p. 14.

[38]See, e.g., King and Squillante (2005), pp. 195 et seq.

[39]See, e.g., generally, Kimball (2010).

license agreements, however, with regard to their subject matter they fall under the same category of outsourcing and hosting agreements.[40] SLAs in the Cloud are different as they depend entirely on customer's demand.[41] The Cloud has brought an increased number of intermediaries and different types of Cloud providers to fulfill the QoS.

Therefore, the main idea of this chapter is to propose a more flexible template, which is also in compliance with the GDPR. A Smart Contract SLA should provide a sound legal basis for the contracting parties and should follow the PbD approach. If this is not properly developed at early stages of the architectural design of the computer code—at least for functions that select suitable Cloud services from an available pool—it may cause harm and unexpected side effects to the involved parties.

For large buyers of Cloud, certain terms of the Smart SLA may be negotiable depending on the Cloud provider and how interested they are in keeping the company as a client.[42] For small buyers, however, these terms are usually drafted on a "take it or leave it" basis. Not to mention the "legalese" complexities of the terms of service that a customer must grapple with. The importance and difficulty of this has been examined by the House of Commons Science and Technology Committee in the UK describing them as "more complex than Shakespeare."[43]

They found out that consumers generally just sign up the agreements without knowing exactly what these terms really mean.[44] Evidence of this is the Article 29 Data Protection Working Party recommendation to Google to clarify its privacy policy so as to avoid "indistinct language."[45] Another example of this problem is revealed in the recent study of Facebook's Data Policy, which concluded that it was unclear to which extent user's data is shared with other companies and third party partners.[46]

4 Choice Architectures, Nudges and Legal Compliance

Following the foregoing discussion, the overarching idea in this chapter is to alter the choice architecture of computer software systems and frame key legal questions that can automatically influence certain positive behavior and lead to legal compliance.

---

[40] Bragg (2006), p. 49; Svirkas (2004), pp. 96 et seq.

[41] Carstensen et al. (2012), p. 244.

[42] Griggs (2013).

[43] Anderson (2015), p. 159.

[44] Anderson (2015), p. 159.

[45] Anderson (2015), p. 159; see also, letter from the Article 29 Data Protection Working Party to Google on Google Privacy Policy (Appendix: List of Possible Compliance Measures. Ref. Ares (2014) 3113072).

[46] Anderson (2015), p. 159; see also Van Alsenoy et al. (2015).

The end goal is thus not to "hardcode" open legal norms, but to *nudge* Cloud providers in achieving a greater level of compliance taking into account those legal rules.[47]

According to Olislaegers, compliance software consists of primarily "hardcoded legal knowledge on the one hand, and, when the law cannot be hardcoded, of nudging mechanisms on the other hand."[48] Therefore certain nudging techniques can help business comply with the legal requirements of e.g., the GDPR.

Over the past decades, behavioral economics has been a growing force in various fields of social sciences including many important legal domains.[49] Behavioral law and economics blends the traditional economic analysis of law and places greater emphasis on behavioral psychology. Its main premises stem from the innate human propensity to "err" in making decisions focusing on the understanding of human behavior. This approach may help us to better understand the difficulties of decision-making and find a better solution to improve the legal environment.[50]

The idea of this integrated normative framework was popularized by Richard Thaler and Cass Sunstein,[51] in their book *Nudge: Improving Decisions about Health, Wealth and Happiness*.[52] Their main argument is that improved choices and information disclosure could prevent individuals from making mistakes, enabling them to be better off.[53] This includes the ideas behind Nudge Theory. The definition of a nudge is "any aspect of the overall choice architecture that alters people's behavior in a predictable way without forbidding any options or significantly changing their economic incentives."[54] In other words, this refers to "every small feature in the environment that attracts our attention and influences the decisions that we make."[55]

The person who manipulates such environment is called a "choice architect." By and large, choice architects arrange the context that affects individual's decision-making.[56] Nudges are therefore those small changes in the choice architecture.[57] To count as a nudge, this intervention must be easy, inexpensive,[58] and most importantly, it must respect people's autonomy without coercing them to comply.[59] A well-designed architecture is only useful if it helps the involved parties to make better decisions, which is also necessary for developing a consistent and consolidated contractual framework.

---

[47] See, e.g., Olislaegers (2012), p. 80.
[48] See, e.g., Olislaegers (2012), p. 80.
[49] See, e.g., generally, Jolls (2010); Diamond and Vartiainen (2007) (eds).
[50] See, e.g., generally, Zamir and Teichman (2014) (eds).
[51] Sunstein (2000) (ed); Sunstein (2014b).
[52] See Thaler and Sunstein (2009).
[53] Corrales and Jurčys (2016), p. 533.
[54] Briggs et al. (2016), p. 117.
[55] Willis (2015).
[56] Bernheim et al. (2015), p. 35.
[57] Whyte et al. (2015), p. 171.
[58] Cwalina et al. (2015), p. 78.
[59] Schweizer (2016), p. 111.

Therefore, the very center idea of this research study is to encourage choice architects to transform the online environment and improve the choices that we have. This can be achieved by making small changes in the overall architecture design of Smart SLAs. Thaler and Sunstein defend the thesis that small changes in choice architectures are indispensable to improve individual's welfare. This notion of choice architecture embraces various dimensions. Examples of this abound in different fields, which show how making small changes can make a big difference such as: one-sized or double-sized printing, automatic enrollment of organ donation or pension funds, or customized reminders deadlines to qualify for a student loan.[60]

By way of illustration consider the example related to the choice of post-mortem organ donation.[61] Two widely accepted default systems exist: (a) opt-out system, whereby consent is automatically assumed; (b) opt-in system, which requires explicit consent from the deceased.[62] In the first system this means that you are a donor by default, whereas in the second system this means that you need an active choice.[63] The procedure differs from country to country.

For example, in some areas of the U.S., this requires the deceased having previously enrolled in a state registry. In other countries, such as Japan and most European countries, however, individuals are given this choice when they get or renew their driving license. In this case they can check a box as an opt-in or opt-out rule.[64] In countries with an opt-in default system—such as Denmark and the Netherlands—the percentage of organ donation is very low[65] in comparison to opt-out systems—such as Spain, Austria, France, Hungary, Poland and Portugal.[66] The reason for this is that people tend to prefer options that do not require mental effort (i.e., deliberation costs).[67]

Another meaningful example for embedding nudging techniques in the design of (software) architectures is the default settings of printer machines. Double-sized or single-sized printing might require users to click a button in the printer "preferences" or even the "advanced properties" settings. People use a lot more papers with single-sized prints.[68] However, this can also be selected as a standard double-sized default rule, thereby being more environmentally friendly and more cost-effective for the society.

---

[60]Corrales and Jurčys (2016), p. 533.

[61]Ben-Porath (2010), p. 11.

[62]Heshmat (2015), p. 243; Detels and Gulliford (2015), p. 782.

[63]Detels and Gulliford (2015), p. 782.

[64]Detels and Gulliford (2015), pp. 23 and 108; see also John (2013), p. 104; Quigley and Stokes (2015), p. 64; Thaler (2009); Hamilton and Zufiaurre (2014), p. 18.

[65]European Commission (2014), Journalist Workshop on Organ Donation and Transplantation: Recent Facts and Figures. Available at: http://ec.europa.eu/health/sites/health/files/blood_tissues_organs/docs/ev_20141126_factsfigures_en.pdf. Accessed 13 April 2017.

[66]Leitzel (2015), p. 137.

[67]Cahn (2013), p. 148.

[68]Corrales and Jurčys (2016), p. 533.

A few years ago, an empirical research study carried out at Rutgers University in the U.S. adopted a double-sized default. The study revealed a significant reduction of 44% in paper consumption during the first 3 years. This is the equivalent of 55 million paper sheets, which amounts to 4,650 trees. This shows how relatively small changes embedded in the architecture design of computer software can have an immediate effect and produce a large impact in the long run.[69]

5   Smart Disclosures in Automated Smart Contracts

According to the Behavioral Law and Economics literature one of most powerful nudging techniques are *information disclosures*. Information disclosure is about giving people just the right piece of information that may influence their decisions in one way or another.[70] The message contained in the "information nudge" may activate a certain schema in people's brains. One concept, which is part of such schema, can trigger other concepts in the same schema.[71]

For example, "eco-labeling" schemes often inform consumers about the sustainability of the product.[72] One way this type of information disclosure may function as a nudge is when the individual has a sort of "self-identity" related to environmental issues. The information contained in the eco-label may activate a thought that reminds the person of his or her eco-friendly self-identity. Applying eco-labeling schemes therefore help consumers to better understand the options they have and to make informed decisions. This can also raise a wider eco-friendly awareness among consumers and promote environmental responsibility among producers.[73]

For the purposes of Smart Contracts, we need to adopt "smart disclosure" strategies to provide objective information and allow end-users to quickly assess the attributes and legal compliance of Cloud providers. The idea of "smart disclosure" has been a recurrent subject over last years, which is kindling interest in various fields of law as a measure for improving consumer choices.[74]

The term "smart disclosure" in this sense refers to "the timely release of complex information and data in *standardize, machine readable formats* [emphasis added] in ways that enable consumers to make more informed decisions."[75] Smart disclosures are adaptive, interoperable and innovative to markets.[76] The role of smart disclosures

---

[69] Sunstein (2015), p. 26.

[70] Lindahl and Stikvoort (2015), p. 45.

[71] Lindahl and Stikvoort (2015), pp. 28–30.

[72] Lindahl and Stikvoort (2015), pp. 28–30.

[73] Lindahl and Stikvoort (2015), pp. 28–30.

[74] Tereszkiewicz (2016), p. 177; Bar-Gill (2012), p. 41.

[75] Sunstein (2014a), p. 98.

[76] Marc et al. (2015), p. 529.

should be to provide more alternatives the consumer did not consider before or remind them to take something into account but they may have forgotten.[77]

Examples of smart disclosures exist across various regulatory fields such as: product safety, finance, energy regulation, employment law, environmental law and health law.[78] One of the most powerful smart disclosure techniques is when data on products or services (including algorithms) is merged with personal data (such as customer location data) into "choice engines" (such as mobile applications in the Cloud) that allow end-users to make better contractual decisions. There are four general categories where smart disclosure applies as follows[79]:

(i) *When government discloses information about products or services*: For example, when the U.S. Health Department releases hospital quality ratings, or when the Security and Exchange Commission discloses public financial data in machine-readable format.[80]

(ii) *When government discloses personal data about citizens*: For example, when the Internal Revenue Service (IRS) provides citizens with online access to their electronic track records.[81]

(iii) *When a private company discloses information about products or services in machine-readable formats*: For instance, when a company launches a website with relevant information and applications that can empower consumers to calculate their taxes and improve their finances.[82]

(iv) *When a private company releases personal information about usage to a consumer*: For example, when a power company provides utility customers with user-friendly and secure access to its energy usage data through e.g., the "Green Button."[83]

Currently, one of the most promising regulatory strategies consists of "targeted disclosure." This urges choice architects to disclose simplified information at the time when consumers have to make decisions. Restaurant sanitation grading is a good example that has empowered consumers and incentivized restaurant owners to improve their sanitation conditions in order to reduce risks for foodborne illness (such as salmonella) caused by bacteria, parasites, toxins and viruses.[84]

A simple notice displayed at the restaurant entrance, which summarizes sanitation information with a certification ranking system ("A", "B", or "C") can reduce the information gap and nudge the involved parties along.[85] In this sense, targeted disclosures are a direct response to the so-called "behavioral market failures" and

---

[77] Lindahl and Stikvoort (2015), pp. 28–30.

[78] See, e.g., generally, Ho (2012), pp. 574–688.

[79] Howard (2012).

[80] Howard (2012).

[81] Howard (2012).

[82] Howard (2012); see, e.g., http://www.hellowallet.com.

[83] Howard (2012); see, e.g., http://www.greenbuttondata.org.

[84] Ho (2012), pp. 574–575.

[85] Ho (2012), pp. 574–575.

provides a justification for the government to intervene.[86] This improves not only transparency but allows consumers to compare the choices that they have.[87]

In other words, these kinds of smart disclosures help consumers to select restaurants based on health risks, which in turn urges restaurants to clean up.[88] The Mayor of New York City Michael Bloomberg introduced restaurant inspection and grading system in 2010 arguing that this helped to improve food safety practices and reduce foodborne illness outbreaks.[89] Furthermore, this information (about specific restaurant grading) is available online as open data and can be retrieved and portrayed to end-users through mobile applications. Archon Fung et al. have also documented how these embedded smart disclosures have played a significant role in improving restaurant hygiene in the city of Los Angeles.[90]

Following these theoretical and empirical examples, one of the main objectives of this study is about the importance of choosing the right institutions and mechanisms when addressing such behavioral market failures in the context of Smart Contracts. The sections below propose a unique way of urging Cloud providers to disclose relevant information, which could be pursued to address the emerging challenges in the Cloud Computing market.

6 A Unified Modeling Language for Checking Legal Compliance

This section presents the elaboration and capabilities of a Unified Model Language (UML) as an extension to the overall contractual framework of Cloud software architectures. The UML-description includes a selection tool that exports their options through a Graphical User Interface (GUI). This will allow end-users to select the most favorable options they have.

UML is a standardized "general-purpose language for modeling object-oriented systems,"[91] which allows software architects to "specify, visualize, build and document the artifacts of software-intensive systems."[92] The idea behind such a language is to model software systems before its construction, and simultaneously, to automate and improve the quality process. Thus, reducing transaction costs and shortening time to market.[93]

---

[86]For more details on "behavioral market failures" and default rules as nudging strategies see, e.g., Sunstein (2015), pp. 206 and 218.

[87]Busch (2016), p. 231. According to Daniel Ho, however, this grading system contains serious flaws and does not guarantee 100% cleanliness down the road. See Ho (2012), pp. 574–688.

[88]Ho (2012), pp. 574–575.

[89]Grynbaum and Taylor (2012).

[90]Fung et al. (2007), pp. 44, 50–51, 59–62, 68, 82–83, 120, 179.

[91]Overgaard (1999), p. 99.

[92]Debbabi et al. (2010), p. 37.

[93]Debbabi et al. (2010), p. 37.

Considering that UML language is very specific and formal, it became one of the most common standard modeling languages that facilitates communication and reduces uncertainty between analysts and people.[94] Just like architects have their own standards for representing their technical graphs and designs, software developers have also developed a unified and universally accepted modeling language.[95] Therefore, UML is specially adapted to support the architectural design of software systems.[96] With respect to end-user input and interface, this could be done via web forms, which can directly export schema files and create the necessary options. There are many tools for this that can enable a simpler and more user-friendly interface and design.[97]

The UML-description schema will aid in checking the legal compliance, which is necessary for choosing a Cloud provider and outsourcing data in an automated fashion. This can serve as the basis for expanding the scope of SLAs and making strategic choices of Cloud providers a global reality. This idea was taken from the ARTIST project[98] and can be implemented as an adjunct to any SLA framework for reducing the information gap and improving the understanding between the involved parties.

The ARTIST project comprises a certification model with a set of legal questions that certifies whether the migrated software is compliant with the legal requirements or not. Similar to the example of the restaurant sanitation grading system explained in the previous section, the major goal of the ARTIST certification model is to elicit answers to a set of questions that can then be translated into a rating system for the used software (such as Gold, Silver and Bronze).[99] This component is fundamental for increasing end-user's trust in software applications considering certain parameters (categories) to be evaluated.[100]

In the context of this chapter, however, the conclusion would be more straightforward and it would be of a "True" and "False" nature. Thus, it is either legally compliant or not. The questions are set as closed and pre-defined options since there are in principle only two possible responses: "Yes" or "No." "Yes" means that the answer to the question is either "Yes" or "Configurable in the SLA." The latter answer will allow Cloud service providers to effect any necessary changes within their own SLAs.

---

[94] Patel (2005), p. 206.

[95] Galis (2000), p. 87.

[96] Muresan (2009), p. 233.

[97] See, e.g., generally, Hennicher and Koch (2001), pp. 158–172.

[98] Advanced Software-based Service Provisioning and Migration of Legacy Software (ARTIST). This project was partially funded by the European Commission under the Seventh (FP7—2007–2013) Framework Program for Research and Technological Development. For more details about the ARTIST project, see: http://www.artist-project.eu/content/r12-certification-model#sthash.zpJSBZ9t.dpuf. Accessed 18 May 2016.

[99] ARTIST R12 Certification Model. Available at: http://www.artist-project.eu/content/r12-certification-model. Accessed 10 December 2016.

[100] ARTIST R12 Certification Model. Available at: http://www.artist-project.eu/content/r12-certification-model. Accessed 10 December 2016.

This is where framing questions to disclose information based on Nudge Theory comes to the fore. These questions could effectively be embedded in a coordinated fashion at different layers, especially if one follows a programming logic approach according to which one can check automatically the legal compliance. These questions would aim at nudging Cloud providers to disclose relevant information urging them to make further modifications in the SLAs and its underlying software.

Questions vary depending on the nature of the Cloud services required and the legal needs of the involved parties. They were designed to answer a broad range of legal issues in an automated fashion based on—primarily—the legal requirements of the GDPR. Depending on the nature of the service, questions range from privacy, data protection and data security. No free text is allowed, but pre-defined selections. This will enable the writing of the computer code, which has the ability to internally process the answers and produce an automatic result.

In this way, a pseudo-code has been created in order to communicate the legal requirements based on the requests made by the concerned parties. If the service provider cannot meet these legal requirements, end-users should be able to decide whether they still want to use the software application. If not, they should be able to migrate and choose another service. The section below explains in more detail the features of the pseudo-code.

7 Nudging Cloud Providers Through a Pseudo-Code

As hinted above in the introduction of this chapter, the pseudo-code describes how the designer would implement an algorithm without getting distracted by the syntactical language details.[101] The pseudo-code is essentially a generic text containing some keywords that provide specific instructions to write the programming language itself. This way the pseudo-code can then easily be translated into the specific source code[102] and thus implemented both in the preliminary and detailed architectural design stages.[103] In other words, it is like a flowchart, but without the graphics.[104] In this context the prefix "pseudo" means that it is not the actual source code, but the synthetic expression of it.[105]

During the elaboration of the pseudo-code, the software architect uses short English language words that follow a structural logical order. Phrases such as: "If-Then-Else, and End" are keywords used to design the structure of the programming language. Hyphens are used to link keywords to describe the control flow, while other English words are used to describe the processing actions.[106] For example: If

---

[101] Ford (2015), p. 163; ISRD Group (2007), p. 192; ITL Education Solutions (2006), p. 222.

[102] Brooks (1997), p. 27.

[103] Agarwal et al. (2010), p. 130.

[104] Myler (1998), p. 37.

[105] Agarwal et al. (2010), p. 130.

[106] Agarwal et al. (2010), p. 130.

A = B, Then C = A, Else C = D. The best way to explain a pseudo-code in simple terms is by describing step-by-step the process of making a cup of coffee as follows:

PROGRAM (name): "Make a cup of coffee"

   i. Fetch and organize all the necessary utensils and ingredients.
  ii. Plug the coffee machine.
 iii. Put the filter inside the coffee machine.
 iv. Put coffee grains inside the filter of the coffee machine.
  v. Fill the coffee machine with water.
 vi. Wait 10 min until coffee is ready.
 vii. Get a mug.
viii. Fill the mug with coffee.
 ix. Add milk and/or sugar.
  x. Serve.

END

As shown in the example above, the first step when designing a program is to choose a name. In this case the name is "Make a cup of coffee." Then, one needs to follow the instructions step by step until the "end" point. Each of these steps is called a "sequence." Now, the question is what happens if one has to make a choice in step "ix" between adding milk and/or sugar? The answer is to include a "selection switch" in the sequence. For instance, IF (sugar is needed), THEN add sugar, ELSE do not add sugar.[107]

In the context of this chapter we want to write the pseudo-code for a computer software that can nudge Cloud service providers to improve their choice architectures and check automatically the legal compliance of their SLAs. Therefore, a good name for the program would be: "Check Legal Compliance." The pseudo-code will then follow the same general conditional formula IF (condition to be checked) THEN (if condition is true) ELSE (if condition is false) ENDIF, as set out in the "Make a cup of coffee" example above.

All in all, the pseudo-code is a good tool especially for lawyers as it takes less time and effort than developing any other programming tool. It also allows more flexibility since there are no strict rules to come up with the pseudo-logic. As a rule of thumb, the simpler the statements, the better.[108] This process would also enable feeding the described pseudo-code to software developers in a more direct manner for the formal implementation of the respective code. This way interdisciplinary endeavors requiring collaboration between legal and computer science professionals could be made significantly clearer and more unambiguous.

---

[107]Gries and Gries (2005), pp. 84–86; Barlow and Barnett (1998), p. 99.
[108]Myler (1998), p. 37.

8 Legal Questions for the Elaboration of a Pseudo-Code: Check Legal Compliance

In order to extract a conclusion from the pseudo-code, one should elaborate first a list of questions related to specific legal issues. A table of all relevant legal questions has been included in Table 1. The table includes a set of 15 questions related to a range of legal and technical issues including, privacy, data protection and data security. This is mainly relevant for two reasons. First, it is important to cover a wide range of legal and technical issues. Second, in some cases, partial aspects of one question are related and follow the previous questions.

This set of questions has been customized and carefully crafted to include some of the main legal issues related to the new GDPR requirements as explained above in Sect. 2. It is important to note, however, that these questions are not exclusively related to the SLA specifications, but also to the general process or design of an application/usage of the underlying resources.

Table 1 Legal questions for the extraction of the pseudo-code

(1) (L001) Does your SaaS application deal with sensitive/personal data?
(2) (L002) Does your SaaS application support native encryption/protection of the data and authentication?
(3) (L003) Does your SaaS application give the choice of EU-based data storage location?
(4) (L004) Is your SaaS application dynamically configured for using IaaS/PaaS services?
(5) (L005) Are the data or metadata "ownership" rights clearly defined and clarified in the contract/SLA?
(6) (L006) Do you offer notifications in case you change the terms and conditions?
(7) (L007) Do you offer notifications in case your underlying PaaS/IaaS provider changes the terms and conditions?
(8) (L008) Do you offer the ability to the end-users to virtually be under more control over their own data ensuring data portability (e.g., migration, extraction and reuse of their data) and interoperability within the Cloud?
(9) (L009) Do you offer the ability to the end-users the right to delete/eliminate their data (so-called "Right to be Forgotten") in the original used service?
(10) (L010) Does your underlying PaaS/IaaS provider use Standard Contractual Clauses (SCCs) with you and other parties?
(11) (L011) Has your underlying PaaS/IaaS provider been certified for their Binding Corporate Rules (BCR) clauses by a EU DPA?
(12) (L012) Do you take measures to prevent data loss (regular backups, replication, etc.)?
(13) (L013) Are you using your own resources to run your application?
(14) (L014) Do you restrict access of data (without prior consent of the data subject) to third parties for specific purposes?
(15) (L015) Is there any auditing mechanism through which the data subject can be informed (e.g., in case of data breach or data access) about disclosure of their data and when?

Following the legal analysis and the programming code developed in the OPTI-MIS toolkit[109] and ARTIST project, a pseudo-code has been created as depicted in Table 2. The pseudo-code follows a logical order where a number of values have been assigned to each legal question. For example, question 1 has been substituted for (L001), question 2 for (L002), question 3 for (L003), etc. Then, the pseudo-code has been broken down in categories in a logical linear manner, there is a specific category assigned to the legal compliance. The result of a legal analysis has been made explicitly clear and has a binary form answering the questions "Yes" or "No" (i.e., "legally compliant" or "not legally compliant"). Table 2 shows a fragment of the pseudo-code.

The Table 2 may seem complicated to the eyes of the traditional lawyer. This is, however, very simple if we learn how to break down the statements in parts. Conditional logical statements: "If (condition, *true, false*)" are often used to choose upon regular activities of our daily life even though we do not often recognize it.

As a way of illustration, consider the fact that we usually go to work during the week and rest during the weekends. In this typical scenario, the conditional formula would be represented as follows: If (it is the weekend, *stay in bed, get up and go to work*). The condition is "If" it is the weekend. If the condition is "true", then you can *stay in bed*. If the condition is "false" (it is not the weekend), then you need *to get up and go to work*.[110]

Conditional logical formulas are also used in various fields for checking one or more conditions on a regular basis. A good example of this is in the accounting sector using the Excel Worksheet program. Accountants often use this method in the Excel sheet to calculate the commissions and bonuses of each employee. This way the Excel conditional formatting function helps to better visualize and calculate relevant data.[111]

In a similar fashion, the way this pseudo code has been designed is to assume that it is legally compliant until one condition is broken and it also works with a conditional "If" formula. In order to make the statements simpler, the legal questions have been substituted for a shorter formula. These are the legal questions (or conditions) that need to be checked in order to be compliant with the new provisions enshrined in the GDPR.

In programming language, the Boolean data type is primarily associated with conditional statements and is denoted as "True" or "False." This can help to understand and check whether certain legal criteria are met or not. If the answer to one question is NO, then it triggers the following statement: "set compliance = false return compliance," which automatically stops the legal analysis and the transaction (e.g., the data transfer) can not be made. However, if the answer to the question is YES, then there is no need to do anything as this is already set as a "True" statement thus legally compliant with the GDPR.

---

[109]Chulani et al. (2012).

[110]Weale (2001), p. 6.

[111]Blanc and Vento (2007), p. 192.

Table 2 Pseudo-code: check legal compliance

```
PROGRAM: "Check Legal Compliance"
//compliance refers primarily to the GDPR
//YES means that the answer to the question is either YES or Configurable in the
//SLA
// The symbol "//" implies a comment line, meaning the text after // does not
//affect execution, it is only used to explain the specific program line and enhance
//code readability
// The word " LEGAL_COMPLIANCE" is a variable, meaning a position in the
//memory structure of the computing system that holds the value (outcome of the
//analysis: true or false for being legally compliant)
// The symbol "=" is an assignment operator, meaning that the value at the right of
//the "=" is stored in the memory position that is indicated by the (variable) name
//on the left of the "="
//The symbol "==" indicates equality between the elements (variables and/or
//values) to the  left and right of the symbol
//The word "Return  LEGAL_COMPLIANCE" means stop executing and return
//the value of the variable  LEGAL_COMPLIANCE at that point

LEGAL_COMPLIANCE=True;

If (L001==YES){
                If ((L002==NO)OR(L005==NO)OR(L006==NO)OR(L007==NO)
                OR(L008==NO)OR(L012==NO)){
                        LEGAL_COMPLIANCE=False;
                        Return  LEGAL_COMPLIANCE;  //stop legal  analysis,
                        final conclusion is reached
}

If (L003==NO){ //if not based in the EU, you need to be certified for BCR for EU
usage
        If (L011==NO){
                LEGAL_COMPLIANCE=False;
                Return  LEGAL_COMPLIANCE;  //stop  legal  analysis,  final
                conclusion is reached
}

If (L003==YES){// if based in the EU,
                If (L009==YES){ //and you can offer the possibility to delete data
                        //do nothing, legal compliance has been set to true before
                                }
```

(continued)

Table 2 (continued)

```
                    }else{
                            LEGAL_COMPLIANCE=False;
                            Return  LEGAL_COMPLIANCE;   //stop  legal
                            analysis, final conclusion is reached
                    }
            }
    }

If (L001==YES){ //if your SaaS application deals with sensitive/personal data
        If (L003==YES){// if based in the EU,
                If (L014=YES){ //if you restrict access of data to third parties
                        //do nothing, legal compliance has been set to true before
                        }
        }else{
                LEGAL_COMPLIANCE=False;
                Return  LEGAL_COMPLIANCE;  //stop  legal  analysis,  final
                conclusion is reached
        }

}
If (L001==YES){ //if your SaaS application deals with sensitive/personal data
        If  (L015=YES){  //if  there  is  any  auditing  mechanism  about  data
disclosures
                //do nothing, legal compliance has been set to true before
                        }
        }else{
                LEGAL_COMPLIANCE=False;
                Return  LEGAL_COMPLIANCE;  //stop  legal  analysis,  final
                conclusion is reached
        }

}

Return LEGAL COMPLIANCE;

//continuous iteration section

If ((L004==YES)OR(L013==YES) { // Reiterate the code below continuously
        while (true){
                If (L003==NO { //you need to be either in white list with SCC or
```

Table 2 (continued)

```
               wherever with BCR
               If              ((Countries         in            White
               List==true)AND((L010==YES))OR(L011==YES){
               //do nothing since legal compliance is already set to True
        } else {
               LEGAL_COMPLIANCE=False;
               Return LEGAL_COMPLIANCE;
        }
    }
}
```

Question 1: *Does your SaaS application deal with sensitive/personal data?* This question refers to sensitive and personal data. This is a very important question that falls directly within the scope of the GDPR. Since the pseudo-code follows a logical order, this question is also related to other questions, especially when it comes to sensitive data such as health or genetic data. In this respect, the GDPR urges data controllers and processors to implement data security measures to prevent unauthorized access and data loss. This involves legal requirements with regard to the encryption and anonymization of personal data and to take the necessary security measures to prevent the loss, disclosure, access or alteration of data.[112] However, such obligations are not enough. They must be implemented into technical standards. Therefore, the following question is more of a technical nature.

Question 2: *Does your SaaS application support native encryption/protection of the data and authentication?* According to Article 32 (1) (a) of the GDPR, "…the controller and the processor shall implement appropriate technical and organizational measures to ensure a level of security appropriate to the risk, including inter alia as appropriate: pseudonymization and encryption[113] of personal data."[114] This may include different authentication and encryption techniques during data transfer or storage with a range of strength options (i.e., bits used for the encryption) and/or security certification provided and validated by an external third party authority. It is important to note that the Cloud provider does not need to publish the strategy itself, but the ability to comply with this legal and technical requirement.[115]

We often experience this when we use, for example, online banking systems from commercial banks. Most online banking services require their customers to

---

[112]See, e.g., Barnitzke et al. (2011), pp. 51–55.

[113]For further details with regard to encryption in the scope of the GDPR, see, e.g., Spindler and Schmechel (2016), pp. 163–177.

[114]See Article 32 (1) (a) of the GDPR; regarding these protective measures see also Recitals 74, 75, 76, 77 and 83 of the GDPR.

[115]Kousiouris et al. (2013), pp. 61–72.

change their passwords on a regular basis. Nevertheless, for security and practical reasons they use other techniques such as automatic passwords generators known as "tokens."[116] Some banks even distribute to their customers some devices that look much like electronic calculators. These devices automatically generate a digit code, which must be used together with the username and password of the client. This method rules out the necessity to choose a password manually every time, saving transaction and deliberation costs. With this new token system, the passcode changes automatically on a regular basis and helps to keep customers' data safe from malicious hackers.[117] This is also a good example of the PbD and Privacy by Default approach[118] set out in the GDPR.

Question 3: *Does your SaaS application give the choice of EU-based data storage location?* This question was designed to cope with the new provisions established in the GDPR, which sets out strict rules for the transferring of personal data to third countries outside of the EU. This question is relevant to establish a location constraint mechanism and the ability of the Cloud provider to receive and fulfill requests regarding geographic location of service placement. If the Cloud provider decides to transfer data outside of the EU/EEA Member States, it must ensure that the proper agreements/authorizations are in place prior to the federation.[119] This question is also related to questions 10 and 11 as explained below.

Question 4: *Is your SaaS application dynamically configured for using IaaS/PaaS services?* This question is more of a technical nature, which may have some legal consequences. It refers to the relationship between the software service provider (SaaS) and the infrastructure and platform providers (IaaS and PaaS). It could happen that during the course of the service provisioning the SaaS provider may need to change or move to another Cloud service (IaaS and PaaS). Therefore, the SLA specifications should include a kind of dynamic rating certification scheme as this would imply re-applying the legal conclusion selection.

Question 5: *Are the data or metadata "ownership" rights clearly defined in the contract/SLA?* This question refers to the potential ability of Cloud applications to generate new data out of the data submitted to the Cloud. For example, data mining tools, Artificial Intelligence (AI), data statistics, etc. It is a common practice that some Cloud services do not often specify "ownership" rights of such "derivative" data. Thus, this question would allow end-users to select other Cloud providers in case they prefer a provider with a clear data "ownership" rights policy.

Questions 6 and 7 refer to the problem in which some Cloud providers do not notify consumers when they change their terms and conditions. Cloud providers often reserve the right to change the terms of service unilaterally, at will and at any time. They usually change the terms of services in their website without previous notification to the end-users. This situation was confirmed in the survey carried out in

---

[116]Caelli et al. (1989), p. 144.

[117]Williams (2007), p. 12.

[118]Hustinx (2010), pp. 253–255; Chulani et al. (2012), pp. 7–10.

[119]Kousiouris et al. (2013), pp. 61–72.

the Cloud Legal Guidelines Report of the OPTIMIS project.[120] These policies need to be re-examined when they change, especially when this is related to customers' data.[121] Therefore, the objective of embedding these legal questions in the Smart SLAs is to urge Cloud providers to implement an automated mechanism, which can communicate effectively their customers of any changes in the terms of the SLA.

One humorous anecdotal example refers to the so-called "immortal soul clause," when in 2010 a British on-line videogame retailer (GameStation) temporarily and playfully added a special clause to its terms and conditions.[122] The clause stated that customers granted GameStation the right to claim their "immortal soul." The clause was included in the terms and conditions on the 1st of April (April Fool's Day) as a joke.[123] The result was that the overwhelming majority of customers (88%) voluntarily agreed with the terms and conditions of this click-through agreement.[124] This is the equivalent to seventy-five hundred souls "sold" (or "captured") on that single day.[125] This was obviously a joke, however, the company made a serious point: no one reads the fine print, especially if they are suddenly included in the terms and conditions of the contract without previous notification to the users.[126]

Another interesting fact regarding this anecdote, is that the customers were given the choice to tick a box as an opt-out option. That is, the default rule was to automatically grant their "immortal souls" with an option to opt-out. Very few did and the company rewarded them with a £5 voucher. This is in line with the behavioral law and economics claim that "default rules tend to stick" as discussed above in Sect. 4. At the end of April Fool's Day, the company said that it would not be enforcing "ownership" rights (of their immortal souls), and planned to send an email to their customers revoking such rights.[127]

Question 8: *Do you offer the ability to the user to migrate/extract and reuse their data without any specific and proprietary technology?* This question refers to the data portability and availability issue. The problem is that much emphasis has been laid down in focusing only on strictly technical issues toward increasing interoperability development. There is currently little guidance on how to resolve complex legal

---

[120]Forgó et al. (2013), p. 20.

[121]See, e.g., Pearson and Charlesworth (2009), p. 137.

[122]House of Commons, Great Britain Parliament, 2014, Responsible Use of data, p. 21, House of Commons, Science and Technology Committee, Fourth Report of Session 2014–15.

[123]The contract read: "By placing an order via this Web site on the first day of the fourth month of the year 2010 Anno Domini, you agree to grant Us a non transferable option to claim, for now and for ever more, your immortal soul. Should we wish to exercise this option, you agree to surrender your immortal soul, and any claim you may have on it, within 5 (five) working days of receiving written notification from gamesation.co.uk or one of its duly authorized minions." See: Fox News Tech, 7,500 Online Shoppers Unknowingly Sold Their Souls. Available at: http://www.foxnews.com/tech/2010/04/15/online-shoppers-unknowingly-sold-souls.html. Accessed 10 December 2016.

[124]Lori (2012), p. 175.

[125]Lindstrom (2011), p. 225.

[126]Molinaro (2016), p. 35; Goodman (2015), p. 90.

[127]Luzak (2010); Rosenthal (2012).

issues that arise with regard to data portability.[128] Before developing this criticism in more detail, consider the following hypothetical situation to illustrate this point further: Assume a federated Cloud scenario. In this scenario there is one customer and one service provider both located in the U.K. and an array of infrastructure providers (IPA, IPB, IPC and IPD) located in different jurisdictions. Each of which has its own legislation. Assume further that one of the infrastructure providers, in which end-user's data is stored goes bankrupt. What are the chances of the end-user to recover his or her data if these kinds of circumstances have not been clarified in the contract and the state's legislation of the infrastructure provider in question is debtor friendly?

On a more theoretical level, this could be clarified in the contractual terms i.e., that in cases of bankruptcy the Cloud provider compromises to restore the client's data and agrees to facilitate the means for data migration to another provider. On a more practical level, however, SLAs do not allow much room for negotiation. If the contractual framework provided by the SLA, is also able to clarify data portability issues as a legal concept, as in the bankruptcy example, this will allow the customers to maximize the number of Cloud providers. Another example would be the so-called "data hostage" clause, which requires the customer to pay a fee in cases of termination of the contract if the customer wants his or her data to be returned.[129] This sort of clause provides essentially a risk of data lock-in and customers should be able to recover and migrate their data without further hindrances.

Question 9: *Do you offer the ability to the end-users the right to delete/eliminate their data (so-called "Right to be Forgotten") in the original use service?* This question refers to the deletion or removal of personal data, which is grounded in the provisions enshrined in the previous EU data protection scheme.[130] However, the GDPR explicitly includes the "Right to the Forgotten" as an important legal innovation and not only as codification of the existing law.[131] In this sense, the GDPR refers to this new right as the data subject's right "to obtain from the controller the erasure of personal data concerning him or her without undue delay" and the data controller's obligation "to erase personal data without undue delay" under specific circumstances[132] as laid down in Art. 17. The rationale behind this right is to enable individuals to request the deletion or removal of any kind of personal data[133] where there is no compelling reason for its continued processing. It is therefore not an absolute right and the GDPR provides a list of specific grounds for its removal/deletion.[134]

---

[128]See, e.g., generally, Zanfir (2012), pp. 149–162.

[129]See, e.g., Carpenter (2010), pp. 1–14.

[130]See also *Google Spain SL, Google Inc. v Agencia Española de Protección de Datos (es), Mario Costeja González*, number C-131/12.

[131]Lindsay (2014), p. 311.

[132]See Article 17 of the GDPR; see also Lindsay (2014), p. 311.

[133]La Fors-Owezynik (2017), p. 129.

[134]See Article 17 (1) (2) (3) of the GDPR.

Questions 10, 11 and 13 refer to the transfer of data to third countries. The use of unmodified Standard Contractual Clauses (SCCs) and Binding Corporate Rules (BCRs) are valuable legal requirements in the framework of the GDPR. Incorporating such options in the SLA framework provides further evidence of an additional safeguard imposed by the law. The pseudo-code it is therefore intended to check a specific instantiation of an SLA (meaning if a specific configuration with given options is legal) or to check if this option is configurable in the SLA. For checking the instantiated SLA, the Cloud provider should add a country/region field and include specific options in the SLA.

In this case, the pseudo-code urges Cloud providers to allow programmatically the inclusion of SCCs and BCRs as a legal text. The BCRs for instance are internal rules (such as a Code of Conduct) adopted by a group of multinational companies who wish to transfer data across different jurisdictions.[135] The automated SLA framework should be able to kick in immediately and stop the processing of data in case the Cloud provider makes a mistake and attempts to make a transfer to a processor or sub-processor that is located outside the group of companies. These checks may include the location of the federated infrastructure provider using a location constraint mechanism. If the target infrastructure provider is inside the jurisdiction of the EU/EEA Member States, then the outsourcing of data may be fulfilled with minimal intervention taking into account the GDPR.[136] If the infrastructure provider is located outside the boundaries of any of the EU/EEA Member States, and, therefore, outside of the scope of the GDPR, then the federation cannot be performed if these checks are not in place in advance.

Question 12: *Do you take measures to prevent data loss (regular backups, replication, etc.)?* Data replication for backup purposes might be seen as one of the main benefits of the Cloud as this prevents data loss in cases of accident. Even from a legal standpoint this might be taken as beneficial if we were to consider data protection and data security issues. However, this also represents a hurdle if we have to consider data location and jurisdictional issues, assuming the customer is not fully aware of where the data has been replicated. In this case the pseudo-code advocates the inclusion of Data Management (DM) specific technical options such as replication rate in the infrastructure. This would allow end-users to track back-up and replication jobs when the databases and Virtual Machines (VMs) grow too fast and may be quickly depleted on the target repository. This will provide greater control for end-users to monitor where their data is located in automated Cloud environments.

Question 15: *Is there any auditing mechanism through which the data subject can be informed (e.g., in case of data breach or data access) about disclosure of their data and when?* This question refers to the data breach notification requirement introduced by the GDPR. According to Art. 33 "in the case of personal data breach,

---

[135] Reform of EU Data Protection Rules. EU Commission. Available at: http://ec.europa.eu/justice/data-protection/reform/index_en.htm. Accessed 3 July 2014.
[136] Kousiouris et al. (2013), p. 63.

the controller shall without undue delay and, where feasible, not later than 72 h after having become aware of it, notify the personal data breach to the supervisory authority...”[137] Therefore, the pseudo-code attempts to make sure that Cloud providers understand the obligation they have and ensure that they have an effective breach detection and robust auditing mechanism in place.[138]

Finally, the process of checking whether the provider answers are valid can be fully automated if the pseudo-code needed fields (answers to the questions) are captured in a machine understandable format like JavaScript Object Notation (JSON) or eXtensible Markup Language (XML)—or translated to such after exposure of the questions through a relevant user interface—which will enable the automatic inclusion of the needed processing in the general software process. An example of a formal input that would be needed follows for a specific question (question 1):

```
{
    "questionNumber":1,
    "questionText":" Does your SaaS application deal with sensitive/personal data?"
    "answer":true
}
```

Therefore, if the provider has answered the entire set of 15 questions and has included it in a document (such as a text file) following the previous format, the process can be fully automated. For aiding the process, a software developer can also define a schema, meaning the necessary structure for the overall document that would be needed. The schema for this case appears in Table 3. The most important things to observe from this schema is the fact that it dictates those exactly 15 core elements (such as the previously described question 1) need to be included in the document (in order to cover for the entire range of the questions), and each element requires three fields, one with a number value (for the respective question number, with a range from 1 to 15), one text (character string) value for the question text and one Boolean field for indicating the true/false.

---

[137] See also Articles 33, 34, 83 and Recitals 85, 87 and 88 of the GDPR; Article 29 Working Party, Guidelines on Personal data breach notification under Regulation 2016/679 adopted on 3 October 2017; Müthlein (2017), p. 78.

[138] See, e.g., generally, ENISA Report on “Data breach notifications in the EU.” Available at: https://www.enisa.europa.eu/topics/data-protection/personal-data-breaches/personal-data-breach-notification-tool. Accessed 30 October 2017.

Table 3 JSON Schema definition for retrieving provider answers

```
{
      "type":"object",
      "$schema": "http://legalcompliance.cloud/schema",
      "id": "http://legalcompliance.cloud",
      "required":true,
      "properties":{
            "0": {
                  "type":["object","array"],
                  "minitems": "15",
                  "maxitems": "15",
                  "id": "http://legalcompliance.cloud",
                  "required":true,
                  "properties":{
                        "answer": {
                              "type":"boolean",
                              "id": "http://legalcompliance.cloud/0/answer",
                              "required":true
                        },
                        "questionNo": {
                              "type":"number",
                              "minimum": "1",
                              "maximum": "15",
                              "id": "http://legalco...nce.cloud/0/questionNumber",
                              "required":true
                        },
                        "questionText": {
                              "type":"string",
                              "id": "http://legalcompliance.cloud/0/questionText",
                              "required":true
                        }
                  }
            },

      }
}
```

9 Conclusion

The idea of embedding this set of questions into a contractual framework has been inspired by the behavioral approach to law and economics (Nudge Theory). In the opinion of Sunstein and Thaler, *smart disclosure* is one of the most powerful nudging techniques, which can influence a positive behavior or response. Hence, helping individuals to make the "right" choice. These new choices can later be exported through a Graphical User Interface (GUI), for end-users to select which options they need. As a result, this framework will enable a well-designed architecture, which is necessary for developing a consistent and consolidated Smart Contract SLA framework.

Smart Contracts are a key component to next-generation technology. While a typical contract is written using natural language, Smart Contracts are written in computer code using specific programming languages. Such languages use strict algorithms and can be very complicated for non-programmers (such as lawyers).

Therefore, this chapter presents the process of creating a *pseudo-code*, which is an intermediate stage between planning and programming. It is essentially a step-by-step outline of the code, which can later be transcribed into any programming language. The whole purpose of a pseudo-code is to make things simpler instead of using real and complex syntax programming language.

The proposed pseudo-code follows a programming logic that allows the implementation of embedding legal concepts into the user interface and related systems. It has been developed in a way to be compliant with the new legal requirements of the GDPR. The design of the pseudo-code includes a set of specific legal and technical questions. These questions are intended to *nudge* Cloud providers and prompt them to disclose relevant information to comply with the new legal requirements set out in the GDPR.

This could be used in the Blockchain realm as a piece of code together with the normal Blockchain code that validates the right of an entity to access a given asset. For example, even if the owner of the asset (the person owning the data) gives the right to the Cloud provider to access the data, the framework could demand from the provider the answers to the specified pseudo-code questions in order to validate if the specific provider can access the data and therefore protect the user in a seamless manner.

Acknowledgements This work has been partially supported by the EU within the 7th Framework Program under contract ICT-257115—OPTIMIS (Optimized Infrastructure Services) project. The authors would also like to thank all the researchers involved in the certification model of the ARTIST (Advanced Software-based Service Provisioning and Migration of Legacy Software) project. Without their technical explanations and support, this chapter would not contain a practical contribution to the state of the art.

References

Agarwal B, Tayal M, Gupta S (2010) Software engineering and testing. Jones and Bartlett Publishers, Sudbury (MA)

Anderson D (2015) A question of trust. Williams Lea Group, London

Asharaf S, Adarsh S (2017) Decentralized computing using blockchain technologies and smart contracts: emerging research and opportunities. IGI Global, Hershey PA

Balasubramanyam S (2013) Cloud-based development using classic life cycle model. In: Mahmood Z, Saeed S (eds) Software engineering frameworks for the cloud computing paradigm. Springer, London

Bar-Gill O (2012) Seduction by contract: law, economics, and psychology in consumer markets. Oxford University Press, Oxford

Barlow R-J, Barnett A-R (1998) Computing for scientists: principles of programming with Fortran 90 and C++. Wiley, Chichester

Barnitzke B et al (2011) Legal restraints and security requirements on personal data and their technical implementation in clouds. In: Workshop for E-contracting for clouds. eChallenges. http://users.ntua.gr/gkousiou/publications/eChallenges2011.pdf. Accessed 1 Sept 2016

Ben-Porath S (2010) Tough choices: structural paternalism and the landscape of choice. Princeton University Press, Princeton

Bernheim R et al (2015) Essentials of public health ethics. Jones and Bartlett Learning, Burlington (MA)

Blanc I, Vento C (2007) Performing with microsoft office 2007: Introductory. Cengage Learning, Boston

Bragg S (2006) Outsourcing: A guide to selecting the correct business unit, negotiating the contract, maintaining control of the process, 2nd edn. Wiley, Hoboken

Briggs P, Jeske D, Coventry L (2016) Behavior change interventions for cybersecurity. In: Little L, Sillence E, Joinson A (eds) Behavior change research and theory: psychological and technological perspectives. Academic Press, Amsterdam

Brooks D (1997) Problem solving with Fortram 90: for scientists and engineers. Springer, New York

Busch C (2016) The future of pre-contractual information duties: from behavioral insights to big data. In: Twigg-Flesner C (ed) Research handbook on EU consumer and contract law. Edward Elgar Publishing, Cheltenham

Caelli W, Longley D, Shain M (1989) Information security for managers. Stockton Press, New York

Cahn N (2013) The new kinship: constructing donor-conceived families. New York University Press, New York

Carnevale C (2017) Future of the CIO: towards an enterpreneurial role. In: Bongiorno G, Rizzo D, Vaia G (eds) CIOs and the digital transformation: a new leadership role. Springer, Cham

Carpenter R (2010) Walking from cloud to cloud: the portability issue in cloud computing. Wash J Law Technol Arts 6(1):1–14

Carstensen J, Morgenthal J, Golden B (2012) Cloud computing: assessing the risks. IT Governance Publishing, Cambridgeshire

Cavoukian A (2015) Evolving FIPPs: proactive approaches to privacy, not privacy paternalism. In: Gutwirth S, Leenes R, de Hert P (eds) Reforming European data protection law. Springer, Dordrecht

Chulani I et al (2012) Technical implementation of legal requirements, exploitation of the toolkit in use cases and component licenses, p 23, Cloud Legal Guidelines, OPTIMIS Deliverable 7.2.1.3. Accessed 10 Oct 2017. http://www.optimis-project.eu/sites/default/files/content-files/document/d7213-cloud-legal-guidelines.pdf

Corrales M, Jurčys P (2016) Cass Sunstein, Why nudge: the politics of libertarian paternalism, New Haven/London: Yale University Press, 2014, 208 pp, pb, £10.99. Modern Law Rev 79(3):533–536

Cwalina W, Falkwoski A, Newman B (2015) Persuasion in the political context: opportunities and threats. In: Stewart D (ed) The handbook of persuasion and social marketing, vol 1: Historical and social foundations. Praeger, Santa Barbara (CA)

D'Aquisto et al. (2015) Privacy by design in big data: an overview of privacy enhancing technologies in the era of big data analytics. European Union Agency for Network and Information Security (ENISA)

Debbabi M et al (2010) Verification and validation in systems engineering: assessing UML/SysML design models. Springer, Berlin

Detels R, Gulliford M (2015) Oxford textbook of global public health, 6th edn, vol 1. Oxford University Press, Oxford

Diamond P, Vartiainen H (2007) Behavioral economics and its applications. Princeton University Press, Princeton

Ford W (2015) Numerical linear algebra with applications: using MARLAB. Elsevier, Amsterdam

Forgó N, Nwankwo I, Pfeiffenbring J (2013) Cloud legal guidelines final report, Deliverable 7.2.1.4. OPTIMIS European funded project

Fung A, Graham M, Weil D (2007) Full disclosure: the perils and promise of transparency. Cambridge University Press, Cambridge

Galis A (2000) Multi-domain communication management systems. CRC Press, Boca Ratón

Gjermundrød H, Dionysiou I, Costa K (2016) privacyTracker: A Privacy-by-Design GDPR-compliant framework with verifiable data traceability controls. In: Casteleyn S, Dolog P, Pautasso C (eds) Current trends in web engineering. ICWE 2016 international workshops DUI, TELERISE, SoWeMine, and Liquid Web, Lugano Switzerland, 6–9 June 2016, Revised Selected Papers. Springer, Cham

Goodman M (2015) Future crimes: inside the digital underground and the battle for our connected world. Transworld Publishers (Bantam Press), London

Gries D, Gries P (2005) Multimedia introduction to programming using Java. Springer, New York

Griggs S (2013) 5 Hidden problems with cloud SLAs. http://www.thewhir.com/blog/5-hidden-problems-cloud-slas. Accessed 10 May 2017

Grynbaum M, Taylor K (2012) Bloomberg defends grading system derided by restaurateurs, The New York Times. http://www.nytimes.com/2012/03/07/nyregion/restaurant-grading-system-under-fire-gets-mayors-backing.html. Accessed 10 May 2017

Hamilton D, Zufiaurre B (2014) Blackboards and bootstraps: revisioning education and schooling. Sense Publishers, Rotterdam

Hennicker R, Koch N (2001) Modeling the user interface of web applications with UML. In: Evans A et al (eds) Practical UML-based rigorous development methods—countering or integrating the eXtremists, Workshop of the pUML-Group held together with UML 2001, Toronto, Canada. GI, Gesselschaft für Informatik, Bonn

Heshmat S (2015) Addiction: a behavioral economic perspective. Routledge, New York

Hijmans H (2016) The European union as guardian of internet privacy: the story of art. 16 TFEU. Springer, Cham

Ho D (2012) Fudging the nudge: information disclosure and restaurant grading. Yale Law J 122(3):574–688

Hogan J (2017) Lawyers learning to code? To do or not to do, that is the question! https://www.cli.collaw.com/latest-on-legal-innovation/2017/08/16/should-lawyers-learn-to-code. Accessed 10 Oct 2017

Horrigan J (2008) Use of cloud computing applications and services. http://www.pewinternet.org/2008/09/12/use-of-cloud-computing-applications-and-services/. Accessed 10 Oct 2017

Hossain S (2013) Cloud computing terms, definitions and taxonomy. In: Bento A, Aggarwal A (eds) Cloud computing service and deployment models: layers and management. Business Science Reference (IGI Global), Hershey (PA)

Howard A (2012) What is smart disclosure? "Choice engines" are helping consumers make smarter decisions through personal and government data. http://radar.oreilly.com/2012/04/what-is-smart-disclosure.html. Accessed 10 May 2017

Hustinx P (2010) Privacy by design: delivering the promises. Identity Inf Soc 3(2):253–255

ISRD Group (2007) Structured system analysis and design. Tata McGraw-Hill Publishing, New Delhi

ITL Education Solutions (2006) Introduction to information technology. Dorling Kindersley, New Delhi

John P et al (2013) Nudge, nudge, think, think: experimenting with ways to change civic behavior. Bloomsbury, London

Jolls C (2010) Behavioral economics and the law. Found Trends Microecon 6(3):176–263

Kamthane A, Kamal R (2012) Computer programming and IT. ITL Education Solutions Ltd., New Delhi

Kimball G (2010) Outsourcing agreements: a practical guide. Oxford University Press, Oxford

King A, Squillante M (2005) Service level agreements for web hosting systems. In: Labbi A (ed) Handbook of integrated risk management for e-business: measuring, modeling, and managing risk. J. Ross Publishing, Boca Ratón

Kost de Sevres N (2016) The blockchain revolution, smart contracts and financial transactions. https://www.dlapiper.com/en/uk/insights/publications/2016/04/the-blockchain-revolution/. Accessed 10 Oct 2017

Kousiouris G, Vafiadis G, Corrales M (2013) A cloud provider description schema for meeting legal requirements in cloud federation scenarios. In: Douligeris et al (eds) Collaborative, trusted and privacy-aware e/m-services. Proceedings of 12th IFIP WG 6.11 conference on e-business, e-services, and e-society, I3E 2013, Athens, Greece. Springer, Heidelberg

La Fors-Owezynik K (2017) Profiling 'Anomalies' and the anomalies of profiling: digitilized risk assessments of Dutch youth and the new European data protection regime. In: Adams S, Purtova N, Leenes N (eds) Under observation: the interplay between ehealth and surveillance. Springer, Cham

Leitzel J (2015) Concepts in law and economics: a guide for the curious. Oxford University Press, Oxford

Lessig (2001) The Future of ideas, 1st edn. Random House, New York

Lessig L (2006) Code. Version 2.0. Basic books, New York

Lindahl T, Stikvoort B (2015) Nudging—The new black in environmental policy? Tryckt hos ScandBooks, Falun

Lindsay D (2014) The right to be forgotten in European data protection law. In: Witzleb N, Lindsay D, Paterson M (eds) Emerging challenges in privacy law. Cambridge University Press, Cambridge

Lindstrom M (2011) Brandwashed: tricks companies use to manipulate our minds and persuade us to buy, 1st edn. Crown Business, New York

Lori A (2012) I know who you are and i saw what you did: social networks and the death of privacy. Free Press, New York

Luzak J (2010) One click could save your soul, recent developments in European consumer law. http://recent-ecl.blogspot.jp/2010/05/one-click-could-save-your-soul.html. Accessed 10 Dec 2016

Lynskey O (2015) The foundations of EU data protection law. Oxford University Press, Oxford

Marc et al. (2015) Indexing publicly available health data with medical subject headings (MeSH): an evaluation of term coverage. In: Sarkar I, Georgiou A, Mazzoncini de Azevedo Marques, P (2015) MEDINFO 2015: eHealth-enabled Health, Proceedings of the 15th World congress on health and biomedical informatics. IOS Press, Amsterdam

Mc Nealy J, Flowers A (2015) Privacy law and regulation: technologies, implications and solutions. In: Zeadally S, Badra M (eds) Privacy in a digital, networked world: technologies, implications and solutions. Springer, Cham

Millham R (2012) Software asset re-use: migration of data-intense legacy system to the cloud computing paradigm. In: Yang H, Liu X (eds) Software reuse in the emerging cloud computing era. Information Science Reference (IGI Global), Hershey

Molinaro V (2016) The leadership contract: the fine print to becoming an accountable leader. Wiley, Hoboken

Morabito V (2017) Business Innovation Through Blockchain: The B3 Perspective. Springer, Cham

Moskowitz S (2017) Cybercrime and business: strategies for global corporate security. Elsevier, Oxford

Mougayar W (2015) Understanding the blockchain: we must be prepared for the blockchain's promise to become a new development environment. https://www.oreilly.com/ideas/understanding-the-blockchain. Accessed 10 Jan 2019

Muresan G (2009) An integrated approach to interaction design and log analysis. In: Jansen B, Spink A, Taksa I (eds) Handbook of research on web log analysis. Information Science Reference (IGI Global), Hershey

Müthlein T (ed) (2017) Datenschutz-Grundverordnung—general data protection regulation. Datakontext, Frechen

Myler H (1998) Fundamentals of engineering programming with C and Fortram. Cambridge University Press, Cambridge

Naughton J, Dredge S (2011) Cloud computing: the lowdown. https://www.theguardian.com/technology/2011/nov/06/cloud-computing-guide-history-naughton. Accessed 10 Oct 2017

Olislaegers S (2012) Early lessons learned in the ENDORSE project: legal challenges and possibilities in developing data protection compliance software. In: Camenish J et al (eds) Privacy and identity management for life. Springer, Heidelberg

Oveergaard G (1999) A formal approach to collaborations in the unified modeling language. In: France R, Rumpe B (eds) Proceedings of the second international conference on UML'99—The unified modeling language: beyond the standard for collins, CO, USA, 28–30 Oct. Springer, Berlin

Patel N (2005) Critical systems analysis and design: a personal framework approach. Routledge, New York

Pearson S, Charlesworth A (2009) Accountability as a way forward for privacy protection in the cloud. In: Jaatun M, Zhao G and Rong C (eds) Proceedings of 1st international conference on cloud computing, CloudCom 2009, Beijing, China, December 2009. Springer, Berlin

Post D (2009) In search of Jefferson's Moose: notes on the state of cyberspace. Oxford University Press, Oxford

Quelle C (2016) Not just user control in the general data protection regulation: on the problems with choice and paternalism, and on the point of data protection. In: Lehmann A et al (eds) Privacy and identity management: facing up to next steps. Springer, Cham

Quigley M, Stokes E (2015) Nudging and evidence-based policy in Europe: problems of normative legitimacy and effectiveness. In: Alemanno A, Sibony A-L (eds) Nudge and the law: a European perspective, modern studies in European Law. Hart Publishing, Oxford

Rosenthal E (2012) I Disclose...Nothing. The New York Times. http://www.nytimes.com/2012/01/22/sunday-review/hard-truths-about-disclosure.html?_r=0. Accessed 10 Dec 2016

Schweizer M (2016) Nudging and the principle of proportionality. In: Mathis K, Thor A (eds) Nudging—possibilities, limitations and applications in European law and economics. Springer, Cham

Sobkow B (2016) Forget me, forget me not—redefining the boundaries of the right to be forgotten to address current problems and areas of criticism. In: Schweichhofer E et al (eds) Privacy technologies and policy, 5th Annual Privacy Forum, APF 2017, Vienna, Austria, 7–8 June 2017, Revised selected papers. Springer, Cham

Spindler G, Schmechel P (2016) Personal data and encryption in the European general data protection regulation. JIPITEC 7:163–177

Sunstein C (2000) (ed) behavioral law & economics. Cambridge University Press, Cambridge

Sunstein C (2014a) Simpler: the future of government. Simon & Schuster, New York

Sunstein C (2014b) Why nudge? The politics of libertarian paternalism, Storrs lectures on jurisprudence. Yale University Press, New Haven

Sunstein C (2015) Choosing not to choose: understanding the value of choice. Oxford University Press, Oxford

Svantesson D (2013) Extraterritoriality in data privacy law. Ex Tuto Publishing, Copenhagen

Svirskas B (2004) Dynamic management of business service quality in collaborative commerce systems. In: Mendes M, Suomi R, Passos C (eds) Digital communities in a networked society: e-commerce, e-business and e-government. Kluwer Academic Publishers, New York

Swan M (2015) Blockchain: blueprint for a new economy, 1st edn. O'Reilly, Sebastopol (CA)

Tereszkiewicz P (2016) Neutral third-party counselling as nudge toward safer financial products? In: Mathis K, Tor A (eds) Nudging—possibilities, limitations and applications in European law and economics. Springer, Cham

Thaler R (2009) Opting in vs. Opting out, The New York Times. http://www.nytimes.com/2009/09/27/business/economy/27view.html?_r=0. Accessed 20 Dec 2016

Thaler R, Sunstein C (2009) Nudge: improving decisions about health, wealth, and happiness. Penguin Books Ltd., London

Thouvenin F (2017) Big data of complex networks and data protection law: an introduction to an area of mutual conflict. In: Dehmer M et al (eds) Big Data of Complex Networks. CRC Press, Boca Ratón

Van Alsenoy B et al (2015) From social media service to advertising network: analysis of Facebook's revised policies and terms, report, draft version 1.2

Varshney A (2017) Types of blockchain—public, private and permissioned. https://blog.darwinlabs. io/types-of-blockchain-public-private-and-permissioned-5b14fbfe38d4. Accessed 10 Jan 2018

Villaronga F (2018) Legal frame of non-social personal care robots. In: Husty M, Hofbaur M (eds) New trends in medical and service robots: design, analysis and control. Springer, Cham

Voigt P, von dem Bussche A (2017) The EU general data protection regulation (GDPR): a practical guide. Springer, Cham

Wattenhofer R (2016) The science of the blockchain. Inverted Forest Publishing, s. l.

Weale D (2001) The smart guide to excel 2000 further skills: a progressive course for more experienced users. Continuum, London

Whyte K et al. (2015) Nudge, nudge or shove, shove—the right way for nudges to increase the supply of donated cadaver organs. In: Caplan A, Mc Cartney J, Reid D (eds) Replacement parts: the ethics of procuring and replacing organs in humans. Georgetown University Press, Washington (DC)

Williams G (2007) Online business security systems. Springer, New York

Willis O (2015) Behavioral economics for better decisions, ABC.net. http://www.abc.net. au/radionational/programs/allinthemind/better-life-decisions-with-behavioural-economics/ 6798918. Thaler Accessed 25 June 2015

Wisman T (2017) Privacy, data protection and e-commerce. In: Lodder A, Murray A (eds) EU regulation of e-commerce. Edward Elgar Publishing, Cheltenham

Zamir E, Teichman D (2014) (eds) The Oxford handbook of behavioral economics and the law. Oxford University Press, Oxford

Zanfir G (2012) The right to data portability in the context of the EU data protection reform. Int Data Privacy Law 2(3):149–162

"When People Just Click": Addressing the Difficulties of Controller/Processor Agreements Online

Sam Wrigley

Abstract Under the new General Data Protection Regulation, data controllers are only allowed to recruit data processors who provide "sufficient guarantees" that they will comply with data protection law. However, given the wide definitions of the terms "processing," "controller" and "processor," it is likely that we will see many situations where at least one of those parties is not acting in a professional capacity, but still comes under the remit of the GDPR (e.g., if the personal data is being processing in a Blockchain). This creates the risk that parties will simply agree to contracts without having read or understood them, leading to significant legal liabilities for both parties and a lack of sufficient protection for data subjects. This chapter will look at how parties should arrange their contracts to provide the best possible chance of complying with data protection law. It will also consider how controllers can use technological and other non-contractual solutions to compliment those agreements while still respecting each party's autonomy and freedoms. Finally, it will examine the regulatory strategies that can be used to allow amateur controllers to exist without unnecessarily risking data subject rights and freedoms.

Keywords Data protection · Controller · Processor · Contracts · Smart contracts

1 Introduction

When thinking about the processing of personal data, we may have a number of assumptions about how that processing will actually take place. In the early days of data protection law, we may have expected that regulated processing would take place in a commercial setting (hence the inclusion of the household exception to the regime) and that, therefore, the parties actually processing the data will be professional actors.

S. Wrigley (✉)
Faculty of Law, University of Helsinki, Helsinki, Finland
e-mail: sam@thewrigleys.com

Given this, we would probably also have assumed that those parties have (or should have) access to legal advice and that they know their business, so that we could therefore fairly and reasonably attribute them with the ability to comply with their legal obligations and responsibilities.

Under the General Data Protection Regulation (GDPR),[1] as under the Data Protection Directive (DPD),[2] these obligations and responsibilities are (largely) distributed through the concepts of "controller" and "processor." As the names would imply, these are the parties who actually have control over the processing and (if the controller does not actually perform the processing itself) the party who processes the data on behalf of the controller. These concepts have been described as playing a "crucial role" in the regime[3] and the way that we interpret them will have a significant impact on the way that the law functions. The problem addressed in this chapter, however, is that the original assumptions—that controllers and processors can be assumed to readily and reliably know their legal obligations—does not necessarily hold true in a modern digital environment.

Under the DPD, we already saw a willingness to hold that amateur actors (i.e., those not acting in a professional capacity) can be controllers.[4] This alone can cause difficulties given that such amateur controllers will often be acting without realizing that they are within the remit of data protection law and are unlikely to know their obligations. To compound this issue, recent trends have also raised the issue of amateur actors acting as processors, either with amateur or professional actors as the controller. As with amateur controllers, this poses difficulties since these amateur processors are unlikely to know their legal obligations and duties. Equally difficult is that the GDPR places certain obligations on a controller's use of a processor. As will be explored below, the law regulates the recruitment of processors, along with elements of the form and content of the relationship between the controller and the processor. This chapter seeks to consider the relationship between these legal provisions and the existence of amateur controllers/processors.

In Sect. 2, this chapter will look at the legal concepts of controllers and processors and some of the relevant obligations and rules relating to them. Section 3 will then consider some possible technological scenarios where private individuals may find themselves acting as a controller or a processor. Notably, in many of these situations, the private individual may not have any idea about their legal role or its responsibilities. Having laid out the issue, this chapter will begin to examine some potential

---

[1]Regulation (EU) 2016/679 of the European Parliament and of the Council of 27 April 2016 on the protection of natural persons with regard to the processing of personal data and on the free movement of such data, and repealing Directive 95/46/EC (General Data Protection Regulation) [2016] OJ L119/1.

[2]Directive 95/46/EC of the European Parliament and of the Council of 24 October 1995 on the protection of individuals with regard to the processing of personal data and on the free movement of such data [1995] OJ L281/31.

[3]Article 29 Working Party (2010), p. 1.

[4]C-101/01 *Lindqvist* [2003] ECR I-12971; C-210/16 *Unabhängiges Landeszentrum für Datenschutz Schleswig-Holstein v Wirtschaftsakademie Schleswig-Holstein GmbH* (Grand Chamber, 5 June 2018). Published in the electronic Report of Cases.

solutions. Section 4 will examine how this issue can be addressed through the controller/processor agreement, while Sect. 5 will examine some approaches which go beyond conventional contractual tools which controllers and processors can utilize. Finally, Sect. 6 will briefly examine a regulatory perspective of the problem and Sect. 7 will provide a summary and some conclusions.

2   The Legal Concepts of Controllers and Processors

This section will briefly set out the status of controllers and processors under the GDPR. At the time of writing, the GDPR has only just entered into force and, as a result, there is little direct guidance on how the law should be interpreted. However, as the definitions of both "controller" and "processor" are substantially the same as under the DPD, much of the earlier guidance and commentary will be informative. As will be seen in this part, these roles are drawn very widely. While this is beneficial in some ways, later sections of this chapter will demonstrate some of the difficulties which may arise because of this width. Before coming to the definitions of controller and processor, however, it is important to first examine the definitions of "processing" and "personal data."

2.1   "Processing" and "Personal Data"

Both controllers and processors are defined in relation to the processing of personal data. "Processing" itself is defined under Article 4 (2) as "any operation…which is performed on personal data or on sets of personal data, whether or not by automated means." This is an incredibly wide definition and includes, but is not limited to, collecting, structuring, storing, adapting, altering, using, disclosing or deleting of data. Meanwhile, data is "personal data" under Article 4 (1) if it is "any information relating to an identified or identifiable natural person," whether the identification is direct or indirect. It is not necessary for a party to hold all of the information necessary for identification; information is personal if the chance of identification is not "insignificant" (i.e., it would either be illegal to acquire the extra information or because it would require such a "disproportionate effort in terms of time, cost and man-power" as to be "practically impossible" to do so).[5]

   This provides a relatively low barrier for the application of data protection law. In theory, this is narrowed by Article 2 (2) (c), which states that the GDPR does not apply to the processing of personal data "by a natural person in the course of a purely

---

[5]C-582/14 *Breyer v Bundesrepublik Deutschland* (Second Chamber, 19 October 2016). Published in the electronic Report of Cases, paras. 41–46.

personal or household activity." However, this was interpreted very narrowly under the DPD and it is unlikely that this would change under the GDPR. For example, in *Lindqvist*, the Court of Justice of the European Union (CJEU) found that posting information on a personal website was within the scope of the DPD because it could be accessed by "an indefinite number of people," even when the information was shared as part of a not-for-profit leisure activity.[6] This wide scope of application means that the GDPR will apply to a significantly wider range of activities than individuals may expect (see Sect. 3). The question then becomes: When performing these activities, is one acting as a controller or a processor?

2.2 *"Controller"*

The GDPR, Article 4 (7) defines a controller as the "natural or legal person, public authority, agency or other body which, alone or jointly with others, determines the purposes and means of the processing of personal data." This role, according to the Article 29 Working Party, is intended to "determine who is responsible for compliance with data protection rules."[7] Accordingly, it is not surprising that the CJEU has stated that it should be given a "broad definition" to ensure "effective and complete protection" for data subject rights.[8] The philosophy of comprehensive coverage can also be seen in the legislative history of the term "controller." The predecessor to the DPD, The Convention for the Protection of Individuals With Regard to Automatic Processing of Data,[9] Article 2 (d), did not refer to controllers, but instead used the phrase "controller of the file." As explained by the Article 29 Working Party, when the DPD was being drafted, the language from the Convention was rejected to ensure that the new law had a "wider and more dynamic meaning and scope."[10] We should not, therefore, be surprised that the phrase "controller" has been given a broad meaning.

If a party is a controller, they have a large number of responsibilities. Fundamentally, the controller is required, under Article 24, to make sure that the processing of personal data complies with the GDPR requirements. They are, therefore, responsible for general compliance with the GDPR rules. For the purposes of this chapter, it is also important to highlight that Article 28 states that the controller is only entitled to use a processor if that processor has provided "sufficient guarantees" that it will meet the requirements of the GDPR ("the Article 28 (1) guarantees"), requires that the controller's relationship with a processor must be governed by a contract which sets

---

[6]C-101/01 *Lindqvist* [2003] ECR I-12971, paras 30 and 47. This decision has continued to be endorsed by the CJEU, e.g., in C-25/17 *Tietosuojavaltuutettu v Jehovan todistajat* (Grand Chamber, 10 July 2018). Published in the electronic Report of Cases, para. 42.

[7]Article 29 Working Party (2010), p. 4.

[8]C-131/12 *Google Spain SL v Agencia Española de Protección de Datos (AEPD)* (Grand Chamber, 13 May 2014). Published in the electronic Reports of Cases, para. 32

[9]Convention for the Protection of Individuals With Regard to Automatic Processing of Data, ETS No. 108, Strasbourg 28/01/1981.

[10]Article 29 Working Party (2010), p. 3.

out set out certain terms ("the controller/processor agreement"), and mandates the controller to provide the processor with documented instructions on how to process the data.

For the amateur controller (i.e., a controller who is not acting in a professional capacity), complying with the GDPR can be an intimidating task. While the DPD was 20 pages long, with 72 recitals and 34 articles, the GDPR is 88 pages long, containing 173 recitals and 99 articles (and this is before beginning to look at the supporting case law, soft law and other interpreting documents). The amateur controller must, in theory, understand all of these rules and ensure that both they and the processor comply with them. This seems like an ambitious requirement. Individuals actors have frequently shown a lack of familiarity with data protection laws and policies, even when acting in the comparatively simple role of data subject. In a Eurobarometer study performed under the DPD, only 34% of respondents stated that they read privacy policies and understood what they were reading. This is compared to 24% of respondents who read the policies, but did not understand them. Meanwhile, 25% said that they do not read policies, while 8% said that they ignore them altogether and 5% stated that they did not know where to find the policies.[11] One must wonder: If two-thirds of respondents freely admitted that they either did not read or did not understand privacy policies under the older, simpler law, when acting in the comparatively passive role of data subject, how likely are amateur controllers to be able to discover, understand and carry out their obligations under the new law (particularly where this involves drawing up privacy policies of their own)?

2.3 *"Processor"*

A party acts as a processor under Article 4 (8) if they are a "natural or legal person, public authority, agency or other body which processes personal data on behalf of the controller." Unlike the controller, a processor can never determine the purposes and means of the processing; if they do so, Article 28 (10) states that they "shall be considered a controller in respect of that processing." Instead, the processor serves the interests of the controller, with the controller delegating certain tasks to them.[12] This does not, however, mean that the processor cannot make any decisions relating to the processing. For example, the UK Information Commissioner's Office (ICO) stated that the instructions may allow for a "considerable degree of discretion" (particularly in relation to technical expertise).[13]

The exact status of each party depends on a careful factual examination, with potentially small differences deciding whether a party is a processor or a joint controller. As a result, it can be very hard to generalize about processor status—the strongest statement that can be said about any hypothetical relationship is that we

---

[11] Eurobarometer (2011), pp. 112–113. The remaining 4% responded with "Don't know."

[12] Article 29 Working Party (2010), p. 25.

[13] UK Information Commissioner's Office, paras. 21–22.

would typically expect party A to be a controller and party B to be a processor, but that the specific facts of the case may lead to a different result.

Under the GDPR, processors have considerably more responsibilities than they did under the DPD. In addition to the obligations to act only on instructions from the controller and to implement "appropriate technical and organizational measures to protect personal data" (which did exist under the DPD), processors are obliged to, inter alia, keep certain records of the processing (Article 30 (2)), co-operate with the Supervisory Authority (Article 31), ensure that the processing is performed safely and securely (Article 32) and notify the controller about data breaches (Article 33). A particularly significant difference between the DPD and the GDPR is that processors may be liable for remedies, liabilities and penalties under Chap. 8 (although, under Article 82 (2), processors are only liable for damage caused if they failed to comply with an obligation specifically directed at processors or if it acted outside of the controller's lawful instructions). This means that processors will be required to take a much more assertive position towards their processing of personal data in order to avoid being fined.

In theory, it may be easier for amateur processors to learn about their obligations than amateur controllers. Although they have a lot of responsibilities, many of these are laid out in the controller/processor agreement and so are directly presented to the processor. Meanwhile, because controllers are only allowed to use processors who provide sufficient guarantees that they will comply with the GDPR, there should be a check to prevent ignorant processors from entering the field (assuming that the controller complies with this requirement). Article 28 (3) contains a long list of elements that must be included in the controller/processor agreement, some of which overlap with the processor's statutory obligations (e.g., Article 28 (3) (c), relating to the security of processing or (d), relating to the engaging of sub-processors). The problem is that there is a risk that amateur processors will simply treat the contract and any communication from the controller in the same way that data subjects do privacy policies—while some may read and understand them, the majority will simply agree without internalizing (or even caring about) what they are being told.

2.4 *"Joint Controllers"*

The GDPR, Article 26 states that where two or more parties "jointly determine the purposes and means of processing," those parties shall be considered joint controllers. Joint controllers are required to "determine their respective responsibilities for compliance with the obligations under [the GDPR]," although data subjects "may exercise" their rights against any joint controller.

Issues of joint controllership are largely outside of the scope of this chapter, but it is important to note a few issues. As stated in the discussion on processors above, it may not always be clear whether a second party should be considered a processor or a joint controller. In *Unabhängiges Landeszentrum für Datenschutz Schleswig-*

Holstein,[14] the CJEU stated that the administrator of a "fan page" on Facebook should be considered a joint controller of Facebook's processing since the administrator is the one who actually chose to give Facebook the opportunity to process the data, even though the processing is almost entirely managed by Facebook. The court was careful to note that "the mere fact of making use of a social network" does not make one a joint controller[15] and that joint responsibility does not necessarily imply equal responsibility,[16] but it is clear that the barrier for joint controllership may be relatively low.

3   Controller/Processor Roles Online

As seen in the previous section, the GPDR has a very wide application. In an online environment, private individuals are used to taking the role of data subject—one's data is processed in one way or another during most interactions online. Individuals may also be used to acting as amateur controllers hiring professional processors, e.g., if they purchase a service which includes data processing. Equally, many companies are used to acting as controllers and/or processors.[17] More unusual, however, is the idea that an individual acting in an individual capacity may be a processor. There is a clear reason for this—if a processor is subservient to the controller and acts on their behalf, there is no (traditional) incentive for a private person, acting in a non-professional capacity, to fulfill this role. This dynamic changes in an online environment, as will be explored below.

This section will examine a number of scenarios and identify the likely controllers and processors in each. As this analysis is incredibly fact-specific, it should not be taken as a statement that the conclusions reached here will always apply; a small change in the way that a particular example works may change whether a party is a controller or a processor. Nevertheless, this section will identify some reasonable possibilities which can then be examined in Sects. 4 and 5. It will begin by looking at the "classic" scenarios from the online environment, with a single (usually long-term or permanent) server distributing information to several clients. After doing this, it will examine a number of different ad hoc, or peer-to-peer methods of processing data.

---

[14]C-210/16 *Unabhängiges Landeszentrum für Datenschutz Schleswig-Holstein v Wirtschaftsakademie Schleswig-Holstein GmbH* (Grand Chamber, 5 June 2018). Published in the electronic Report of Cases.

[15]C-210/16 *Unabhängiges Landeszentrum für Datenschutz Schleswig-Holstein v Wirtschaftsakademie Schleswig-Holstein GmbH*, para. 35.

[16]C-210/16 *Unabhängiges Landeszentrum für Datenschutz Schleswig-Holstein v Wirtschaftsakademie Schleswig-Holstein GmbH*, para. 43.

[17]As they are not natural persons, a company can never be a data subject.

3.1 "Classic" Dedicated Server Hosting

A common method of processing personal data in the online environment is simply to host it on a server, whether as a web page or as some other service. A conventional website is, at its core, a collection of files that are stored on a publicly accessible server. When a user wishes to browse a website (i.e., access the information in those files), the server transfers a temporary copy of the relevant files to the client device.[18] This same basic principle applies to most server technology, with the main conceptual difference being the exact nature of the files that are being transferred and the exact protocol being used to transfer them.

The CJEU has already stated in *Lindqvist* that the inclusion of personal data on a webpage, even if that website is not run in a professional capacity, will qualify as "processing" personal data.[19] In such a scenario, the controller will typically be the one who owns the website, or who controls the content. Although the controller may host the server themselves, they will typically contract a professional service provider to do so. If the controller chooses this option, that external service provider will, by necessity, process the data. In some cases, this service provider may be acting as a joint controller (e.g., where the service provider provides additional services which analyze user traffic). Where, however, the service provider simply offers basic hosting services, it is likely that they are acting as a processor—although they may make some technical decisions as to the exact hardware and software used, the party who runs the webpage is the only one acting as a controller. A website owner must, therefore, ensure that their agreement with the service provider complies with the various GDPR requirements.

When small actors approach large service providers, it may be somewhat artificial to say that the controller will be able to set out the terms of the agreement. Notably, this is the case with both professional and amateur controllers. Rather, what will often happen is that the processor provides the controller with their standard contractual terms on a "take it or leave it" basis, which the must then return as "instructions." Nevertheless, that party may still be considered a processor. While the Article 29 Working Party has stated that parties cannot designate who is the controller or processor in a contract,[20] the mere fact that a contract is on the service provider's standard

---

[18]Notably, where a person outside of the EU is accessing a website, the downloading of the files will not qualify as a transfer to a third country. This is because such a finding would mean that the "special regime" governing such international data transfers would become a regime of "general application" to online activitiy: C-101/01 *Lindqvist*, para. 69. This should not be taken to mean that all transfers of files from servers are not transfers of data (for example, a file sent under the FTP protocol, which is typically intended to be stored on a more permanent basis than files in an HTML page, would undoubtedly be considered a transfer), nor is it necessarily clear whether, under *Lindqvist*, accessing a webpage from within the EU should be considered a "transfer" of data (although it would be strange if it were not). For the purposes of this chapter, it is not necessary to resolve such questions; it is sufficient to focus on the mere hosting of the information on a server.

[19]C-101/01 *Lindqvist*, paras. 27 and 47

[20]Article 29 Working Party (2010), p. 9.

terms is not, by itself, enough to mean that the service provider is now a controller.[21] The question remains whether, in practice, the host controls the purpose and means of the processing.

Commercial server hosting is a well-established model and, beyond the question of standard terms and conditions, is unlikely to provide much difficulty for the controller/processor relationship. We must, however, also consider the situation of amateur server hosting. It is relatively easy for an individual (particularly one who is technically minded) to create a server on their personal computer and then offer hosting capabilities to others.[22] While this may be done professionally, it may also be done informally, with a person offering web space to friends or family members. In this situation, the host is performing substantially the same role as a commercial web server (i.e., they are processing information on behalf of another party without determining the purpose and means of that processing) and it would seem strange not to consider them a processor. However, especially if the agreement to host is informal, it is very unlikely that there will be any contractual relationship between the two individuals—and neither may be aware that it is necessary for them to reach such an agreement. This problem arises, in part, because there is an incredibly low barrier to entry; anybody with enough time or patience can follow the included documentation and create a server with little or no prior training or knowledge.[23]

3.2 Distributed Computing

In 1999, scientists at the University of California, Berkeley released a program called SETI@home. The purpose of this program was to scan signals from space for signs of intelligent extraterrestrial life. Rather than using specially-built supercomputers, the SETI@home project was designed to use "distributed computing"—a "virtual supercomputer" using the processing power of a network of personal computers from around the world.[24] In terms of aggregating computing power, SETI@home was incredibly successful: Researchers were able to process their data without the need for expensive machines, while individuals were able to assist in scientific research without any cost or burden. Notably, the individuals donating their power never interacted with the data personally; everything was done behind the scenes by their computer by the SETI@home program. The technology behind SETI@home now forms the basis for the platform BOINC.[25]

---

[21] Article 29 Working Party (2010), p. 26.

[22] This can be done easily by, for example, using the freely available Apache server software: https://httpd.apache.org/. Accessed 22 January 2018.

[23] A person's ability to make their server accessible from the Internet will depend, to some extent, on their agreement with their Internet Service Provider ("ISP"). However, this cannot be taken to mean that this is not a realistic scenario for at least some people.

[24] About SETI@home. Available at: https://setiathome.berkeley.edu/sah_about.php. Accessed 10 January 2018.

[25] For more information, see: boinc.berkeley.edu. Accessed 10 January 2018.

There is no conceptual reason to prevent someone from using a distributed-computing system (whether BOINC or another similar system) to analyze personal data. In such a scenario, it will often be easy to assign roles. The organizer of the project is acting as the controller as they control the purposes and means of the processing. Meanwhile, the individuals who donate their processing power may, by virtue of their contributions of the project, be storing, using, deleting or otherwise processing personal data. Although these individuals can choose, for example, on what computer they install the client software, this is a limited choice that is technical in nature. They are, therefore, probably only acting as processors, unless there is some special feature of the particular system that gives them control. It should be noted that this does not require the primary purpose of the project to involve the processing of personal data; as long as some personal data is included in the dataset which is downloaded to client machines, this will apply.

While those who create the projects may be used to acting as data controllers, those who download the program will often be people using their personal computer who simply want to contribute to a project. Further, as those individuals may not ever actually interact directly or manually with the data, they may be unaware that they are actually processing personal data in the first place. This could cause significant legal difficulties.

3.3   Listen Servers

Often, a developer will build a program that is designed to transfer data between two computers, but does not wish to pay for a dedicated server to host or manage this communication. This is particularly common in video games. If a developer or publisher wishes for the game to include multiplayer functionality, there must be some way of letting different players' computers communicate.[26] This can be done by paying for a commercial host—a server responsible for, inter alia, determining who is doing what at any one given moment and coordinating this information between the players. However, hosting a dedicated server is an expensive and long-term commitment which a publisher may wish to avoid. Many games will, therefore, avoid this by using a listen server. Under this system, an ad hoc server is set up where one of the players' computer will act as the host. This player's machine will receive information from the different players, determine what is happening in the game and then redistribute this information to the other client machines, in much the same way as a traditional dedicated server would, except that it is owned and operated by one of the players rather than by the publisher.[27] It should be noted that this kind of

---

[26]While it is possible for games to fill this role by having every client exchange information with every other client, this requires a lot of duplicate work and is considerably slower than running all of the information through a single host. It is, therefore, not a viable option for many developers.

[27]For more information on different types of video game servers, see Fiedler (2010).

technology is not limited to video games and could be used for communicating any kind of data.

Players who are acting as hosts will typically, at the very least, be processing the IP addresses of other players. Depending on the software in question, they may also be processing other forms of personal data, such as real names or account details. Whether or not the host will be acting as a controller or a processor will likely depend on the particular software. Hosting software may not typically give any meaningful choices to the players in terms of the actual processing of data—this will be performed automatically. It may, therefore, be considered as analogous to a situation where the server is hosted by a dedicated third party, with the physical host merely acting as a processor. However, there may be situations where the host does have sufficient choices over how and why the data is processed that they should be considered a controller, or where it may be found that, by electing to use the service, the host has enabled the processing of personal data and, therefore, had sufficient control.[28] Equally, it is important to emphasize that simply providing software that can be used to host a server does not mean that the developer or publisher is the controller—this must depend on whether, in the factual circumstances in question, that party determines the purposes and means of the processing. This, then, is a potentially difficult scenario in which to ascribe general roles—and actors must be very careful to identify their positions and obligations in a particular factual scenario.

3.4 Peer-to-Peer File Sharing

In Windows 10, Microsoft introduced a feature called Delivery Optimization. This feature meant that once a computer had downloaded an update for the Windows operating system, it could be shared with other Windows computers on the same network.[29] This is a form of peer-to-peer distribution—instead of each user downloading the files from a central server owned by the controller, they download it from other users who already have a copy of the files. Windows is not alone in using peer-to-peer protocols to release or patch their software; it is a relatively common alternative to using dedicated servers. This is especially popular with not-for-profit companies or

---

[28] In this way, the situation may be seen as analogous to that in C-210/16 *Unabhängiges Landeszentrum für Datenschutz Schleswig-Holstein.*

[29] For more information, see Windows (2017) Configure Delivery Optimization for Windows 10 updates. Available at: https://docs.microsoft.com/en-us/windows/deployment/update/waas-delivery-optimization. Accessed 10 January 2018.

developers. For example, many Linux distributions encourage their users to download software via the torrent network to avoid having to host large and expensive file servers.[30] Equally, it is very easy for individuals to create such a system. There are many easy ways to share large files through torrenting software.[31] Torrent files are also a useful option for amateur developers. If one creates a program and releases updates for that program, but does not wish to (or cannot afford to) pay for server space to host those updates, a peer-to-peer patching system can be a sensible and effective way of distributing those updates. Such a system is cheap, relatively easy to establish and efficient at distributing data (provided that the userbase has enough peers).

At its most overt level, these files may simply contain personal data, in which case participating in the peer-to-peer network will, by necessity, involve the processing of that information. This is not, however, the only personal data that may be involved. A typical peer-to-peer network will involve a direct connection between peers, which requires the software client to know the IP address of the other people who are connected. Depending on the peer-to-peer software in question, it may also transfer things like usernames or other potentially personal information. When any of these occur, the client may be transferring, storing, using or otherwise processing personal information. The question is whether they are doing so as a controller or as a processor.

Often, the body which initiates the distribution, or who is responsible for deciding to use the peer-to-peer system, should be treated as a controller, since they are the party who determines the purpose and means of the processing. Whether or not the client will be acting as a controller or a processor will depend on the system itself. For example, if the peer-to-peer protocol operates in the background of a patching program, the users will have no control over what happens and it is likely that they will merely be considered a processor. Equally, it is argued that a user would still be a processor if they were simply able to decide whether they wanted to turn off the peer-to-peer connections; or could choose how much bandwidth to use, or how many peers could connect. This is because they would not have any real choices about the purpose and means of the processing—their choices would be limited to technical decisions. The more control which the user gains, however, the more likely it is that they would be considered a controller.

---

[30] See, e.g., Debian. Downloading Debian CD images with BitTorrent. Available at: https://www.debian.org/CD/torrent-cd/. Accessed 10 January 2018.

[31] See, e.g., the instructions on creating a torrent with the Vuze client. Available at: https://blog.vuze.com/2014/01/23/vuze-101-how-to-create-a-torrent-file/. Accessed 22 January 2018.

3.5 Blockchain

Blockchain technology[32] is a way of storing and maintaining a database without the need to have a single authoritative version of that database.[33] Instead of keeping the database in a single location with a single administrator, the information is shared between multiple computers and servers.[34] When a change is made, it is then propagated to other clients, who share it with others.[35] As a result, individuals who maintains a copy of the Blockchain will download, store, verify and share the details of every transaction.[36] We can assume that there will be Blockchains which contain personal data (which could be as subtle as the IP address of the person who added a particular block,[37] or as overt as a Blockchain which contains the names and addresses of certain individuals). Where this occurs, each act of downloading, storing, verifying and sharing information will constitute a processing of that data.

The question which remains is, when personal data is stored in a Blockchain, who is the controller and who is the processor? As with peer-to-peer file sharing, this will largely depend on the factual circumstances in question. There are many situations where a controller may wish to create a Blockchain, but will not allow the peers who maintain it to actually add to the record or use the information in any way.[38] This may be done if, for example, the system uses a Blockchain in the backend of the service. Since more peers will increase the data integrity in the Blockchain, a controller may wish to require anybody who uses their service to maintain a copy. These users will not make any decisions about the purpose and means of the processing, so will likely only be considered as processors. By contrast, if the Blockchain is designed in such

---

[32]It could be argued that, given the fundamental incompatibilities between Blockchain and the right to erasure, nobody will be willing to place personal data in a Blockchains. Even assuming that this is true (which is not guaranteed, since it ignores actors who do not know or care about the GDPR, or actors who mistakenly believe that the information is not personal), for the purposes of this chapter, the term "Blockchain" should be taken to include "Blockchain-like" technologies. This could include, for example, a system which uses similar protocols but which has been designed to allow for the removal of information in certain circumstances.

[33]This database is often described as a "distributed ledger." See, e.g., UK Government Office for Science (2016).

[34]UK Government Office for Science (2016), p. 5.

[35]Key to Blockchain technology is the way in which it protects the integrity of the record despite the lack of any authoritative version. While interesting, an examination of this aspect (and the legal problems surrounding it) is outside of the scope of this Chapter.

[36]There is a difference between so-called "full clients" and "node clients," with the former maintaining a complete record of the Blockchain and the latter only containing partial records. If a node client needs data which it does not hold, it will download a copy from an authorized node. Assuming that not all records contain personal data, it is less likely that node clients will contain personal data (by virtue of holding fewer records), but it is not necessary to distinguish between the two for the purposes of this chapter.

[37]Dynamic IP addresses were confirmed as capable of being personal data by the CJEU in C-582/14 *Breyer*. They are also likely to be considered "online identifiers" for the purposes of Article 4 (1).

[38]This could be done with a permissioned Blockchain, where only certain, authorized users are able to add new blocks. Any changes made by non-authorized users will be rejected.

a way that every peer will be able (or even expected) to write new information and to freely decide when (and how) to use the data in the Blockchain, it is more likely that they will be considered controllers. Most cases will likely be somewhere in the middle of these two extremes.

3.6 The Implications of Amateur Processors

Each of the situations set out above demonstrates the potential benefits of using amateur actors as controllers or processors. By expanding the different forms of processing, we enable more opportunities, which can provide both economic benefits (e.g., where it is more efficient to use a listen server than a dedicated one) and social ones (e.g., the ability for researchers to use distributed computing rather than needing to have a dedicated super computer). However, as noted in Sect. 2, these amateur actors are likely to have difficulty in understanding their legal obligations under the GDPR. In another situation, an analysis may at this point turn to the oft-repeated maxim *ingorantia juris non excusat*: Ignorance of the law excuses not. If you make a mistake and unknowingly break the law, you must bear the consequences of that action. As a result, if you do not perform the necessary research before becoming a controller or a processor, you cannot (legally) complain if you end up being penalized for failing to meet your obligations.

There are, however, difficulties applying this maxim here. Even assuming that we can agree that it is right for the law to punish individuals for failing to comply with incredibly complicated regulations, this situation would vastly undermine the practical effectiveness of the GDPR. As one of the purposes of the provisions in the GDPR is to provide a "consistent and high level of protection" for data subjects,[39] it is insufficient to simply say that amateur actors will be punished for failing to comply with their obligations if we cannot reliably assume that this punishment will lead to an increase in compliance.

The situation is further complicated by the requirements of the Article 28 (1) guarantee. As outlined above, there are many situations where a person or company, acting as a controller, may wish to utilize processors who do not necessarily understand their legal obligations (or even realize that they are processors). In another area of law, one may be satisfied with laying out the counterparty's obligations in a contract; if the counterparty does not read it and agrees anyway, the first party has done all that they can reasonably do to ensure compliance and the relevant liability rests with the counterparty. The requirement of the Article 28 (1) guarantee, however, means that controllers cannot rely on this approach. Recital 81 states that the guarantee should relate, "in particular," to "expert knowledge," "reliability and resources" and the ability to "implement technical and organizational measures" which ensure safe and compliant processing. This has been described as a "high bar";[40] simply

---

[39] The GDPR, Recital 10.
[40] Webber (2016), p. 11.

requiring a processor to agree that they "agree to the terms and conditions" is unlikely to be sufficient. As a result, there is a risk that the GDPR could curtail the desirable usage of such amateur processors.

Fortunately, the GDPR does make some steps to resolving these issues. Under Article 28 (3), the relationship between controllers and processors must be governed by a contract. If used correctly, this contract can be a very powerful tool for helping amateur processors to understand their obligations under the law. Further, there are other tools which controllers can take which will allow them to ensure that amateur processors are acting within the law. The next two sections will examine these approaches, before Sect. 6 turns to wider regulatory discussions.

4   The Contractual Approach

Under Article 28 (3), all processing by a processor "shall be governed by a contract or other legal act…that is binding on the processor."[41] The article further sets out a number of provisions which must be included in the controller/processor agreement, including details about the processing and a number of the processor's legal responsibilities. This agreement will be easier to implement in some of the circumstances identified in Sect. 3 than in others.

4.1   Entering into the Controller/Processor Agreement

The starting point for this analysis should be that the requirements are more likely to be implemented in cases involving at least one professional actor (whether as a business or an individual acting professionally). This is because, although not necessarily the case, professional actors are more likely to have legal advice and, therefore, actually know when it is necessary to implement such a contract. By contrast, amateur actors are less likely to obtain legal advice before processing information, or even necessarily be aware that they should do so. Increasing the likelihood of amateur awareness must, therefore, be a priority. Supervisory Authorities must ensure that they are promoting the spread of information about controller's responsibilities, as well as helping to provide guidance about when an individual is an amateur controller or processor.[42] Another way to raise awareness may also be to encourage developers

---

[41] It is assumed for the purposes of this chapter that the controller will take the necessary steps to ensure that the contract is legally valid and enforceable. Due to the fact that these requirements vary from jurisdiction to jurisdiction, methods of integrating these steps into the contract are outside of the scope of this chapter.

[42] It is notable that the guidance for controllers given by the UK Information Commissioner's Office website is largely presented under a section entitled "For organization": https://ico.org.uk/. Accessed 13 September 2018. The same is also true of the Finnish Supervisory Authority: https://tietosuoja.fi/en/home. Accessed 13 September 2018.

who create software to include a notice for users: "If you use this program, you may be acting as a controller or a processor under the GDPR and should be aware of your legal responsibilities." Outside of increased education, it is difficult to see many ways to reliably improve this issue.

Assuming that the controller is aware of their obligation to enter into a contract with the processor, the next challenge is how they will actually enter into the controller/processor agreement. Article 28 (9) explicitly states that this agreement can be in an electronic form, although it must be in writing. With a professional processor, this should be relatively easy, even when the controller is acting in an amateur capacity—as noted above, many professional processors will provide the agreement as part of their standard terms and conditions, particularly where they market their services to individuals. With an amateur processor, however, this may be more difficult.

In many of the situations involving an amateur processor outlined in Sect. 3, the processor will be processing the information with software that is distributed by the controller. Here, it should be comparatively easy for the controller to integrate the agreement into the normal use of that software. One way to do this may be by presenting the agreement in a "click-wrap" form, where the user is not able to run the program, or at least certain elements of it, until they have agreed to the contract. This agreement could either be displayed at the time of installing the program, when the program is first used, or when the user first attempts to use certain features of the service. Many pieces of software use click-wrap agreements to display the End User License Agreement (EULA) and it would be relatively trivial to add the controller/processor agreement to these screens. Alternatively, it may be possible to host the contract online, either as part of an account creation process or when users are downloading the software. However, unless the software has some way of verifying that the agreement has been made (e.g., the user must log into an account), this may have a low success rate as it does not account for individuals who get the software from other sources (e.g., from unofficial download mirrors, or simply from another person).

Entering into these agreements may be difficult where the software used to process the personal data is not provided by the controller. For example, where the processor is a web host, they will typically use their own server software and only receive the content (e.g., in the form of HTML files) from the controller. Although it may be possible to hide the files behind some sort of agreement, this will not always be feasible. Where this applies, the controller will have to actively engage with the processor in order to get them to agree to the controller/processor agreement. The difficulty of this will depend on the exact nature of the relationship between the parties (e.g., how they communicate or how the files are transferred to the processor).

These solutions will work more easily in some situations than others. For example, new software can include these agreements as part of the original design and old software with the necessary patching function can (relatively easily) add these agreements to existing installations. However, this will not help with the large amounts of existing software which may involve the user acting as a processor but which has no way of updating itself. This is a problem as the GDPR will apply to all controller-processor relationships, regardless of when the relationship was formed or the age of the software which forms the basis of that relationship. Controllers whose programs operate in this way will need to come up with an inventive solution for the implementation of the necessary formalities.

4.2 Using the Controller/Processor Agreement to Promote GDPR Compliance

Let us assume that we have a controller who, first, is aware that they are acting as a controller, secondly, is aware that the counterparty is acting as a processor, thirdly, is aware of their legal obligations and, finally, is able to enter into a contract with that party contract (either by actively reaching out to the processor, or by including it as part of the processing software). Once we have reached this point, the controller/processor agreement offers an important opportunity for the controller. Under Article 28 (1), the controller may only use processors who can guarantee that they will meet the requirements of the GDPR and that they will ensure the protection of the data subjects. However, it should be assumed that most amateur processors will not immediately volunteer the necessary guarantees (not least because they may not know that they are required to do so) and that the controller will need to prompt them to provide them. One approach for doing this will be to simply include these guarantees as part of their contracts with the processor (either in the same contract or as a separate agreement).

The problem with this approach is that, as discussed above, many users do not read or understand privacy policies. If amateur processors have similar attitudes as they do when acting as data subjects, it is likely that many (if not most) would simply enter into the agreement without understanding or even actually reading it. As a result, simply requiring a user to click a box which says "I will comply with the requirements of the GDPR" or "I will comply with my above obligations" is unlikely to result in any real protection for data subjects and, therefore, is unlikely to be sufficient to provide the Article 28 (1) guarantees. What, then, can controllers do to increase the possibility of obtaining sufficient guarantees?

Despite the concerns about amateur actors neglecting to read the agreement properly, the first step to dealing with an amateur processor's lack of knowledge must be to explicitly tell them what they are required to do. Where an amateur processor has no legal knowledge or training, just telling the person that they are acting as a processor will not be sufficient as they are unlikely to understand what this actually entails. Equally, telling such a processor that they must comply with their GDPR obligations is unlikely to be enough—not least because there is no guarantee that the processor will be able to find out what these obligations are.

The difficulty will be to try and present this information in a way which maximizes engagement from the user. Merely copying and pasting the text of the GDPR into the contract (or some related document) is unlikely to actually inform an amateur processor—instead, it will simply result in long block of text which the user is increasingly unlikely to read and internalize. In order to ensure that an amateur processor will properly internalize their obligations, the contract must be laid out in an accessible way.

One technique which could be useful is the creation of standard contractual terms for use with amateur processors. This would, at the very least, be helpful in situations where both the controller and the processor are acting in an amateur role (e.g., the person who borrows space on a friend's server to host their blog) and may not know how to draft the required agreement. There would also be advantages for professional controllers dealing with amateur processors. Ideally, these terms would be drafted in a way that is easy to understand and follow, even for amateur actors. A controller would also be able to show that these terms are generally recognized as being understandable by processors and, therefore, the guarantees that are provided under them are more reliable. Equally, if an amateur processor acts on behalf of many controllers, standard terms between those agreements will help to simplify compliance and, hopefully, increase the chances that they take in their obligations.

Controllers would also do well to consider adapting various techniques used to make privacy notices more accessible. Under the GDPR, controllers must communicate with data subjects in an accessible way, using clear and plain language.[43] There is no legal obligation to present information to a processor in such a way and there are valid arguments against imposing such an obligation.[44] Nevertheless, even if there is no strict legal obligation to do so, controllers who wish to utilize amateur processors would be well-advised to write both their controller/processor agreements and any other communications in plain and clear language. This will help to ensure that the amateur processor is able to read, engage with and internalize the controller/processor agreement, which will make it easier to obtain the necessary guarantees.

For privacy notices, the ICO has recommended that controllers use a layered approach to drafting. This involves a first layer, containing the key information; a second (longer) layer, providing more detailed information; and, potentially, a third layer, which explores specific issues.[45] Layering the information in this way prevents readers from becoming overwhelmed and ensures that the information is accessible. This method could easily be transferred to controller/processor agreements. A click-wrap license could, for example, state "The processor agrees to comply with their obligations under the General Data Protection Regulation. Click here for more

---

[43] See, e.g., the conditions for consent under Article 7, the principle of transparency under Article 5 (1) as described in Recitals 39 and 58, and the communication of a personal data breach to a data subject under Article 34.

[44] Whereas data subjects are always natural persons who are protected by their human right to data protection under the EU Charter, Article 8, processors are often likely to be commercial entities. Any attempts to implement such a restriction on business-to-business transactions would likely be considered too strong an infringement on the freedom of contract.

[45] UK Information Commissioner's Office. Where should you deliver privacy information to individuals? Available at: https://ico.org.uk/for-organisations/guide-to-data-protection/privacy-notices-transparency-and-control/where-should-you-deliver-privacy-information-to-individuals/. Accessed 16 January 2018.

details." Clicking on the link would then take the reader to a section of the contract which contains the GDPR text (whether by jumping to an appendix; displaying the information in a dynamic, pop-out window; or through some other method). This approach is not limited simply to the general GDPR provisions with which the processor must comply, but can apply to most of the topics required to be included in the controller/processor agreement.

Another tool which could be used is the addition of images used to illustrate or summarize the agreement. This approach has already been endorsed in other areas of the GDPR: Article 12 (7) states that information which must be given to data subjects may be provided "in combination with standardized icons in order to give...a meaningful overview of the intended processing." It further states that the icons can be used if they give that overview in "an easily visible, intelligible and clearly legible manner." As with layered privacy notices, there is no reason why this should be restricted to controller-data subject interactions. The use of icons has been very effective with, for example, the Creative Commons licensing scheme.[46] This approach naturally encourages combination with layered privacy notices; an icon can be used to help represent the first layer, with more detail being available. Assuming that some form of standard icons can be found, it may be possible to allow amateur processors to identify the terms of the contract more quickly.

A more extreme possibility is the use of "comic contracts."[47] These are contracts where "the parties to the contract are represented by the characters; the content of the agreement is represented by the visual interaction of the parties, and is signed by the parties."[48] It is unclear how useful this may be with controller/processor agreements. While some GDPR obligations may be easy to explain in comic format (e.g., providing of information to supervisory authorities, or certain arrangements relating to security of processing), others are often quite precise or technical. If it is possible to represent these terms in comic form, this may be an extremely useful tool (particularly with younger processors), but the challenge will be finding a way that does this more clearly than using text and symbols, as described above.

It should, however, be noted that the use of novel contractual forms cannot be taken too far as Article 28 (3) requires that the controller/processor agreement be made "in writing." While, therefore, a controller may wish to utilize these tools to help obtain the Article 28 (1) guarantee, they cannot be relied upon for the requirements under Article 28 (3) itself. Nevertheless, it would be strange to find that the inclusion of symbols and comics means that the contract is no longer "in writing," provided that the represented terms are also explicitly laid out in text. In this way, comics and images may be useful as a layering tool, but should not be relied upon to form the entire agreement.

---

[46]Creative Commons. About the Licenses. Available at: https://creativecommons.org/licenses/. Accessed 16 January 2018.

[47]See Haapio et al. (2017).

[48]Haapio et al. (2017), p. 6.

4.3 The Problem with the Contractual Approach

The contractual tools laid out above may go some way to helping to ensure that amateur processors fulfill their obligations under the GDPR. However, it is argued that this approach is still relatively unreliable and may not be capable of providing the sufficient guarantees required. For example, while each of the approaches to improving user engagement discussed above may increase the chances of an amateur processor reading, understanding and acting upon their contractual (or statutory) obligations, it is doubtful that any of them will be enough to reach the "high level" required by Article 28 (1). Lannerö attempted to create a "Common Terms" system, under which a website would allow users to click a button to preview the terms and conditions, without having to read the entire agreement. While testing this system, Lannerö found that, without any option to preview the terms, only 1–2% of users would click to open the full terms and conditions, whereas when the system was implemented, 10% of users would take advantage of the ability to preview the terms.[49] This is a relatively large increase, which shows that users do respond to attempts to make terms and conditions more accessible. However, 10% of users is still far from the GDPR's standard of "shall only use processors providing sufficient guarantees"—and there is nothing to support a proposition that any of the above tools will be able to persuade the equivalent of Lannerö's remaining 90% to engage. Given the stiff fines for failing to meet the GDPR requirements,[50] it would seem foolish for a controller to rely solely on any of the approaches described in this section unless they were confident that 100% of processors will read, understand and comply with the obligations laid out in the agreement.

Further, while a court may be tempted to interpret Article 28 (1) as being satisfied by mere contractual terms (and while doing so would certainly make sense on both practical and commercial grounds), it is argued that this would not be in line with the underlying principles of the GDPR. If we start with the assumption that the number of amateur processors who read and understand the contract will be similar to those who read and understood privacy policies[51] (which, given Lannerö's findings, may itself be optimistically high), then assume (arguably fairly optimistically) that the use of layered notices, graphical representations and standard terms will further increase these numbers, it is still incredibly unlikely that we will ever reach 100% reading, comprehension and compliance. Inevitably, this will lead to data breaches and harm for data subjects. It would seem incompatible with the high protection required for data protection (as a human right, and as regularly stated is the goal of the GDPR) to allow controllers to claim that they were complying with the GDPR when they brought such processors onboard. While it may, therefore, be very business-friendly,

---

[49]Lannerö (2013), p. 19.

[50]Under Article 83 (4), infringement of the controller and processor obligations under Article 28 can be subject to a fine of up to €10,000,000 or 2% of total worldwide annual turnover of the preceding financial year, whichever is higher.

[51]See the discussion on the Eurobarometer study in Sect. 2.2.

we should reject any suggestion that such contractual terms are of sufficient reliability in relation to amateur actors.[52]

Contractual tools per se, then, are an important and necessary inclusion in the controller/processor relationship, but should not be relied upon as the only approach. When dealing with amateur processors, there is simply no guarantee that they will read, understand and comply with the terms of the agreement. Given the controller's liability if the processor fails to meet their various legal obligations, other tools must be employed. Section 5 will examine some different options which may be available.

5 Beyond Conventional Contracts

Having entered into a contract with an amateur processor, there are a number of extra steps that can be entered into to help obtain the Article 28 (1) guarantees. These steps can be broken down into two main approaches: The controller can either implement the measures on behalf of the processor (often by automating them as part of the processing software) or can help to make it as easy as possible for the processor to implement their own measures. This section will examine some examples where these approaches could be used.

5.1 Automated Measures

One of the biggest issues highlighted above is that controllers can present amateur processors with a list of their obligations, but there is no guarantee that the processor will actually read and comply with them. One solution to this issue is automation. Where the processor is not needed to actually perform an action, but instead simply must not interrupt certain automatic procedures, the controller can be much more certain that the event in question will occur, even if the processor has not actually read the agreement. Some of the approaches discussed below could be defined as a form of "Smart Contract." Smart Contracts have been given a range of definitions, with some simply requiring that the agreement be executed automatically,[53] and others insisting that the term should be reserved for contracts which are automated as part of a Blockchain.[54] It is the position of this chapter that it is unnecessary to artificially narrow the definition of "Smart Contracts" to those functioning through a particular technological approach. Further, for our purposes, it largely unnecessary to discuss the legally binding nature of Smart Contracts. The controller is not interested

---

[52] It should be stressed that this analysis does not extend to professional processors, where different presumptions and considerations are likely to be relevant. In such a situation, contractual terms may be considerably more reliable and may be satisfactorily found to be sufficient guarantees.

[53] See, e.g., Raskin (2017).

[54] See, e.g., Savelyev (2016).

in whether they can enforce any of the automated procedures ex post, but simply whether the automation ex ante provides a stronger guarantee that the process will occur.[55] This section will examine some of the different processor obligations under the GDPR and whether they could be automated.

One question which may be asked is whether a Smart Contract alone would be sufficient to fulfill the requirements of Article 28 (3) in a wider sense. Whether or not this may be theoretically (or legally) possible, it is argued that the controller should always include explicit, human-readable contractual arrangements. There are two main reasons for this. The first is that even if the amateur processor is acting on behalf of a professional controller, they are still natural people with an expectation of their human rights to privacy and home life. Many of the automating provisions that could be used to fulfill the GDPR obligations may be extremely invasive in a user's computer and could involve installing additional monitoring software, or software which restricts a person's use of their computer in some way. In order to ensure that these actions are proportionate to the processor's own expectations of privacy, the processor must be made aware (at least nominally) of what the programs are actually doing. The second reason is that by including these terms and provisions in both a "Smart Contract" and a "conventional contract," it is more likely that the obligation will be fulfilled through one route or the other. This will, therefore, make their guarantees more reliable, which will both allow the controller to be more confident that they are complying with Article 28 (1) and allow for a stronger protection for data subjects.

5.1.1 Documented Instructions

Under Article 28 (3) (a), the controller/processor agreement states that the processor will only process personal data "on documented instructions" from the controller. It does not provide any clarification for what form this documentation must take, although the ICO interprets this as requiring that they be written.[56] This lack of clarification has led to a lack of certainty. In interviews with Milla Keller, several legal practitioners said that they were unsure how to include instructions to processors in their contracts and how detailed these should be. One lawyer further wondered if online training could qualify as "instructions."[57]

When the processing takes place as part of software distributed by the controller, the code which constitutes that software could be considered as "instructions." Prima facie, this would fit with the text of the GDPR: Code is documented and does act as a set of instructions for the processor's computer. Where the processor has no real

---

[55] One may ask why the controller does not simply attempt to replace the entire controller/processor agreement with a Smart Contract. The reason for this, as will be demonstrated below, is simply that it would not be possible to automate all of the requirements in Article 28 (3).

[56] See UK Information Commissioner's Office. Contracts. Available at: https://ico.org.uk/ for-organisations/guide-to-the-general-data-protection-regulation-gdpr/accountability-and-governance/contracts/. Accessed 18 January 2018.

[57] Keller (2017), p. 55.

opportunity for manual interaction with the data, other than running the software on their machine (e.g., as in the case of BOINC software, or where the processor is hosting a listen server for a video game), the only instructions which are necessary are those relating to the software's code—the processor has no input over the processing and any further instructions would serve no purpose. This interpretation also allows for accountability as, provided that the code is not set to delete itself, it will be possible to review the record of the instructions. Finally, even if we accept the ICO's requirement that the documentation be written, this will be satisfied—albeit the instructions will be written in a programming language, rather than in English, Finnish or German etc. This interpretation, therefore, allows for a simple execution of the legal requirements, without sacrificing the level of protection to data subjects.

This becomes more ambiguous if the user has the ability to interact with the data, or if the software is designed to make more dynamic choices, meaning that it may not always be so easy to determine the consequences of the processing simply by reading the code. Certainly, where the data subject has the option to interact, they should be given some form of instruction on how to interact. However, this type of instruction could also, in theory, be integrated into the program itself (e.g., through the inclusion of a help menu).

It is unclear in the GDPR how specific the instructions must be. Clearly, they cannot be so vague as to mean that the controller no longer determines the purposes and means of the processing; if this were the case, the parties would be joint controllers, rather than controller and processor. Nevertheless, it is argued that "catch-all" instructions should be considered valid. Requiring the instructions to be specific to each instance or circumstance of processing would be extremely onerous for controllers and processors and unlikely to be practically feasible. Further, such a requirement would not be in keeping with other provisions in the GDPR. It must be noted that records of processing activities (discussed below) do not need to relate to each individual processing act—rather, it is acceptable to record, for example, the "categories" of data subjects and personal data for each purpose of processing and a "general description" of the technical and organizational security measures. It would, therefore, be strange that the requirements for instructions are stricter than the requirements for records. This is particularly so as one of the reasons that the recording obligations were drawn as they are is due to concern about the onerous nature of keeping records[58]; this concern would be irrelevant if the parties already had incredibly detailed instructions which could easily be modified into records of processing. Whether or not the code is sufficient as "instructions" will, therefore, depend on the scope of direct interaction open to the processor, but we should not assume that even simply interaction will render the code insufficient.

---

[58] European Parliament LIBE Committee (2012), p. 326.

5.1.2 Records of Processing Activities

Article 30 (2) states that processors must "maintain a record of all categories of processing activities carried out on behalf of a controller." While the controller is not required to include this obligation in the controller/processor agreement, it is covered by the Article 28 (1) guarantee. The difficulty is that, given the potentially onerous nature of making records, many amateur processors may be unable to consistently comply with this requirement (particularly if they are acting as a volunteer). However, it would be extremely easy for this obligation to be automated by a processing program which is downloaded from the controller. For example, the controller could create the program so that these records are generated when the program is run, saving the output on the processor's computer, or even automatically transferring them to the controller.

Where this has been done, the controller simply needs a sufficient guarantee that the processor will run the client without disabling this function. The starting point for this is the inclusion of a term in the controller/processor agreement informing the processor that the software has this feature and that they should not disable it. Where the program is closed source, this should be relatively easy—the controller simply needs to ensure that there is no option to turn off the logging and the guarantee should be sufficiently reliable to satisfy the requirements of Article 28 (1). Where the program is open sourced, or where it is easy for the processor to modify the code, it may be more difficult. In such a situation, the controller would need to obtain some sort of extra guarantee from the processor that they will not modify this portion of the code, or that (if they do) they will leave the function intact.[59] The nature of this guarantee would depend on the exact processing in question; while it may be possible to automate checks for recording in some scenarios, it may not be possible in others.

5.1.3 Security of Processing

Article 28 (c) requires the controller/processor agreement to include a term stating that the processor will take "all measures required" to ensure the security of the processing under Article 32. In turn, Article 32 states that, "taking into account the state of the art, the costs of implementation and the nature, scope, context and purpose of the processing," as well as the level of risk for data subject rights, the controller and processor will implement "technical and organizational measures" that are "appropriate to the risk." This is a very flexible provision. Where the information is particularly sensitive or the chances of the information being leaked is potentially very high, it will require a lot of precautions. However, where the processing is more banal and the information is not particularly sensitive, the processor and the controller will have to do considerably less.

---

[59]In some scenarios, a party who alters the processing software may actually be considered to have become a controller for the sake of the processing. This will depend on the exact factual scenario and would free the controller of their obligation to obtain the Article 28 (1) guarantees.

In some situations, it may be relatively easy to integrate Article 28 (c) into the processing client. This may arise if, for example, all that is required is that the information be stored in an encrypted form and that the computer which performs the processing has an up-to-date antivirus service. In this scenario, the controller could create a program which will automatically encrypt and decrypt any personal data which it creates and uses, and which will not run unless it detects that the processor has such an antivirus installed. Importantly, it would not be necessary for the controller in this scenario to actually force the automatic installation of an anti-virus—all the program needs to do is ensure that the user cannot act as a processor if they do not have one installed. It must be remembered that the controller is not under an obligation to enact the processor's compliance, rather they are forbidden from using a processor who does not comply. In some cases (as with the maintenance of records discussed above), it may be sensible to create the program in such a way that it automates compliance for the processor. These will be cases where such automation is relatively easy and unobtrusive to implement, or where it would be difficult to find amateur processors without doing so. Nevertheless, there is a limit to what controllers should do. As noted above, processors have their own expectations of privacy. While it would be easy to bundle an antivirus installer with a client program, this would be extremely intrusive (and, depending on the antivirus in question, potentially quite invasive). One possible test is whether the automation is strictly related to the processing in question. While software which produces a record of processing runs exclusively as part of the processing and is not concerned with the amateur processor's other activities, an antivirus software would monitor the entire computer and would run even when the processing is not taking place. It should, therefore, be considered excessive and unduly invasive.

Where the requirements for compliance with Article 32 are more complicated, it may be impossible to automate compliance. For example, if the security of the processing requires that the processor take certain steps that cannot be automatically executed (e.g., not running the program while others are in the room to avoid them reading data from the screen, or using a dedicated password for the controller's website), there is no way for this to be integrated into the program. In such a scenario, controllers must try and find other ways of gaining the required guarantees.

5.1.4 Deletion or Returning of Personal Data

The GDPR, Article 28 (3) (g) states that the controller/processor agreement must include a provision stating that, at the controller's choice, the processor must delete or return all personal data to the controller at the end of the provision of processing services. As with record-keeping under Article 30 (2), this can be automated—software can be built such that, when it is closed, uninstalled or some other criteria occurs, the personal data that has been saved on the processor's computer is deleted. However, this does not necessarily mean that all of the personal data will actually be deleted. For example, depending on how and where the information is saved, it may be possible for a processor to make a copy of the information. Notably, it does not necessarily matter if this is done deliberately (e.g., by a processor who wishes to take a copy of that information for later consultation) or accidentally (e.g., simply by a back-up system saving the files to a storage location). If the processor has taken such a copy of the information and fails to delete or return it at the end of the processing services, they will be in breach of the controller/processor agreement.

We must, therefore, consider whether an agreed contractual term that the processor will delete or return the information, along with the inclusion of an auto-deleting function in the processing client and an agreement that the processor will not interfere with this process, is enough to constitute a sufficient guarantee. It is argued that this should be sufficient, provided that the agreement is sufficiently clear and the deletion procedure sufficiently reliable. To require a more active participation from the controller would be an unnatural interpretation of the phrase "sufficient guarantee" and would likely result in an incredibly invasive search of the amateur processor's computer. By providing the processor with a relevant tool and integrating its use into the agreement and the processing software, the controller can be sure that the processor has sufficient "reliability and resources" as per Recital 81. Further, the program itself should qualify as technical measures implemented by the processor, even if the tools were provided as a bundle by the controller. As a result, although it is not 100% certain that deletion will occur as contracted, the controller should be regarded as having received the sufficient guarantees from the processor under Article 28 (1).

5.2 Other Measures for Increasing Compliance

Where it is not possible for the controller to implement the technical or organizational measures on behalf of the processor, they should aim to make it as easy as possible for the processor to implement those measures on their own. As above, this is not because it is an active obligation for the controller, but rather because it will greatly increase the reliability of the guarantees from amateur processors and increase the likelihood that the guarantees will be sufficient (thus decreasing the controller's potential liability). Further, this will be a key element to increasing compliance where automation is insufficient (e.g., when the processor has the ability to disable logging, or when the security of processing requires physical steps be taken to secure a computer).

The GDPR, Article 28 (5) states that approved codes of conduct or certificates may be used as "an element to demonstrate compliance." It is incredibly unlikely that amateur processors will go through the effort and cost of obtaining a certificate to prove that they are compliant with the GDPR (not least because most of the situations described in Sect. 3 will not provide any direct remuneration for processors). However, it may be possible to encourage amateur processors to follow a code of conduct. Ideally, this code would be written in a way that is simple and easy to understand for amateur actors and may involve many of the elements discussed in Sect. 4 (e.g., the use of clear and plain language, or infographics).

Importantly, it may be possible to portray this code of conduct to the user in a way that is more accessible than a contract. For example, a processor may be more likely to read through the code if it is presented to them as a guide or instruction manual, rather than as a series of terms and conditions. Equally, unlike a contract, there is no requirement, per se, that the information be presented and agreed to at the start of the processing. The details of the code could be made easily available to processors, with controllers prompting them to read it at various stages (either as tooltips during the processing, or by integrating it as a click-wrap element, as discussed above). The difficulty with these codes, as with the contract, will be ensuring that they are designed in a way which maximizes processors' reading and engagement.

Unfortunately, a difficulty with codes of conduct is that the Article 29 Working Party (now replaced with the European Data Protection Board) has rejected codes for, inter alia, failing to use sufficient amounts of GDPR terminology. In a response to the mHealth Code of Conduct, the Working Party stated that while it "appreciates the effort to use a non-legalistic language," they were concerned that "if the language…differs too much from the GDPR, it will not provide enough clarification about the GDPR and may even not comply with it."[60] While staying within the terminology of the GDPR would ensure that the code was accurate, there is a concern that requiring too close a following of the GDPR's language will reduce the utility of codes of conduct. One of the most useful features of a code of conduct is the ability to allow people who do not understand legal terminology to comply with the rules without needing to consult a lawyer. There is, therefore, a need to ensure that codes of conduct can be written in a way that accurately reflects the GDPR requirements, but which does not necessarily get bogged down with the same complications and uncertainties.

Even where formal codes of conduct are not used, the guarantee is more likely to be sufficient if it does not have to rely on an amateur processor taking an unprompted initiative. This could, for example, take the form of prompts for users that appear as part of the processing program. For example, every time the program is run, a pop-up could appear which reminds the processor to check that they are in a private environment or perform some other action. These simple prompts will increase the reliability that a processor will perform their obligations, since it will no longer rely on an essentially untrained actor remembering all of their (potentially complicated) legal obligations. Equally, a controller can often introduce simple and easy-to-use tools to help an amateur processor act. For example, to help to guarantee that a processor will comply with their obligation to report data breaches under Article 33, the controller can create a simple messaging tool or provide an easily found email address.

Finally, depending on the processing in question, controllers may simply wish to help spread educational tools about a processor's GDPR obligations. This could be as simple as links to resources created by Supervisory Authorities or as advanced as creating educational videos that are specifically targeted to their processing. These

---

[60] Article 29 Working Party (2018), p. 3.

systems will help to provide a general level of education to processors and should help to increase the reliability of any guarantees.

6 The Regulatory Perspective

Sections 4 and 5 have laid out a number of ways that controllers can attempt to integrate their relationships with amateur processors into the GDPR structure. However, for the reasons outlined above, no matter how many steps a controller takes to increase the probability of compliance, we can still expect that an amateur processor is less likely to fulfill their obligations than a professional one. When an amateur processor does violate the agreement, the fact that the controller may have a claim against them will often be of little use—amateur processors are highly unlikely to be able to afford the huge sums of fines and damages dealt with by the GDPR. Nevertheless, as highlighted in Sect. 3, there are many valid, useful and desirable situations in which a controller may want to (or need to) utilize amateur processors. It is not, therefore, desirable to simply say that controllers should avoid using amateur processors.

Thus far, the chapter has largely approached the situation from the assumption that amateur processors will largely be subject to the same rules and requirements as professional processors. It is, however, worth considering whether they should be treated differently. One possible way to explore this issue is if the decision in *Lindqvist* were either narrowed or held to not apply to the GDPR. As the decision was made under the DPD, it is not technically binding under the GDPR (even though the wording of the DPD, Article 3 (2) and the GDPR, Article 2 (2) (c) are the same). If this were accepted, we could simply find that some of the individuals do not fall under the legal regime and, therefore, all of the difficulties discussed in Sects. 4 and 5 become irrelevant.

The requirement in Article 2 (2) (c) is that the person is acting "in the course of a purely personal or household activity." The use of the word "purely" implies that this would, therefore, only be capable of covering situations which involved both an amateur processor and an amateur controller. Already, then, a change to the rule arising from *Lindqvist* would not cover many of the scenarios raised in Sect. 3. Regardless, it is relatively unlikely that such a reversal would occur. Since *Lindqvist*, the Charter of Fundamental Rights of the European Union has come into force, which contains the human right to data protection in Article 8. The concern in *Lindqvist* (that publishing information online allows it to be accessed by in indefinite number of people)[61] still exists and poses a risk to this right. It would, therefore, seem strange if the decision would be reversed.

Another possible solution could be to embrace the position that was argued by Hon, Millard and Walden. This argument, which was made under the DPD, is that the mere provision of technical equipment should not be enough to mean that the provider is considered a processor (assuming that the party does not also provide storage for that data). The reasoning behind this argument is that the provider does

---

[61]C-101/01 *Lindqvist*, para. 47.

not actually "process" the information in a true sense; rather, the controller processes the information on hardware which happens to belong to another party.[62] Under this argument, the user who allows a publisher to host a game server on their computer, or the individual who lends their processing power to a BOINC project would not be considered a processor—simply the provider of a computer which is being used by the controller.

The difficulty with this approach is that, as with a reversal of *Lindqvist*, it would significantly weaken the protection for data subjects. Even if the information were not saved permanently on the machine, it would still exist on that computer for a period of time, at which point it is vulnerable. In order to ensure an adequate protection for data subjects, we may need to impose certain obligations on the person who is responsible for that machine (e.g., in relation to security of the processing, or the obligation to only process the data as instructed). Under the GDPR, this is achieved by treating that person as a processor and, if we were to exclude the owner from that class without another way of imposing obligations, this would leave a serious hole in the regulatory regime. This argument is endorsed by recent case law. Under the DPD, a mere temporary caching will qualify as processing.[63] Assuming that this applies to the GDPR (and there is no reason to rebut this assumption), this will automatically bring the provider of equipment within the definition of a "processor."[64]

Attempts to remove amateur processors from the GDPR's scope altogether are, therefore, unlikely to be particularly successful or desirable. The Article 29 Working Party pointed out that the concept of "processor" was created to prevent controllers from reducing the level of protection by having others perform the processing.[65] As the potential harm suffered by data subjects will be the same whether their data is processed by amateur or professional processors, this justification applies equally in both scenarios. Moreover, this justification arguably becomes even stronger—the controller will often be using amateur processors as a free alternative to a professional one and, as has been shown, amateur actors are less likely to know how to deal with personal data in a way that the law deems sufficient, thus meaning that harm may be more likely. It would, therefore, seem strange that we would allow the controller to avoid the legal obligations by electing to choose the cheaper and less secure option.

Although we, therefore, should reject options which take amateur processors outside of the GDPR, it may still be possible to ease the regulatory burden. During the discussions in Sects. 4 and 5, a number of ambiguous scenarios were highlighted, where controllers may be able to take certain steps towards compliance, but where it is uncertain if these will satisfy the legal requirements (e.g., whether code can qualify as instructions). Where such ambiguities exist, it would be incredibly helpful if some guidance were issued which resolved the issues in a way which allows for controllers to safely deal with amateur processors. This could come from, for example, the

---

[62] Hon et al. (2012), pp. 9–11.

[63] C-131/12 *Google Spain SL v Agencia Española de Protección de Datos (AEPD)*, paras. 24–28.

[64] For the sake of fairness, it should be highlighted that this decision was given after Hon, Millard and Walden's article was published.

[65] Article 29 Working Party (2010), p. 24.

European Data Protection Board or the CJEU. Equally, it would be helpful if the Board, the Commission and the local Supervisory Authorities promoted the creation of appropriate codes of conduct and standard contractual terms which could be used in these scenarios. Ultimately, the most helpful regulatory approach will simply be adopting an interpretive stance that recognizes that amateur processors are a desirable part of data processing and attempts to enable, rather than discourage, their use.

7 Conclusion

The growth of both amateur controllers and amateur processors is inevitable in the online environment. Given the Internet's removal of the barriers between companies and individuals, and the increasingly attractive opportunities for individuals to process data on behalf of other people, it is likely that this trend will only increase as time goes on. The difficulty, as shown by this chapter, is integrating these amateur actors into a relatively complicated legal regime.

In some situations, this will not create novel situations. Amateur controllers have been interacting with professional processors for a long time. Although these relationships look a little atypical (as the processor, practically speaking, may hold much more power than the controller), they have already been integrated into the law. Although these situations can be difficult for amateur controllers, professional processors may often be able to help guide the controller to ensure that their relationship is legally compliant.

The analysis in this chapter has suggested that the more difficult situations are those involving amateur processors. The first situation is where both the controller and the processor are acting in an amateur fashion. While these actions may sometimes be outside of the scope of the GDPR, many processing activities will still fall under the law. This creates the risk that neither party will know their obligations and will have no chance of complying with the law. This is an unfortunate situation, but one which can only be resolved with general education of the public.

The majority of this chapter has focused on situations involving a professional controller and an amateur processor. It is worth emphasizing that the analysis of this relationship will, largely, also apply to situations involving an amateur controller, assuming that this amateur controller is actually aware of their legal obligations. The risk in this situation is that the amateur processor will act in much the same way as the majority of data subjects—they will agree to the controller's terms and conditions, but will not read or understand them. As controllers are obligated under the law to only use processors who have agreed to certain terms and who offer sufficient guarantees of GDPR compliance, this is insufficient. Clearly, in some situations, such processing activities should be ceased if it is impossible to ensure appropriate protection for data subjects. Notwithstanding these instances, this chapter has explored a number of ways which can allow amateur processors to be used, including the use of simple contractual language, the strategic positioning of contractual terms, the inclusion of smart-contract-like tools to automate processor obligations, and the creation of tools and guidelines intended to help processors understand and enact their obligations.

This chapter finished by looking at the issue from a regulatory perspective. It is important that these actors remain within the scope of the GDPR so that data subjects retain sufficient protection; we must, therefore, make sure that the law is interpreted in a way which enables them to act in a realistic manner. It is desirable that we do not create a regulatory situation which imposes a de facto ban on amateur processors, who can make valuable contributions to society.

Ultimately, this chapter finds that amateur controllers and processors can be integrated into the existing GDPR structure. What is important is that all of the relevant actors are aware of the ways in which these parties differ from professional controllers and processors—and that they take this into account when ensuring that they are providing adequate protection for data subjects.

References

Article 29 Working Party (2010) Opinion 1/2010 on the concepts of "controller" and "processor"

Article 29 Working Party (2018) Letter to Mr. Graux, "Subject: your letter of 7th December 2017 and a new draft code of conduct with the request of a positive opinion from the WP29 under the Data Protection Directive" http://ec.europa.eu/newsroom/article29/item-detail.cfm?item_id=625391. Accessed 11 July 2018

Bitcoin (2018) Bitcoin Developer Guide https://bitcoin.org/en/developer-guide. Accessed 9 Jan 2018

Eurobarometer (2011) Special Eurobarometer 359: Attitudes on Data Protection and Electronic Identity in the European Union http://ec.europa.eu/public_opinion/archives/ebs/ebs_359_en.pdf. Accessed 12 Jan 2018

European Parliament LIBE Committee (2013) Report on the proposal for a regulation of the European Parliament and of the Council on the protection of individuals with regard to the processing of personal data and on the free movement of such data (General Data Protection Regulation). COM(2012)0011- C7-0025/2012–2012/0011(COD), A7-0402/2013 http://www.europarl.europa.eu/sides/getDoc.do?pubRef=-//EP//NONSGML+REPORT+A7-2013-0402+0+DOC+PDF+V0//EN. Accessed 17 Jan 2018

Fiedler G (2010) Game Networking https://gafferongames.com/categories/game-networking/. Accessed 12 Jan 2018

Haapio H, Plewe D, de Rooy R (2017) Contract continuum: from text to images, comics and code. https://ssrn.com/abstract=2928604. Accessed 27 Sept 2018

Hon W, Millard C, Walden I (2012) Who is responsible for 'personal data' in cloud computing?—The cloud of unknowing. Part 2. Int Data Privacy Law 2(1):3–18

Keller M (2017) Data processor's responsibilities under the general data protection regulation. LLM Thesis, University of Helsinki, Helsinki

Lannerö P (2013) Fighting the biggest lie on the internet: common terms beta proposal. http://www.commonterms.net/commonterms_beta_proposal.pdf. Accessed 16 Jan 2018

Raskin M (2017) The law and legality of smart contracts. Georgia Law Tech Revue 1:305–341

Savelyev A (2016) Contract Law 2.0: "Smart" contracts as the beginning of the end of classic contract law. Russian National Research University Higher School of Economics Working Paper. WP BRP 71/LAW/2016//ssrn.com/abstract = 2885241. Accessed 18 Jan 2018

UK Government Office for Science (2016) Distributed Ledger Technology: beyond block chain

UK Information Commissioner's Office. Data controllers and data processors: What the difference is and what the governance implications are https://ico.org.uk/media/1546/data-controllers-and-data-processors-dp-guidance.pdf. Accessed 10 Jan 2018

UK Information Commissioner's Office. Contracts https://ico.org.uk/for-organisations/guide-to-the-general-data-protection-regulation-gdpr/accountability-and-governance/contracts/. Accessed 18 Jan 2018

UK Information Commissioner's Office. Where should you deliver privacy information to individuals? https://ico.org.uk/for-organisations/guide-to-data-protection/privacy-notices-transparency-and-control/where-should-you-deliver-privacy-information-to-individuals/. Accessed 16 Jan 2018

Webber M (2016) The GDPR's impact on the cloud service provider as a processor. Privacy Data Protect Law 16(4):11–14

The Lawyer of the Future as "Transaction Engineer": Digital Technologies and the Disruption of the Legal Profession

Mark Fenwick and Erik P. M. Vermeulen

Abstract This chapter introduces two connected arguments about the future of the legal profession. First, the ongoing "digital revolution" will continue to disrupt legal work as it has traditionally operated. Various aspects of this disruption are outlined. Second, in contrast to previous technological revolutions, the "deployment" of disruptive innovation in the context of the digital revolution seems unlikely to be primarily "state-led." Instead, new technologies will be deployed by a coalition of diverse private actors (entrepreneurs, technologists, consultants, and other professionals) working in collaboration. Crucial amongst these actors will be the lawyer of the future operating as "transaction engineer." The chapter outlines this transaction engineer function and its importance in the deployment of emerging digital technologies.

Keywords Blockchain · Digital revolution · Disruptive innovation · Lawyers · Legal profession · Smart contracts

1 "Digital Revolution"

Over the last half-century, digital technologies have transformed the world. Code is the invisible architecture structuring everyday life.[1] This development is the essence of the digital transformation . As such, the "digital revolution" refers to the shift from

---

[1] See, e.g., Lessig (2006), Mitchell (1995).

M. Fenwick (✉)
Graduate School of Law, Faculty of Law, Kyushu University, Fukuoka, Japan
e-mail: mdf0911@gmail.com

E. P. M. Vermeulen
Department of Business Law, Tilburg University, Tilburg, The Netherlands

E. P. M. Vermeulen
Legal Department, Philips Lighting, Amsterdam, The Netherlands

© Springer Nature Singapore Pte Ltd. 2019
M. Corrales et al. (eds.), *Legal Tech, Smart Contracts and Blockchain*,
Perspectives in Law, Business and Innovation,
https://doi.org/10.1007/978-981-13-6086-2_10

"analog," electronic and mechanical devices to computer-based, "digital" technologies. This process began in earnest with the launch of the Intel microprocessor in California in the early 1970s and is ongoing.

"Digitalization" has been driven by a series of technological developments. Most significantly:

i. Cheaper and smaller digital hardware (first PCs and, more recently, smartphones);
ii. Global communication networks and mass connectivity (the Internet);
iii. Cloud-based data storage and automated algorithms;
iv. Emerging digital technologies (e.g., robots/automation, AI, the Internet of Things, and "Blockchain").

Crucially, these technologies "amplify" each other, that is to say, they are "self-reinforcing."[2] There are significant synergies *between* technologies that feed the exponential growth of further new technologies, as well as create new business opportunities. As such, we live in an age of constant fast-moving technological innovation. The economic, cultural, and social impact of these changes is so significant that it makes sense to speak of a "digital transformation" or "revolution."

This chapter makes two connected arguments about the future of the legal profession. First, the ongoing "digital revolution" will continue to disrupt legal work as it has traditionally operated. Various aspects of this disruption are outlined (Sect. 2). Second, in contrast to previous technological revolutions, the "deployment" of disruptive innovation in the context of the digital revolution seems unlikely to be primarily "state-led." Instead, new technologies will be deployed by a coalition of diverse private actors (entrepreneurs, technologists, consultants, and other professionals) working in collaboration. Crucial amongst these actors will be the business lawyer of the future operating as "transaction engineer." The chapter outlines this transaction engineer function and its importance in the deployment of emerging digital technologies (Sect. 3).

2 The Legal Profession Disrupted

New technologies are disrupting traditional legal practice and create new challenges and opportunities for the reinvention of the profession. Three aspects of this disruption are highlighted here: "Legal Tech" and the disruption of legal practice (Sect. 2.1); digital technologies and the disruption of transactions and organizations (Sect. 2.2); and, the proliferation of transnational legal risk and the disruption of traditional state-centered forms of legal expertise (Sect. 2.3). As a consequence of these changes, the lawyer of the future will operate under conditions of permanent cognitive and normative uncertainty.

---

[2]Fenwick and Vermeulen (2018).

2.1 "Legal Tech" and the Disruption of Legal Practice

Legal technology—or "Legal Tech"—is changing many aspects of how lawyers practice law. In this context, Legal Tech refers to platforms, IT services, and software that first made law firms and lawyers more efficient in performing their core activities.[3] Practice management, document storage, and automated billing and accounting software are prominent examples of how technology has affected such core tasks. Legal Tech also plays an increasingly important part in assisting legal professionals in the due diligence and discovery processes.

Legal Tech has evolved from support systems to fully integrated and automated services for lawyers that increasingly disrupt the practice of law. Legal Tech can now be understood broadly as including information technology services and software, as well as platforms and their applications. Since the 1970s, with the invention of the first legal databases. Legal Tech has supported the need for additional lawyers to evaluate the new and increasing numbers of legal materials made available faster and more easily accessible by technology.

At first, Legal Tech made law firms and lawyers more efficient in performing their activities. Examples include automated billing, document storage, practice management, and accounting software. In the early 2010s, Legal Tech became more advanced and started to incorporate technology that assisted legal professionals in due diligence and e-discovery processes. Since 2015, Legal Tech has continued to evolve in unprecedented ways. Multiple start-up companies and their investors have started to capitalize on technologies, and their applications are already replacing some junior lawyers and disrupting the existing parameters for the practice of law.

Four categories of start-ups in Legal Tech can be distinguished. The first category includes start-up companies that offer a range of online legal services, removing the in-person legal consultation process and guidance process for clients. The second legal start-up category involves online "matching" platforms that connect lawyers with clients. Such platform start-ups help consumers find a fitting lawyer without the costly involvement of a law firm. The third category entails start-ups that use AI tools to take over their lawyer time consuming and expensive legal research activities such as reviewing, understanding, evaluating, and reapplying contracts. Finally, start-ups with expertise in Blockchain technology attempt to replace lawyers as intermediaries in certain types of transactions.

The decentralization of law that is a central part of the start-up companies' purpose and that disrupts existing legal practices has broad repercussions for the legal profession. First, existing legal services are rendered increasingly irrelevant or will be replaced by Legal Tech. Junior legal professionals and legal support staff are likely to be the first victims of the Legal Tech evolution. Legal Tech applications will be able to perform most of the junior lawyers' work soon without the human elements that create imprecision, flaws, inaccuracies, possible lawsuits, and delay. Second, and more importantly, the legal profession will be forced by such start-up companies to innovate in perpetuity, a task that is not easily accomplished by overextended

---

[3] American Bar Association (2016).

and—often—cumbersome legal organizations that have, over time, lost the capacity for rapid re-invention.

Most radically, Legal Tech has the potential to rapidly transform law firms and legal departments into virtual law firms. Virtual law firms may dominate in the future. A virtual law firm is a platform with an emphasis on connecting legal and other professionals in a collaboration. When implemented successfully, the effect of the platform model will be the creation of a flexible and accessible community of professionals with different skills and experience. The bigger the community, the easier it is to offer solutions tailored to the needs of the clients. The virtual law firm model attracts a broad spectrum of law firms. One extreme is represented by the traditional law firm characterized by a hierarchy with partners at the top and varying levels of associates, paralegals, and non-lawyers below them. On the other end of the spectrum are those firms that adopt an "Airbnb-type" platform organization, mainly providing a matchmaking/coordination service. Enormous variations exist between the two extremes, depending on the level of implementation of Legal Tech.

Legal platforms adopt a variety of approaches. For instance, UpCounsel offers entrepreneurs on-demand access to experienced lawyers. LawyerlinQ in the Netherlands and Digitorney in Germany offer law firms the possibility to insource special knowledge and skills for more complex projects. Digitorney is one of the earliest start-ups known to the authors that also realized very quickly the need to bring law students into the new reality of virtual law firms early. Accordingly, Digitorney established the so-called "Junior Pool," as a way for law students to work very early in their careers on international mandates and help them develop a track record of excellence in a virtual law firm setting that allows them to take on more senior roles earlier in their careers. LexSemble is a crowdsourcing platform that allows multiple users to edit legal knowledge entries. The information gathered from the Cloud helps the platform to develop a machine learning analytics engine. This engine can be used to assist in legal decision-making and prediction activities.

Legal Tech is replacing the traditional role of legal professionals. Legal professionals play a crucial role in establishing trust and truth in legal transactions. They negotiate, draft, and interpret contracts and help enforce them; create laws and regulations that protect the weaker parties; and design structures that enable the registration and transfer of tangible property and intellectual property. Well-drafted legal contracts help establish trust and confidence in the validity of the transaction and the economic benefits of the transaction for the contracting parties. Important matters, such as the truth about ownership and control, the transfer of ownership, and the allocation of risk and control, are typically covered in a contract. However, the dealmaking, matchmaking, gatekeeping, and enforcing roles are increasingly performed by technology. This trend is likely to accelerate soon, enabled by new technologies (such as Blockchain technology) and Smart Contracts.

But it will not stop here. Near future technological advances—most obviously, machine learning and deep learning—have already started to replace lawyers and other legal professionals. Artificial intelligence tools help clients to review, understand and even draft legal documents. Data analytics, machine learning, and deep learning are not only used to do legal research but also assist in legal decision-making and the prediction of legal cases. As such, there is no doubt that Legal Tech will automate a lot of legal work, such as contract drafting, legal risk management, and dispute resolution. If legal work will be dependent on and performed by algorithms in the future, it is crucial for the future lawyers (and lawyers who are at the start of their careers) to get a better understanding of "data analytics" and "artificial intelligence."

2.2 Smart Contracts and the Disruption of Transactions and Organizations

The term "Smart Contracts" was first introduced by Nick Szabo, a computer scientist, and legal theorist, in 1994.[4] A Smart Contract is a computer program code that enables the verification, execution, and enforcement of specific terms and conditions of a contractual arrangement. An often-cited example is the "purchase" of music through Apple's iTunes platform. A computer code ensures that the "purchaser" can only listen to the music file on a limited number of Apple devices.

A Smart Contract could also be an essential part of, for instance, a car loan. If the borrower misses a payment (tracked via a Blockchain-like technology), the contract will not allow the use and operation of the car ("enforced" via networked technologies that "disable" the car automatically, rather than a "repo man" physically depriving a driver of access to their car). Such Smart Contracts will become more prevalent in the growing world of the Internet of Things. As more devices are connected, the more "Smart Contracts" will be used to execute and enforce "legal transactions."

Smart Contracts will become more prevalent in the growing world of the Internet of Things. The more devices are connected to each other, the more "Smart Contracts" will be used to execute and enforce "legal transactions." There is no doubt that Smart Contracts are already disrupting traditional legal assumptions, doctrines, and concepts. For instance, it will give a boost to the sharing economy (with its implications for property law).

Moreover, Smart Contracts can be utilized to set up so-called "decentralized autonomous organization" (DAO) built on software, code, and Smart Contracts. Such organizations can challenge traditional corporation laws and disrupt our concept of organizations.[5] The idea was to set up a corporate-type organization using computer code without using conventional hierarchal and centralized structures. The DAO didn't have any directors, managers or employees. The governance structure was built with Smart Contracts that ran on the Blockchain platform, Ethereum.

This project launched in 2016 in Germany under the leadership of Christoph Jentzsch. The DAO intended to automate governance and was based on the idea that since "people" don't always follow the rules, it might be better to use computer code to manage an organization. In the DAO, this automated structure was intended to give participants ("investors") direct real-time control over decisions about how

---

[4] Szabo (1994).
[5] Jentzsch (2016).

contributed funds would be distributed to start-up projects. Investors could participate by purchasing DAO Tokens during a kind of crowdfunding campaign, an Initial Coin Offering.

DAOs are "merely" computer code. They don't have any directors, managers or employees. The governance structure is built with and on software, code and Smart Contracts that ran on a public decentralized Blockchain platform (in most cases Ethereum). This automated structure is intended to give "participants"/"investors" in the DAO direct real-time control over contributed funds and where such funds would be distributed.

Unfortunately, fundamental flaws in the DAO code made it possible for "hackers" to transfer one-third of the total contributed funds (US$150 million) to a subsidiary account. This and other technological limitations meant the end of the initiative. Some saw the failure as evidence that digital technologies will not easily solve corporate governance issues and it highlights concerns above about "untried technologies."[6]

Nevertheless, we shouldn't dismiss DAOs too quickly. DOAs fit in the flatter, decentralized and automated world that is slowly "eating away" at the old world of centralized and hierarchical organizations and authorities.[7]

More generally, similar technology-driven disruption can be seen across multiple sectors of the economy and society. Consider the following examples of how distributed ledger technology, for instance has the potential to disrupt various areas of social life and have important implications for the legal profession:

i. *Health and Wellbeing*: Blockchain technology will transform healthcare, giving the patient more control in the healthcare ecosystem by increasing the security, privacy, and interoperability of health data;

ii. *Agriculture and Food Security*: Consumers increasingly favor "clean" food. It is usually difficult to verify the integrity of products. A distributed ledger replacing the current supply chain would provide transparency. Fair price-setting and fast payments systems would also be facilitated;

iii. *Safe, Clean and Efficient Energy Supplies*: We are facing an aggressive growth in distributed energy resources. Think rooftop solar and electric vehicles, for example. Governments, utilities, and other stakeholders need new ways to regulate better the electricity grid. Blockchain has the potential to offer a reliable, low-cost solution for financial or operational transactions to be recorded and validated across the distributed network with no central point of authority.

In each case, a societal problem can be addressed via the use of Blockchain technology or Smart Contracts. With software code automating procedures and tasks, the focus of "knowledge work" is shifting from the routine "application of procedures" to designing the systems and standardized functions that are then performed by machines . In this way, the way tasks of lawyers are being disrupted and a more

---

[6]Birkinshaw (2018).
[7]Fenwick and Vermeulen (2018).

"tech-savvy" legal service provider is increasing required and expected. As the fields in which technology operate continues to expand, the demand for such legal services will only increase.

2.3 *"Net-Widening" and Expanding Transnational Legal Risk*

More generally, the broader context in which lawyers work is also changing. For example, there is the increase in normative uncertainty and complexity created by legal globalization and the expansion in transnational legal risk.[8] Again, the effect of expanding legal risk is to disrupt the traditional operations of many legal service providers.

Take as an example of expanding legal risk the increased extra-territorial application of many regulatory offences in fields such as environmental law, labor law or health and safety law.[9] In its most basic sense, this simply refers to the fact that the substantive norms of a particular jurisdiction are applied to corporate conduct that has occurred overseas. More recently, however, the territorial reach of corporate criminal law has extended further and the law of a particular jurisdiction is also applied to any corporation that issues securities or simply conducts part of its business in that jurisdiction, irrespective of where that corporation was established, where the firm's center of operations is located, or where the alleged wrongdoing took place. A company that has been established and has its center of operations in one jurisdiction, but issues shares in a UK-based stock exchange, for example, may be exposed to criminal liability in the UK for conduct occurring in either the UK, the companies home jurisdiction or a third country.

Consider the example of anti-corruption law. Contemporary efforts to engage with transnational corporate corruption can be traced back to the United States in the mid-1970s when, in the context of diminishing public trust with corporate and other power elites triggered by the Vietnam War, the civil rights movement and Watergate, the Carter administration enacted the Foreign Corrupt Practices Act (FCPA). The FCPA criminalized the payment of bribes to foreign government by any company issuing securities in US-securities markets, irrespective of where the bribe actually took place.[10]

The real complexities arise, however, when multiple jurisdictions extend the reach of their corporate criminal law in this way. The legal requirements of different legal systems may vary significantly or, at least, significant uncertainties may remain as to the precise extent of any overlap. Criminal law retains a strong national character and precise harmonization between substantive norms of jurisdictions is unlikely,

---

[8]Fenwick (2016).

[9]See Slaugher and Zaring (1997).

[10]On the FCPA generally, see Koehler (2012).

even in those cases where there is a shared legal tradition, a broad consensus around the nature of the underlying problem and an international treaty in place. Companies find themselves obliged to comply with the disparate normative requirements of multiple jurisdictions and enforcement agencies are obliged to conduct investigations transnationally and manage the resulting jurisdictional conflicts.

Again, consider the example of corporate corruption. In retrospect, the enactment of the FCPA can be seen as a foundational moment in the history of the new corporate criminal law, both in terms of the substance of the law and the attention that it attracted to the issue of transnational corporate wrongdoing. A series of international treaties followed, e.g., The OECD Anti-Bribery Convention, 1997 and The UN Convention Against Corruption, 2004.[11] More recently, a number of other important jurisdictions have expanded the scope of their domestic criminal laws, including Brazil, China, India and the UK, and a more aggressive attitude towards enforcement has been adopted. However, important differences between the different schemes—on issues such as facilitation payments, for example—still remain and create new complications for corporations.

A final complication arises from the fact that corporate criminal law is constantly changing. New laws are being made and older laws revised. The profile of legal risk for companies is rendered highly unstable and the uncertainties created by the fact of the relentless pace of criminal law reform itself becomes an additional source of legal risk. The instability of contemporary corporate criminal law—the fact that, at any moment, the law somewhere is being revised or reviewed—also has a transnational aspect.

The belief that universal principles—either formal or substantive—can provide a foundation for modern law is no longer credible. Rather, the basis of contemporary corporate criminal law is social "facts"—understood as contingent constructions of a particular social problem—and the political demands that surround those "facts." Crucially, both these "facts" (i.e., the contingent understanding of a particular problem) and the attendant political demands for action are constantly changing as perceptions of transnational corporate wrongdoing evolve.

In the context of political modernity, it has always been the case that the validity of law is a temporary state of affairs, subject to the countervailing wishes of the people as articulated through the legislature. Nevertheless, under contemporary conditions there is acceleration in the temporal instability of the validity of law. Social facts and their associated political demands are constantly changing (driven by a twenty-four hours news cycle and social media) and the profile of legal risk acquires a new instability. This more general shift—which results from economic globalization—adds to the technology-driven disruption of the legal profession outlined above.

---

[11] See Jordan (2012).

3   The Lawyer of the Future as "Transaction Engineer"

The result of the above changes is that legal professions now occupy a highly unstable space and are in an ongoing state of transition. In this section, we want to shift focus and discuss a different aspect of this issue and a possible future role for lawyers. We want to suggest, that in contrast to previous technological revolutions, the "deployment" of disruptive innovation in the context of the digital revolution seems unlikely to be "state-led." Instead, new technologies will be deployed by a coalition of diverse private actors (entrepreneurs, technologists, consultants, and other professionals) working in collaboration. Crucial amongst these actors will be the lawyer of the future operating as "transaction engineer." The chapter outlines this transaction engineer function and its importance in the deployment of emerging digital technologies.

3.1   "State-Managed" Deployment of Disruptive Technologies

Clayton Christenson in his classic account of innovation defined disruptive innovation as "an innovation that transforms an existing market or creates a new market, typically by trading off raw performance in the name of simplicity, convenience, accessibility, or affordability."[12] Christenson understood the force of disruption as progressively changing the industrial landscape and—as a consequence—transforming business. In this type of account, disruptors create growth by redefining performance that either brings a simple, cheap solution to the low end of a traditional market or enables "non-consumers" to solve pressing problems in their everyday lives.

Innovative technologies, therefore, disrupt at multiple levels. From the business perspective, a new technology disrupts existing ways of doing business and the configuration of stakeholders and their respective interests that exist within a particular sector at a given point in time. And, as described above, this disruption of business has important implications for multiple stakeholders, including lawyers.

From the perspective of government, innovative technologies disrupt existing regulatory schemes and create new (and possibly unimagined) policy issues.[13] Carlota Perez in her influential account on previous technological revolutions has developed a helpful framework for making sense of what happened during these periods of technology-driven socio-economic change. In particular, Perez identified two "phases" that characterize such "revolutions."[14]

First, there is the so-called "Installation phase." During this first phase, a new technology is discovered, developed and scaled. The core applications of the technology are established and a surrounding infrastructure is built. Second, there is a "Deployment phase." During this second phase, there is a large-scale adoption of

---

[12]Christensen (1997).

[13]See Fenwick et al. (2018a).

[14]Perez (2003). See also Freeman and Louca (2002).

that technology throughout the society. This is when the technology establishes itself as a defining feature of a social transformation and new society.

Consider the major technology-driven "revolutions" of the last 250 years, as described by Perez:

i. The industrial revolution, which began in the 1770s in England with the invention of a water-wheel powered spinning machine and resulted in the first textile factories;

ii. The invention of the steam engine in the 1820s, also in England, and the rapid growth of a railway system that facilitated cheap and fast transportation of raw materials and goods, as well as people;

iii. The emergence in the late 19th century of steel, electricity and heavy engineering in Germany and the US. New technologies included steel ships, transcontinental railways, preserved foods, electrical lighting and a global telegraph network;

iv. The automobile, oil and mass production in the early 20th century was driven by US and companies like Standard Oil and Ford. Improvements in refining technology and cheap mass-produced cars meant that the car became affordable for the expanding middle class.

Each of these revolutions brought far-reaching social change—a new way of life, consumption, production and work. But, what is interesting is what happened *between* "Installation" and "Deployment," i.e., the "turning point" between the two phases. According to Perez and others, all previous technological revolutions seem to have experienced some kind of crisis around twenty or thirty years after "Installation."

Moreover, the causes of these crises are broadly the same. After "Installation," capital is attracted to the new technology, driving fast growth and ever more proliferation. Investment accelerates after the new technology is fully developed and the full possibilities become clear.

However, at some point expectations surrounding that technology quickly outstrip actual capacities. This results in tensions developing within the system. A "bubble" is created that, at some point "bursts," promoting a difficult process of retreat and collapse. Consider the following historical examples of such crises:

i. The excitement of canal mania, ending in the "Canal Panic" of 1793;

ii. "Railway mania" and the railway panic of 1848;

iii. The advent of cheap steel, from the 1860s led to the Age of Heavy Engineering—civil, chemical, electrical, naval. Panics occurred in Australia, Argentina and other Southern hemisphere countries triggering a crisis in London;

iv. In 1908, Ford's model-T triggered the Age of the Automobile and Mass Production in the United States. The great crash of 1929 ended the frenzy of the Roaring Twenties and led to the longest post-collapse recessive period to date: the 1930s.

However, soon after each of these crises there was a period of rapid economic growth:

i. A short recession after the "canal panic" was followed by the Great British leap in the early decades of the C19th;

ii. Two years after the Two years later, the Victorian Boom began;
iii. The revival after the steel crises brought the Belle Époque in Europe and the so-called 'Progressive Era' in the USA;
iv. The experience of government-industry collaboration during World War II to enable acceptance of the full Welfare State and the Keynesian policies and institutions that facilitated the greatest economic boom in history.

Venture capitalist, Chris Dixon, summarizes this process as follows:

> Each revolution begins with a financial bubble that propels the (irrationally) rapid installation of the new technology. Then there's a crash, followed by a recovery and then a long period of productive growth as the new technology is "deployed" throughout other industries as well as society more broadly. Eventually the revolution runs its course and a new technological revolution begins.[15]

Crucially, in all previous technological revolutions post-1750, government worked with business leaders to perform the crucial role in helping society move from "Crisis" to "Deployment." i.e., Market failure triggered government intervention and regulation.

This state-driven intervention involved a reactive process of "fact-finding" (gathering all relevant information/evidence regarding a new technology), "understanding" (identifying and evaluating the risks) and, finally, "regulation" (the imposition of a new regulatory framework that would control how, when and where a new technology would be deployed). In this way, a "Crisis" provided a vital opportunity for state-managed "learning" about, and "understanding" of, new technology. Technologies could then be disseminated in a controlled and responsible way. Table 1 summarizes this process.

Table 1 Previous technological revolutions

	Where and when?	Installation period and bubble	"Turning point"/Recession	Deployment period/Golden age
The industrial revolution	UK, 1770s	Canal Mania	1793–97	Great British leap
Age of steam and railways	UK, 1820s	Railway Mania	1848–50	Victorian boom
Age of steel	UK/US/Germany, 1870s	London Funded "Globalization"	1890–95	Progressive Era (US) Belle Epoque (Europe)
Age of oil and mass production	US, 1910s	Roaring Twenties	1929–45	Post-war boom

---

[15]Dixon (2013).

3.2 The "Digital Revolution"

But what about the "Digital Revolution?" If we apply this framework to the present technological revolution, we would have already expected to have entered the deployment phase. The installation phase of the latest revolution stated in the early 1970s with the emergence of personal computers and microprocessors. Thirty years later followed the dot.com crash of 2000 and the 2008 Financial Crisis. These crises could be seen as the turning point. If the existing model holds true, we would expect to see a process of state-managed "readjustment," which in turn would result in deployment and "new ways of living," "new ways of producing," "new ways of communicating" and "new ways of working."

In earlier technological revolutions, risk was allowed to unfold, to be revealed—culminating, in each case, in a crisis. The crisis then triggered a process of re-adjustment that utilized that crisis as a trigger for a state-led learning opportunity. This cycle seems to have relatively settled: Installation—Expansion—Crisis—Learning—Readjustment—Deployment.

However, this type of pattern does not seem applicable in the context of the digital revolution. As such, there are several good reasons to think that things might be different this time. And these differences matter, in the sense that state-led "re-adjustment" and state-managed "deployment" are not a feasible option.

First, this is because technology and attendant risk are increasingly beyond human understanding.[16] In a digital age, there is a shift from a world of risks—established facts about technologies and their dangers—to a world of uncertainties—a world where it is much harder to establish facts that can form the basis of regulation. In part, this is a function of the fact that technology is increasingly incomprehensible. Some facts about new technologies may be difficult to empirically establish or are highly contested, even amongst experts in a field. The task of establishing facts about new technology may be made difficult by the lack of an adequate sample or other reliable data on the effects of new technology.[17] Identification of relevant or irrelevant facts may also be distorted or otherwise influenced by the concerns of entrenched interests about new (and commercially threatening) technologies. Finally, other facts may be "unknown unknowns." We simply lack the information, experience or imagination to predict what negative possibilities may be associated with a piece of new technology.[18]

In this respect, the "relevant facts" that form the basis of regulation and deployment are never going to be obvious or settled. The regulation of any disruptive new

---

[16]See Arbesman (2017) for an overview of the challenge of navigating a digital world that is too complex for human understanding.

[17]See Mandel (2013), p. 62: "Given the uncertainty surrounding an emerging technology's development and risks, there will be inherent limitations concerning how specific a framework can be developed at early stages."

[18]See Kaal (2013), p. 799: "Anticipation of unknown future contingencies and the pre-emption of possible future crises do not play a significant role in the current regulatory framework or in the literature on financial regulation."

technology is increasingly going to be reactive and based on an uncertain and politicized factual basis.

A second factor significantly raising the difficulties of state-led deployment is the speed of contemporary technological change. As mentioned above, the "amplification effects" created as a result of multiple *simultaneous* technological advances have triggered an exponential development of technologies that—as a result of globalization—then proliferate rapidly. In such circumstances, state regulators struggle to keep up with the fast-paced character of contemporary technological change.

Many commentators have commented on the "pacing problem" that such a situation has created:

> Moore's Law notoriously states that the 'functional capacity of ICT products roughly doubles every 18 months,' with the same dynamics manifesting in biotechnology, and namely in sequencing human genome. As a result, regulating innovation involves what is called a 'pacing problem' in the academic literature from the US, or the 'challenge of regulatory connection' or 'regulatory disconnection' in European-based scholarship.[19]

The "pacing problem" refers to a situation when technology develops faster than the corresponding regulation, the latter hopelessly falling behind:

> The 'pacing problem' is an attempt to understand the struggle to 'keep up' with technology. There is more than one way to describe the 'pacing problem'. One can look at the types of legal and regulatory problems that arise as a result of technological change including the need to manage new negative impacts and risks, the need to manage uncertainty in the application of existing laws, the need to adapt regulatory regimes that may be over-inclusive or under-inclusive when applied in the new context and the need to manage obsolescence. Alternatively, Brownsword distinguishes between descriptive and normative disconnection, and between productive and unproductive disconnection. These line-up to some extent, although there are differences in emphasis. On a simplistic level, numerous scholars point to hare and tortoise metaphors to explain the difficulties faced by 'law' when interacting with 'technology.' On a deeper level, new technologies can force us to question our commitment to and interpretation of important concepts and values, such as democracy.[20]

This metaphor of "the hare and the tortoise" is frequently used to describe this situation. As summed up by Marchant and Wallach, "at the rapid rate of change, emerging technologies leave behind traditional governmental regulatory models and approaches which are plodding along slower today than ever before."[21]

The last two decades offer multiple examples of such regulatory struggles:

> Emerging technologies such as nanotechnology, biotechnology, personalized medicine, synthetic biology, applied neuroscience, geoengineering, social media, surveillance technologies, regenerative medicine, robotics and artificial intelligence present complex governance and oversight challenges. These technologies are characterized by a rapid pace of development, a multitude of applications, manifestations and actors, pervasive uncertainties about risks, benefits and future directions, and demands for oversight ranging from potential health and environmental risks to broader social and ethical concerns. Given this complexity, no

---

[19] Allenby (2011), p. 3.

[20] Bennett Moses (2013), p. 7.

[21] Butenko and Larouche (2015), p. 66.

single regulatory agency, or even group of agencies, can regulate any of these emerging technologies effectively and comprehensively.[22]

The conclusion? Deployment—i.e., designing and putting in place a regulatory framework that is appropriate for the new realities of a digital age—is by no means easy and modern states lack the means and capacities to perform this function. Particularly when such a framework needs to ensure the safety of consumers and the public, whilst facilitating the commercial use and consumer enjoyment of disruptive innovation. This is especially true in contemporary settings, where innovation is quicker and the global dissemination of new technology is much faster and harder to manage.[23] Expecting the nation-state to provide strong leadership—as it did with previous technological revolutions—seems fanciful. Nevertheless, some action is required.

The limits of nation states and regulators to manage the installation of new technologies does not mean that such a process will not occur. Rather, it means that more diverse coalitions of actors providing "contingent" solutions will become the new normal.

Michel Callon the French sociologist, for example, has emphasized how regulatory decisions should no longer be thought of as "final events" (to be made for all-time and from which we "all move on").[24] Rather, we should think of them as "measured decision-making." i.e., regulatory choices are open-ended and highly contingent choices that form one stage in a longer process and not the "final word" on a particular issue. Regulators need to abandon a fixation on finality and legal certainty and embrace contingency, flexibility and an openness to the new.[25]

Similarly, Gralf-Peter Caliess and Peer Zumbasen's concept of "rough consensus and running code" developed in the context of transnational business law also highlights a new contingency as a defining feature of contemporary "law"-making in transnational settings.[26]

We can expand this line of thought to suggest that diverse coalitions of private actors utilizing transnational polycentric normative orders will become more important in managing the deployment of highly complex technologies. Table 2 provides a schematic overview of this shift from the state-led deployment of new technologies to diverse coalitions of actors "co-creating" a digital future using more contingent, diverse and often transnational regulatory forms.

---

[22]Marchant and Wallach (2013), p. 136.

[23]McGrath (2013).

[24]See Callon (2009).

[25]See Kaal (2014), p. 46: "The 'Institutional Infrastructure' for rule-making was geared towards the creation of rules for governing a relatively stable society with less upward mobility and relatively stable economic and market environments."

[26]Calliess and Zumbansen (2010).

Table 2 From "state-led deployment" to the "co-creation of a digital future"

	Traditional state-led "deployment" of New Technology	"The co-creation of a digital future"
Role and goal of state	Responsible and precautionary public leadership and "control" over the mass dissemination of a new technology	Dynamic "participation"—along with multiple other actors—in the on-going project of "co-creating" the future together
Key actors and relationships	Delegation of regulatory design to a "legitimate" combination of state politicians and bureaucrats working with information provided by industry and scientific community to identify and then mitigate risk	Flat, fluid and inclusive "eco-system" built around technology companies, involving diverse stakeholders, including the state
When and what to regulate	"Crisis" as opportunity for learning and trigger for ex post state regulatory action	"Data-driven" ex ante regulatory action
Method	A reactive process of risk mitigation via: (i) "fact-finding" (gathering all relevant knowledge/evidence regarding a new technology), (ii) "understanding" (identifying and evaluating the risks) and, (iii) finally, "regulatory design" (the selection and imposition of a new legal framework that would control/regulate how a new technology would be deployed)	Design and installation of "touch points"/"sensors" in society that facilitate meaningful dialogue and collaboration with innovator-entrepreneurs aimed at promoting responsible deployment of innovation
Form of regulation	National "law": static, fixed, general norms targeting individuals and companies with sanctions for non-compliance; punish and persuade; command and control	Polycentric/de-centred/plurality of regulatory forms/combination of iterative strategies/transnational: (i) individualized and negotiated regulation via "sand-boxes", "test-beds"; (ii) offering incentives via investment funds and regulatory advantages; diffusion of responsibility across national and supranational, state and non-state (industry standards, market based instruments); hybrid forums
Substance of regulation and enforcement	Universal standards policed by state gatekeepers/intermediaries. Reporting, "comply or explain"	Experimentation
Risks	Minoritarian bias and agency capture	Lack of transparency and accountability as transnational regulation "disappears"

3.3 The Lawyer of the Future as "Transaction Engineer"

Crucially, lawyers can play an important role in co-creating solutions around the deployment of new technologies. In this context, the history of the legal profession can provide some guidance as to the type of role that lawyers can play.

Historically, lawyers have been at their most effective—and socially useful—when they have operated as "transaction engineers" that facilitate new forms of business and other social relationships. Take the development and growth of Silicon Valley as a center for digital technologies in the early 1970s. While the idea of the "clustering" of similar businesses was a significant source of innovation, there is a broad consensus that the legal industry was also important in the development of technology firms and facilitating innovation.[27]

For example, lawyers were responsible for drafting the innovative contractual provisions that protected high-risk investors—for instance, angel investors and venture capitalists—from the relational and performance risks associated with investing in young companies and inexperienced founder-entrepreneurs.

Moreover, the involvement of lawyers in both non-legal and legal activities, such as deal making, matchmaking, gatekeeping, and conciliating, also served as an important "sorting device" for entrepreneurs that needed more than just investors to start and scale their young businesses.

Finally, the contractual mechanisms and the lawyer-dominated market for reputation reduced information asymmetries between the entrepreneurs and investors and, as such, were necessary to bring the demand- and supply-side of venture capital" together in a way that was effective and mutually advantageous.

In this sense, we can see from the Silicon Valley example how lawyers functioned as "transaction engineers," i.e., crucial intermediaries that brought together in a "safe" space various parties with different but mutually compatible interests and novel forms of expertise. The often-neglected contribution of local law firms to the institutionalization of venture capital and venture capital contracting helps explain the success of Silicon Valley.

The problem, however, is that lawyers have often failed to perform this function of being active transaction engineers that add-value and they have often become a hindrance or obstacle to transactions. This can happen for multiple different reasons but the tendency to "proceduralize" legal solutions and to employ standard form "templates" is one major factor. Fixed and standardized solutions are often imposed on complex, dynamic transactions resulting in frustration and difficulties.

As a result, lawyers have developed a reputation as one of the least trusted professions. The list of complaints is familiar: lawyers are verbose, they don't listen, they are unresponsive, they charge too much, they don't care about clients, they spend too much time on trivial issues, they don't keep clients informed, they constantly "over-lawyer," and they don't communicate clearly and concisely.

In a highly competitive and fast-changing world, lawyers need to focus on re-discovering their function as effective transaction engineers that can help parties to

---

[27]See Friedman et al. (1989), Chandler (2014).

facilitate interactions and reduce costs. In a modern context, there are many costs need to be cut: agency costs, transaction costs, monitoring costs, regulatory costs and (increasingly) compliance costs. In that respect, the scope for lawyers to "add value" is enormous.

More generally, lawyers can play a crucial role in the "co-creation" of the infrastructure for the deployment of new technologies introduced in the previous section. Such co-creation involving partnerships between multiple actors can be crucial to building a "better" digital future.

In contrast, to this view one can sometimes hear commentators suggesting that the digital transformation may mark the end of lawyers and legal advisors. We certainly don't agree with this argument. Nevertheless, we do think that if the lawyers of the future are to function as effective transaction engineers playing a socially productive role in the deployment of digital technologies, it is very clear that the legal profession is going to need to adapt in various ways.

Firstly, lawyers of the future will need to be able to assume the role of "project managers" or, at least, active participants in new multi-disciplinary teams that are going to design new solutions of the future. As such, the capacity to work in multi-disciplinary teams will take on a much greater significance than has previously been the case for lawyers. The ability to work with and communicate with a more diverse set of "partners" will be increasingly required.

In the digital world, this means that lawyers will not only have to work closely with their traditional professional "partners" such as accountants or financial advisors, but also with engineers, designers, architects and other technological experts and specialists (depending on the particular project/transaction at hand).

In this new model of legal services, law firms will become more like legal "platforms" with an emphasis on connecting legal and other experts and managing the collaboration and transactions.[28] In a new world of platforms, this type of "matchmaking" and project-based partnerships, will mean that lawyers and other legal advisors will need to be aware of the way network technology, and other code-based technologies operate.

Secondly, in pursuing these new solutions, lawyers will be confronted with a very different type of client. Fast-growth technology companies with few assets and fewer employees are central to the digital world. Winning companies have used the opportunities of networked digital technologies to develop new business models. Trust, value and wealth are created through platforms, connections, and networks, instead of the management of workers or physical assets. Crucially, many firms in this new innovation-driven economy adopt new organizational forms and governance structures to deliver their new products and services.

What then are the main features of such organizations? To appeal to Millennial "talent" and consumers, such firms have embraced mission-driven and inclusive organizational cultures and practices in which a "best-idea-wins" culture replaces hierarchies. Significantly, however, many such "new" firms have often struggled to maintain this new governance model and fulfill their initial promise. Lawyers of the

---

[28] See Fenwick et al. (2018).

future will need to understand the opportunities and challenges of the digital world and help firms to re-invent their governance structures to be more open and inclusive.

Thirdly, many of the "solutions" that the lawyer of the future will be expected to help design will be technology based. The transactions that lawyers will be facilitating will be dependent on computer code. It is in this context that blockchain and Smart Contracts become particularly important. To facilitate lawyers in performing this function, legal education will need to undergo some important changes in order to prepare prospective legal professionals to perform this function.

For example, in the context of the digital transformation, an understanding of code is going to be crucial for the lawyer of the future to perform their transaction engineer function effectively.[29]

More and more businesses and industries will revolve around code-based products or services. Since all companies are now increasingly managed by and run on software code, facilitating transactions—i.e., being an active transaction engineer—will inevitably involve coding. This coding will involve multi-disciplinary teams working in collaboration and the capacity of lawyers to actively participate in such teams will be crucial to their success as legal professionals. The development of blockchain technologies and Smart Contracts are particularly relevant in this regard.

Finally, as discussed above, Legal Tech will profoundly disrupt the legal profession and since these technologies are code-based lawyers need to be able to understand and communicate in and about code to participate in the design of such legal technologies and to maximize their usefulness in supporting legal work.

4 Conclusion

We should not feel threatened by the exponential growth of new digital technologies and the subsequent changes in economy, culture and society triggered by technological developments. Rather, we should view them more as opportunities. The opportunities for lawyers and other legal professionals are obvious. If "standardized work" and legal research activities can be performed by algorithms, there will be more time for assisting the client with the new and very specific challenges of the digital world. The new technologies in the digital world will force us to return to the drawing board. This does not mean that business lawyers will become irrelevant but, rather, that the legal profession will need to reinvent itself in order to perform the key function of designing and engineering the new transactions and organizations of a digital future.

---

[29] See Fenwick et al. (2018b).

References

American Bar Association (2016) Commission on the future of legal services. Report on the Future of Legal Services in the United States. American Bar Association, New York

Allenby B-R (2011) Governance and technology systems: the challenge of emerging technologies. In: Marchant G-E, Allenby B-R, Herket J-R (eds) The growing gap between emerging technologies and legal-ethical oversight: the pacing problem. Springer, New York

Arbesman S (2017) Overcomplicated: technology at the limits of comprehension. Penguin, London

Bennett Moses L (2013) How to think about law, regulation and technology: problems with 'technology' as a regulatory target. Law, Innovation & Technol 5(1):1–20

Birkinshaw J (2018) What's the purpose of companies in the age of AI. Harvard Business Rev, August 2013

Butenko A, Larouche P (2015) Regulation for innovativeness or regulation of innovation? Law, Innovation & Technol 7(1):52–82

Calliess G-P, Zumbansen P (2010) Rough consensus and running code: a theory of transnational private law. Hart, London

Callon M, Lasoumes P, Barthe Y (2009) Acting in an uncertain world: an essay on technical democracy. MIT Press, Cambridge

Chandler A (2014) How law made silicon valley. Emory Law Rev 63(3):639–94

Christensen C (1997) The innovator's dilemma: when new technologies cause great firms to fail. Harvard Business Review Press, Boston

Dixon C (2013) The computing deployment phase. http://cdixon.org/2013/02/10/the-computing-deployment-phase/. Accessed 10 Oct 2018

Fenwick M (2016) The new corporate criminal law and transnational legal risk. In: Fenwick M, Wrbka S (eds) Flexibility in modern business law: a comparative assessment. Springer, London

Fenwick M, Kaal W-A, Vermeulen E-P-M (2018a) Regulation tomorrow: what happens when technology is faster than the law. Am Univ Bus Law Rev 6(3):561–84

Fenwick M, Kaal W-A, Vermeulen E-P-M (2018b) Legal education in a digital age: why coding for lawyers matters. University of St. Thomas (Minnesota) Legal Studies Research Paper No. 18–21 https://papers.ssrn.com/sol3/papers.cfm?abstract_id=3227967. Accessed 25 Sept 2018

Fenwick M, McCahery J-A, Vermeulen E-P-M (2018) The end of "corporate" governance: Hello new world of platform governance https://papers.ssrn.com/sol3/papers.cfm?abstract_id=3232663. Accessed 25 Sept 2018

Fenwick M, Vermeulen E-P-M (2018) Technology and corporate governance: blockchain, crypto and artificial intelligence. Lex Research Topics in Corporate Law and Economics Working Paper No. 2018-7 https://papers.ssrn.com/sol3/papers.cfm?abstract_id=3263222. Accessed 25 Sept 2018

Freeman C, Louca F (2002) As time goes by: from the industrial revolutions to the information revolution. Oxford University Press, Oxford

Friedman L-M et al (1989) Law, lawyers and legal practice in silicon valley. Indiana Law Rev 64(3):555–67

Jentzsch C (2016) Decentralized autonomous organization to automate governance https://download.slock.it/public/DAO/WhitePaper.pdf. Accessed 25 Sept 2018

Jordan J (2012) The need for a comprehensive international bribery compliance program, covering A to Z, in an expanding global anti-bribery environment. PA State Law Rev 117(1):89–136

Kaal W-A (2013) Dynamic regulation of the financial services industry. Wake For Law Rev 48:791–828

Kaal W-A (2014) Evolution of law: dynamic regulation in a new institutional economics framework. In: Kaal W-A, Schmidt M, Schartze A (eds) Festschrift Zu Ehren von Christian Kirchner. Mohr Siebeck, Tubingen

Koehler M (2012) The story of the foreign corrupt practices act. Ohio State Law J 73(5):929–1013

Lessig L (2006) Code: Version 2.0. Creative Commons, New York

Mandel G-N (2013) Emerging technology governance. In: Marchant G-E, Abbot K-W, Allenby B (eds) Innovative governance models for emerging technologies. Edward Elgar, London

Marchant G-W, Wallach W (2013) Governing the governance of emerging technologies. In: Marchant G-E, Abbot K-W, Allenby B (eds) Innovative governance models for emerging technologies. Edward Elgar, London

McGrath R (2013) The pace of technology adoption is speeding up. Harvard Bus Rev https://perma.cc/DA8M-7QQV/. Accessed 25 Sept 2018

Mitchell W (1995) City of bits: space. MIT Press, Cambridge (MA), Place and the Infobahn

Perez C (2003) Technological revolutions and financial capital: the dynamics of bubbles and golden ages. Edward Elgar, London

Slaughter A-M, Zaring D (1997) Extra-territoriality in a globalized world http://papers.ssrn.com/sol3/papers.cfm?abstract_id=39380. Accessed 25 Sept 2018

Szabo N (1994) Smart contracts http://www.fon.hum.uva.nl/rob/Courses/InformationInSpeech/CDROM/Literature/LOTwinterschool2006/szabo.best.vwh.net/smart.contracts.html. Accessed 25 Sept 2018

Index

© Springer Nature Singapore Pte Ltd. 2019
M. Corrales et al. (eds.), *Legal Tech, Smart Contracts and Blockchain*,
Perspectives in Law, Business and Innovation,
https://doi.org/10.1007/978-981-13-6086-2